RAVINE™

created by
STJEPAN ŠEJIĆ

written by
STJEPAN ŠEJIĆ & RON MARZ

illustrated by
STJEPAN ŠEJIĆ

lettered by
TROY PETERI

•••••

production by
PHIL SMITH & ADDISON DUKE

•••••

published by

image® & TOP COW® PRODUCTIONS, INC.

~DEDICATION~

To my wife Linda, because all this began
that day in college when I decided to
draw you wearing armor.

-STJEPAN ŠEJIĆ

To my son, Killian, who taught me how
to be a father.

-RON MARZ

IMAGE COMICS, INC.
Robert Kirkman – Chief Operating Officer
Erik Larsen – Chief Financial Officer
Todd McFarlane – President
Marc Silvestri – Chief Executive Officer
Jim Valentino – Vice-President

Eric Stephenson – Publisher
Corey Murphy – Director of Sales
Jeremy Sullivan – Director of Digital Sales
Kat Salazar – Director of PR & Marketing
Emily Miller – Director of Operations
Branwyn Bigglestone – Senior Accounts Manager
Sarah Mello – Accounts Manager
Drew Gill – Art Director
Jonathan Chan – Production Manager
Meredith Wallace – Print Manager
Randy Okamura – Marketing Production Designer
David Brothers – Content Manager
Addison Duke – Production Artist
Vincent Kukua – Production Artist
Sasha Head – Production Artist
Tricia Ramos – Production Artist
Emilio Bautista – Sales Assistant
Jessica Ambriz – Administrative Assistant
IMAGECOMICS.COM

TOP COW PRODUCTIONS, INC.
Marc Silvestri - CEO
Matt Hawkins - President and COO
Betsy Gonia - Managing Editor
Elena Salacedo - Operations Manager
Ryan Cady - Editorial Assistant
Vincent Valentine - Production Assistant
www.topcow.com

RAVINE volume 2 trade paperback,
June 2015. Second Printing. ISBN: 978-1-60706-768-9. $14.99 USD.
Published by Image Comics, Inc. Office of Publication: 2001 Center St., Sixth Floor, Berkeley, CA 94704. RAVINE © 2015 Stjepan Sejic
and Ron Marz. "RAVINE," the RAVINE logos and the likeness of all featured characters are trademarks of Stjepan Sejic and Ron Marz.

PROLOGUE

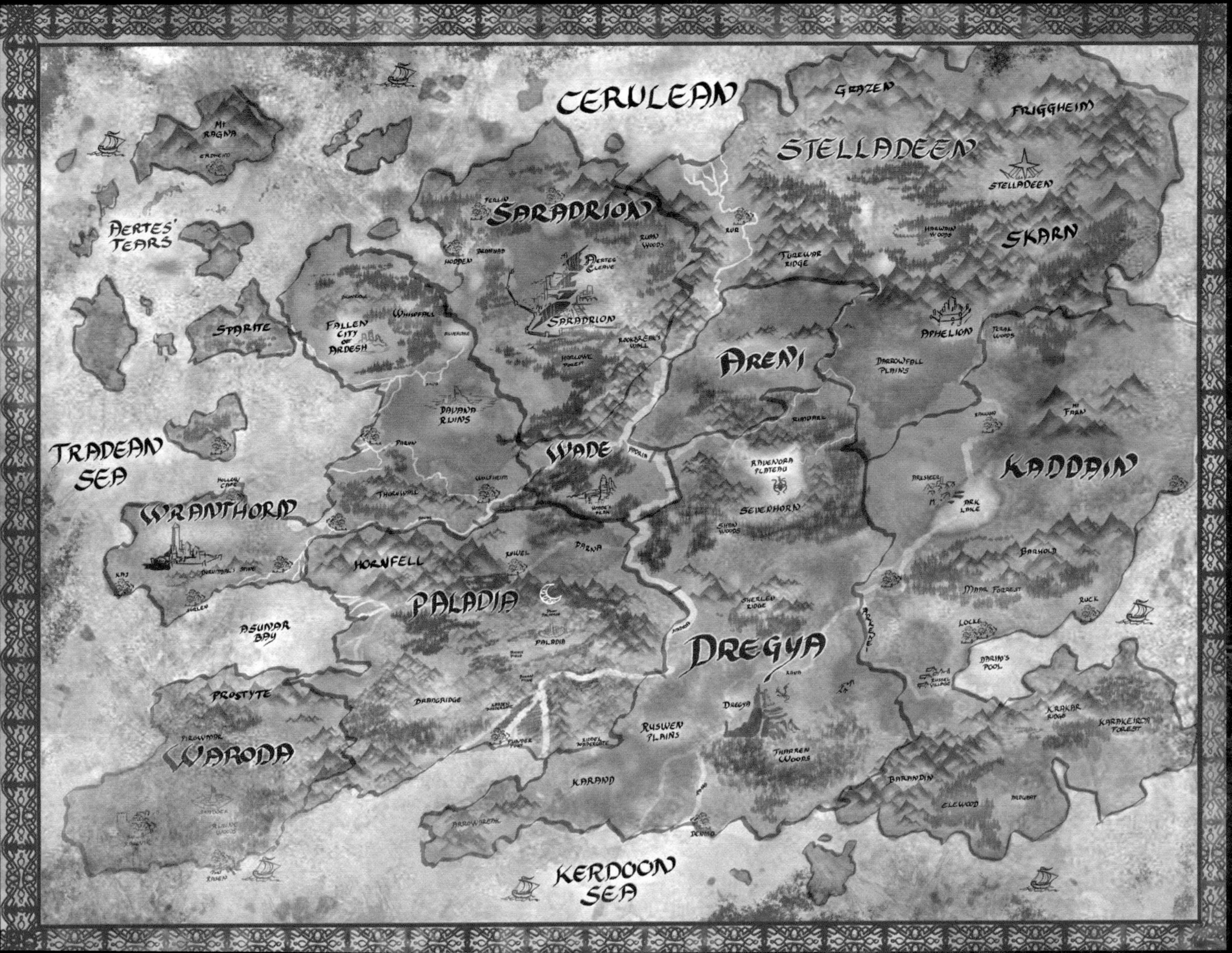
CERULEAN
STELLADEEN
FRIGGHEIM
GRAZEN
STELLADEEN
SKARN
HAWWIN WOODS
TUREWAR RIDGE
RUR
SARADRION
FERLIN
RUIN WOODS
HODDEN
AERTES' CLEAVE
SARADRION
ROOKBREAK'S WALL
HORLOWE FOREST
AERTES' TEARS
MT RAGNA
SPARITE
FALLEN CITY OF ARDESH
WHISFALL
DAVANA RUINS
PARUN
WULFHEIM
THORNWALL
TRADEAN SEA
HOLLOW CAPE
WRANTHORN
KRJ
AREN
APHELION
DARROWFALL PLAINS
TERAL WOODS
MT FARN
RIMDARL
RAVENORA PLATEAU
SEVERHORN
SHAW WOODS
WADE
APDRIA
KADDAIN
ARK LAKE
BARHOLD
MAAR FORREST
RUCK
LOCKE
DARIN'S POOL
HORNFELL
PARNA
PALADIA
PALADIA
ASUNAR BAY
SHERLEN RIDGE
DREGYA
DREGYA
KRAKAR RIDGE
KARAKEIRON FOREST
PROSTYTE
BRANGRIDGE
RUSWEN PLAINS
THARREN WOODS
WARODA
KARAND
ARROWREACH
BARANDIN
ELEWOOD
KERDOON SEA

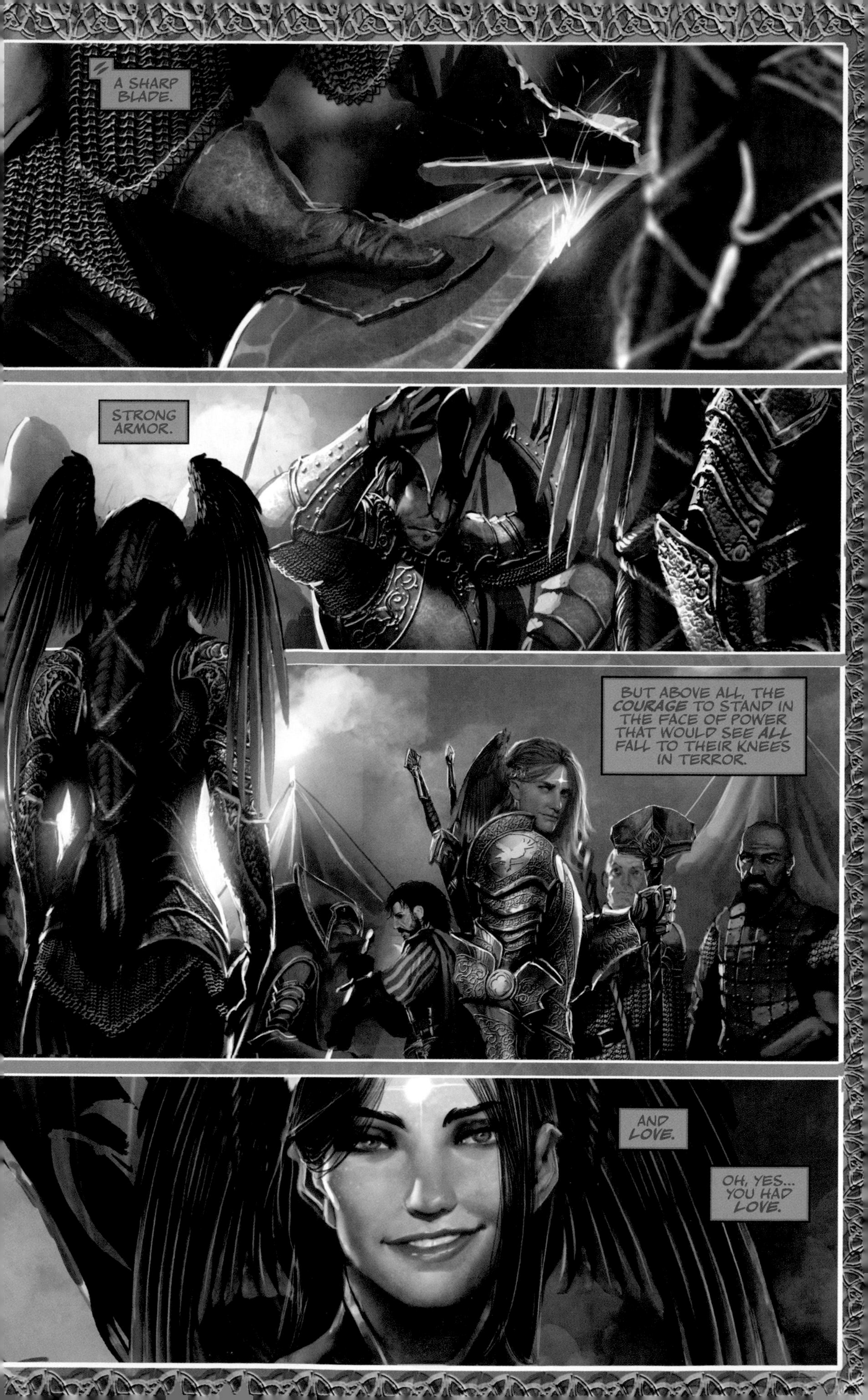
A SHARP BLADE.
STRONG ARMOR.
BUT ABOVE ALL, THE *COURAGE* TO STAND IN THE FACE OF POWER THAT WOULD SEE *ALL* FALL TO THEIR KNEES IN TERROR.
AND *LOVE.*
OH, YES... YOU HAD *LOVE.*

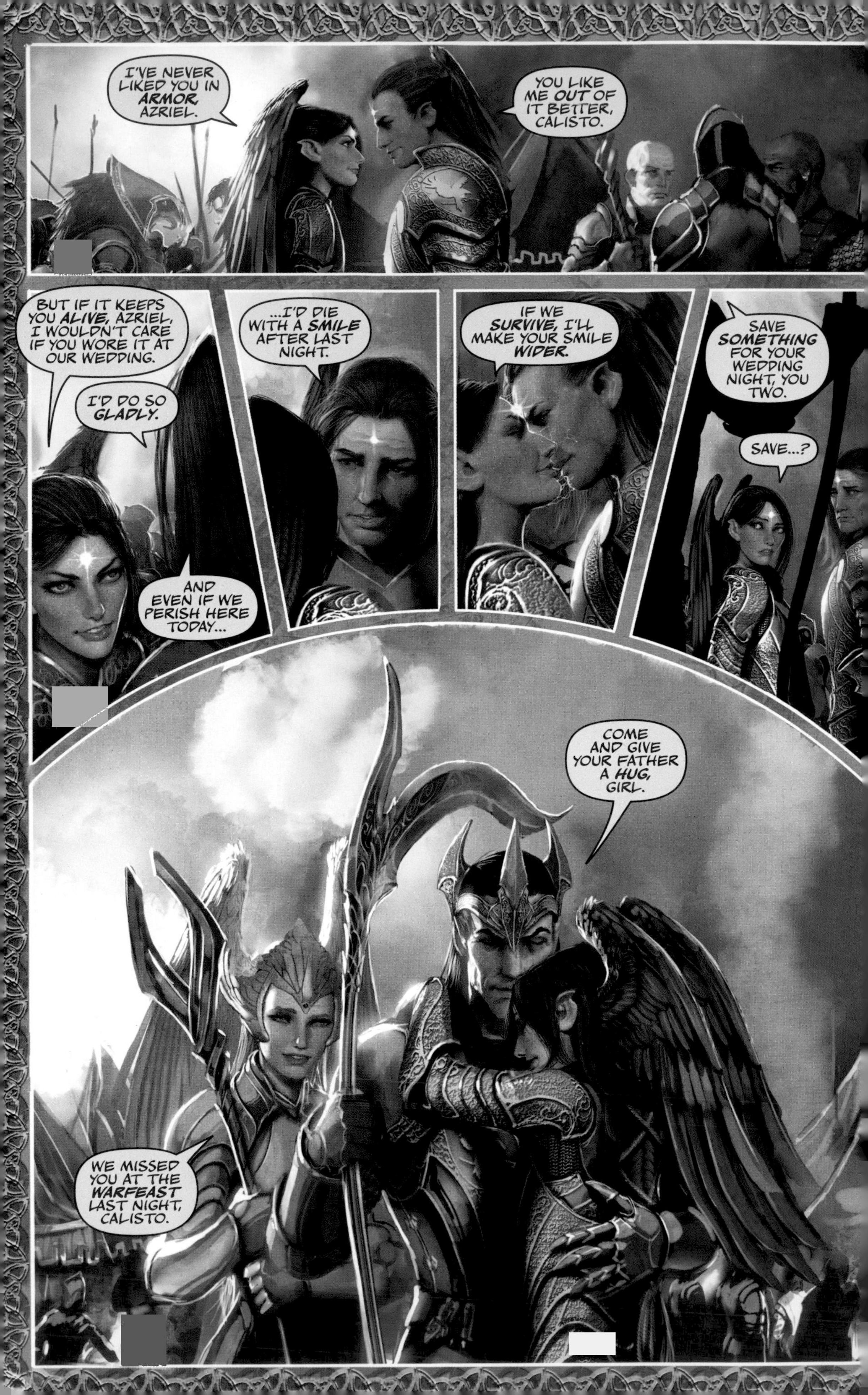
I'VE NEVER LIKED YOU IN ARMOR, AZRIEL.
YOU LIKE ME OUT OF IT BETTER, CALISTO.
BUT IF IT KEEPS YOU ALIVE, AZRIEL, I WOULDN'T CARE IF YOU WORE IT AT OUR WEDDING.
I'D DO SO GLADLY.
AND EVEN IF WE PERISH HERE TODAY...
...I'D DIE WITH A SMILE AFTER LAST NIGHT.
IF WE SURVIVE, I'LL MAKE YOUR SMILE WIDER.
SAVE SOMETHING FOR YOUR WEDDING NIGHT, YOU TWO.
SAVE...?
COME AND GIVE YOUR FATHER A HUG, GIRL.
WE MISSED YOU AT THE WARFEAST LAST NIGHT, CALISTO.

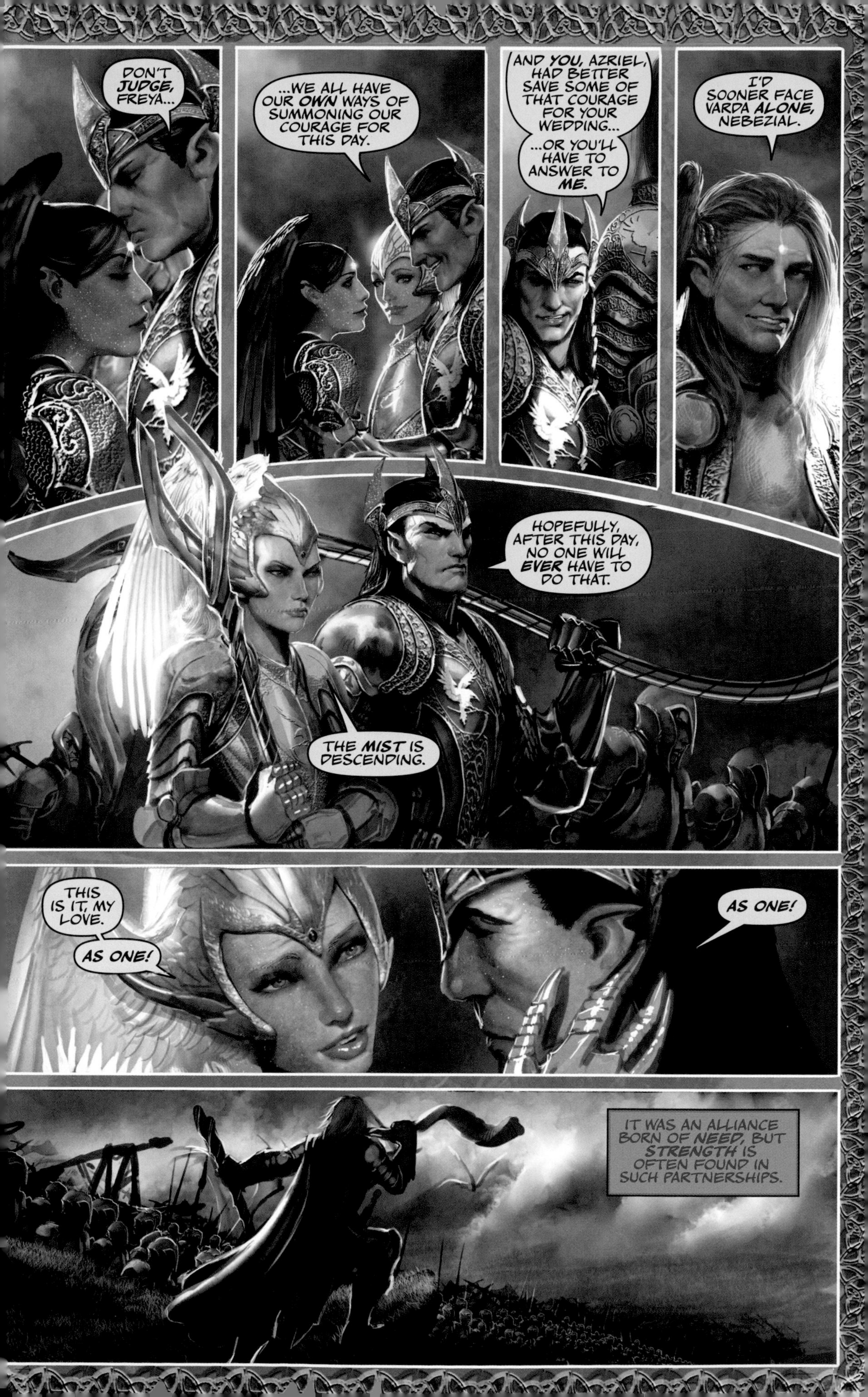
DON'T JUDGE, FREYA...
...WE ALL HAVE OUR OWN WAYS OF SUMMONING OUR COURAGE FOR THIS DAY.
AND YOU, AZRIEL, HAD BETTER SAVE SOME OF THAT COURAGE FOR YOUR WEDDING...
...OR YOU'LL HAVE TO ANSWER TO ME.
I'D SOONER FACE VARDA ALONE, NEBEZIAL.
HOPEFULLY, AFTER THIS DAY, NO ONE WILL EVER HAVE TO DO THAT.
THE MIST IS DESCENDING.
THIS IS IT, MY LOVE.
AS ONE!
AS ONE!
IT WAS AN ALLIANCE BORN OF NEED, BUT STRENGTH IS OFTEN FOUND IN SUCH PARTNERSHIPS.

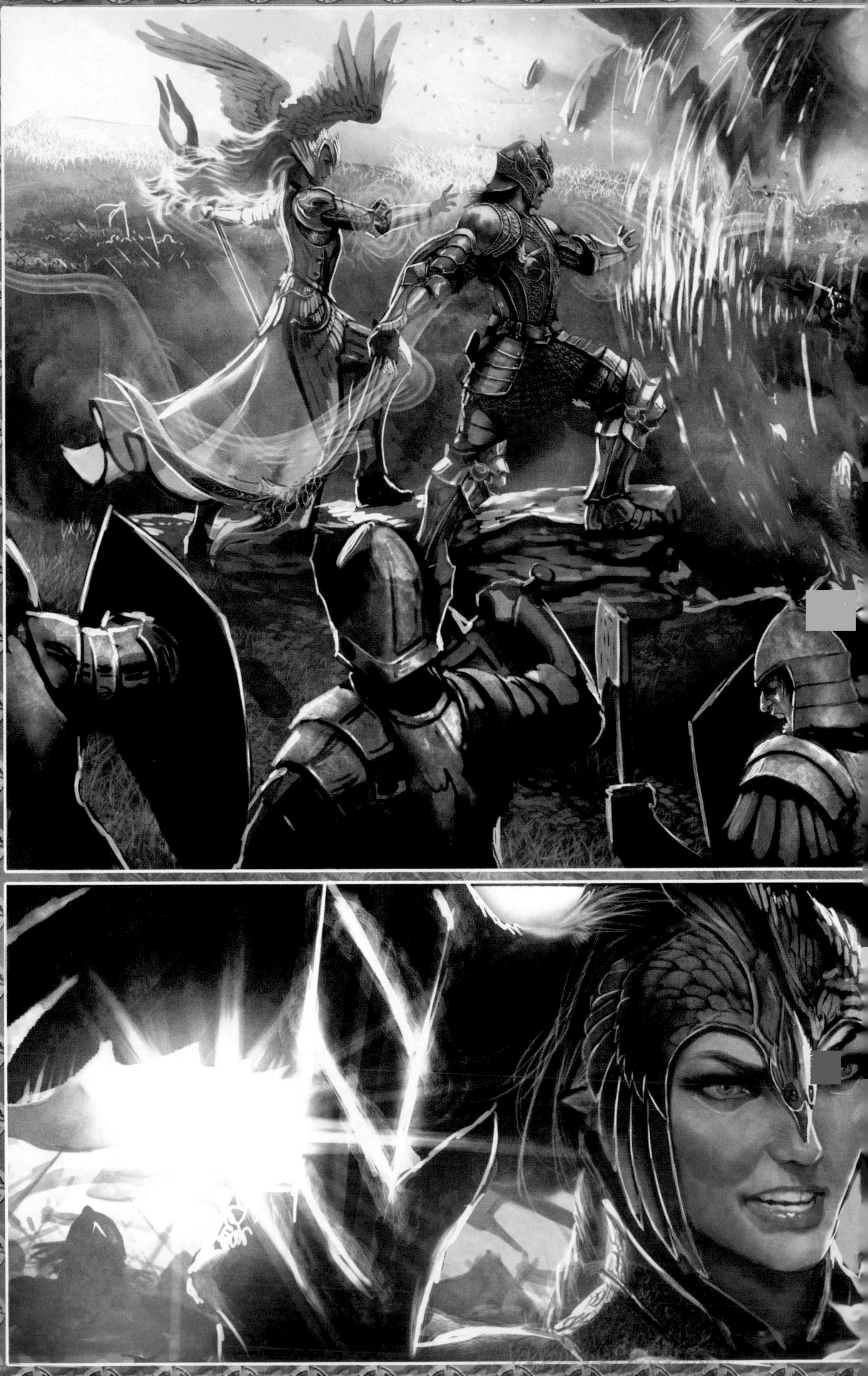

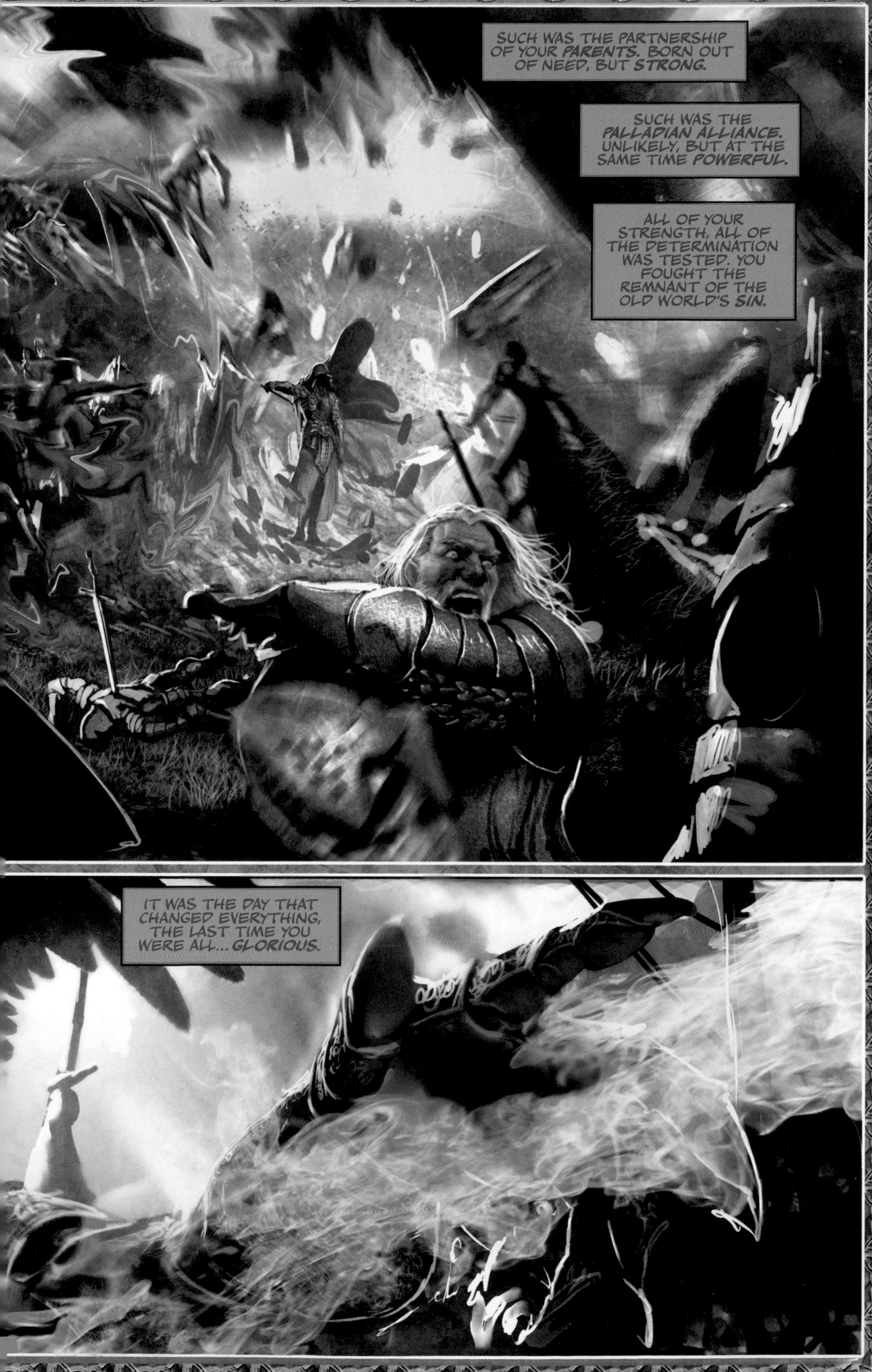
SUCH WAS THE PARTNERSHIP OF YOUR *PARENTS*. BORN OUT OF NEED, BUT *STRONG*.
SUCH WAS THE *PALLADIAN ALLIANCE*. UNLIKELY, BUT AT THE SAME TIME *POWERFUL*.
ALL OF YOUR STRENGTH, ALL OF THE DETERMINATION WAS TESTED. YOU FOUGHT THE REMNANT OF THE OLD WORLD'S *SIN*.
IT WAS THE DAY THAT CHANGED EVERYTHING, THE LAST TIME YOU WERE ALL... *GLORIOUS*.

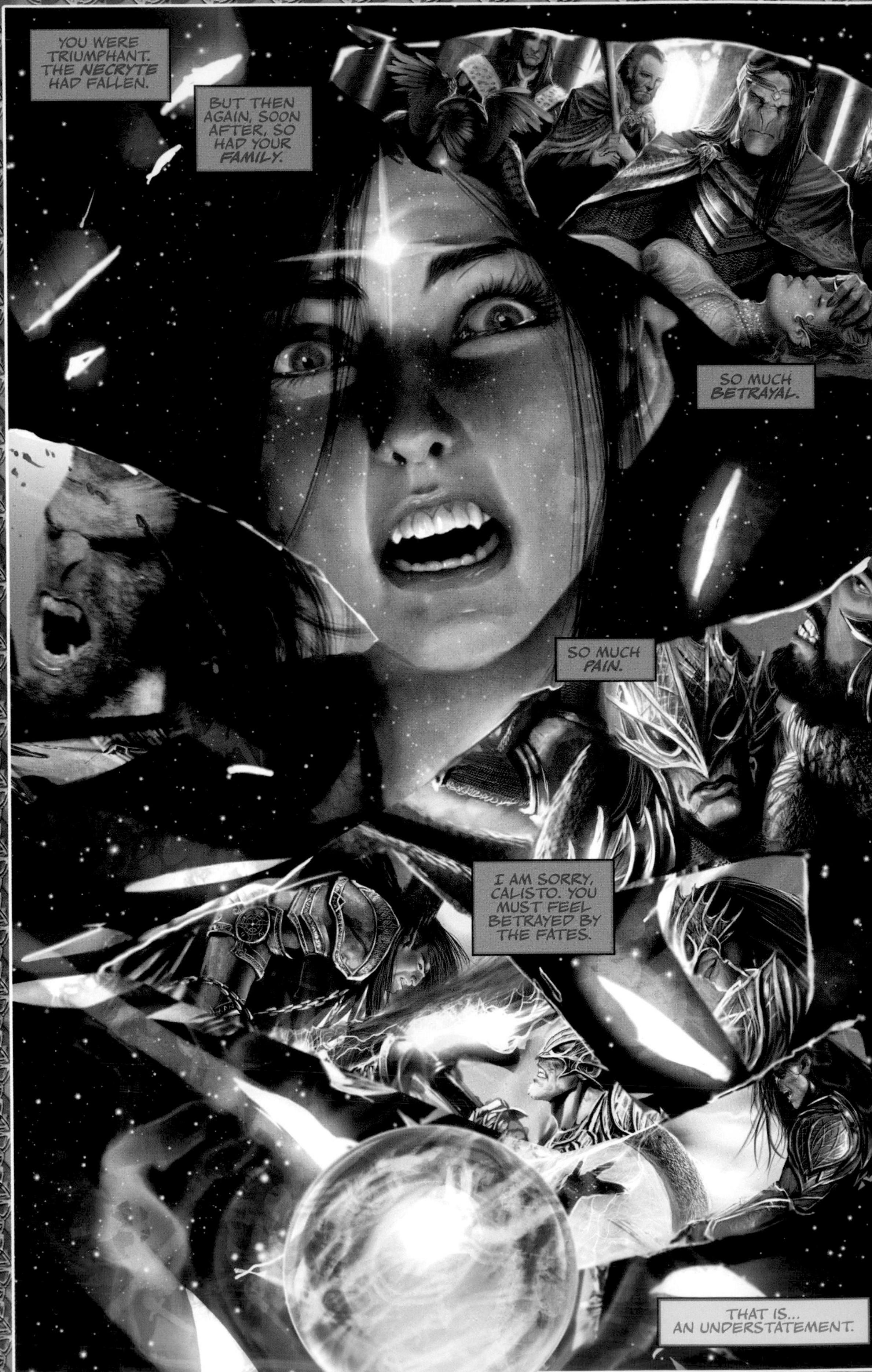
YOU WERE TRIUMPHANT. THE NECRYTE HAD FALLEN.
BUT THEN AGAIN, SOON AFTER, SO HAD YOUR FAMILY.
SO MUCH BETRAYAL.
SO MUCH PAIN.
I AM SORRY, CALISTO. YOU MUST FEEL BETRAYED BY THE FATES.
THAT IS... AN UNDERSTATEMENT.

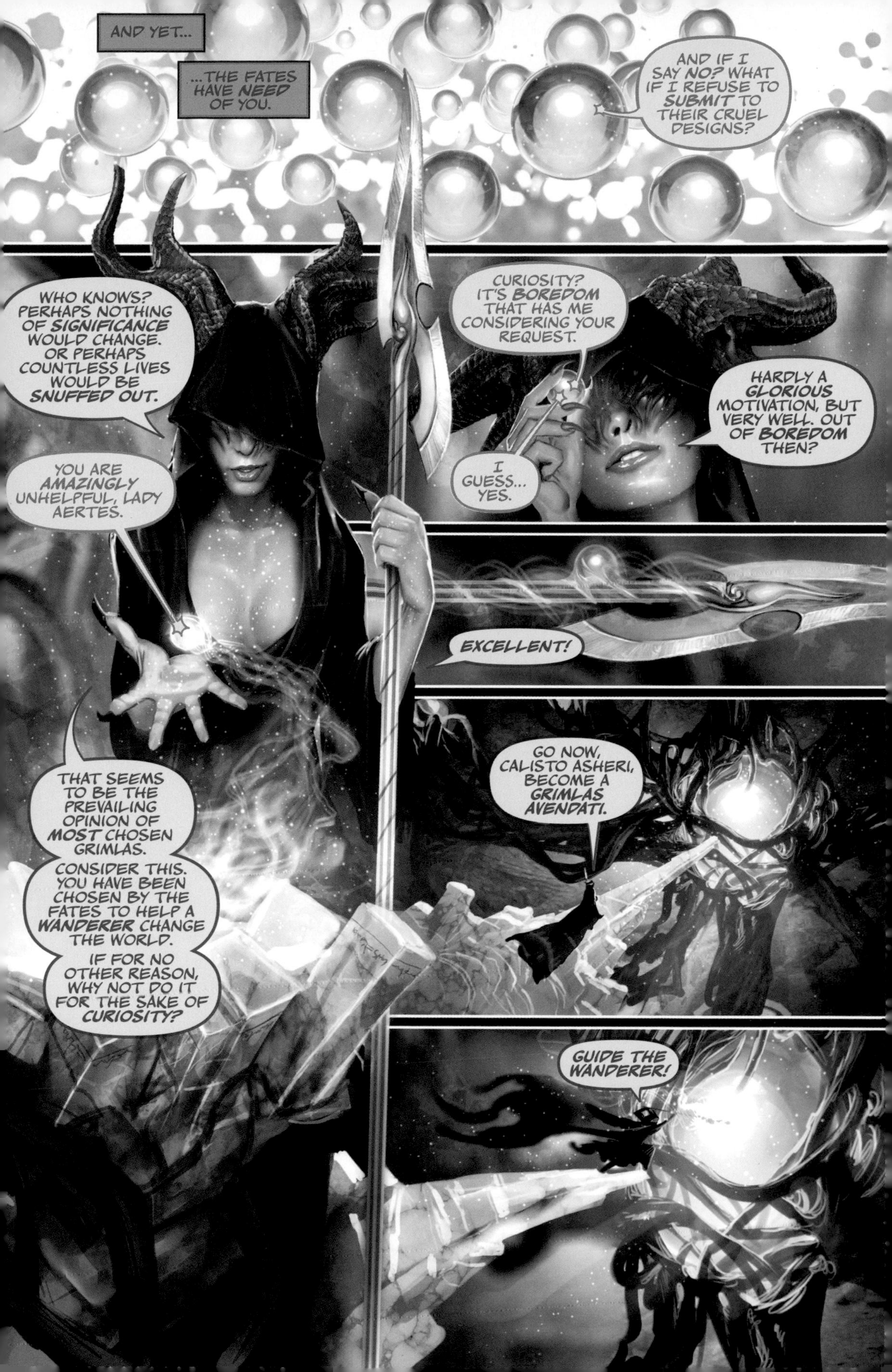
AND YET...
...THE FATES HAVE NEED OF YOU.
AND IF I SAY NO? WHAT IF I REFUSE TO SUBMIT TO THEIR CRUEL DESIGNS?
WHO KNOWS? PERHAPS NOTHING OF SIGNIFICANCE WOULD CHANGE. OR PERHAPS COUNTLESS LIVES WOULD BE SNUFFED OUT.
YOU ARE AMAZINGLY UNHELPFUL, LADY AERTES.
THAT SEEMS TO BE THE PREVAILING OPINION OF MOST CHOSEN GRIMLAS.
CONSIDER THIS. YOU HAVE BEEN CHOSEN BY THE FATES TO HELP A WANDERER CHANGE THE WORLD.
IF FOR NO OTHER REASON, WHY NOT DO IT FOR THE SAKE OF CURIOSITY?
CURIOSITY? IT'S BOREDOM THAT HAS ME CONSIDERING YOUR REQUEST.
HARDLY A GLORIOUS MOTIVATION, BUT VERY WELL. OUT OF BOREDOM THEN?
I GUESS... YES.
EXCELLENT!
GO NOW, CALISTO ASHERI, BECOME A GRIMLAS AVENDATI.
GUIDE THE WANDERER!

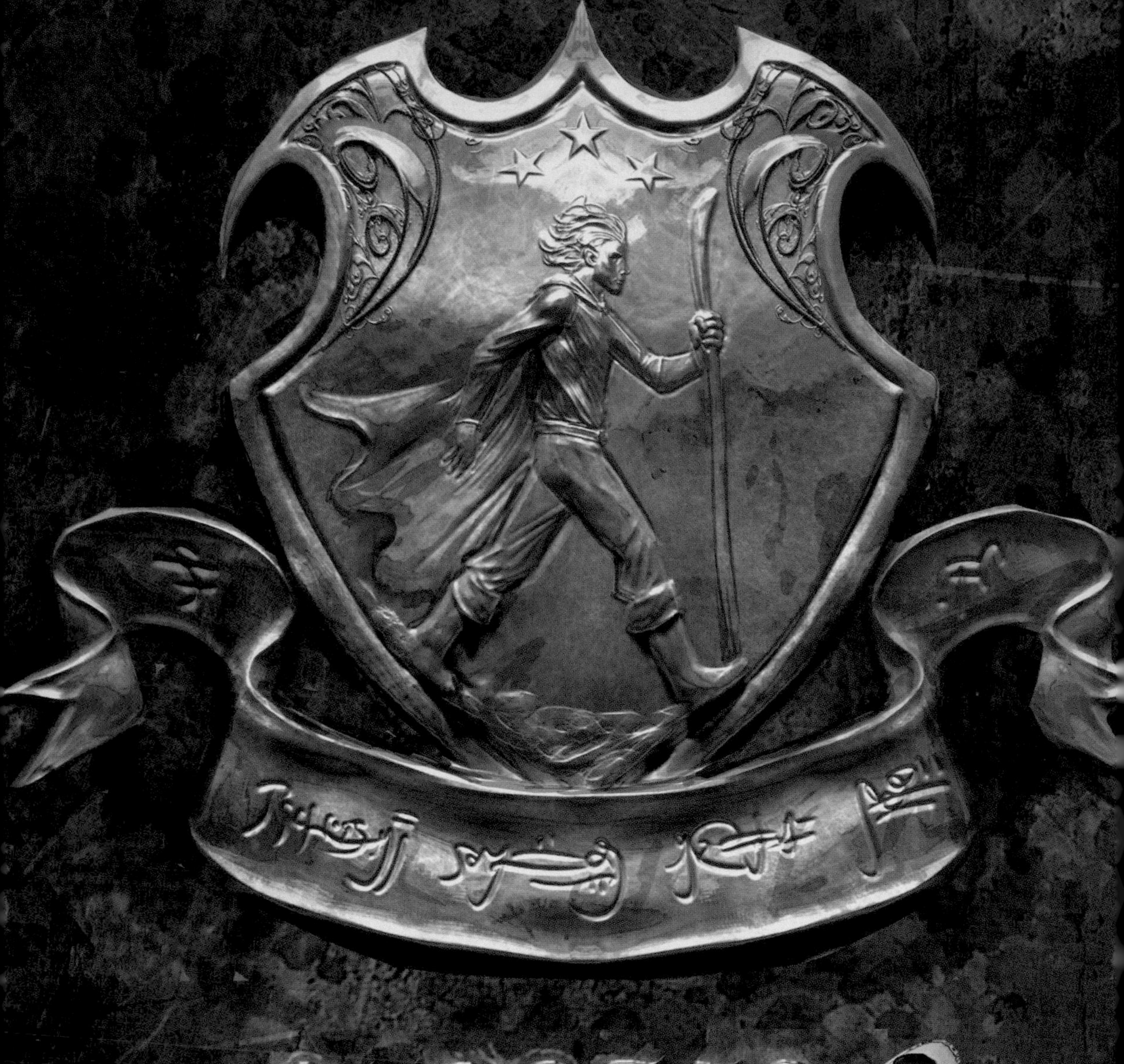

CHAPTER 2
COMPANIONS

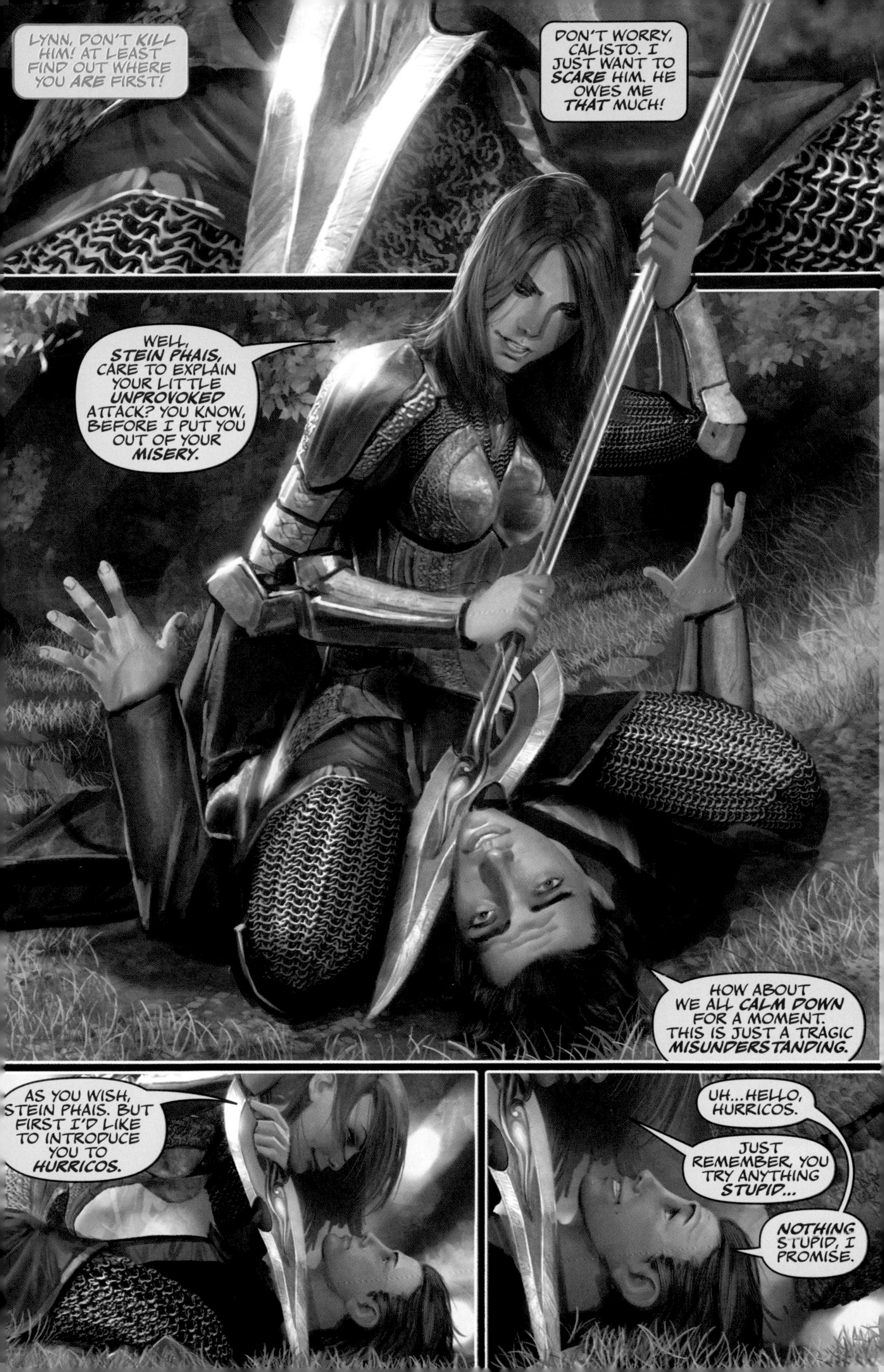
LYNN, DON'T KILL HIM! AT LEAST FIND OUT WHERE YOU ARE FIRST!
DON'T WORRY, CALISTO. I JUST WANT TO SCARE HIM. HE OWES ME THAT MUCH!
WELL, STEIN PHAIS, CARE TO EXPLAIN YOUR LITTLE UNPROVOKED ATTACK? YOU KNOW, BEFORE I PUT YOU OUT OF YOUR MISERY.
HOW ABOUT WE ALL CALM DOWN FOR A MOMENT. THIS IS JUST A TRAGIC MISUNDERSTANDING.
AS YOU WISH, STEIN PHAIS. BUT FIRST I'D LIKE TO INTRODUCE YOU TO HURRICOS.
UH...HELLO, HURRICOS.
JUST REMEMBER, YOU TRY ANYTHING STUPID...
NOTHING STUPID, I PROMISE.

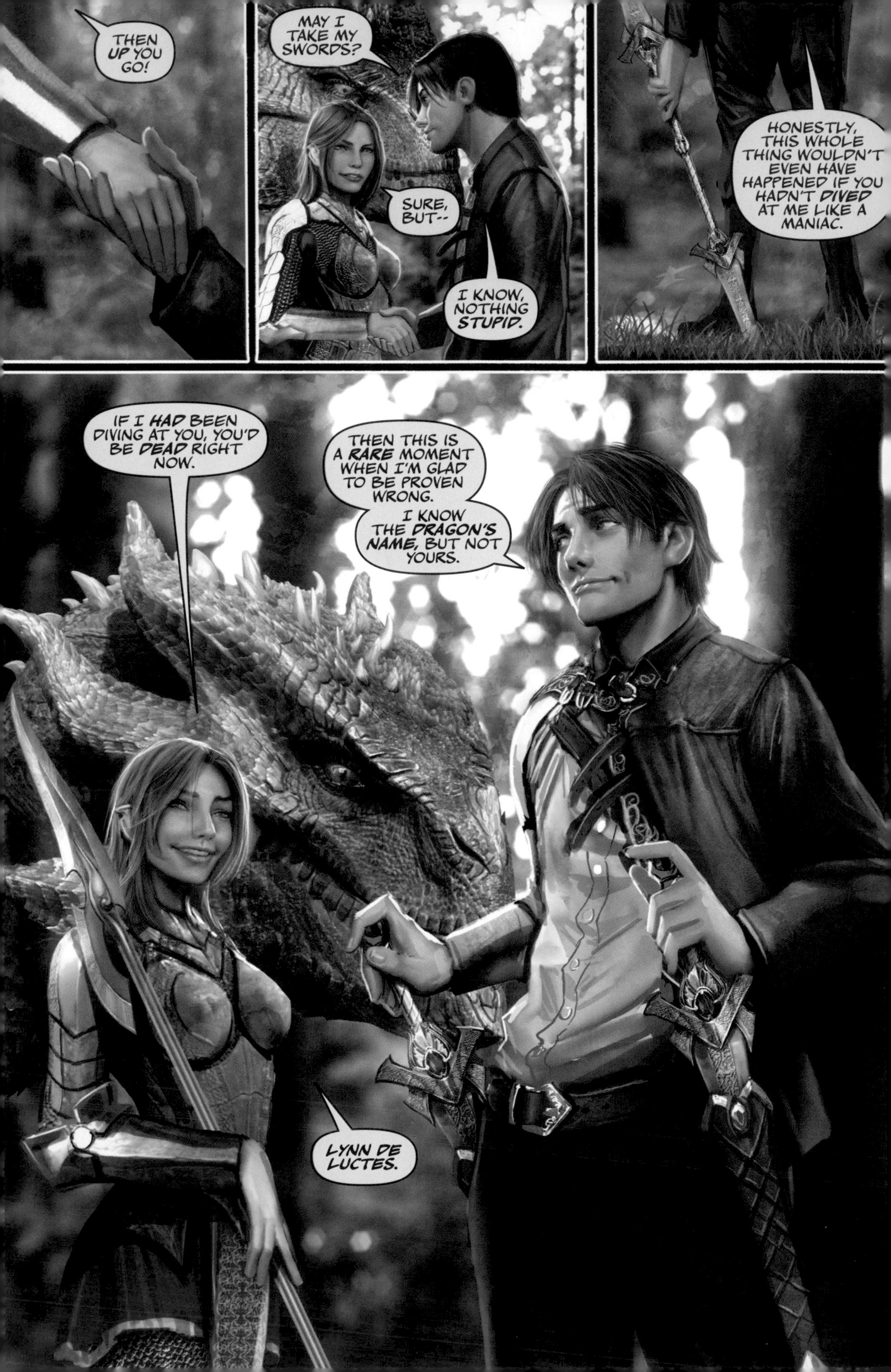
THEN UP YOU GO!
MAY I TAKE MY SWORDS?
SURE, BUT--
I KNOW, NOTHING STUPID.
HONESTLY, THIS WHOLE THING WOULDN'T EVEN HAVE HAPPENED IF YOU HADN'T DIVED AT ME LIKE A MANIAC.
IF I HAD BEEN DIVING AT YOU, YOU'D BE DEAD RIGHT NOW.
THEN THIS IS A RARE MOMENT WHEN I'M GLAD TO BE PROVEN WRONG.
I KNOW THE DRAGON'S NAME, BUT NOT YOURS.
LYNN DE LUCTES.

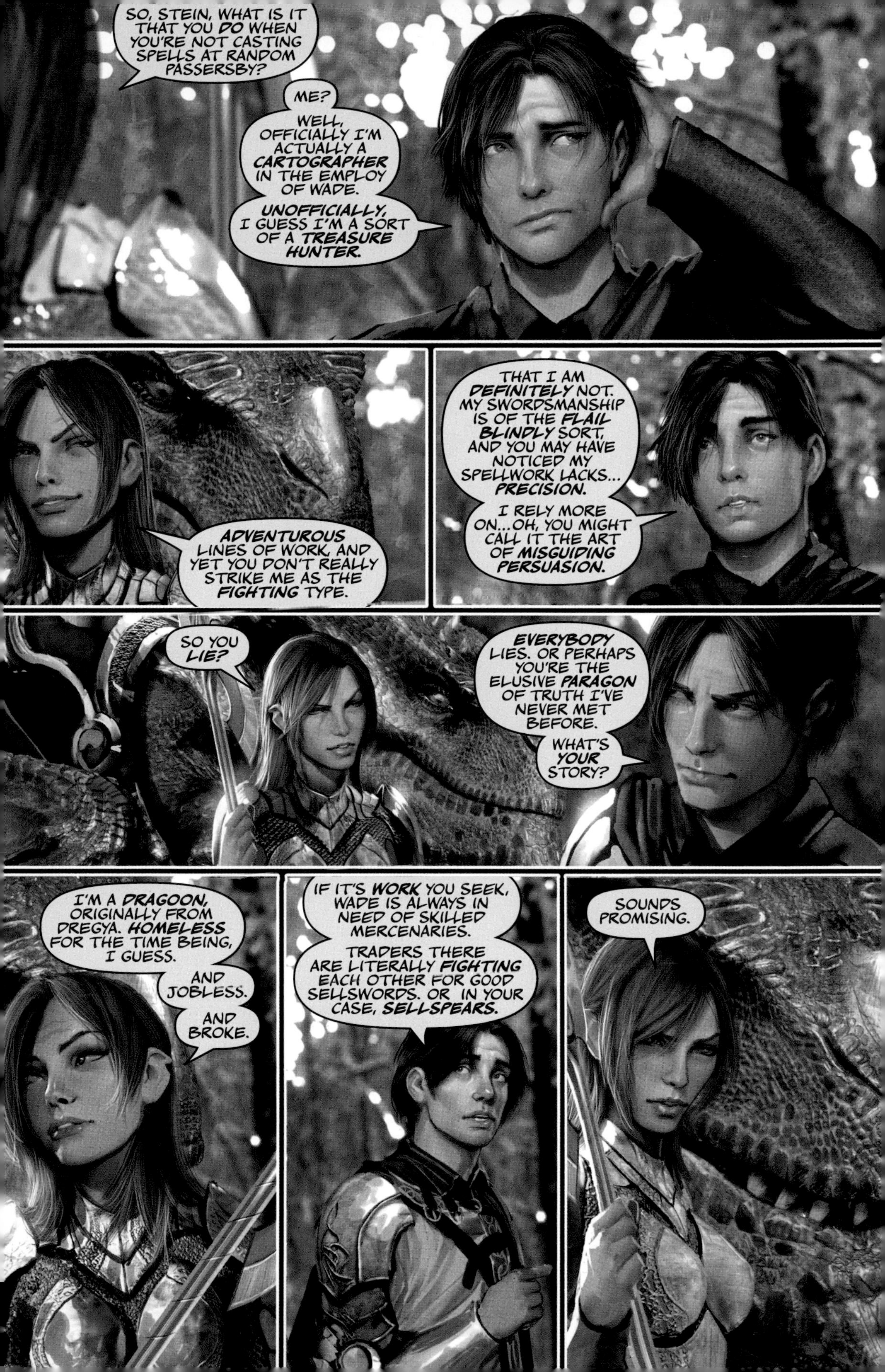
SO, STEIN, WHAT IS IT THAT YOU DO WHEN YOU'RE NOT CASTING SPELLS AT RANDOM PASSERSBY?
ME?
WELL, OFFICIALLY I'M ACTUALLY A CARTOGRAPHER IN THE EMPLOY OF WADE.
UNOFFICIALLY, I GUESS I'M A SORT OF A TREASURE HUNTER.
ADVENTUROUS LINES OF WORK, AND YET YOU DON'T REALLY STRIKE ME AS THE FIGHTING TYPE.
THAT I AM DEFINITELY NOT. MY SWORDSMANSHIP IS OF THE FLAIL BLINDLY SORT, AND YOU MAY HAVE NOTICED MY SPELLWORK LACKS... PRECISION.
I RELY MORE ON...OH, YOU MIGHT CALL IT THE ART OF MISGUIDING PERSUASION.
SO YOU LIE?
EVERYBODY LIES. OR PERHAPS YOU'RE THE ELUSIVE PARAGON OF TRUTH I'VE NEVER MET BEFORE.
WHAT'S YOUR STORY?
I'M A DRAGOON, ORIGINALLY FROM DREGYA. HOMELESS FOR THE TIME BEING, I GUESS.
AND JOBLESS.
AND BROKE.
IF IT'S WORK YOU SEEK, WADE IS ALWAYS IN NEED OF SKILLED MERCENARIES.
TRADERS THERE ARE LITERALLY FIGHTING EACH OTHER FOR GOOD SELLSWORDS. OR IN YOUR CASE, SELLSPEARS.
SOUNDS PROMISING.

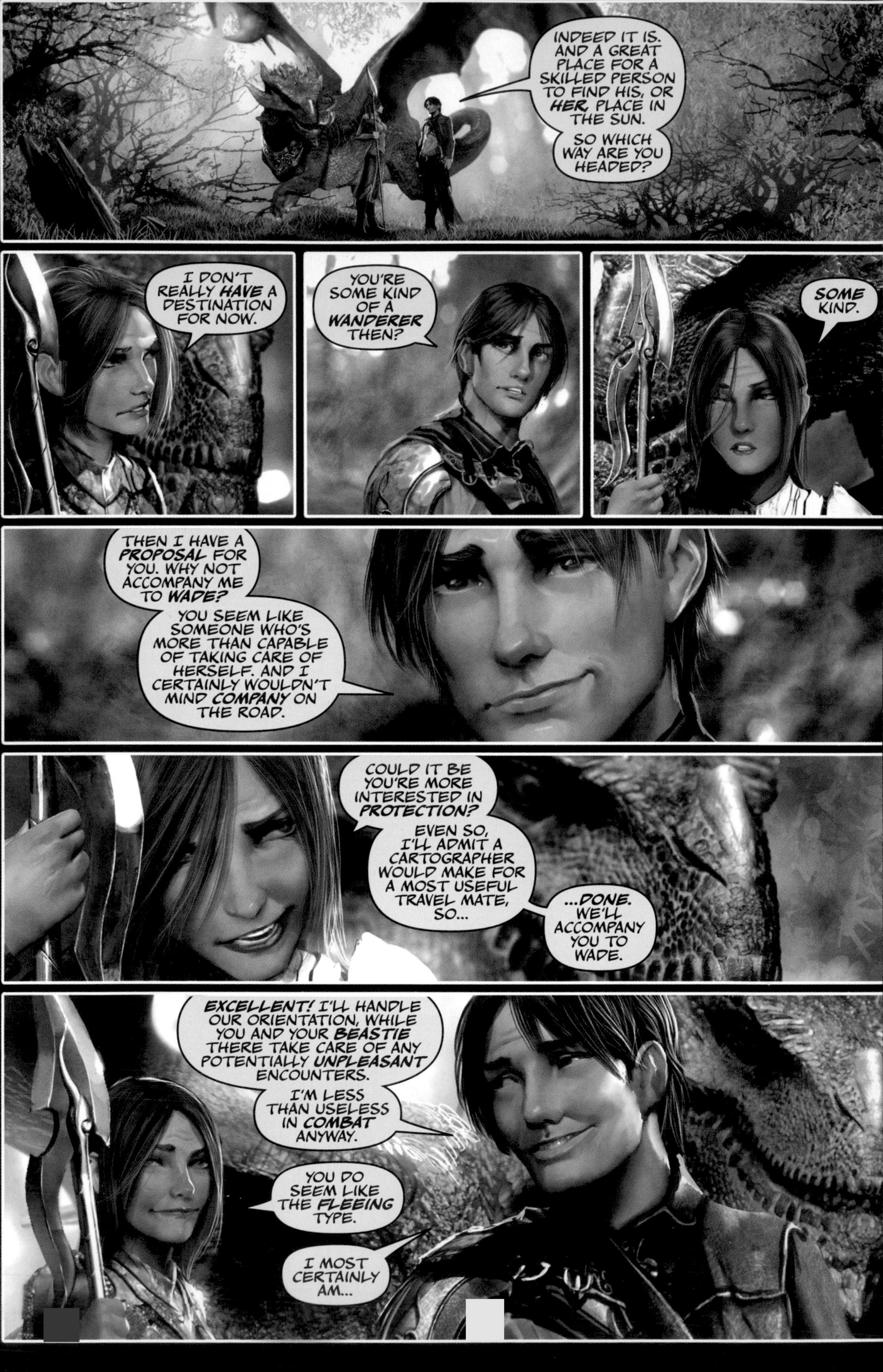
INDEED IT IS. AND A GREAT PLACE FOR A SKILLED PERSON TO FIND HIS, OR *HER*, PLACE IN THE SUN.
SO WHICH WAY ARE YOU HEADED?
I DON'T REALLY *HAVE* A DESTINATION FOR NOW.
YOU'RE SOME KIND OF A *WANDERER* THEN?
SOME KIND.
THEN I HAVE A *PROPOSAL* FOR YOU. WHY NOT ACCOMPANY ME TO *WADE?*
YOU SEEM LIKE SOMEONE WHO'S MORE THAN CAPABLE OF TAKING CARE OF HERSELF. AND I CERTAINLY WOULDN'T MIND *COMPANY* ON THE ROAD.
COULD IT BE YOU'RE MORE INTERESTED IN *PROTECTION?*
EVEN SO, I'LL ADMIT A CARTOGRAPHER WOULD MAKE FOR A MOST USEFUL TRAVEL MATE, SO...
...DONE. WE'LL ACCOMPANY YOU TO WADE.
EXCELLENT! I'LL HANDLE OUR ORIENTATION, WHILE YOU AND YOUR *BEASTIE* THERE TAKE CARE OF ANY POTENTIALLY *UNPLEASANT* ENCOUNTERS.
I'M LESS THAN USELESS IN *COMBAT* ANYWAY.
YOU DO SEEM LIKE THE *FLEEING* TYPE.
I MOST CERTAINLY AM...

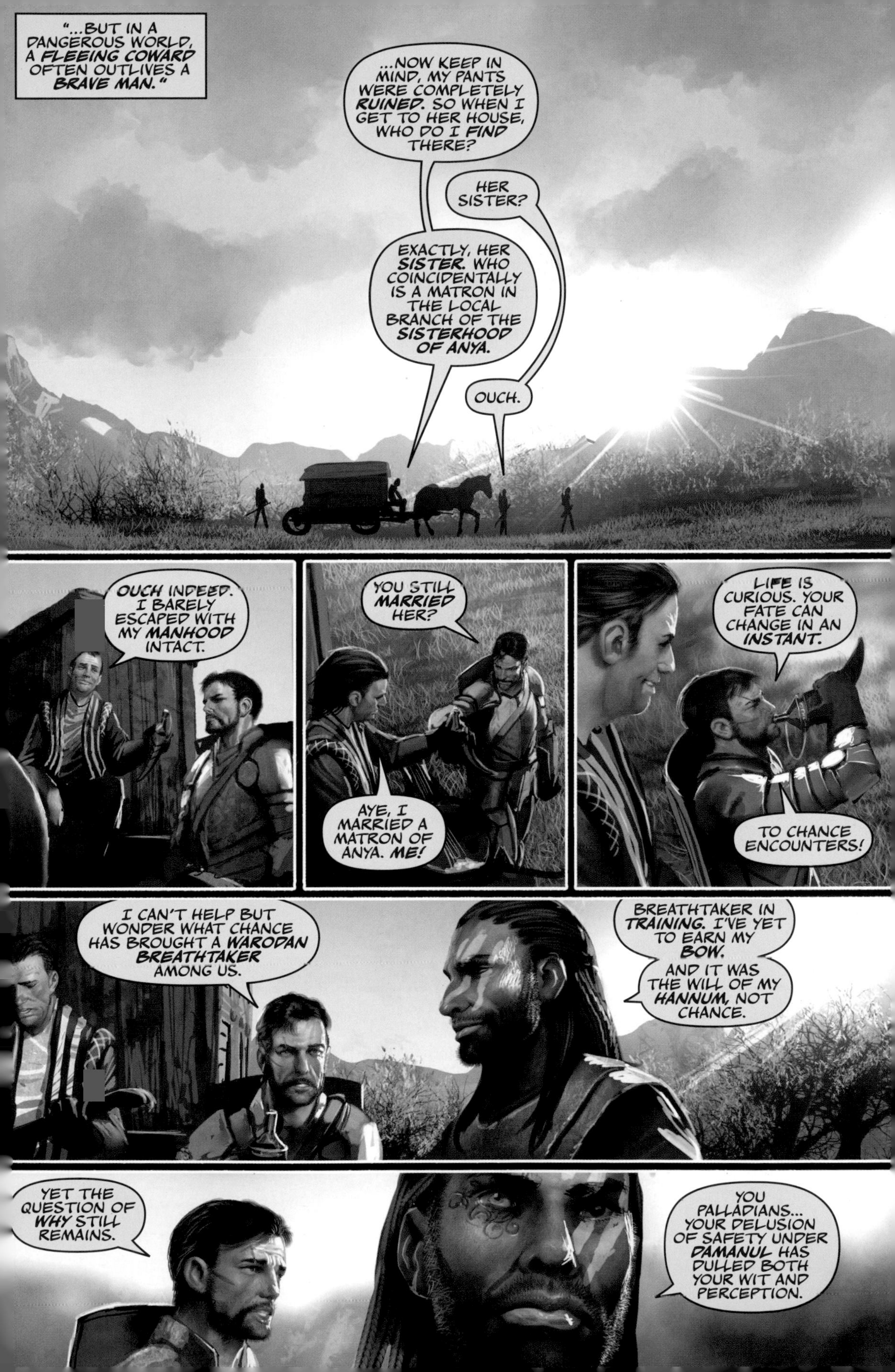
"...BUT IN A DANGEROUS WORLD, A FLEEING COWARD OFTEN OUTLIVES A BRAVE MAN."
...NOW KEEP IN MIND, MY PANTS WERE COMPLETELY RUINED. SO WHEN I GET TO HER HOUSE, WHO DO I FIND THERE?
HER SISTER?
EXACTLY, HER SISTER. WHO COINCIDENTALLY IS A MATRON IN THE LOCAL BRANCH OF THE SISTERHOOD OF ANYA.
OUCH.
OUCH INDEED. I BARELY ESCAPED WITH MY MANHOOD INTACT.
YOU STILL MARRIED HER?
AYE, I MARRIED A MATRON OF ANYA. ME!
LIFE IS CURIOUS. YOUR FATE CAN CHANGE IN AN INSTANT.
TO CHANCE ENCOUNTERS!
I CAN'T HELP BUT WONDER WHAT CHANCE HAS BROUGHT A WARODAN BREATHTAKER AMONG US.
BREATHTAKER IN TRAINING. I'VE YET TO EARN MY BOW.
AND IT WAS THE WILL OF MY HANNUM, NOT CHANCE.
YET THE QUESTION OF WHY STILL REMAINS.
YOU PALLADIANS... YOUR DELUSION OF SAFETY UNDER DAMANUL HAS DULLED BOTH YOUR WIT AND PERCEPTION.

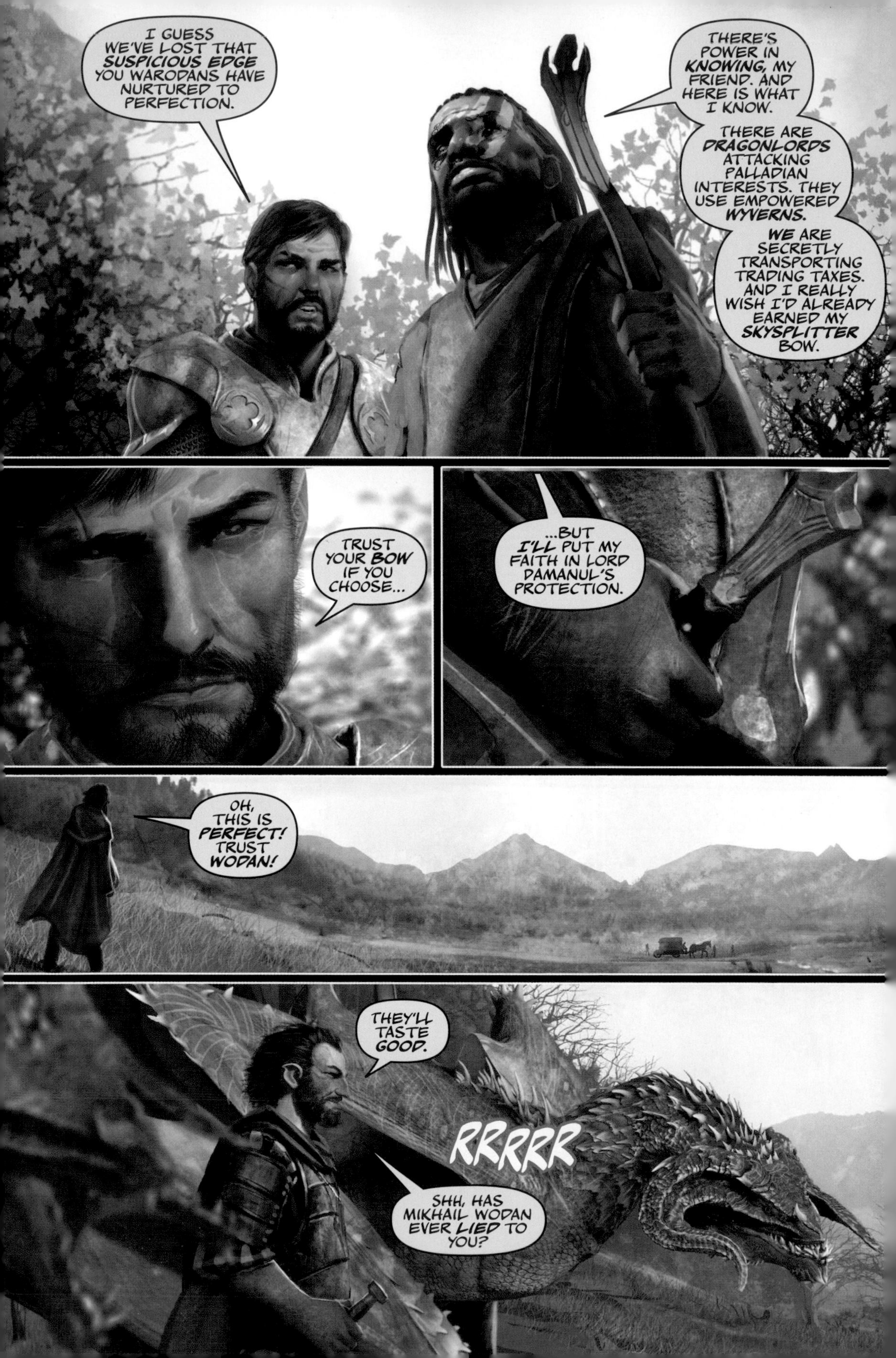
I GUESS WE'VE LOST THAT SUSPICIOUS EDGE YOU WARODANS HAVE NURTURED TO PERFECTION.
THERE'S POWER IN KNOWING, MY FRIEND. AND HERE IS WHAT I KNOW.
THERE ARE DRAGONLORDS ATTACKING PALLADIAN INTERESTS. THEY USE EMPOWERED WYVERNS.
WE ARE SECRETLY TRANSPORTING TRADING TAXES. AND I REALLY WISH I'D ALREADY EARNED MY SKYSPLITTER BOW.
TRUST YOUR BOW IF YOU CHOOSE...
...BUT I'LL PUT MY FAITH IN LORD DAMANUL'S PROTECTION.
OH, THIS IS PERFECT! TRUST WODAN!
THEY'LL TASTE GOOD.
RRRRR
SHH, HAS MIKHAIL WODAN EVER LIED TO YOU?

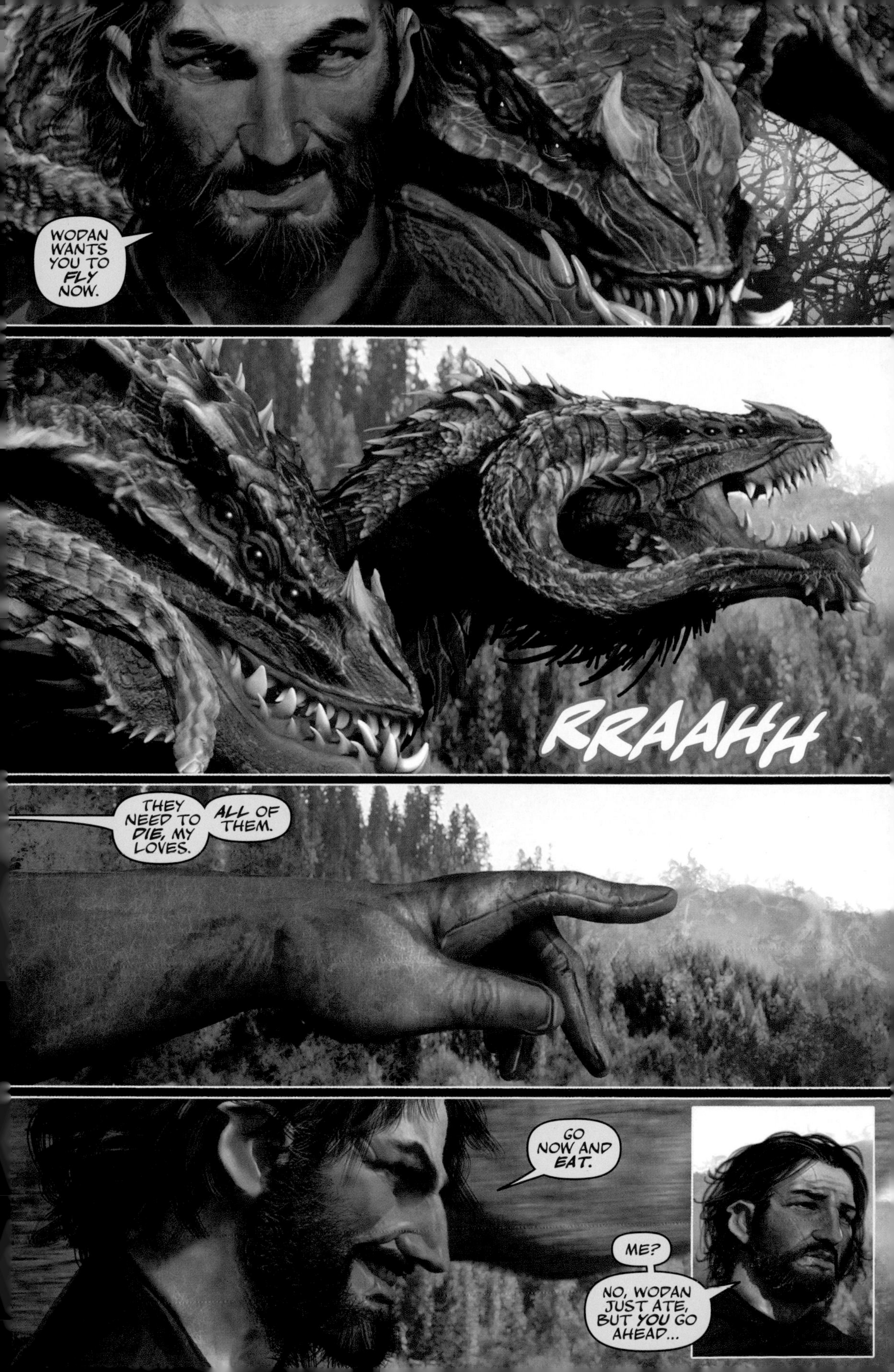
WODAN WANTS YOU TO FLY NOW.
RRAAHH
THEY NEED TO DIE, MY LOVES.
ALL OF THEM.
GO NOW AND EAT.
ME?
NO, WODAN JUST ATE, BUT YOU GO AHEAD...

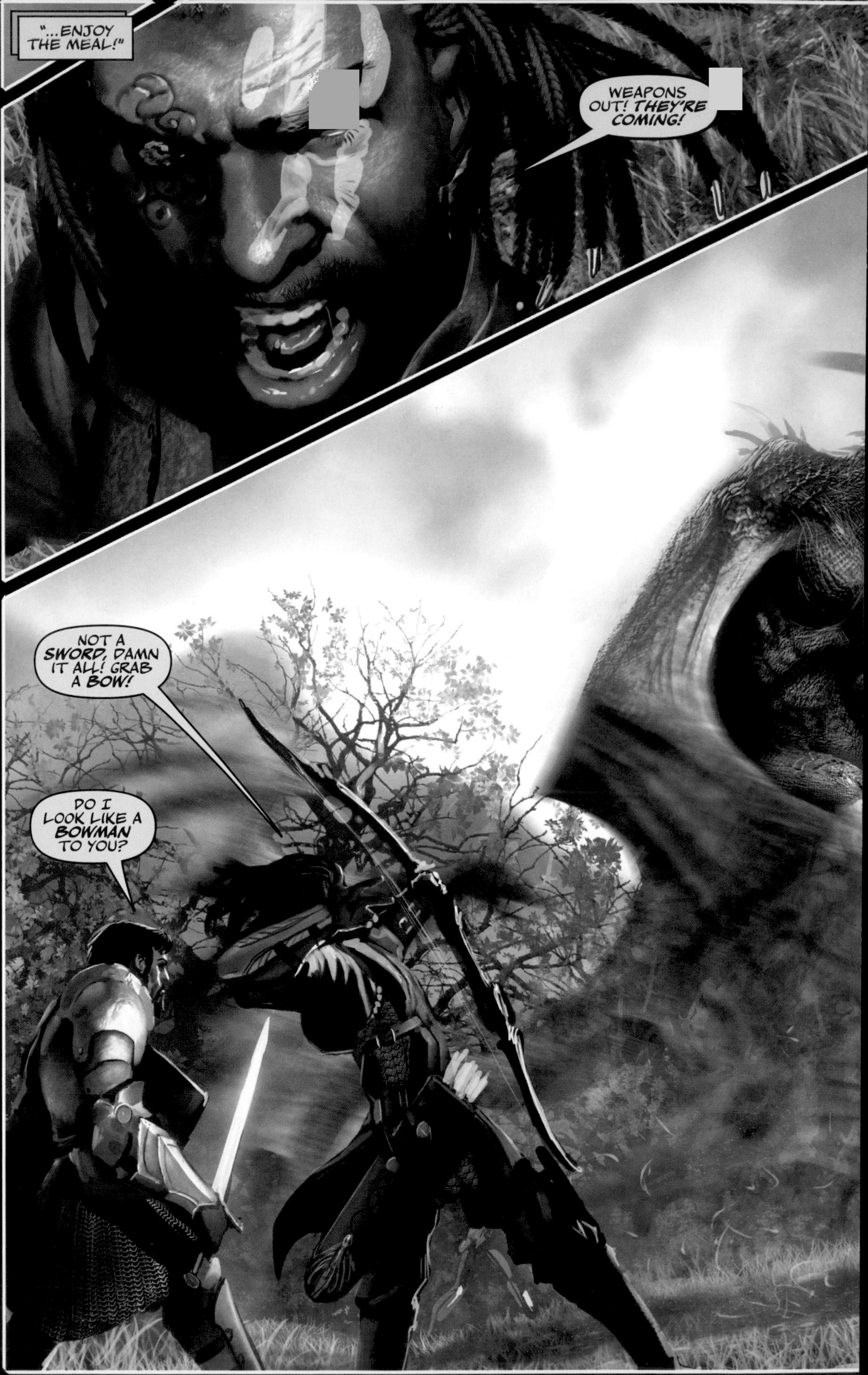
"...ENJOY THE MEAL!"
WEAPONS OUT! THEY'RE COMING!
NOT A SWORD, DAMN IT ALL! GRAB A BOW!
DO I LOOK LIKE A BOWMAN TO YOU?

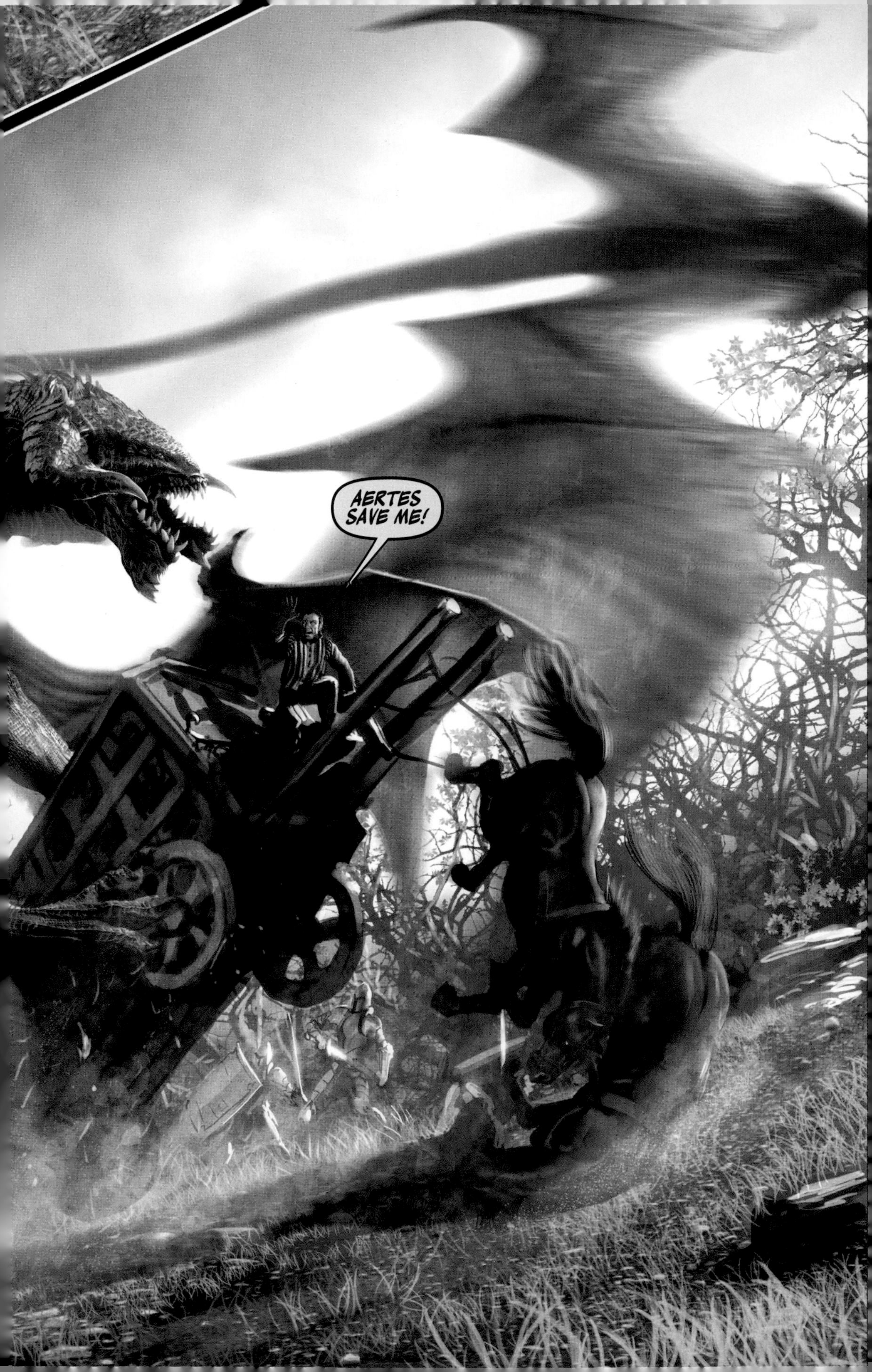
AERTES SAVE ME!

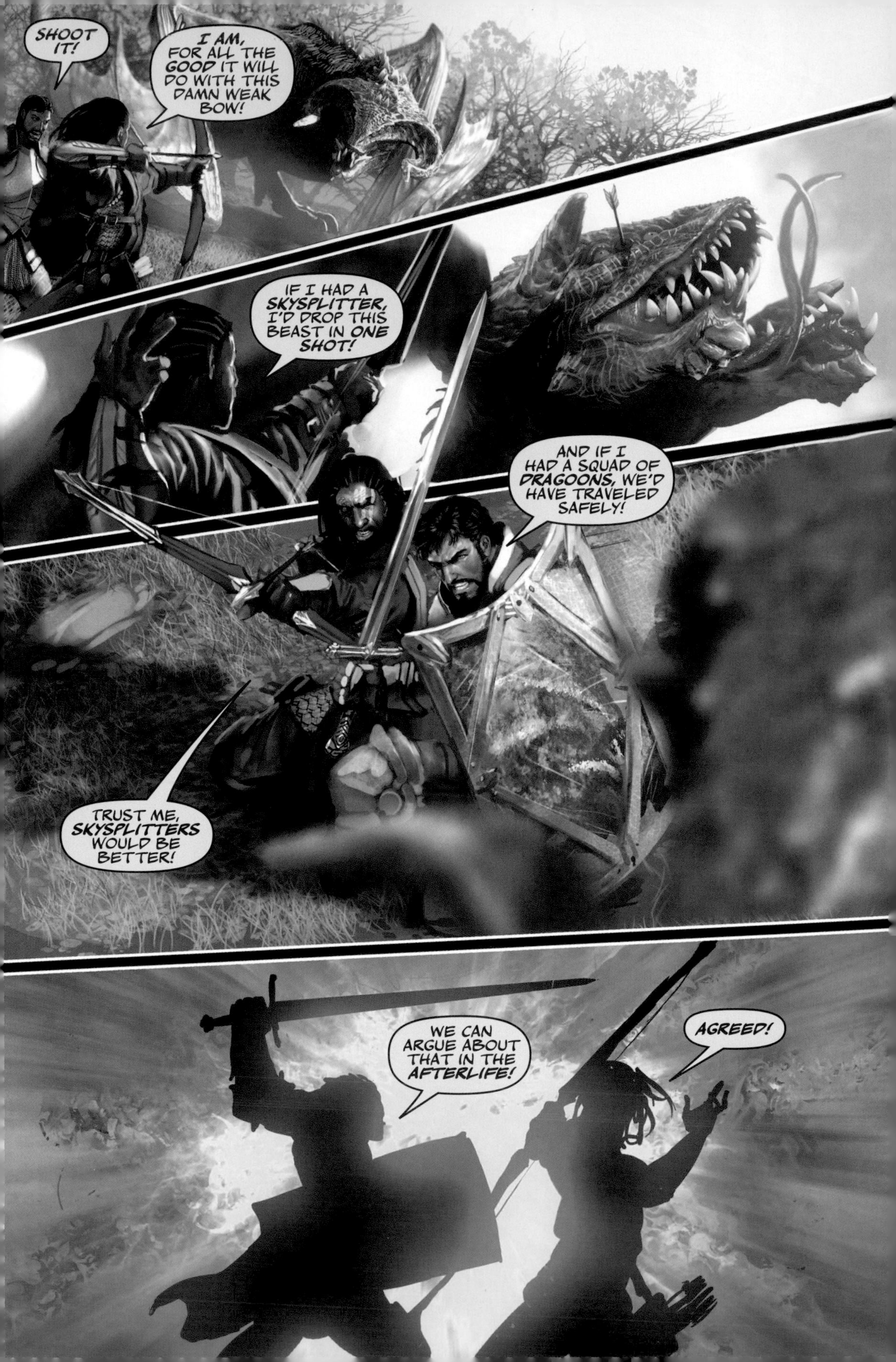
SHOOT IT!
I AM, FOR ALL THE GOOD IT WILL DO WITH THIS DAMN WEAK BOW!
IF I HAD A SKYSPLITTER, I'D DROP THIS BEAST IN ONE SHOT!
AND IF I HAD A SQUAD OF DRAGOONS, WE'D HAVE TRAVELED SAFELY!
TRUST ME, SKYSPLITTERS WOULD BE BETTER!
WE CAN ARGUE ABOUT THAT IN THE AFTERLIFE!
AGREED!

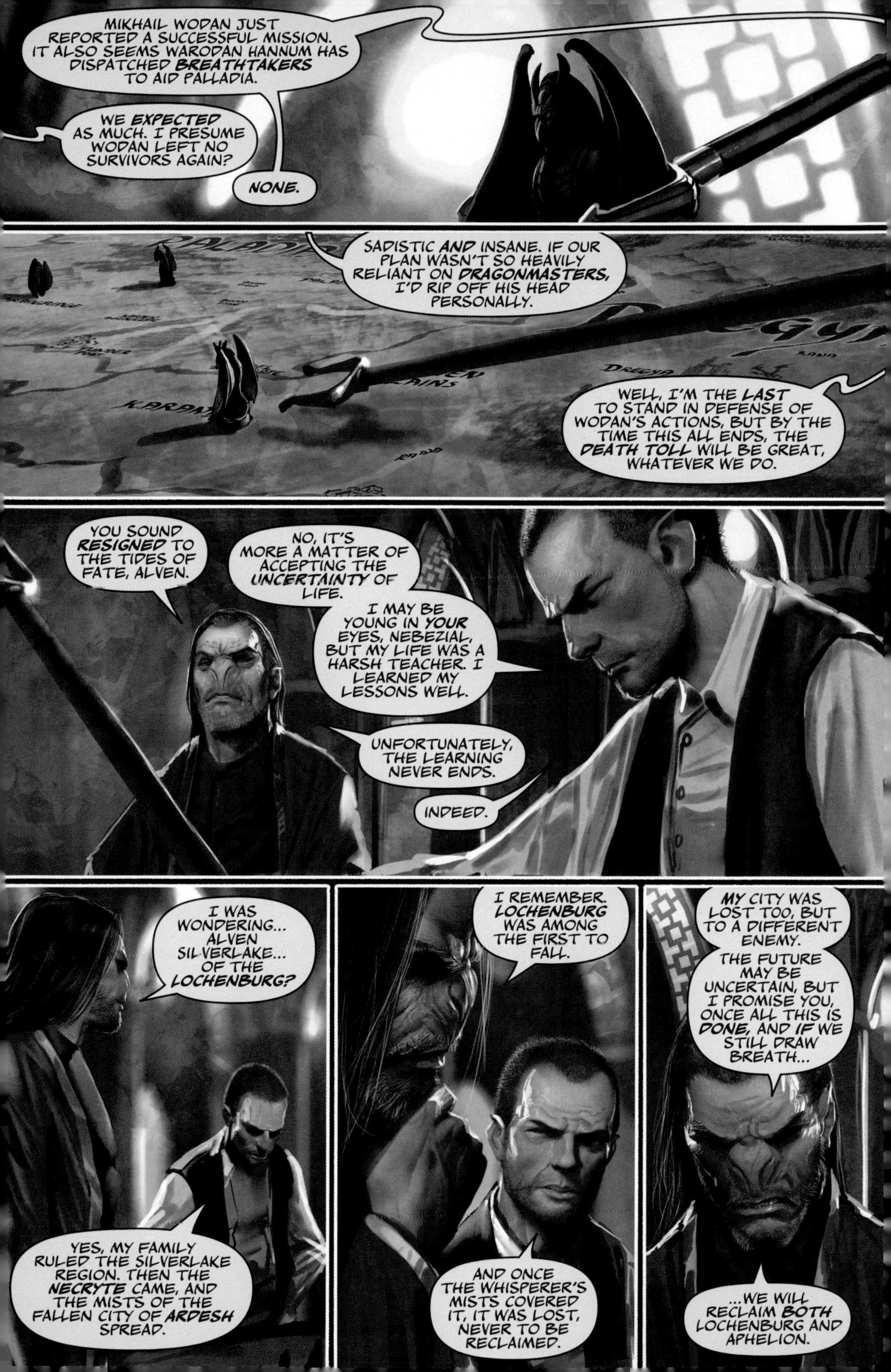
MIKHAIL WODAN JUST REPORTED A SUCCESSFUL MISSION. IT ALSO SEEMS WARODAN HANNUM HAS DISPATCHED BREATHTAKERS TO AID PALLADIA.
WE EXPECTED AS MUCH. I PRESUME WODAN LEFT NO SURVIVORS AGAIN?
NONE.
SADISTIC AND INSANE. IF OUR PLAN WASN'T SO HEAVILY RELIANT ON DRAGONMASTERS, I'D RIP OFF HIS HEAD PERSONALLY.
WELL, I'M THE LAST TO STAND IN DEFENSE OF WODAN'S ACTIONS, BUT BY THE TIME THIS ALL ENDS, THE DEATH TOLL WILL BE GREAT, WHATEVER WE DO.
YOU SOUND RESIGNED TO THE TIDES OF FATE, ALVEN.
NO, IT'S MORE A MATTER OF ACCEPTING THE UNCERTAINTY OF LIFE.
I MAY BE YOUNG IN YOUR EYES, NEBEZIAL, BUT MY LIFE WAS A HARSH TEACHER. I LEARNED MY LESSONS WELL.
UNFORTUNATELY, THE LEARNING NEVER ENDS.
INDEED.
I WAS WONDERING... ALVEN SILVERLAKE... OF THE LOCHENBURG?
YES, MY FAMILY RULED THE SILVERLAKE REGION. THEN THE NECRYTE CAME, AND THE MISTS OF THE FALLEN CITY OF ARDESH SPREAD.
I REMEMBER. LOCHENBURG WAS AMONG THE FIRST TO FALL.
AND ONCE THE WHISPERER'S MISTS COVERED IT, IT WAS LOST, NEVER TO BE RECLAIMED.
MY CITY WAS LOST TOO, BUT TO A DIFFERENT ENEMY.
THE FUTURE MAY BE UNCERTAIN, BUT I PROMISE YOU, ONCE ALL THIS IS DONE, AND IF WE STILL DRAW BREATH...
...WE WILL RECLAIM BOTH LOCHENBURG AND APHELION.

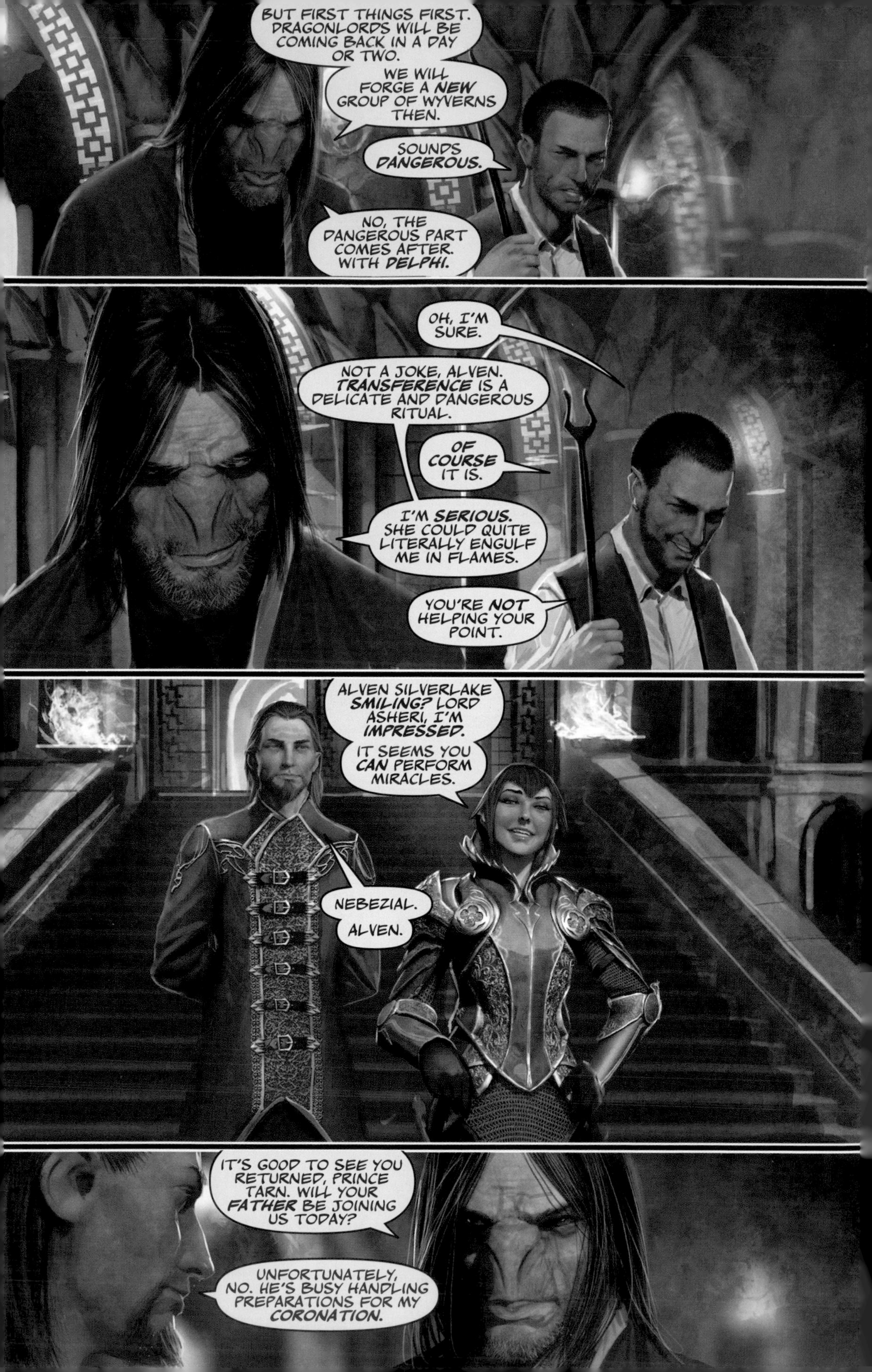
BUT FIRST THINGS FIRST. DRAGONLORDS WILL BE COMING BACK IN A DAY OR TWO.
WE WILL FORGE A NEW GROUP OF WYVERNS THEN.
SOUNDS DANGEROUS.
NO, THE DANGEROUS PART COMES AFTER. WITH DELPHI.
OH, I'M SURE.
NOT A JOKE, ALVEN. TRANSFERENCE IS A DELICATE AND DANGEROUS RITUAL.
OF COURSE IT IS.
I'M SERIOUS. SHE COULD QUITE LITERALLY ENGULF ME IN FLAMES.
YOU'RE NOT HELPING YOUR POINT.
ALVEN SILVERLAKE SMILING? LORD ASHERI, I'M IMPRESSED.
IT SEEMS YOU CAN PERFORM MIRACLES.
NEBEZIAL.
ALVEN.
IT'S GOOD TO SEE YOU RETURNED, PRINCE TARN. WILL YOUR FATHER BE JOINING US TODAY?
UNFORTUNATELY, NO. HE'S BUSY HANDLING PREPARATIONS FOR MY CORONATION.

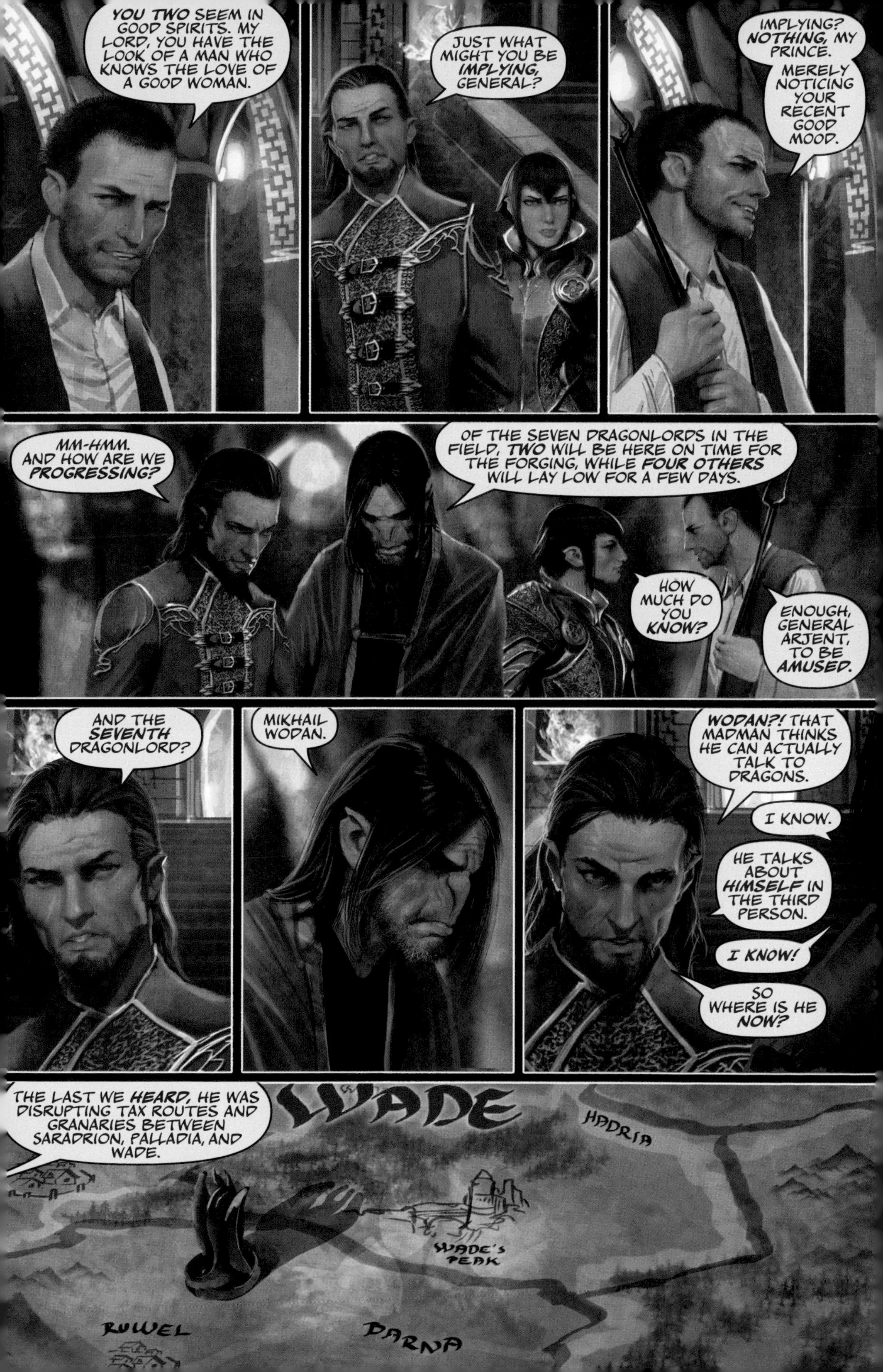
YOU TWO SEEM IN GOOD SPIRITS. MY LORD, YOU HAVE THE LOOK OF A MAN WHO KNOWS THE LOVE OF A GOOD WOMAN.
JUST WHAT MIGHT YOU BE IMPLYING, GENERAL?
IMPLYING? NOTHING, MY PRINCE.
MERELY NOTICING YOUR RECENT GOOD MOOD.
MM-HMM. AND HOW ARE WE PROGRESSING?
OF THE SEVEN DRAGONLORDS IN THE FIELD, TWO WILL BE HERE ON TIME FOR THE FORGING, WHILE FOUR OTHERS WILL LAY LOW FOR A FEW DAYS.
HOW MUCH DO YOU KNOW?
ENOUGH, GENERAL ARJENT, TO BE AMUSED.
AND THE SEVENTH DRAGONLORD?
MIKHAIL WODAN.
WODAN?! THAT MADMAN THINKS HE CAN ACTUALLY TALK TO DRAGONS.
I KNOW.
HE TALKS ABOUT HIMSELF IN THE THIRD PERSON.
I KNOW!
SO WHERE IS HE NOW?
THE LAST WE HEARD, HE WAS DISRUPTING TAX ROUTES AND GRANARIES BETWEEN SARADRION, PALLADIA, AND WADE.
WADE
HADRIA
WADE'S PEAK
RUWEL
BARNA

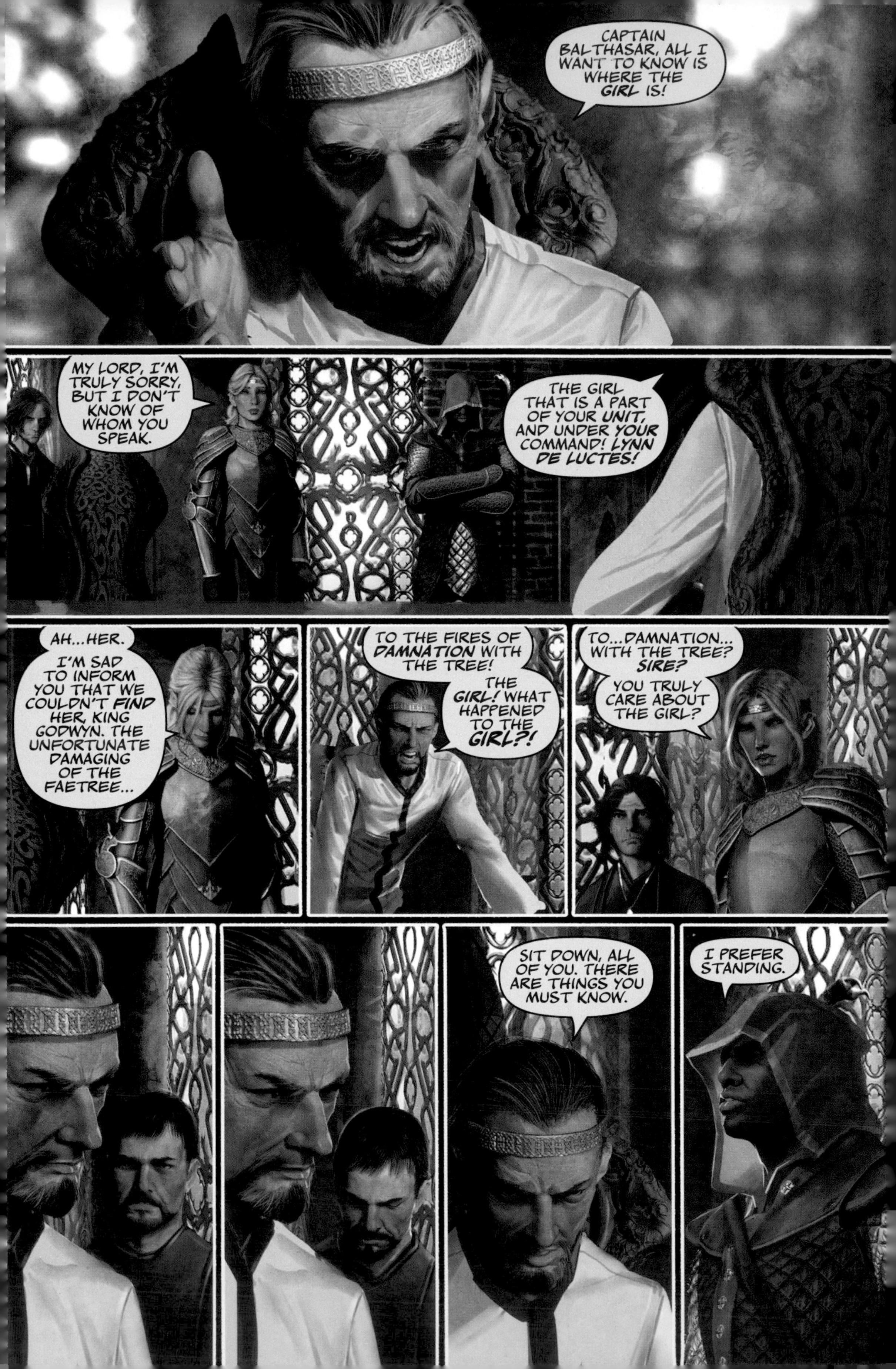
CAPTAIN BALTHASAR, ALL I WANT TO KNOW IS WHERE THE GIRL IS!
MY LORD, I'M TRULY SORRY, BUT I DON'T KNOW OF WHOM YOU SPEAK.
THE GIRL THAT IS A PART OF YOUR UNIT, AND UNDER YOUR COMMAND! LYNN DE LUCTES!
AH...HER.
I'M SAD TO INFORM YOU THAT WE COULDN'T FIND HER, KING GODWYN. THE UNFORTUNATE DAMAGING OF THE FAETREE...
TO THE FIRES OF DAMNATION WITH THE TREE!
THE GIRL! WHAT HAPPENED TO THE GIRL?!
TO...DAMNATION... WITH THE TREE? SIRE?
YOU TRULY CARE ABOUT THE GIRL?
SIT DOWN, ALL OF YOU. THERE ARE THINGS YOU MUST KNOW.
I PREFER STANDING.

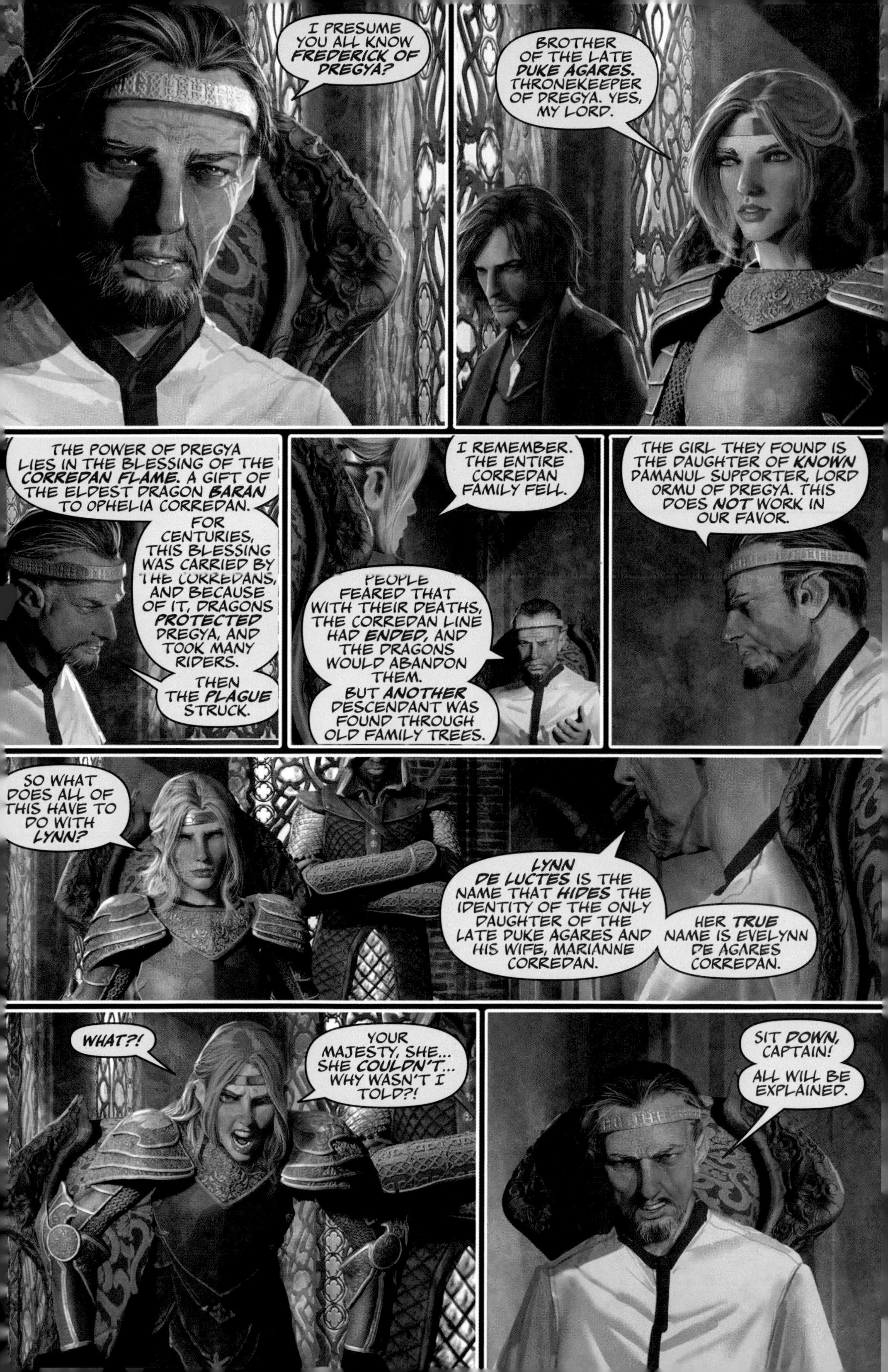
I PRESUME YOU ALL KNOW FREDERICK OF DREGYA?
BROTHER OF THE LATE DUKE AGARES. THRONEKEEPER OF DREGYA. YES, MY LORD.
THE POWER OF DREGYA LIES IN THE BLESSING OF THE CORREDAN FLAME. A GIFT OF THE ELDEST DRAGON BARAN TO OPHELIA CORREDAN.
FOR CENTURIES, THIS BLESSING WAS CARRIED BY THE CORREDANS, AND BECAUSE OF IT, DRAGONS PROTECTED DREGYA, AND TOOK MANY RIDERS.
THEN THE PLAGUE STRUCK.
I REMEMBER. THE ENTIRE CORREDAN FAMILY FELL.
PEOPLE FEARED THAT WITH THEIR DEATHS, THE CORREDAN LINE HAD ENDED, AND THE DRAGONS WOULD ABANDON THEM.
BUT ANOTHER DESCENDANT WAS FOUND THROUGH OLD FAMILY TREES.
THE GIRL THEY FOUND IS THE DAUGHTER OF KNOWN DAMANUL SUPPORTER, LORD ORMU OF DREGYA. THIS DOES NOT WORK IN OUR FAVOR.
SO WHAT DOES ALL OF THIS HAVE TO DO WITH LYNN?
LYNN DE LUCTES IS THE NAME THAT HIDES THE IDENTITY OF THE ONLY DAUGHTER OF THE LATE DUKE AGARES AND HIS WIFE, MARIANNE CORREDAN.
HER TRUE NAME IS EVELYNN DE AGARES CORREDAN.
WHAT?!
YOUR MAJESTY, SHE... SHE COULDN'T... WHY WASN'T I TOLD?!
SIT DOWN, CAPTAIN!
ALL WILL BE EXPLAINED.

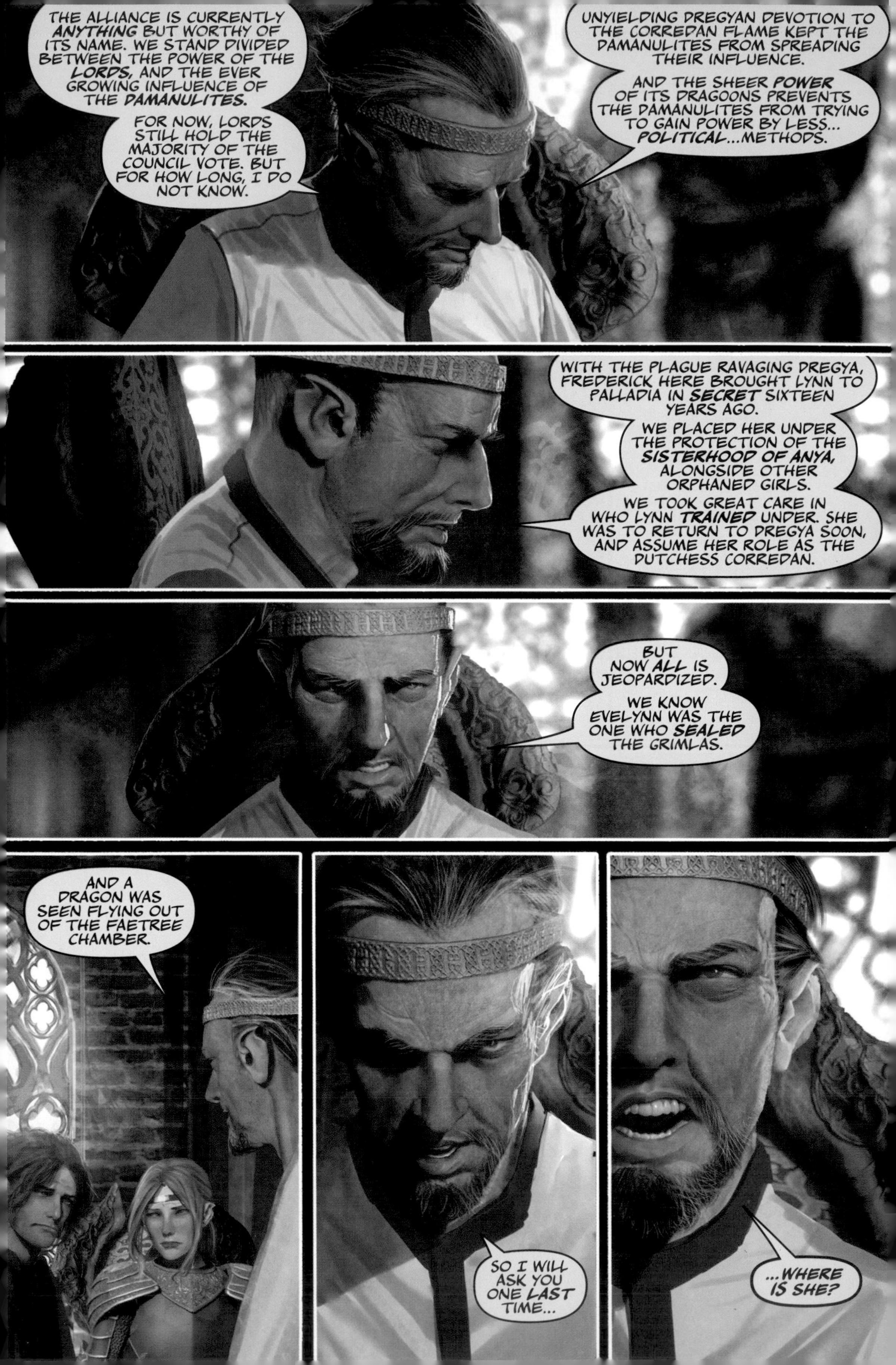
THE ALLIANCE IS CURRENTLY ANYTHING BUT WORTHY OF ITS NAME. WE STAND DIVIDED BETWEEN THE POWER OF THE LORDS, AND THE EVER GROWING INFLUENCE OF THE DAMANULITES.
FOR NOW, LORDS STILL HOLD THE MAJORITY OF THE COUNCIL VOTE. BUT FOR HOW LONG, I DO NOT KNOW.
UNYIELDING DREGYAN DEVOTION TO THE CORREDAN FLAME KEPT THE DAMANULITES FROM SPREADING THEIR INFLUENCE.
AND THE SHEER POWER OF ITS DRAGOONS PREVENTS THE DAMANULITES FROM TRYING TO GAIN POWER BY LESS... POLITICAL...METHODS.
WITH THE PLAGUE RAVAGING DREGYA, FREDERICK HERE BROUGHT LYNN TO PALLADIA IN SECRET SIXTEEN YEARS AGO.
WE PLACED HER UNDER THE PROTECTION OF THE SISTERHOOD OF ANYA, ALONGSIDE OTHER ORPHANED GIRLS.
WE TOOK GREAT CARE IN WHO LYNN TRAINED UNDER. SHE WAS TO RETURN TO DREGYA SOON, AND ASSUME HER ROLE AS THE DUTCHESS CORREDAN.
BUT NOW ALL IS JEOPARDIZED.
WE KNOW EVELYNN WAS THE ONE WHO SEALED THE GRIMLAS.
AND A DRAGON WAS SEEN FLYING OUT OF THE FAETREE CHAMBER.
SO I WILL ASK YOU ONE LAST TIME...
...WHERE IS SHE?

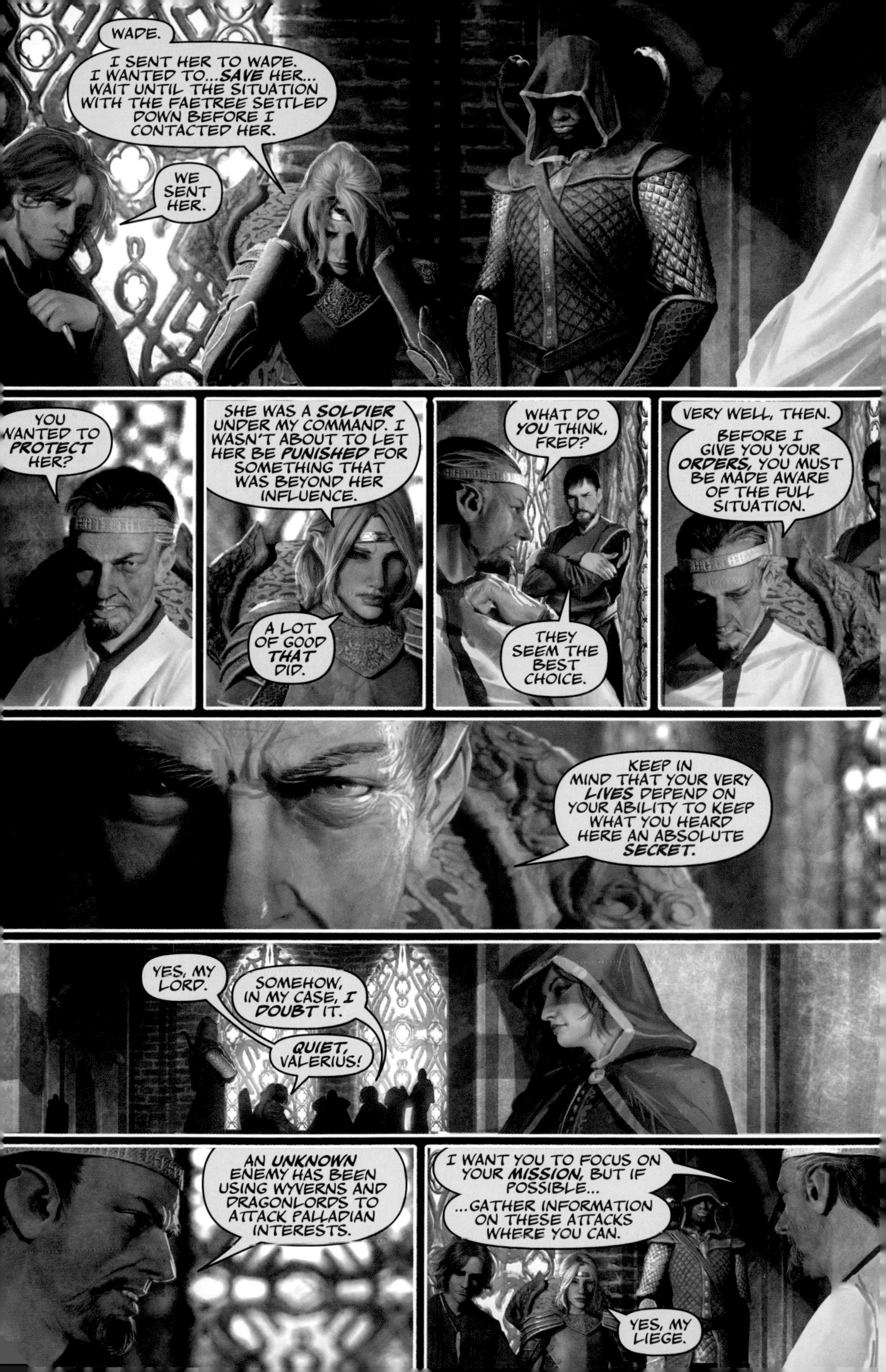
WADE.
I SENT HER TO WADE. I WANTED TO...SAVE HER... WAIT UNTIL THE SITUATION WITH THE FAETREE SETTLED DOWN BEFORE I CONTACTED HER.
WE SENT HER.
YOU WANTED TO PROTECT HER?
SHE WAS A SOLDIER UNDER MY COMMAND. I WASN'T ABOUT TO LET HER BE PUNISHED FOR SOMETHING THAT WAS BEYOND HER INFLUENCE.
A LOT OF GOOD THAT DID.
WHAT DO YOU THINK, FRED?
THEY SEEM THE BEST CHOICE.
VERY WELL, THEN.
BEFORE I GIVE YOU YOUR ORDERS, YOU MUST BE MADE AWARE OF THE FULL SITUATION.
KEEP IN MIND THAT YOUR VERY LIVES DEPEND ON YOUR ABILITY TO KEEP WHAT YOU HEARD HERE AN ABSOLUTE SECRET.
YES, MY LORD.
SOMEHOW, IN MY CASE, I DOUBT IT.
QUIET, VALERIUS!
AN UNKNOWN ENEMY HAS BEEN USING WYVERNS AND DRAGONLORDS TO ATTACK PALLADIAN INTERESTS.
I WANT YOU TO FOCUS ON YOUR MISSION, BUT IF POSSIBLE...
...GATHER INFORMATION ON THESE ATTACKS WHERE YOU CAN.
YES, MY LIEGE.

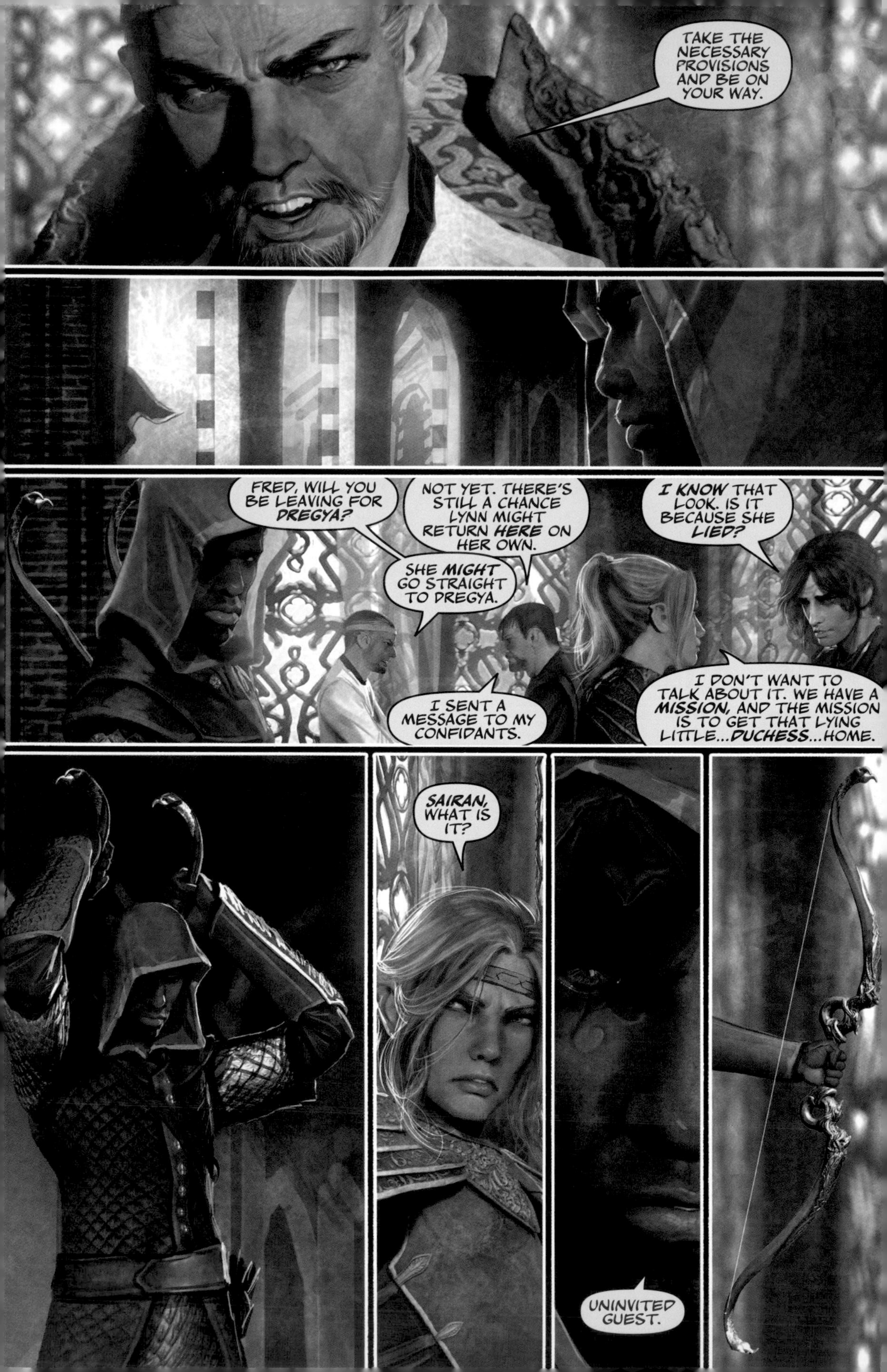
TAKE THE NECESSARY PROVISIONS AND BE ON YOUR WAY.
FRED, WILL YOU BE LEAVING FOR DREGYA?
NOT YET. THERE'S STILL A CHANCE LYNN MIGHT RETURN HERE ON HER OWN.
SHE MIGHT GO STRAIGHT TO DREGYA.
I SENT A MESSAGE TO MY CONFIDANTS.
I KNOW THAT LOOK. IS IT BECAUSE SHE LIED?
I DON'T WANT TO TALK ABOUT IT. WE HAVE A MISSION, AND THE MISSION IS TO GET THAT LYING LITTLE...DUCHESS...HOME.
SAIRAN, WHAT IS IT?
UNINVITED GUEST.

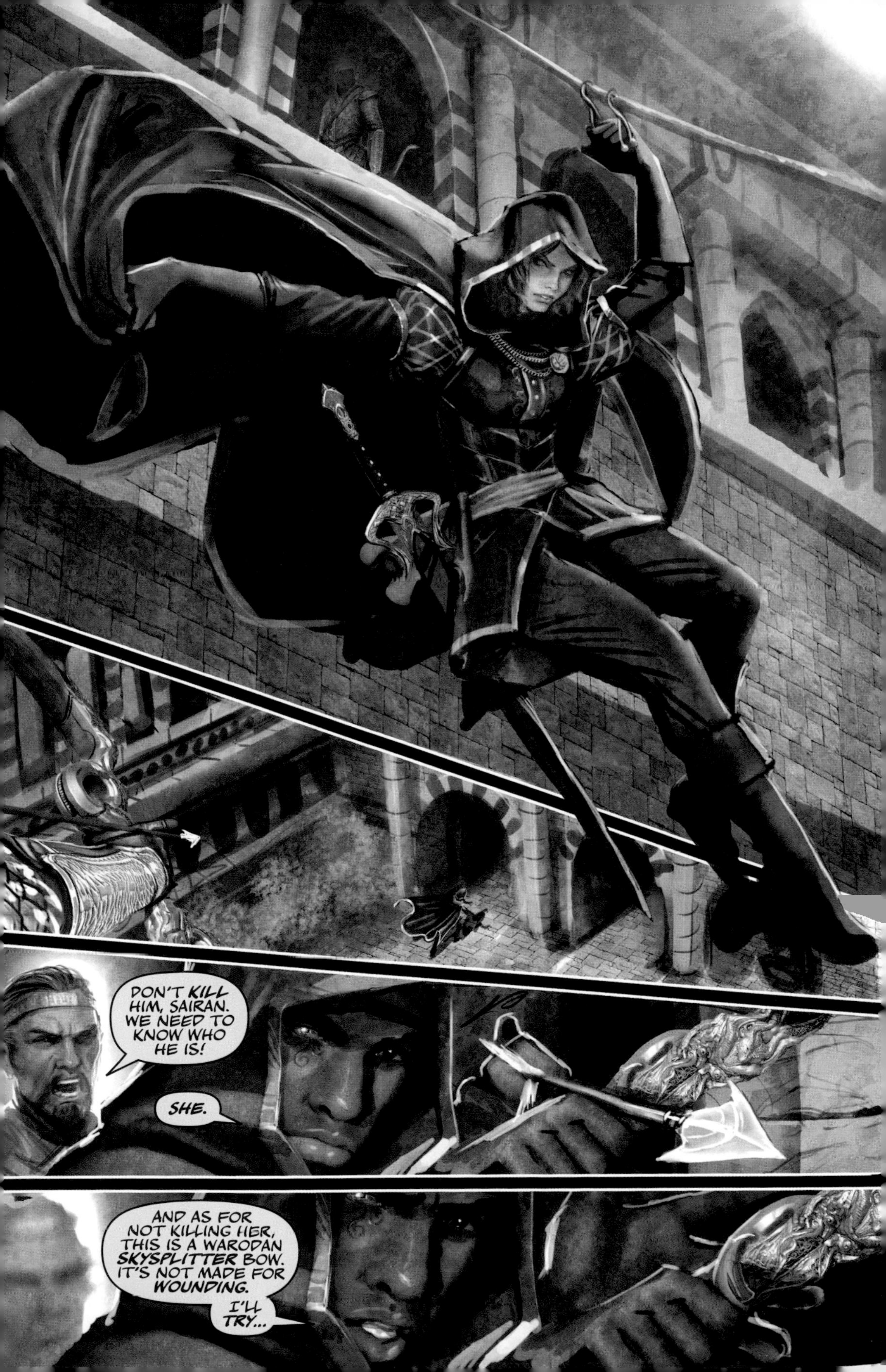
DON'T KILL HIM, SAIRAN. WE NEED TO KNOW WHO HE IS!
SHE.
AND AS FOR NOT KILLING HER, THIS IS A WARODAN SKYSPLITTER BOW. IT'S NOT MADE FOR WOUNDING.
I'LL TRY...

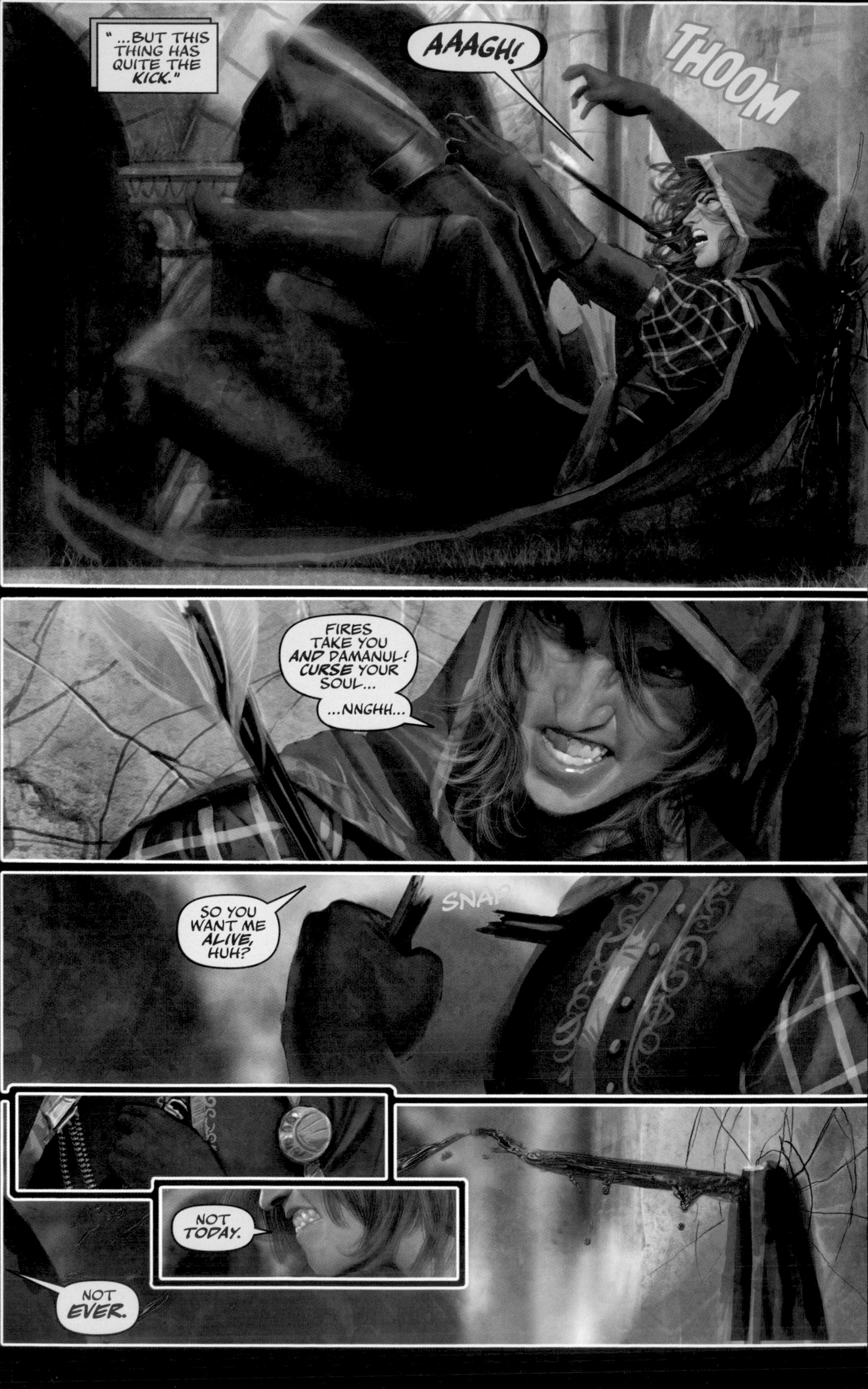
"...BUT THIS THING HAS QUITE THE KICK."
AAAGH!
THOOM
FIRES TAKE YOU AND DAMANUL! CURSE YOUR SOUL...
...NNGHH...
SO YOU WANT ME ALIVE, HUH?
SNAP
NOT TODAY.
NOT EVER.

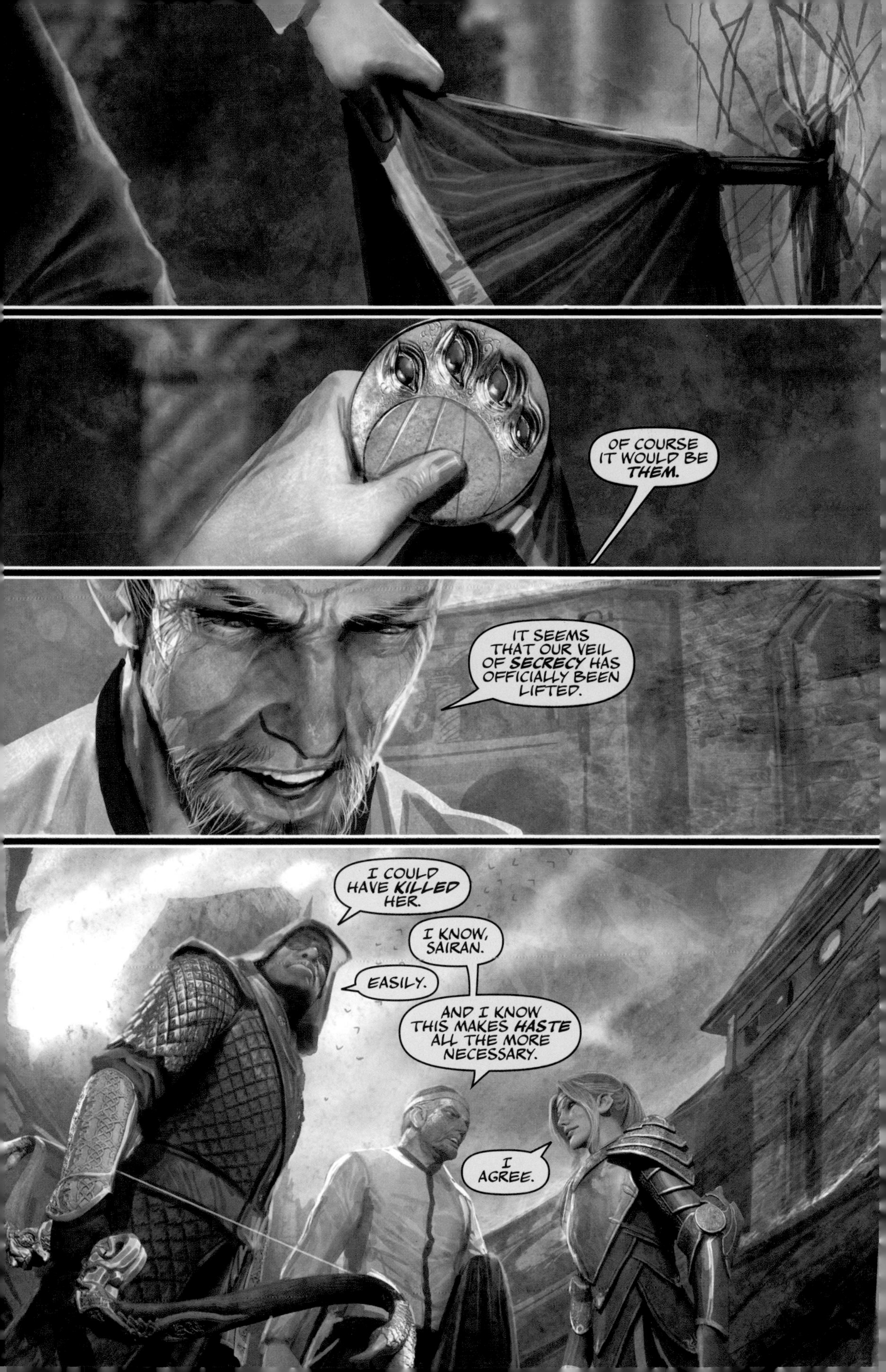
OF COURSE IT WOULD BE THEM.
IT SEEMS THAT OUR VEIL OF SECRECY HAS OFFICIALLY BEEN LIFTED.
I COULD HAVE KILLED HER.
I KNOW, SAIRAN.
EASILY.
AND I KNOW THIS MAKES HASTE ALL THE MORE NECESSARY.
I AGREE.

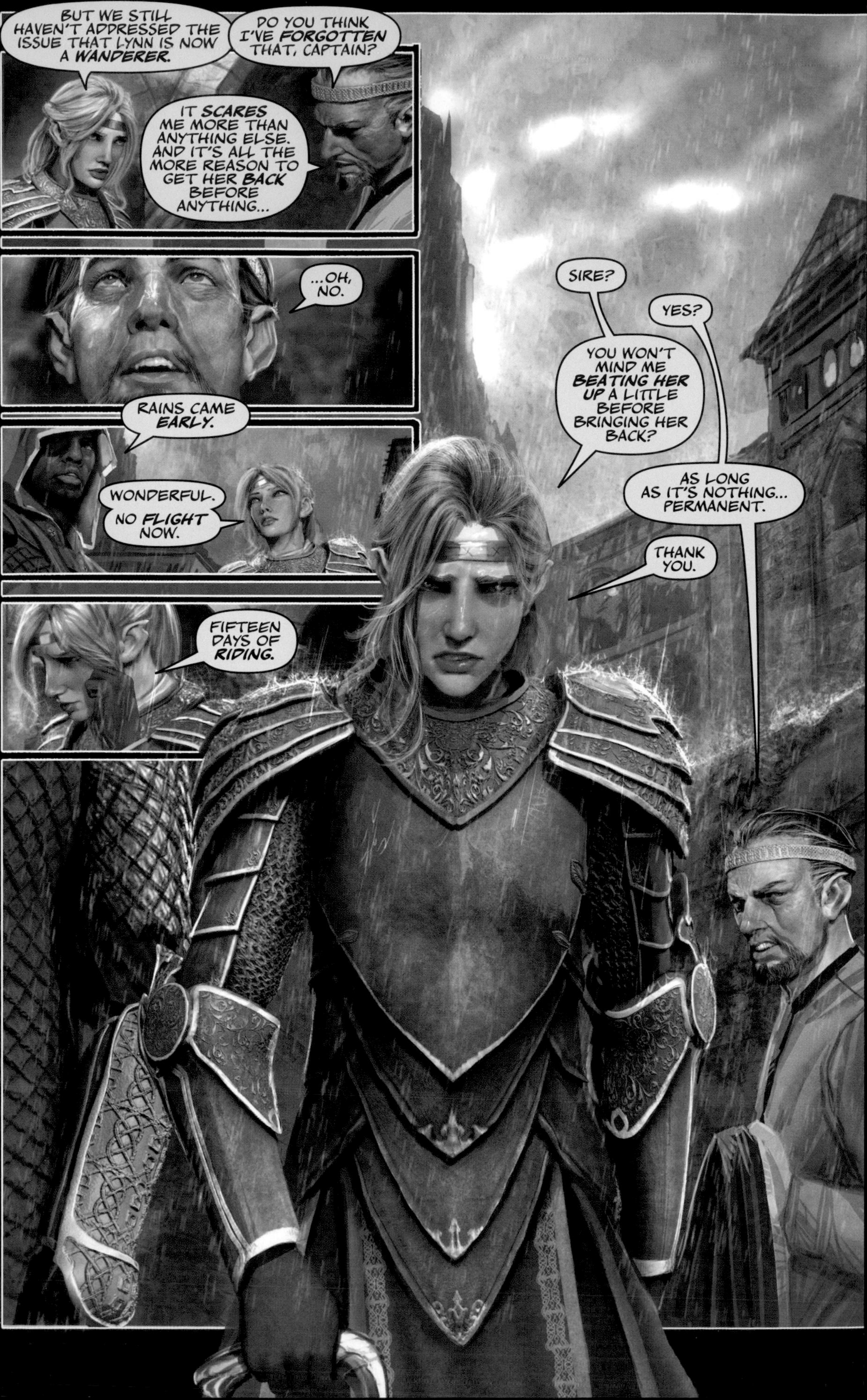

BUT WE STILL HAVEN'T ADDRESSED THE ISSUE THAT LYNN IS NOW A WANDERER.
DO YOU THINK I'VE FORGOTTEN THAT, CAPTAIN?
IT SCARES ME MORE THAN ANYTHING ELSE. AND IT'S ALL THE MORE REASON TO GET HER BACK BEFORE ANYTHING...
...OH, NO.
RAINS CAME EARLY.
WONDERFUL. NO FLIGHT NOW.
FIFTEEN DAYS OF RIDING.
SIRE?
YES?
YOU WON'T MIND ME BEATING HER UP A LITTLE BEFORE BRINGING HER BACK?
AS LONG AS IT'S NOTHING... PERMANENT.
THANK YOU.

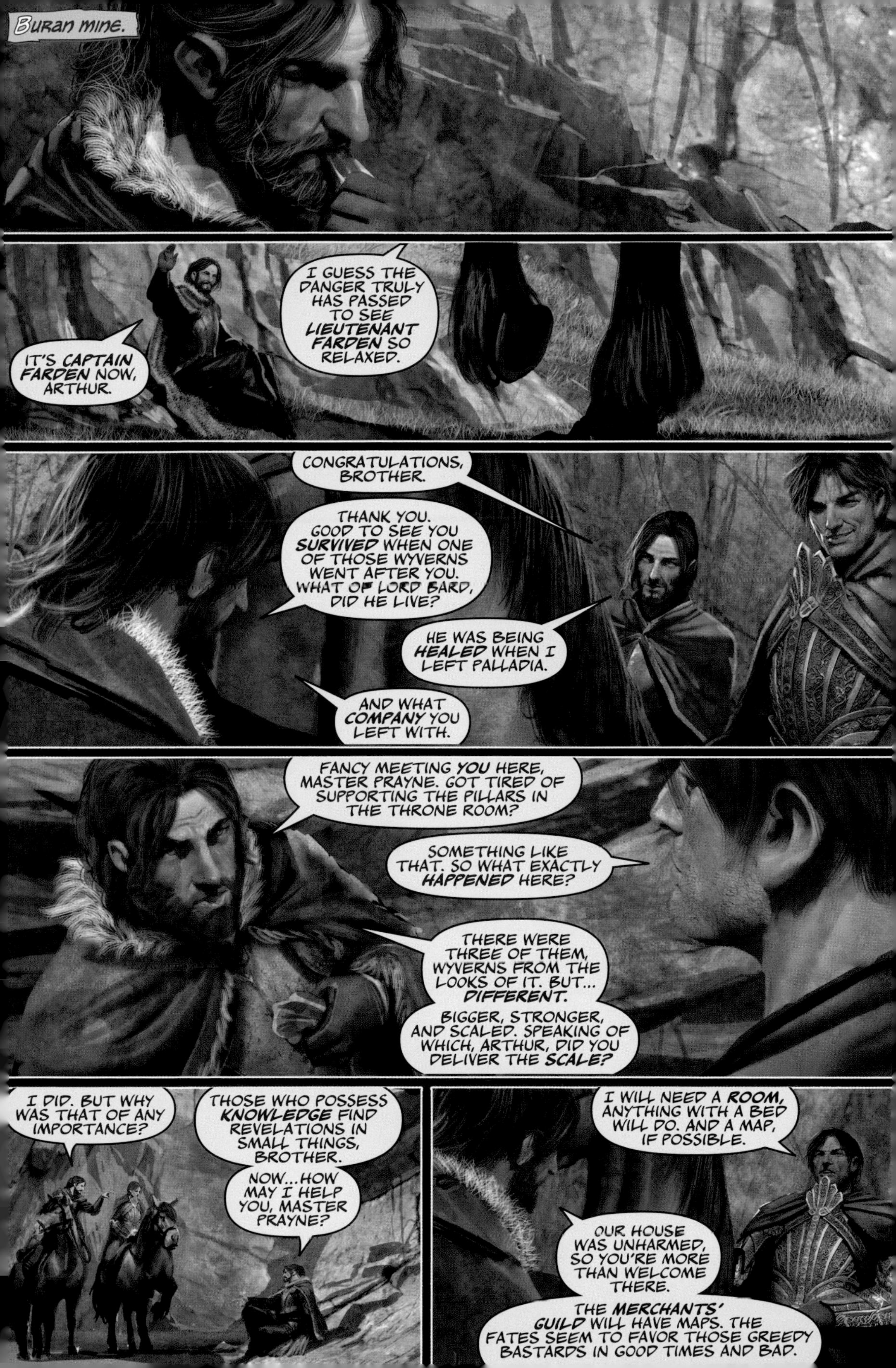
Buran mine.
I GUESS THE DANGER TRULY HAS PASSED TO SEE LIEUTENANT FARDEN SO RELAXED.
IT'S CAPTAIN FARDEN NOW, ARTHUR.
CONGRATULATIONS, BROTHER.
THANK YOU. GOOD TO SEE YOU SURVIVED WHEN ONE OF THOSE WYVERNS WENT AFTER YOU. WHAT OF LORD BARD, DID HE LIVE?
HE WAS BEING HEALED WHEN I LEFT PALLADIA.
AND WHAT COMPANY YOU LEFT WITH.
FANCY MEETING YOU HERE, MASTER PRAYNE. GOT TIRED OF SUPPORTING THE PILLARS IN THE THRONE ROOM?
SOMETHING LIKE THAT. SO WHAT EXACTLY HAPPENED HERE?
THERE WERE THREE OF THEM, WYVERNS FROM THE LOOKS OF IT. BUT... DIFFERENT.
BIGGER, STRONGER, AND SCALED. SPEAKING OF WHICH, ARTHUR, DID YOU DELIVER THE SCALE?
I DID. BUT WHY WAS THAT OF ANY IMPORTANCE?
THOSE WHO POSSESS KNOWLEDGE FIND REVELATIONS IN SMALL THINGS, BROTHER.
NOW... HOW MAY I HELP YOU, MASTER PRAYNE?
I WILL NEED A ROOM, ANYTHING WITH A BED WILL DO. AND A MAP, IF POSSIBLE.
OUR HOUSE WAS UNHARMED, SO YOU'RE MORE THAN WELCOME THERE.
THE MERCHANTS' GUILD WILL HAVE MAPS. THE FATES SEEM TO FAVOR THOSE GREEDY BASTARDS IN GOOD TIMES AND BAD.

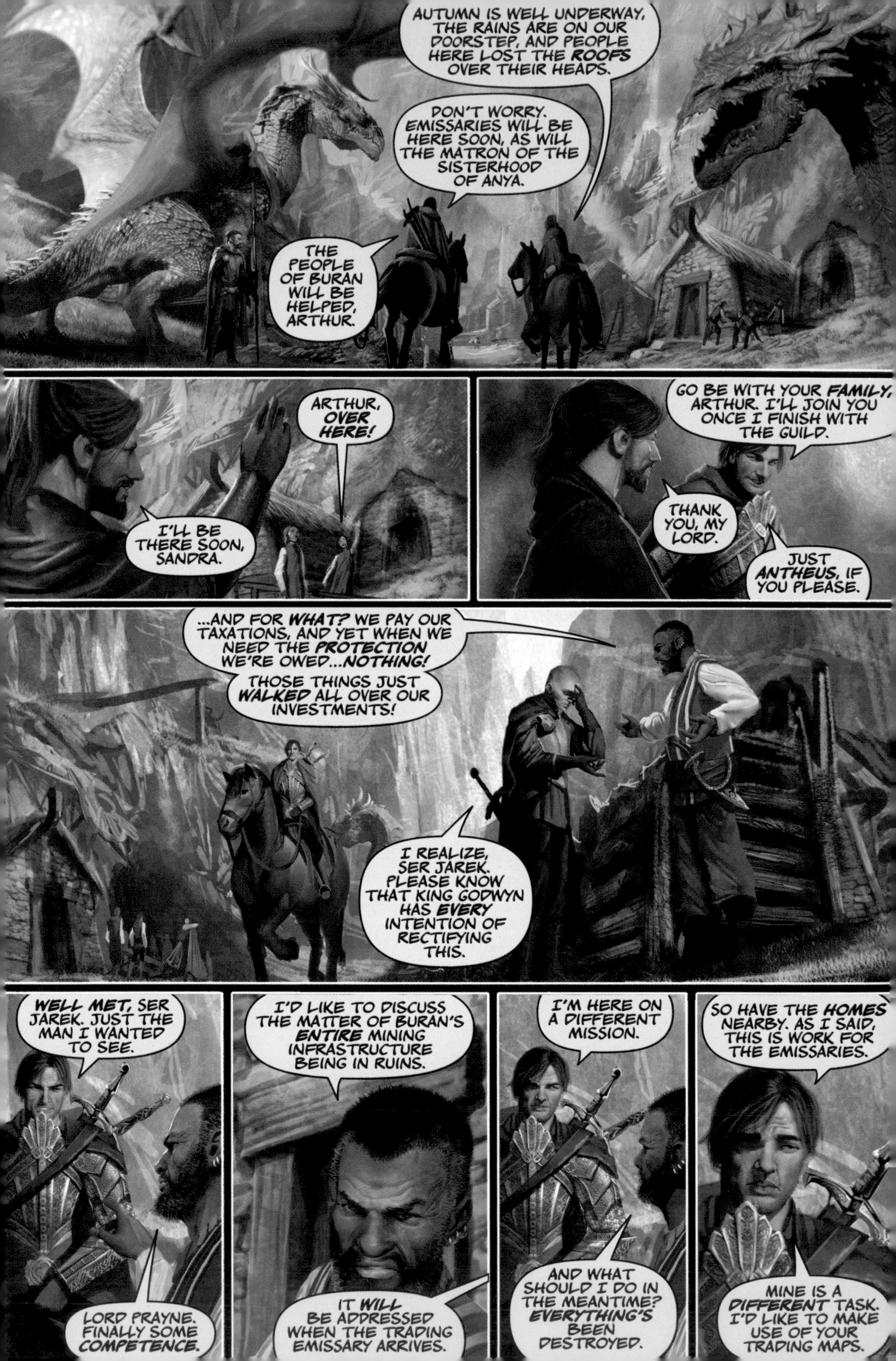
AUTUMN IS WELL UNDERWAY, THE RAINS ARE ON OUR DOORSTEP, AND PEOPLE HERE LOST THE ROOFS OVER THEIR HEADS.
DON'T WORRY. EMISSARIES WILL BE HERE SOON, AS WILL THE MATRON OF THE SISTERHOOD OF ANYA.
THE PEOPLE OF BURAN WILL BE HELPED, ARTHUR.
ARTHUR, OVER HERE!
I'LL BE THERE SOON, SANDRA.
GO BE WITH YOUR FAMILY, ARTHUR. I'LL JOIN YOU ONCE I FINISH WITH THE GUILD.
THANK YOU, MY LORD.
JUST ANTHEUS, IF YOU PLEASE.
...AND FOR WHAT? WE PAY OUR TAXATIONS, AND YET WHEN WE NEED THE PROTECTION WE'RE OWED...NOTHING!
THOSE THINGS JUST WALKED ALL OVER OUR INVESTMENTS!
I REALIZE, SER JAREK. PLEASE KNOW THAT KING GODWYN HAS EVERY INTENTION OF RECTIFYING THIS.
WELL MET, SER JAREK. JUST THE MAN I WANTED TO SEE.
LORD PRAYNE. FINALLY SOME COMPETENCE.
I'D LIKE TO DISCUSS THE MATTER OF BURAN'S ENTIRE MINING INFRASTRUCTURE BEING IN RUINS.
IT WILL BE ADDRESSED WHEN THE TRADING EMISSARY ARRIVES.
I'M HERE ON A DIFFERENT MISSION.
AND WHAT SHOULD I DO IN THE MEANTIME? EVERYTHING'S BEEN DESTROYED.
SO HAVE THE HOMES NEARBY. AS I SAID, THIS IS WORK FOR THE EMISSARIES.
MINE IS A DIFFERENT TASK. I'D LIKE TO MAKE USE OF YOUR TRADING MAPS.

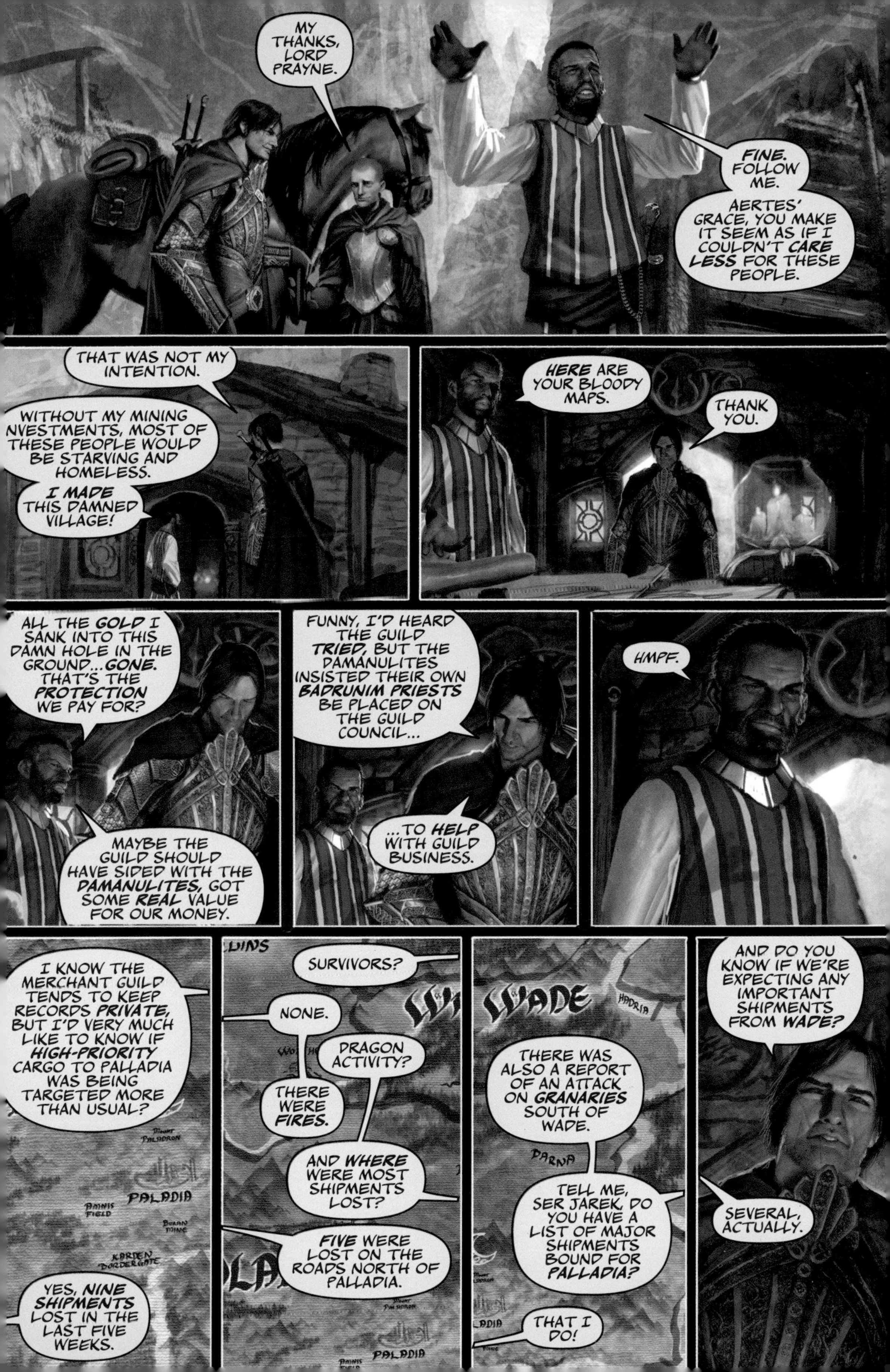
MY THANKS, LORD PRAYNE.
FINE. FOLLOW ME.
AERTES' GRACE, YOU MAKE IT SEEM AS IF I COULDN'T CARE LESS FOR THESE PEOPLE.
THAT WAS NOT MY INTENTION.
WITHOUT MY MINING NVESTMENTS, MOST OF THESE PEOPLE WOULD BE STARVING AND HOMELESS.
I MADE THIS DAMNED VILLAGE!
HERE ARE YOUR BLOODY MAPS.
THANK YOU.
ALL THE GOLD I SANK INTO THIS DAMN HOLE IN THE GROUND...GONE. THAT'S THE PROTECTION WE PAY FOR?
MAYBE THE GUILD SHOULD HAVE SIDED WITH THE DAMANULITES, GOT SOME REAL VALUE FOR OUR MONEY.
FUNNY, I'D HEARD THE GUILD TRIED, BUT THE DAMANULITES INSISTED THEIR OWN BADRUNIM PRIESTS BE PLACED ON THE GUILD COUNCIL...
...TO HELP WITH GUILD BUSINESS.
HMPF.
I KNOW THE MERCHANT GUILD TENDS TO KEEP RECORDS PRIVATE, BUT I'D VERY MUCH LIKE TO KNOW IF HIGH-PRIORITY CARGO TO PALLADIA WAS BEING TARGETED MORE THAN USUAL?
PALADIA
YES, NINE SHIPMENTS LOST IN THE LAST FIVE WEEKS.
SURVIVORS?
NONE.
DRAGON ACTIVITY?
THERE WERE FIRES.
AND WHERE WERE MOST SHIPMENTS LOST?
FIVE WERE LOST ON THE ROADS NORTH OF PALLADIA.
PALADIA
WADE
HADRIA
THERE WAS ALSO A REPORT OF AN ATTACK ON GRANARIES SOUTH OF WADE.
DARNA
TELL ME, SER JAREK, DO YOU HAVE A LIST OF MAJOR SHIPMENTS BOUND FOR PALLADIA?
THAT I DO!
AND DO YOU KNOW IF WE'RE EXPECTING ANY IMPORTANT SHIPMENTS FROM WADE?
SEVERAL, ACTUALLY.

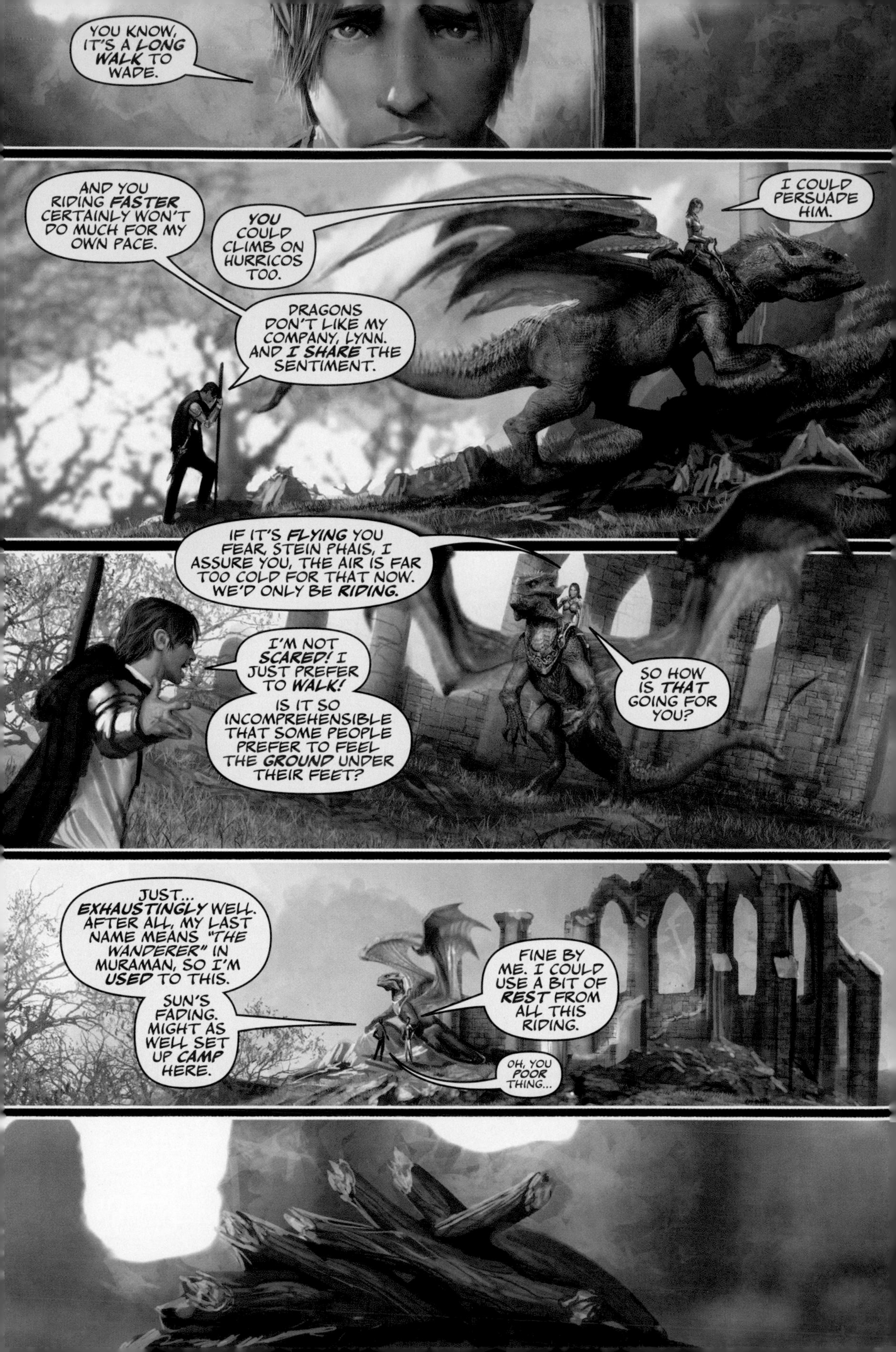

YOU KNOW, IT'S A LONG WALK TO WADE.
AND YOU RIDING FASTER CERTAINLY WON'T DO MUCH FOR MY OWN PACE.
YOU COULD CLIMB ON HURRICOS TOO.
I COULD PERSUADE HIM.
DRAGONS DON'T LIKE MY COMPANY, LYNN. AND I SHARE THE SENTIMENT.
IF IT'S FLYING YOU FEAR, STEIN PHAIS, I ASSURE YOU, THE AIR IS FAR TOO COLD FOR THAT NOW. WE'D ONLY BE RIDING.
I'M NOT SCARED! I JUST PREFER TO WALK!
IS IT SO INCOMPREHENSIBLE THAT SOME PEOPLE PREFER TO FEEL THE GROUND UNDER THEIR FEET?
SO HOW IS THAT GOING FOR YOU?
JUST... EXHAUSTINGLY WELL. AFTER ALL, MY LAST NAME MEANS "THE WANDERER" IN MURAMAN, SO I'M USED TO THIS.
SUN'S FADING. MIGHT AS WELL SET UP CAMP HERE.
FINE BY ME. I COULD USE A BIT OF REST FROM ALL THIS RIDING.
OH, YOU POOR THING...

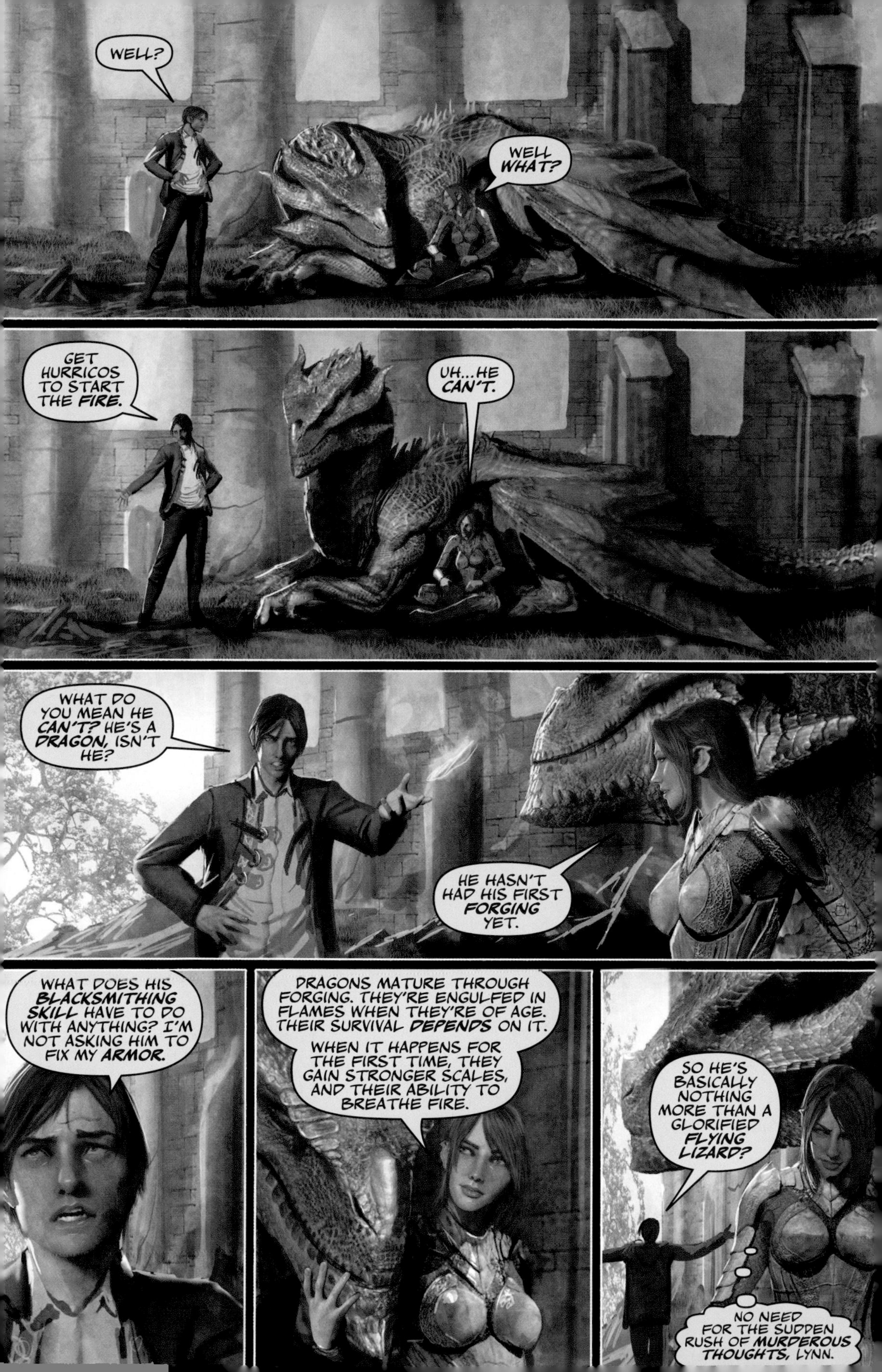
WELL?
WELL WHAT?
GET HURRICOS TO START THE FIRE.
UH...HE CAN'T.
WHAT DO YOU MEAN HE CAN'T? HE'S A DRAGON, ISN'T HE?
HE HASN'T HAD HIS FIRST FORGING YET.
WHAT DOES HIS BLACKSMITHING SKILL HAVE TO DO WITH ANYTHING? I'M NOT ASKING HIM TO FIX MY ARMOR.
DRAGONS MATURE THROUGH FORGING. THEY'RE ENGULFED IN FLAMES WHEN THEY'RE OF AGE. THEIR SURVIVAL DEPENDS ON IT.
WHEN IT HAPPENS FOR THE FIRST TIME, THEY GAIN STRONGER SCALES, AND THEIR ABILITY TO BREATHE FIRE.
SO HE'S BASICALLY NOTHING MORE THAN A GLORIFIED FLYING LIZARD?
NO NEED FOR THE SUDDEN RUSH OF MURDEROUS THOUGHTS, LYNN.

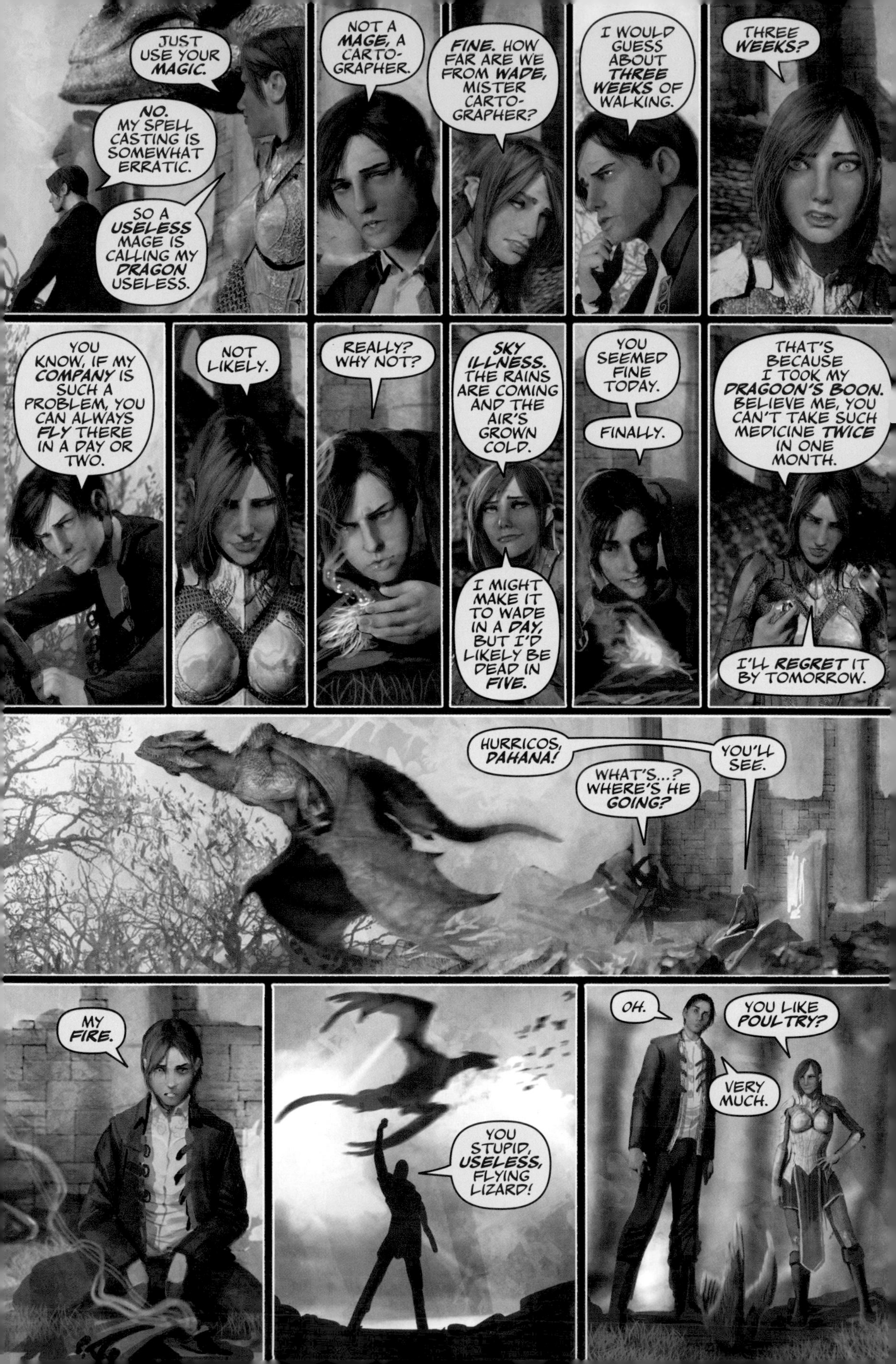

JUST USE YOUR MAGIC.
NO. MY SPELL CASTING IS SOMEWHAT ERRATIC.
SO A USELESS MAGE IS CALLING MY DRAGON USELESS.
NOT A MAGE, A CARTO-GRAPHER.
FINE. HOW FAR ARE WE FROM WADE, MISTER CARTO-GRAPHER?
I WOULD GUESS ABOUT THREE WEEKS OF WALKING.
THREE WEEKS?
YOU KNOW, IF MY COMPANY IS SUCH A PROBLEM, YOU CAN ALWAYS FLY THERE IN A DAY OR TWO.
NOT LIKELY.
REALLY? WHY NOT?
SKY ILLNESS. THE RAINS ARE COMING AND THE AIR'S GROWN COLD.
I MIGHT MAKE IT TO WADE IN A DAY, BUT I'D LIKELY BE DEAD IN FIVE.
YOU SEEMED FINE TODAY.
FINALLY.
THAT'S BECAUSE I TOOK MY DRAGOON'S BOON. BELIEVE ME, YOU CAN'T TAKE SUCH MEDICINE TWICE IN ONE MONTH.
I'LL REGRET IT BY TOMORROW.
HURRICOS, DAHANA!
WHAT'S...? WHERE'S HE GOING?
YOU'LL SEE.
MY FIRE.
YOU STUPID, USELESS, FLYING LIZARD!
OH.
YOU LIKE POULTRY?
VERY MUCH.

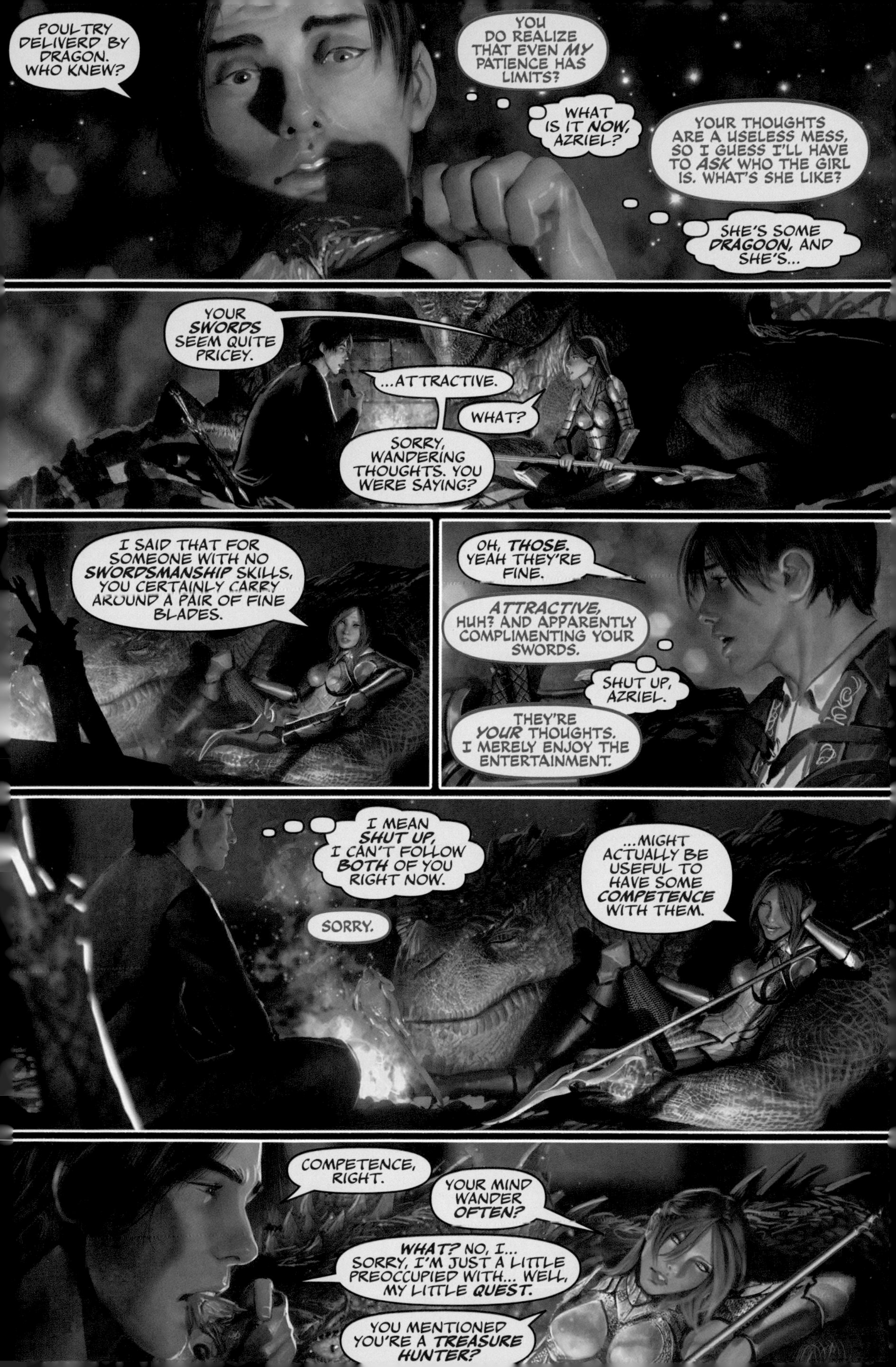
POULTRY DELIVERD BY DRAGON. WHO KNEW?
YOU DO REALIZE THAT EVEN MY PATIENCE HAS LIMITS?
WHAT IS IT NOW, AZRIEL?
YOUR THOUGHTS ARE A USELESS MESS, SO I GUESS I'LL HAVE TO ASK WHO THE GIRL IS. WHAT'S SHE LIKE?
SHE'S SOME DRAGOON, AND SHE'S...
YOUR SWORDS SEEM QUITE PRICEY.
...ATTRACTIVE.
WHAT?
SORRY, WANDERING THOUGHTS. YOU WERE SAYING?
I SAID THAT FOR SOMEONE WITH NO SWORDSMANSHIP SKILLS, YOU CERTAINLY CARRY AROUND A PAIR OF FINE BLADES.
OH, THOSE. YEAH THEY'RE FINE.
ATTRACTIVE, HUH? AND APPARENTLY COMPLIMENTING YOUR SWORDS.
SHUT UP, AZRIEL.
THEY'RE YOUR THOUGHTS. I MERELY ENJOY THE ENTERTAINMENT.
I MEAN SHUT UP, I CAN'T FOLLOW BOTH OF YOU RIGHT NOW.
SORRY.
...MIGHT ACTUALLY BE USEFUL TO HAVE SOME COMPETENCE WITH THEM.
COMPETENCE, RIGHT.
YOUR MIND WANDER OFTEN?
WHAT? NO, I... SORRY, I'M JUST A LITTLE PREOCCUPIED WITH... WELL, MY LITTLE QUEST.
YOU MENTIONED YOU'RE A TREASURE HUNTER?

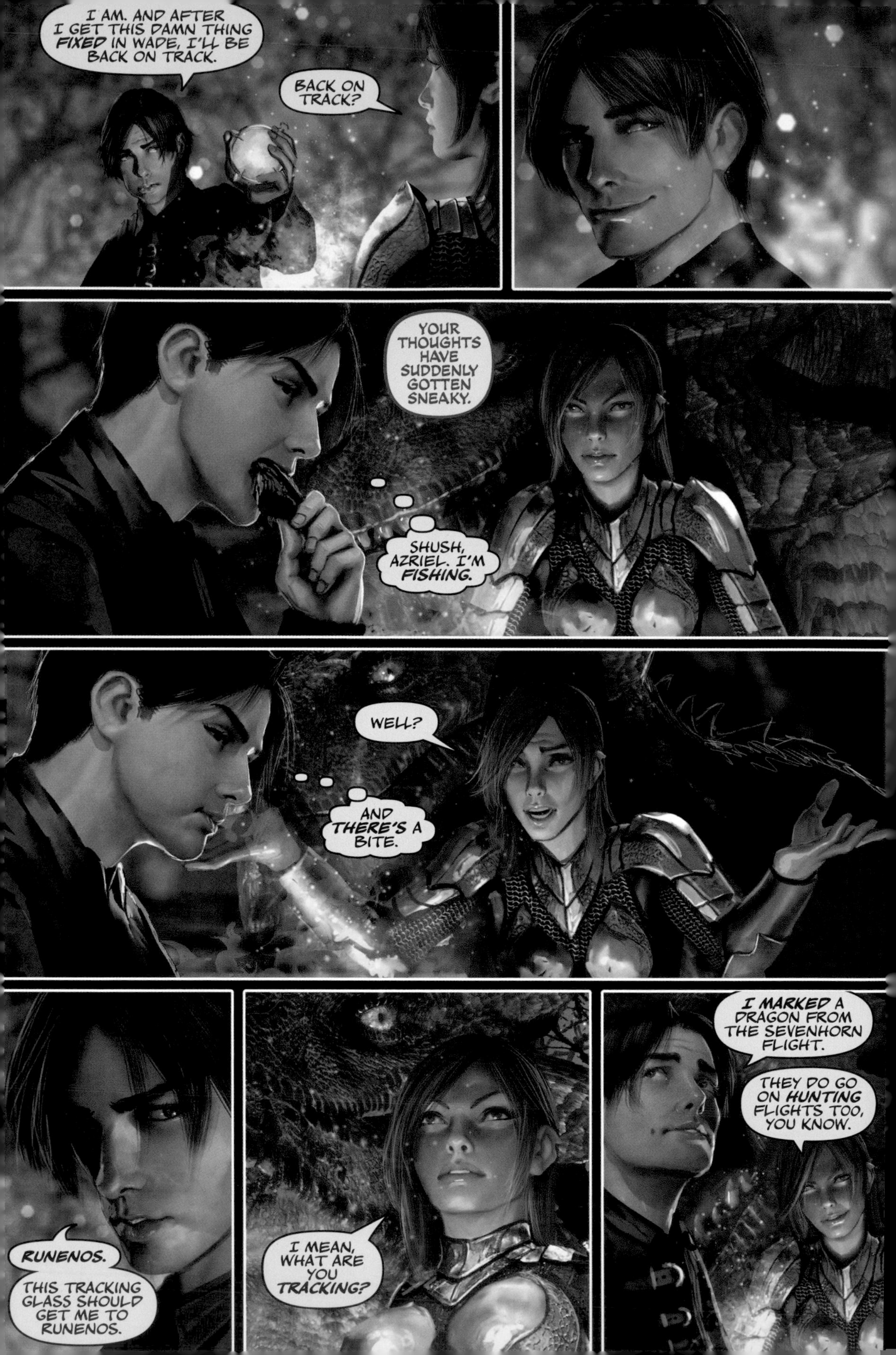

I AM. AND AFTER I GET THIS DAMN THING FIXED IN WADE, I'LL BE BACK ON TRACK.
BACK ON TRACK?
YOUR THOUGHTS HAVE SUDDENLY GOTTEN SNEAKY.
SHUSH, AZRIEL. I'M FISHING.
WELL?
AND THERE'S A BITE.
RUNENOS.
THIS TRACKING GLASS SHOULD GET ME TO RUNENOS.
I MEAN, WHAT ARE YOU TRACKING?
I MARKED A DRAGON FROM THE SEVENHORN FLIGHT.
THEY DO GO ON HUNTING FLIGHTS TOO, YOU KNOW.

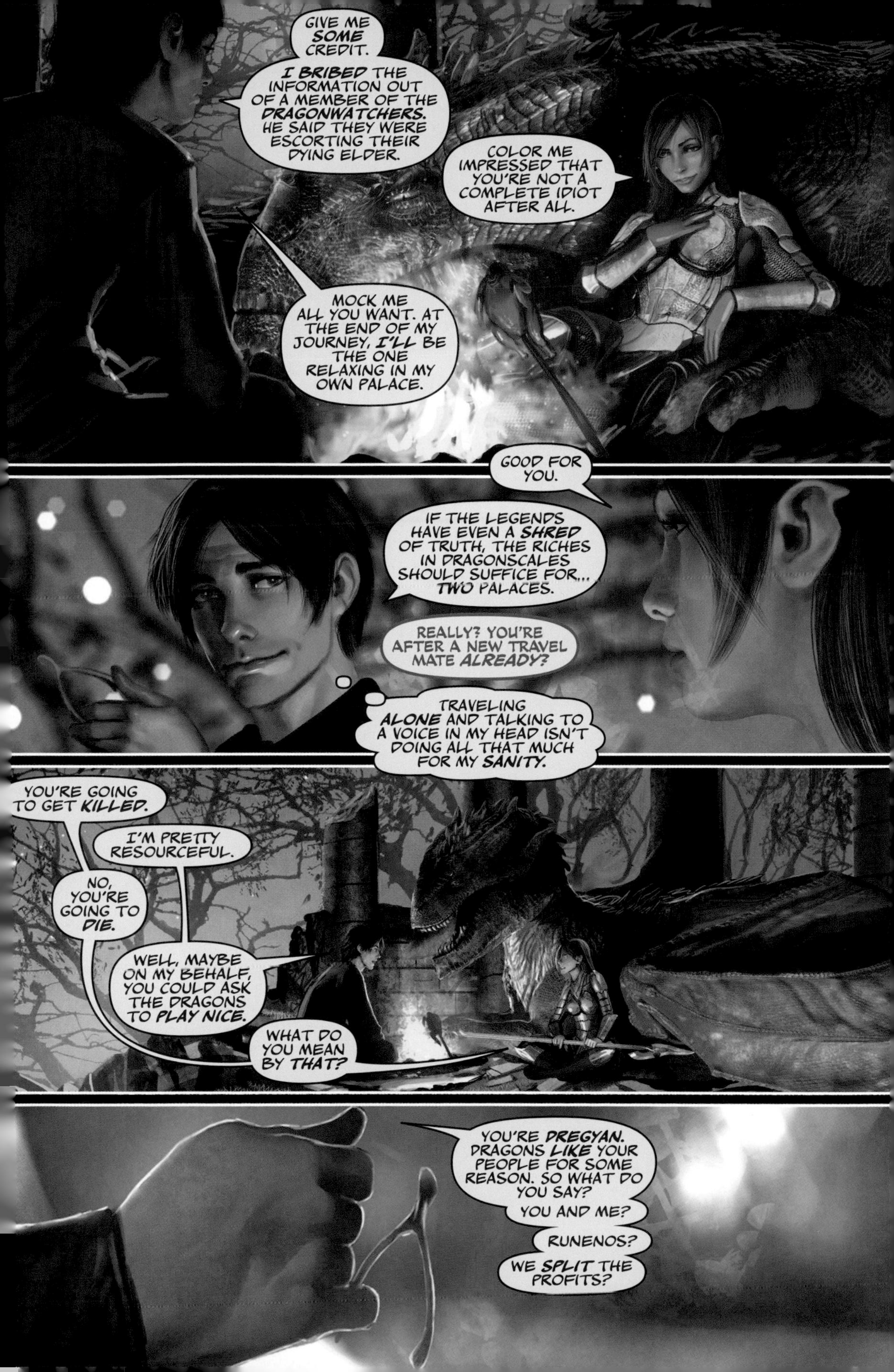
GIVE ME SOME CREDIT.
I BRIBED THE INFORMATION OUT OF A MEMBER OF THE DRAGONWATCHERS. HE SAID THEY WERE ESCORTING THEIR DYING ELDER.
COLOR ME IMPRESSED THAT YOU'RE NOT A COMPLETE IDIOT AFTER ALL.
MOCK ME ALL YOU WANT. AT THE END OF MY JOURNEY, I'LL BE THE ONE RELAXING IN MY OWN PALACE.
GOOD FOR YOU.
IF THE LEGENDS HAVE EVEN A SHRED OF TRUTH, THE RICHES IN DRAGONSCALES SHOULD SUFFICE FOR... TWO PALACES.
REALLY? YOU'RE AFTER A NEW TRAVEL MATE ALREADY?
TRAVELING ALONE AND TALKING TO A VOICE IN MY HEAD ISN'T DOING ALL THAT MUCH FOR MY SANITY.
YOU'RE GOING TO GET KILLED.
I'M PRETTY RESOURCEFUL.
NO, YOU'RE GOING TO DIE.
WELL, MAYBE ON MY BEHALF, YOU COULD ASK THE DRAGONS TO PLAY NICE.
WHAT DO YOU MEAN BY THAT?
YOU'RE DREGYAN. DRAGONS LIKE YOUR PEOPLE FOR SOME REASON. SO WHAT DO YOU SAY?
YOU AND ME?
RUNENOS?
WE SPLIT THE PROFITS?

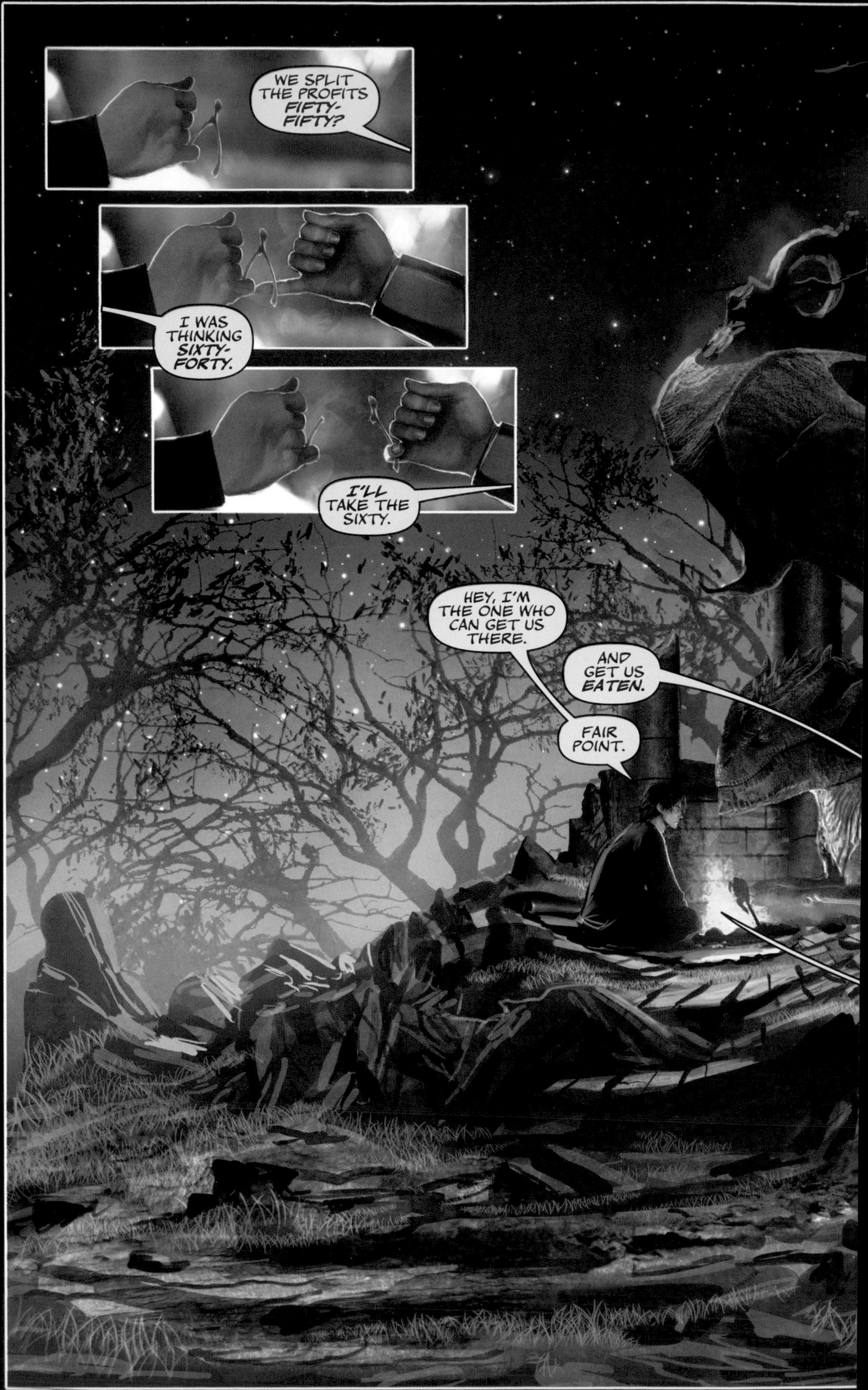
WE SPLIT THE PROFITS *FIFTY-FIFTY?*
I WAS THINKING *SIXTY-FORTY.*
I'LL TAKE THE SIXTY.
HEY, I'M THE ONE WHO CAN GET US THERE.
AND GET US *EATEN.*
FAIR POINT.

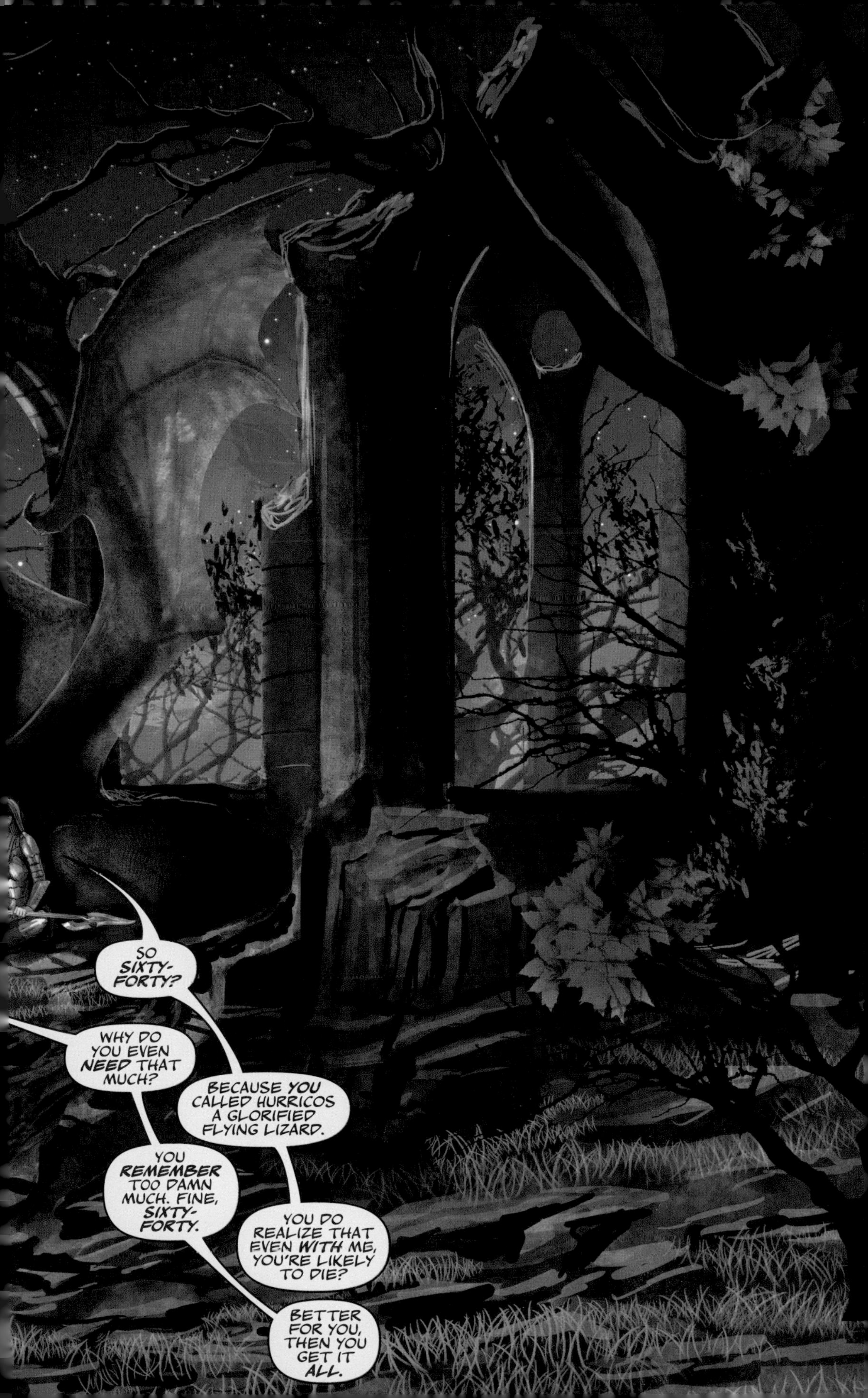
SO SIXTY-FORTY?
WHY DO YOU EVEN NEED THAT MUCH?
BECAUSE YOU CALLED HURRICOS A GLORIFIED FLYING LIZARD.
YOU REMEMBER TOO DAMN MUCH. FINE, SIXTY-FORTY.
YOU DO REALIZE THAT EVEN WITH ME, YOU'RE LIKELY TO DIE?
BETTER FOR YOU, THEN YOU GET IT ALL.

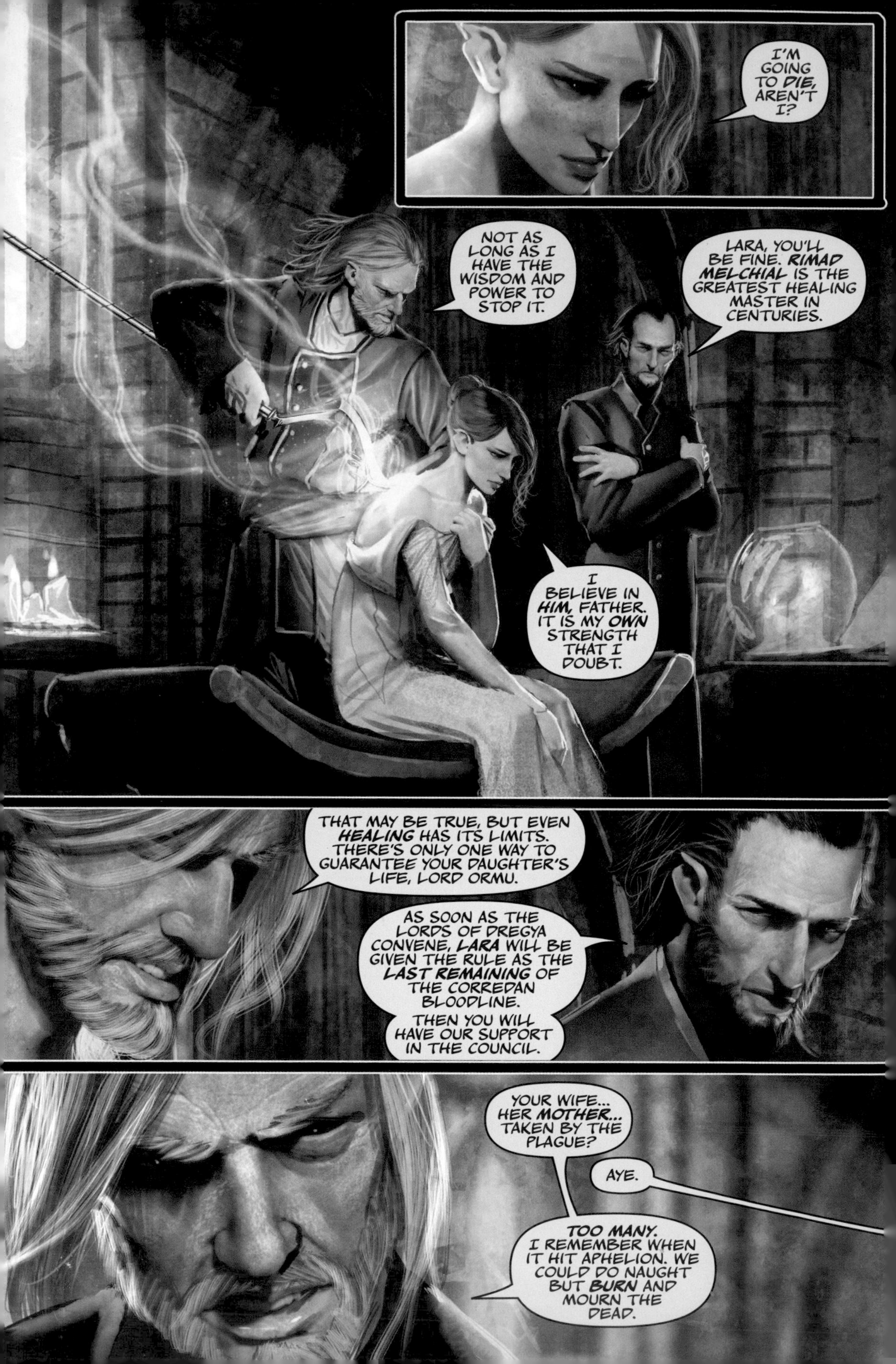
I'M GOING TO DIE, AREN'T I?
NOT AS LONG AS I HAVE THE WISDOM AND POWER TO STOP IT.
LARA, YOU'LL BE FINE. RIMAD MELCHIAL IS THE GREATEST HEALING MASTER IN CENTURIES.
I BELIEVE IN HIM, FATHER. IT IS MY OWN STRENGTH THAT I DOUBT.
THAT MAY BE TRUE, BUT EVEN HEALING HAS ITS LIMITS. THERE'S ONLY ONE WAY TO GUARANTEE YOUR DAUGHTER'S LIFE, LORD ORMU.
AS SOON AS THE LORDS OF DREGYA CONVENE, LARA WILL BE GIVEN THE RULE AS THE LAST REMAINING OF THE CORREDAN BLOODLINE.
THEN YOU WILL HAVE OUR SUPPORT IN THE COUNCIL.
YOUR WIFE... HER MOTHER... TAKEN BY THE PLAGUE?
AYE.
TOO MANY. I REMEMBER WHEN IT HIT APHELION. WE COULD DO NAUGHT BUT BURN AND MOURN THE DEAD.

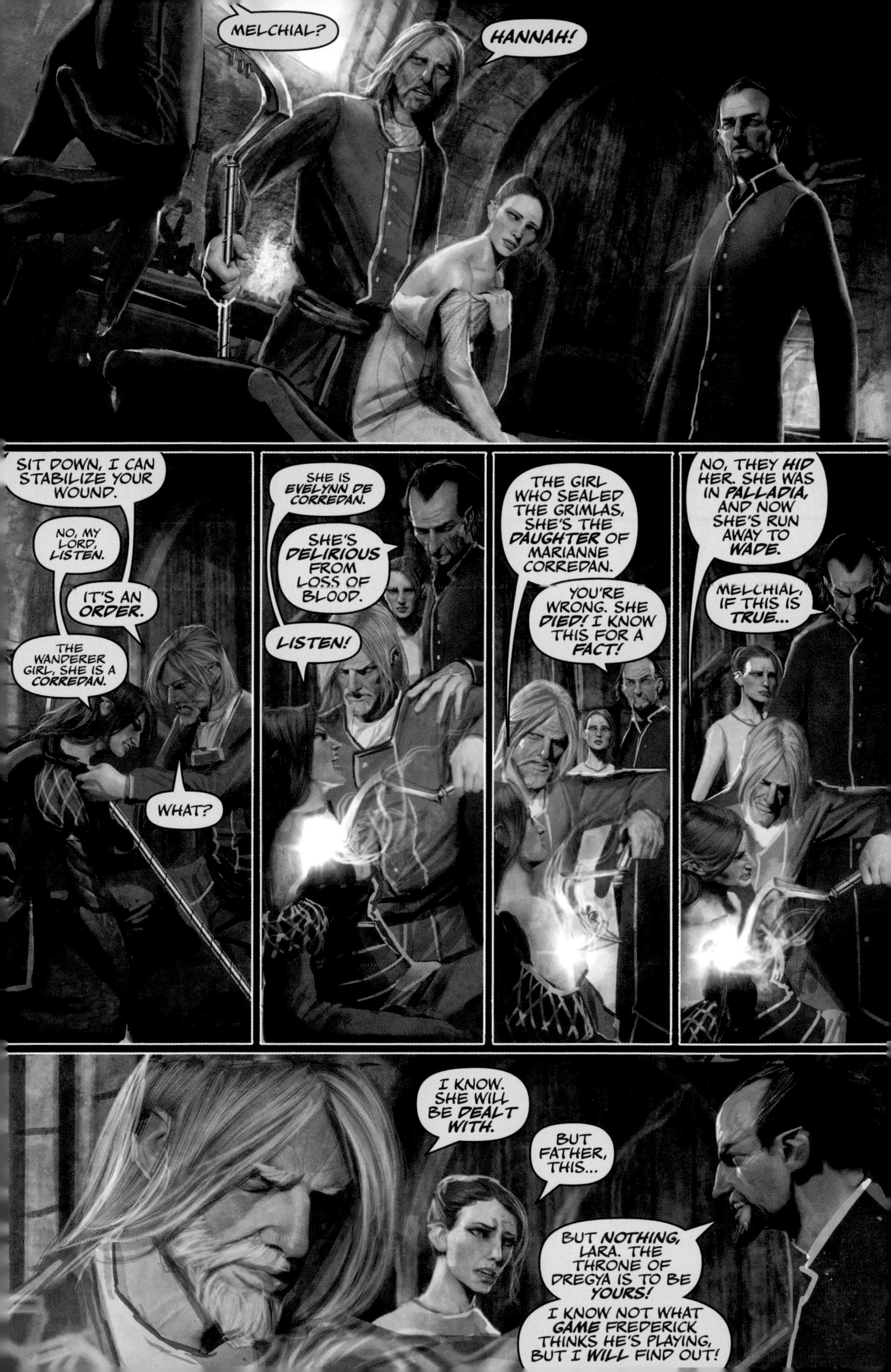

MELCHIAL?
HANNAH!
SIT DOWN, I CAN STABILIZE YOUR WOUND.
NO, MY LORD, LISTEN.
IT'S AN ORDER.
THE WANDERER GIRL, SHE IS A CORREDAN.
WHAT?
SHE IS EVELYNN DE CORREDAN.
SHE'S DELIRIOUS FROM LOSS OF BLOOD.
LISTEN!
THE GIRL WHO SEALED THE GRIMLAS, SHE'S THE DAUGHTER OF MARIANNE CORREDAN.
YOU'RE WRONG. SHE DIED! I KNOW THIS FOR A FACT!
NO, THEY HID HER. SHE WAS IN PALLADIA, AND NOW SHE'S RUN AWAY TO WADE.
MELCHIAL, IF THIS IS TRUE...
I KNOW. SHE WILL BE DEALT WITH.
BUT FATHER, THIS...
BUT NOTHING, LARA. THE THRONE OF DREGYA IS TO BE YOURS!
I KNOW NOT WHAT GAME FREDERICK THINKS HE'S PLAYING, BUT I WILL FIND OUT!

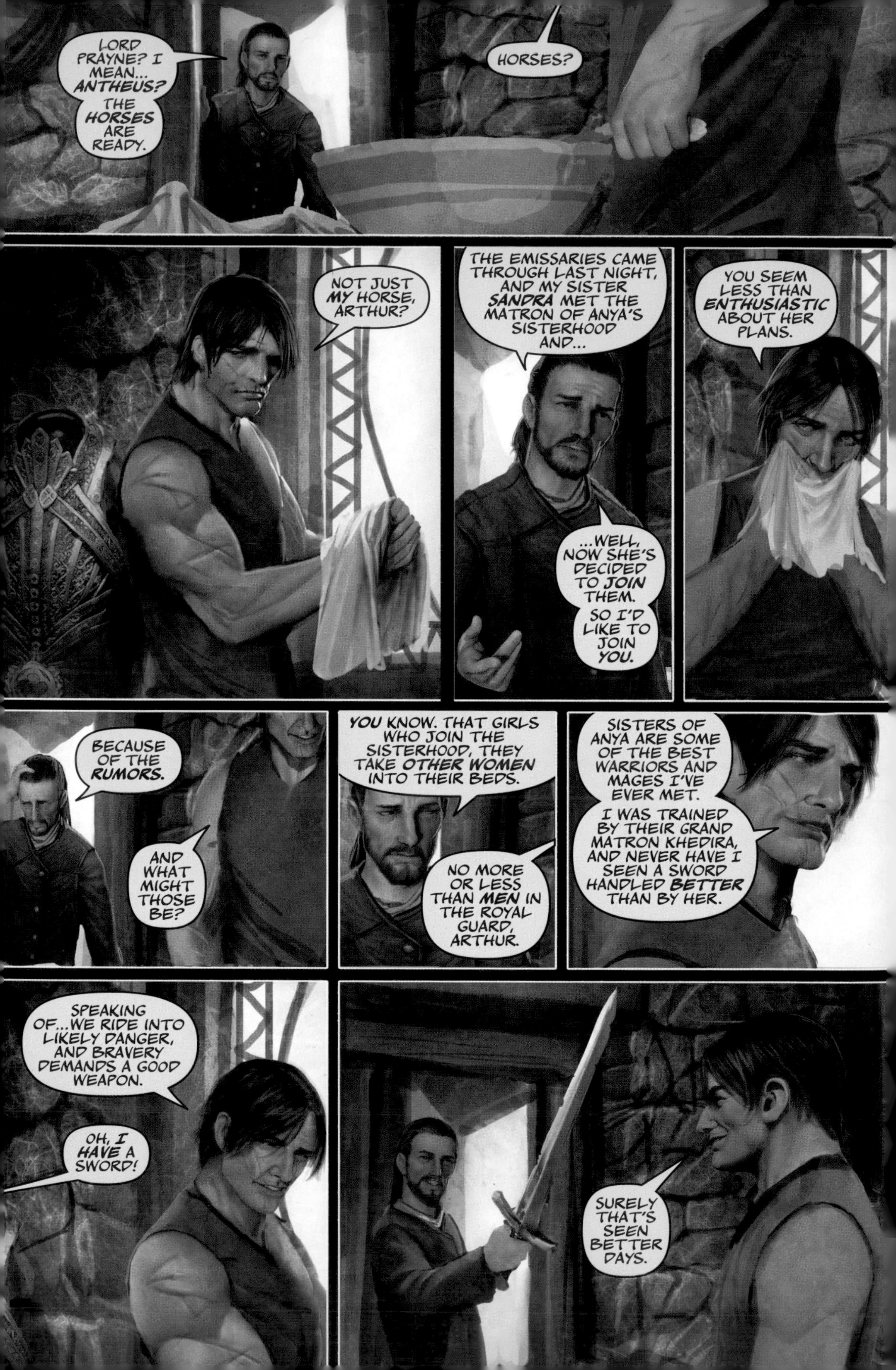
LORD PRAYNE? I MEAN... ANTHEUS? THE HORSES ARE READY.
HORSES?
NOT JUST MY HORSE, ARTHUR?
THE EMISSARIES CAME THROUGH LAST NIGHT, AND MY SISTER SANDRA MET THE MATRON OF ANYA'S SISTERHOOD AND...
...WELL, NOW SHE'S DECIDED TO JOIN THEM.
SO I'D LIKE TO JOIN YOU.
YOU SEEM LESS THAN ENTHUSIASTIC ABOUT HER PLANS.
BECAUSE OF THE RUMORS.
AND WHAT MIGHT THOSE BE?
YOU KNOW. THAT GIRLS WHO JOIN THE SISTERHOOD, THEY TAKE OTHER WOMEN INTO THEIR BEDS.
NO MORE OR LESS THAN MEN IN THE ROYAL GUARD, ARTHUR.
SISTERS OF ANYA ARE SOME OF THE BEST WARRIORS AND MAGES I'VE EVER MET.
I WAS TRAINED BY THEIR GRAND MATRON KHEDIRA, AND NEVER HAVE I SEEN A SWORD HANDLED BETTER THAN BY HER.
SPEAKING OF...WE RIDE INTO LIKELY DANGER, AND BRAVERY DEMANDS A GOOD WEAPON.
OH, I HAVE A SWORD!
SURELY THAT'S SEEN BETTER DAYS.

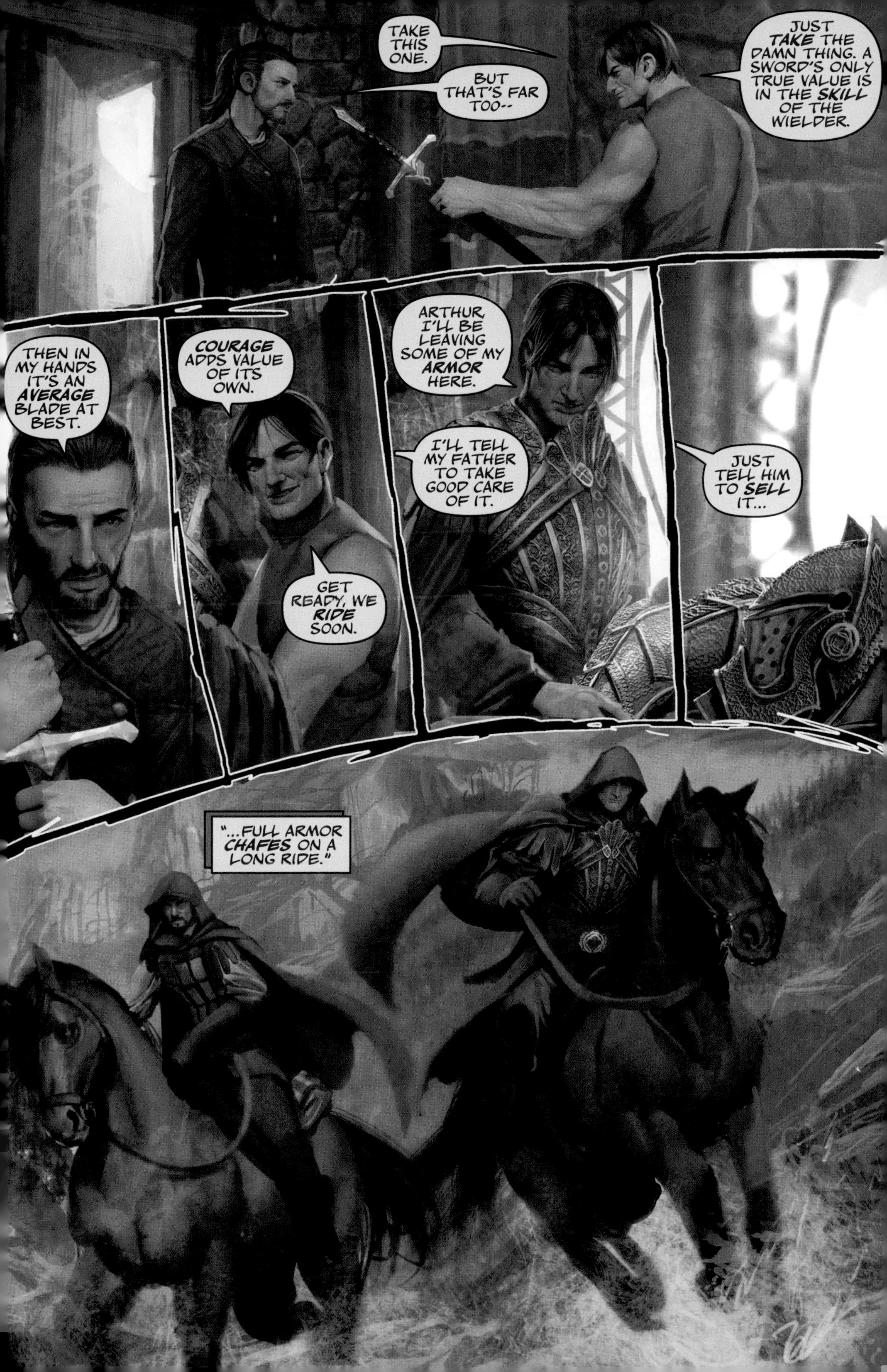
TAKE THIS ONE.
BUT THAT'S FAR TOO--
JUST TAKE THE DAMN THING. A SWORD'S ONLY TRUE VALUE IS IN THE SKILL OF THE WIELDER.
THEN IN MY HANDS IT'S AN AVERAGE BLADE AT BEST.
COURAGE ADDS VALUE OF ITS OWN.
GET READY, WE RIDE SOON.
ARTHUR, I'LL BE LEAVING SOME OF MY ARMOR HERE.
I'LL TELL MY FATHER TO TAKE GOOD CARE OF IT.
JUST TELL HIM TO SELL IT...
"...FULL ARMOR CHAFES ON A LONG RIDE."

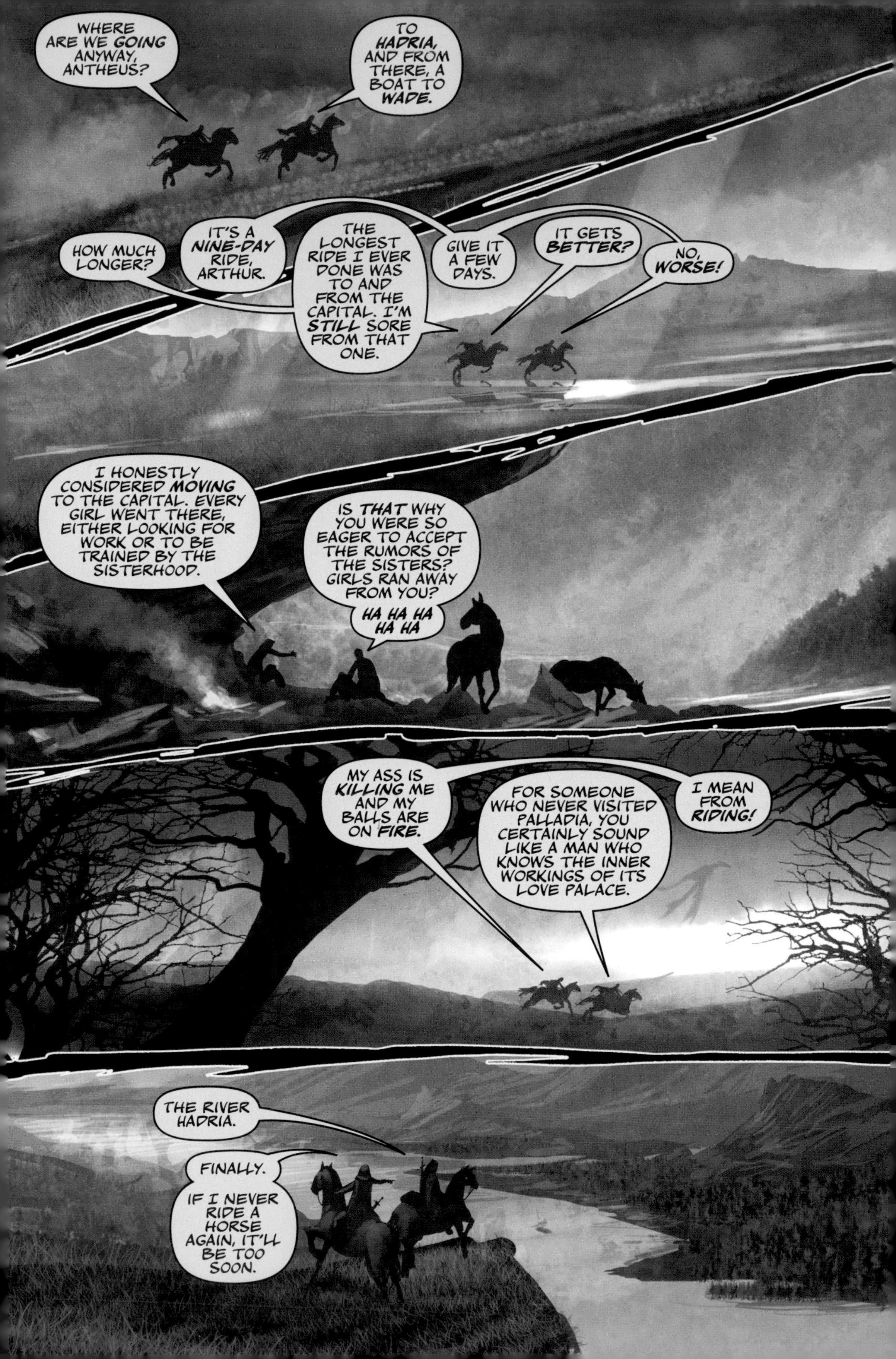

WHERE ARE WE GOING ANYWAY, ANTHEUS?
TO HADRIA, AND FROM THERE, A BOAT TO WADE.
HOW MUCH LONGER?
IT'S A NINE-DAY RIDE, ARTHUR.
THE LONGEST RIDE I EVER DONE WAS TO AND FROM THE CAPITAL. I'M STILL SORE FROM THAT ONE.
GIVE IT A FEW DAYS.
IT GETS BETTER?
NO, WORSE!
I HONESTLY CONSIDERED MOVING TO THE CAPITAL. EVERY GIRL WENT THERE, EITHER LOOKING FOR WORK OR TO BE TRAINED BY THE SISTERHOOD.
IS THAT WHY YOU WERE SO EAGER TO ACCEPT THE RUMORS OF THE SISTERS? GIRLS RAN AWAY FROM YOU?
HA HA HA HA HA
MY ASS IS KILLING ME AND MY BALLS ARE ON FIRE.
FOR SOMEONE WHO NEVER VISITED PALLADIA, YOU CERTAINLY SOUND LIKE A MAN WHO KNOWS THE INNER WORKINGS OF ITS LOVE PALACE.
I MEAN FROM RIDING!
THE RIVER HADRIA.
FINALLY.
IF I NEVER RIDE A HORSE AGAIN, IT'LL BE TOO SOON.

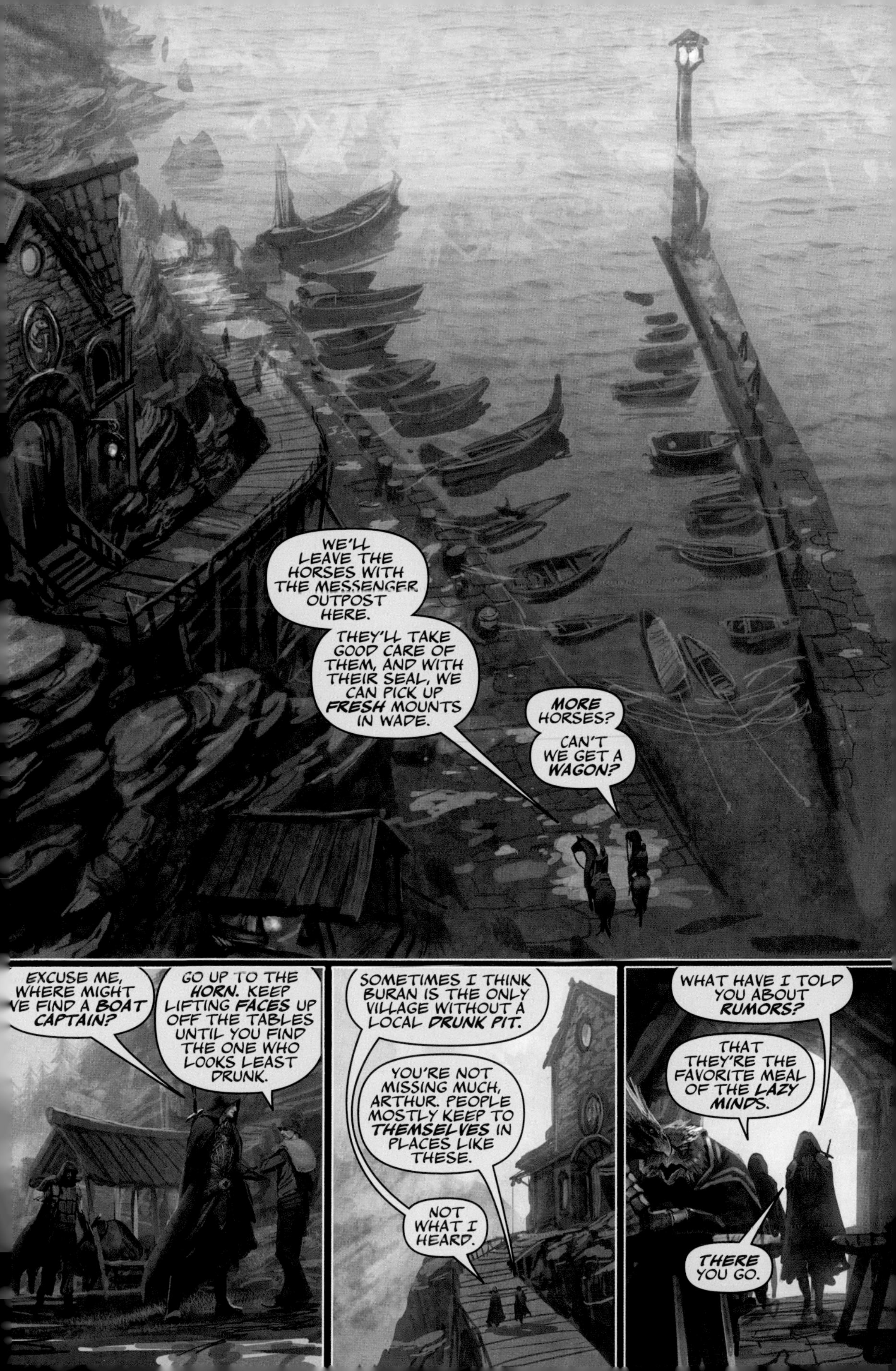
WE'LL LEAVE THE HORSES WITH THE MESSENGER OUTPOST HERE.
THEY'LL TAKE GOOD CARE OF THEM, AND WITH THEIR SEAL, WE CAN PICK UP FRESH MOUNTS IN WADE.
MORE HORSES?
CAN'T WE GET A WAGON?
EXCUSE ME, WHERE MIGHT WE FIND A BOAT CAPTAIN?
GO UP TO THE HORN. KEEP LIFTING FACES UP OFF THE TABLES UNTIL YOU FIND THE ONE WHO LOOKS LEAST DRUNK.
SOMETIMES I THINK BURAN IS THE ONLY VILLAGE WITHOUT A LOCAL DRUNK PIT.
YOU'RE NOT MISSING MUCH, ARTHUR. PEOPLE MOSTLY KEEP TO THEMSELVES IN PLACES LIKE THESE.
NOT WHAT I HEARD.
WHAT HAVE I TOLD YOU ABOUT RUMORS?
THAT THEY'RE THE FAVORITE MEAL OF THE LAZY MINDS.
THERE YOU GO.

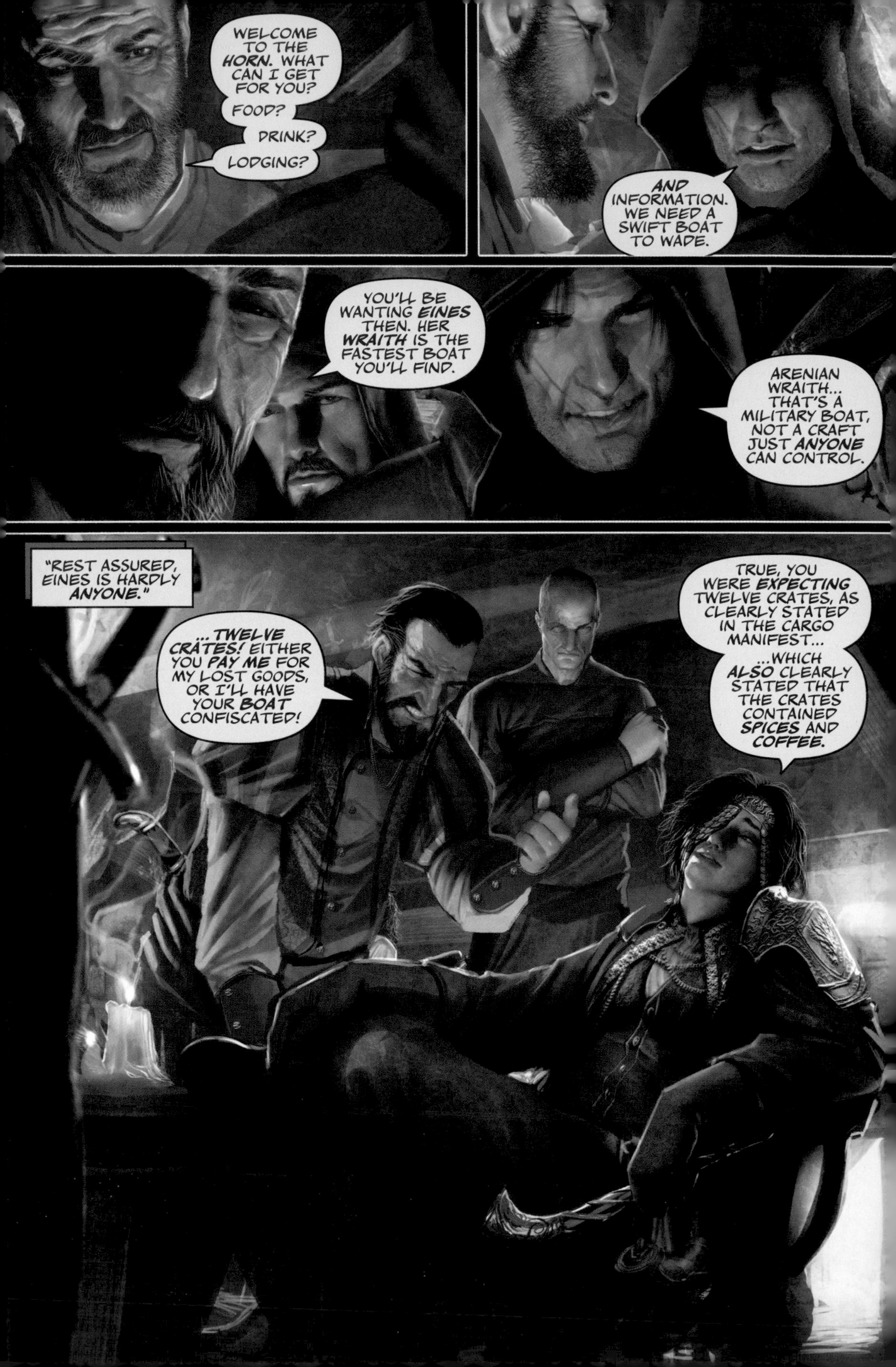
WELCOME TO THE HORN. WHAT CAN I GET FOR YOU?
FOOD?
DRINK?
LODGING?
AND INFORMATION. WE NEED A SWIFT BOAT TO WADE.
YOU'LL BE WANTING EINES THEN. HER WRAITH IS THE FASTEST BOAT YOU'LL FIND.
ARENIAN WRAITH... THAT'S A MILITARY BOAT, NOT A CRAFT JUST ANYONE CAN CONTROL.
"REST ASSURED, EINES IS HARDLY ANYONE."
...TWELVE CRATES! EITHER YOU PAY ME FOR MY LOST GOODS, OR I'LL HAVE YOUR BOAT CONFISCATED!
TRUE, YOU WERE EXPECTING TWELVE CRATES, AS CLEARLY STATED IN THE CARGO MANIFEST...
...WHICH ALSO CLEARLY STATED THAT THE CRATES CONTAINED SPICES AND COFFEE.

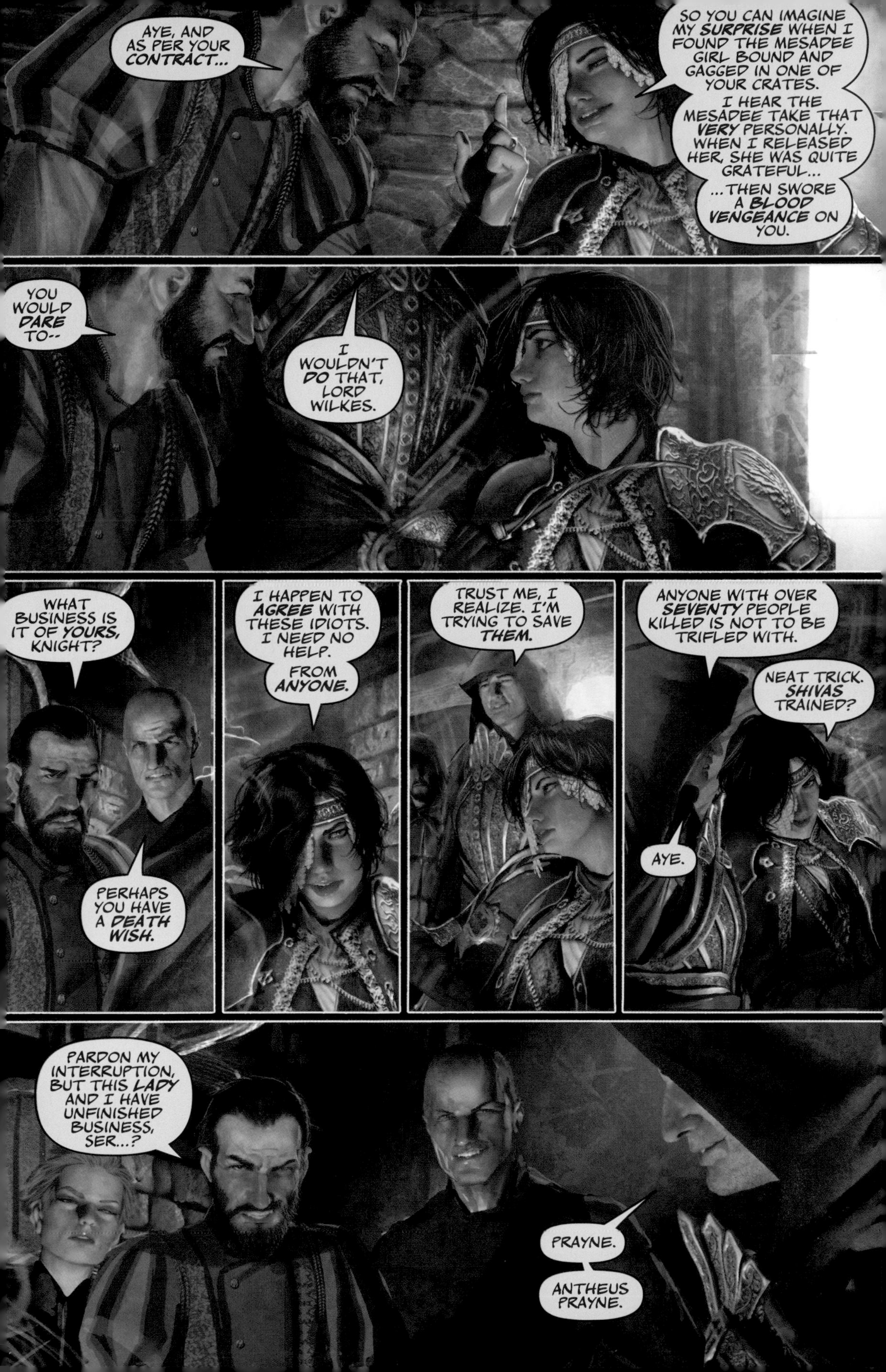
AYE, AND AS PER YOUR CONTRACT...
SO YOU CAN IMAGINE MY SURPRISE WHEN I FOUND THE MESADEE GIRL BOUND AND GAGGED IN ONE OF YOUR CRATES.
I HEAR THE MESADEE TAKE THAT VERY PERSONALLY. WHEN I RELEASED HER, SHE WAS QUITE GRATEFUL...
...THEN SWORE A BLOOD VENGEANCE ON YOU.
YOU WOULD DARE TO--
I WOULDN'T DO THAT, LORD WILKES.
WHAT BUSINESS IS IT OF YOURS, KNIGHT?
PERHAPS YOU HAVE A DEATH WISH.
I HAPPEN TO AGREE WITH THESE IDIOTS. I NEED NO HELP.
FROM ANYONE.
TRUST ME, I REALIZE. I'M TRYING TO SAVE THEM.
ANYONE WITH OVER SEVENTY PEOPLE KILLED IS NOT TO BE TRIFLED WITH.
NEAT TRICK. SHIVAS TRAINED?
AYE.
PARDON MY INTERRUPTION, BUT THIS LADY AND I HAVE UNFINISHED BUSINESS, SER...?
PRAYNE.
ANTHEUS PRAYNE.

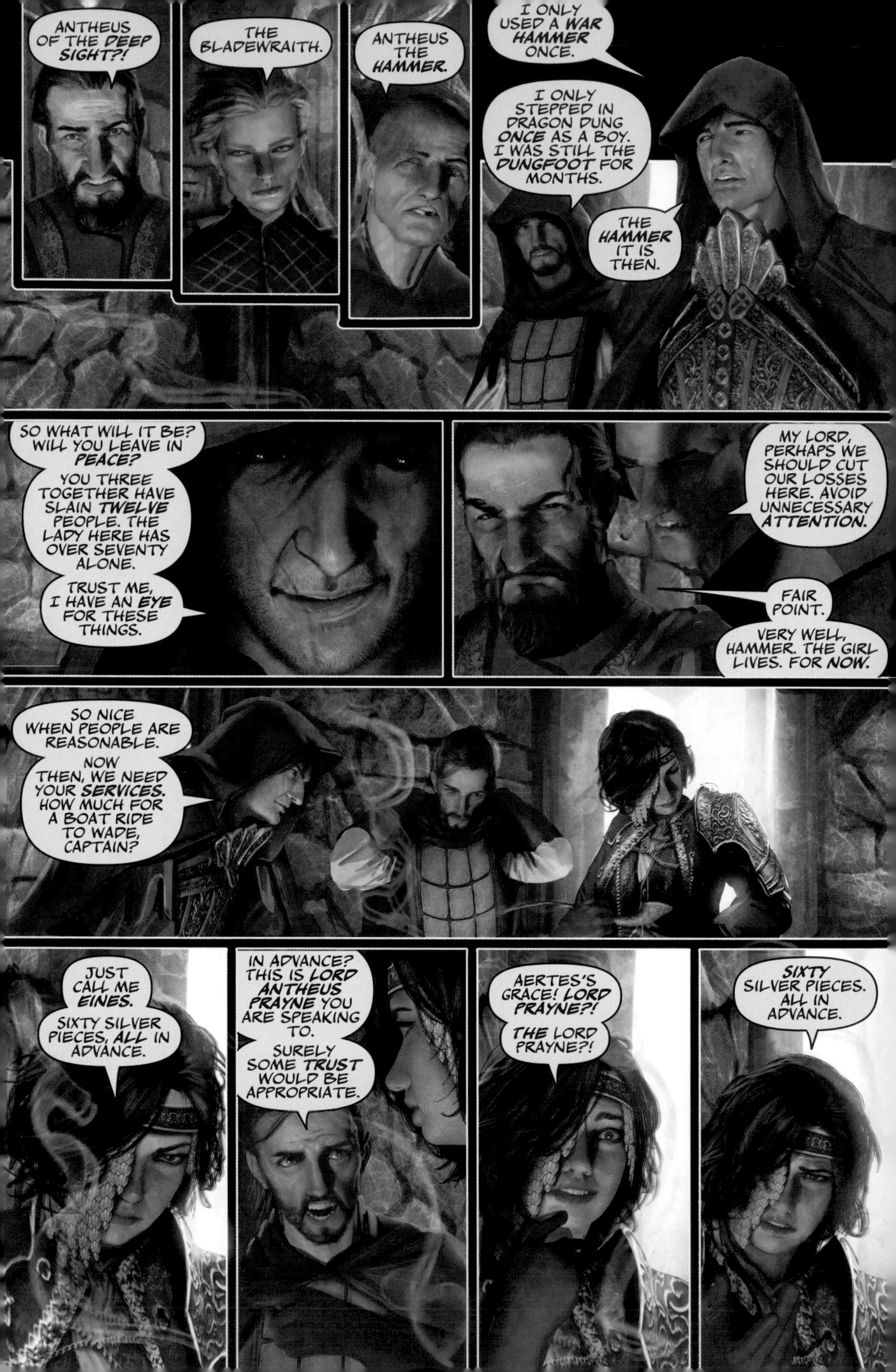
ANTHEUS OF THE DEEP SIGHT?!
THE BLADEWRAITH.
ANTHEUS THE HAMMER.
I ONLY USED A WAR HAMMER ONCE.
I ONLY STEPPED IN DRAGON DUNG ONCE AS A BOY. I WAS STILL THE DUNGFOOT FOR MONTHS.
THE HAMMER IT IS THEN.
SO WHAT WILL IT BE? WILL YOU LEAVE IN PEACE?
YOU THREE TOGETHER HAVE SLAIN TWELVE PEOPLE. THE LADY HERE HAS OVER SEVENTY ALONE.
TRUST ME, I HAVE AN EYE FOR THESE THINGS.
MY LORD, PERHAPS WE SHOULD CUT OUR LOSSES HERE. AVOID UNNECESSARY ATTENTION.
FAIR POINT.
VERY WELL, HAMMER. THE GIRL LIVES. FOR NOW.
SO NICE WHEN PEOPLE ARE REASONABLE.
NOW THEN, WE NEED YOUR SERVICES. HOW MUCH FOR A BOAT RIDE TO WADE, CAPTAIN?
JUST CALL ME EINES.
SIXTY SILVER PIECES, ALL IN ADVANCE.
IN ADVANCE? THIS IS LORD ANTHEUS PRAYNE YOU ARE SPEAKING TO.
SURELY SOME TRUST WOULD BE APPROPRIATE.
AERTES'S GRACE! LORD PRAYNE?!
THE LORD PRAYNE?!
SIXTY SILVER PIECES. ALL IN ADVANCE.

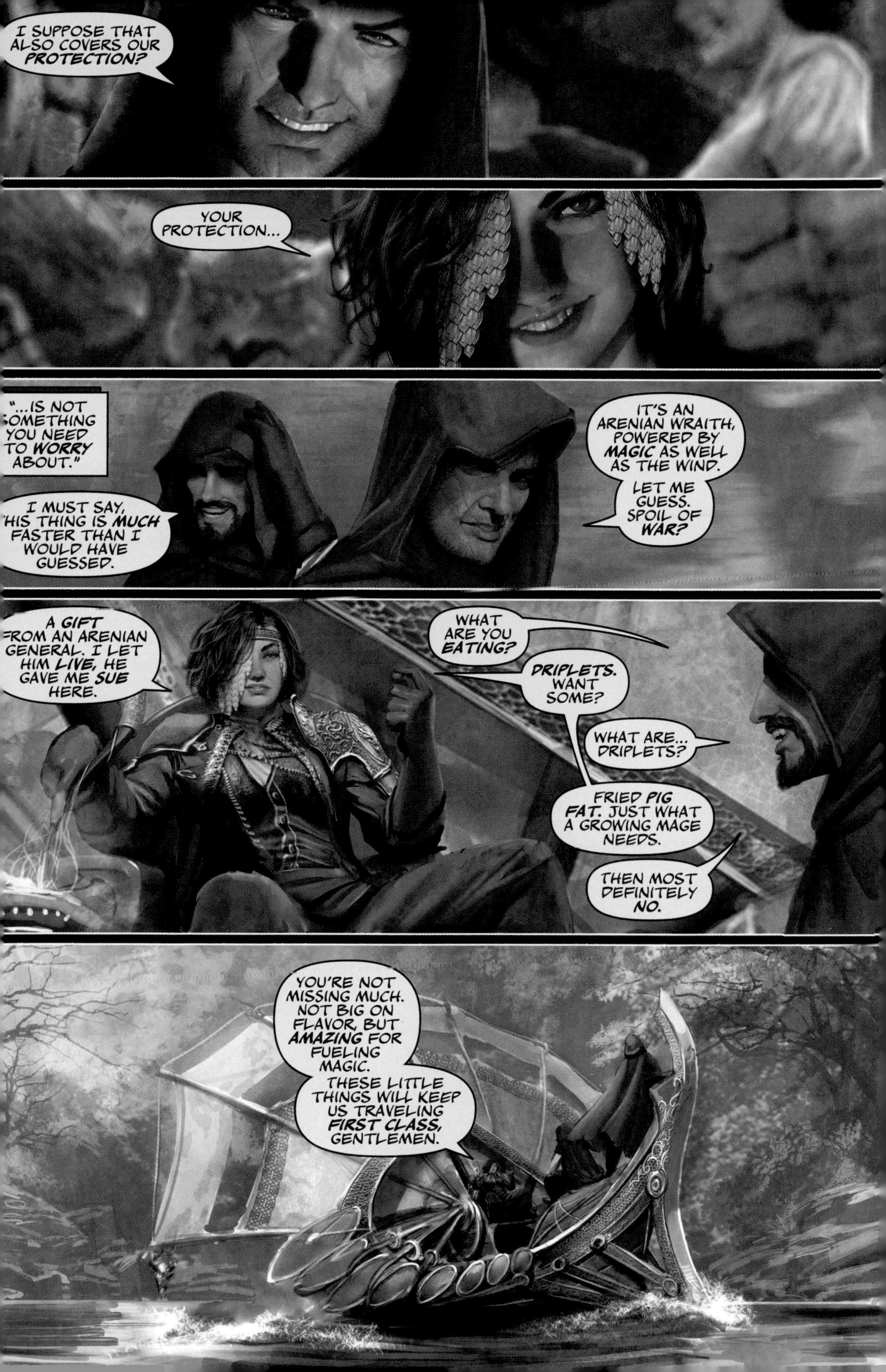
I SUPPOSE THAT ALSO COVERS OUR PROTECTION?
YOUR PROTECTION...
"...IS NOT SOMETHING YOU NEED TO WORRY ABOUT."
I MUST SAY, THIS THING IS MUCH FASTER THAN I WOULD HAVE GUESSED.
IT'S AN ARENIAN WRAITH, POWERED BY MAGIC AS WELL AS THE WIND.
LET ME GUESS. SPOIL OF WAR?
A GIFT FROM AN ARENIAN GENERAL. I LET HIM LIVE, HE GAVE ME SUE HERE.
WHAT ARE YOU EATING?
DRIPLETS. WANT SOME?
WHAT ARE... DRIPLETS?
FRIED PIG FAT. JUST WHAT A GROWING MAGE NEEDS.
THEN MOST DEFINITELY NO.
YOU'RE NOT MISSING MUCH. NOT BIG ON FLAVOR, BUT AMAZING FOR FUELING MAGIC.
THESE LITTLE THINGS WILL KEEP US TRAVELING FIRST CLASS, GENTLEMEN.

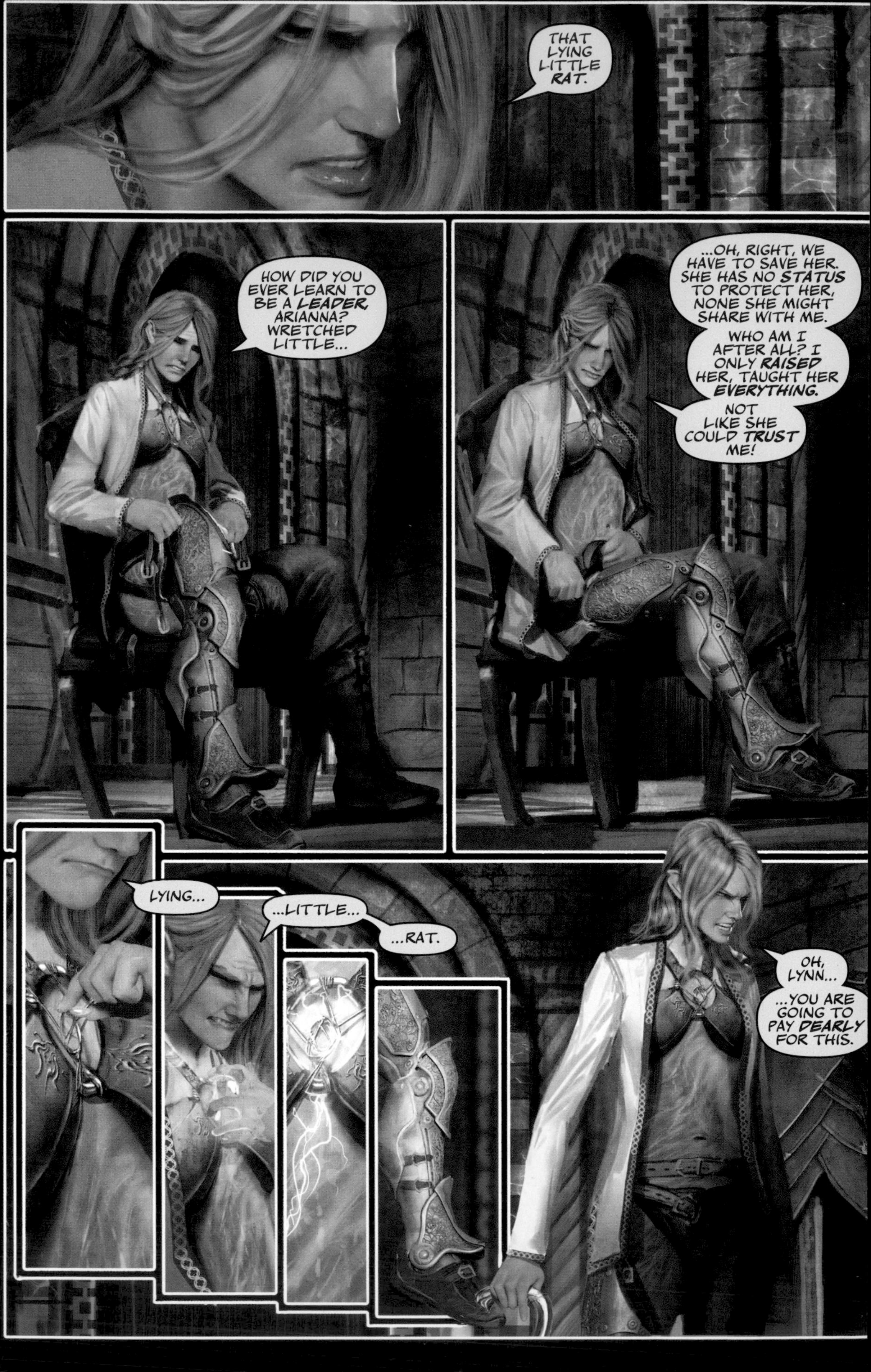
THAT LYING LITTLE RAT.
HOW DID YOU EVER LEARN TO BE A LEADER, ARIANNA? WRETCHED LITTLE...
...OH, RIGHT, WE HAVE TO SAVE HER. SHE HAS NO STATUS TO PROTECT HER, NONE SHE MIGHT SHARE WITH ME.
WHO AM I AFTER ALL? I ONLY RAISED HER, TAUGHT HER EVERYTHING.
NOT LIKE SHE COULD TRUST ME!
LYING...
...LITTLE...
...RAT.
OH, LYNN...
...YOU ARE GOING TO PAY DEARLY FOR THIS.

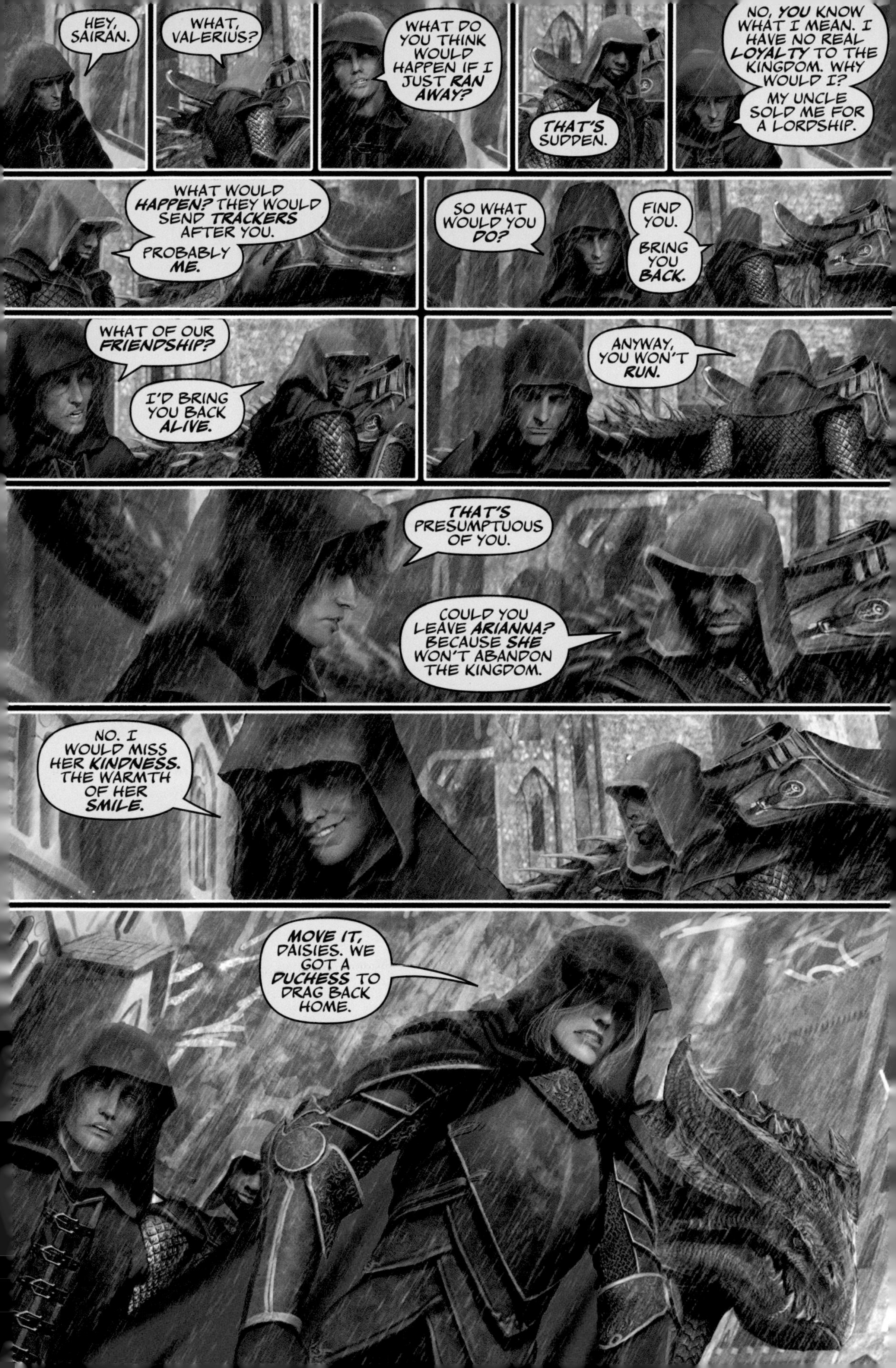
HEY, SAIRAN.
WHAT, VALERIUS?
WHAT DO YOU THINK WOULD HAPPEN IF I JUST RAN AWAY?
THAT'S SUDDEN.
NO, YOU KNOW WHAT I MEAN. I HAVE NO REAL LOYALTY TO THE KINGDOM. WHY WOULD I?
MY UNCLE SOLD ME FOR A LORDSHIP.
WHAT WOULD HAPPEN? THEY WOULD SEND TRACKERS AFTER YOU.
PROBABLY ME.
SO WHAT WOULD YOU DO?
FIND YOU.
BRING YOU BACK.
WHAT OF OUR FRIENDSHIP?
I'D BRING YOU BACK ALIVE.
ANYWAY, YOU WON'T RUN.
THAT'S PRESUMPTUOUS OF YOU.
COULD YOU LEAVE ARIANNA? BECAUSE SHE WON'T ABANDON THE KINGDOM.
NO. I WOULD MISS HER KINDNESS. THE WARMTH OF HER SMILE.
MOVE IT, DAISIES. WE GOT A DUCHESS TO DRAG BACK HOME.

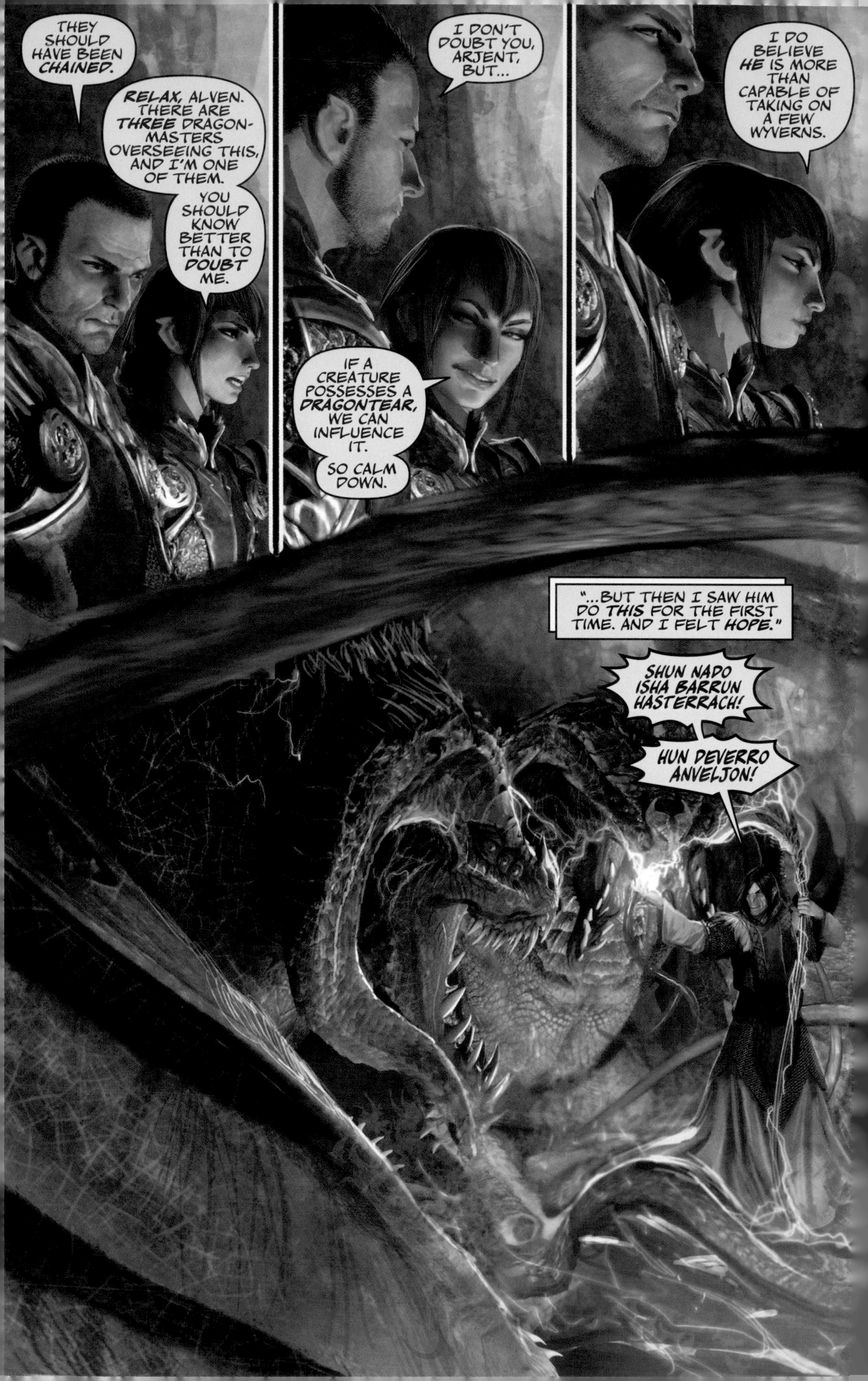
THEY SHOULD HAVE BEEN CHAINED.
RELAX, ALVEN. THERE ARE THREE DRAGON-MASTERS OVERSEEING THIS, AND I'M ONE OF THEM.
YOU SHOULD KNOW BETTER THAN TO DOUBT ME.
I DON'T DOUBT YOU, ARJENT, BUT...
IF A CREATURE POSSESSES A DRAGONTEAR, WE CAN INFLUENCE IT.
SO CALM DOWN.
I DO BELIEVE HE IS MORE THAN CAPABLE OF TAKING ON A FEW WYVERNS.
"...BUT THEN I SAW HIM DO THIS FOR THE FIRST TIME. AND I FELT HOPE."
SHUN NADO ISHA BARRUN HASTERRACH!
HUN DEVERRO ANVELJON!

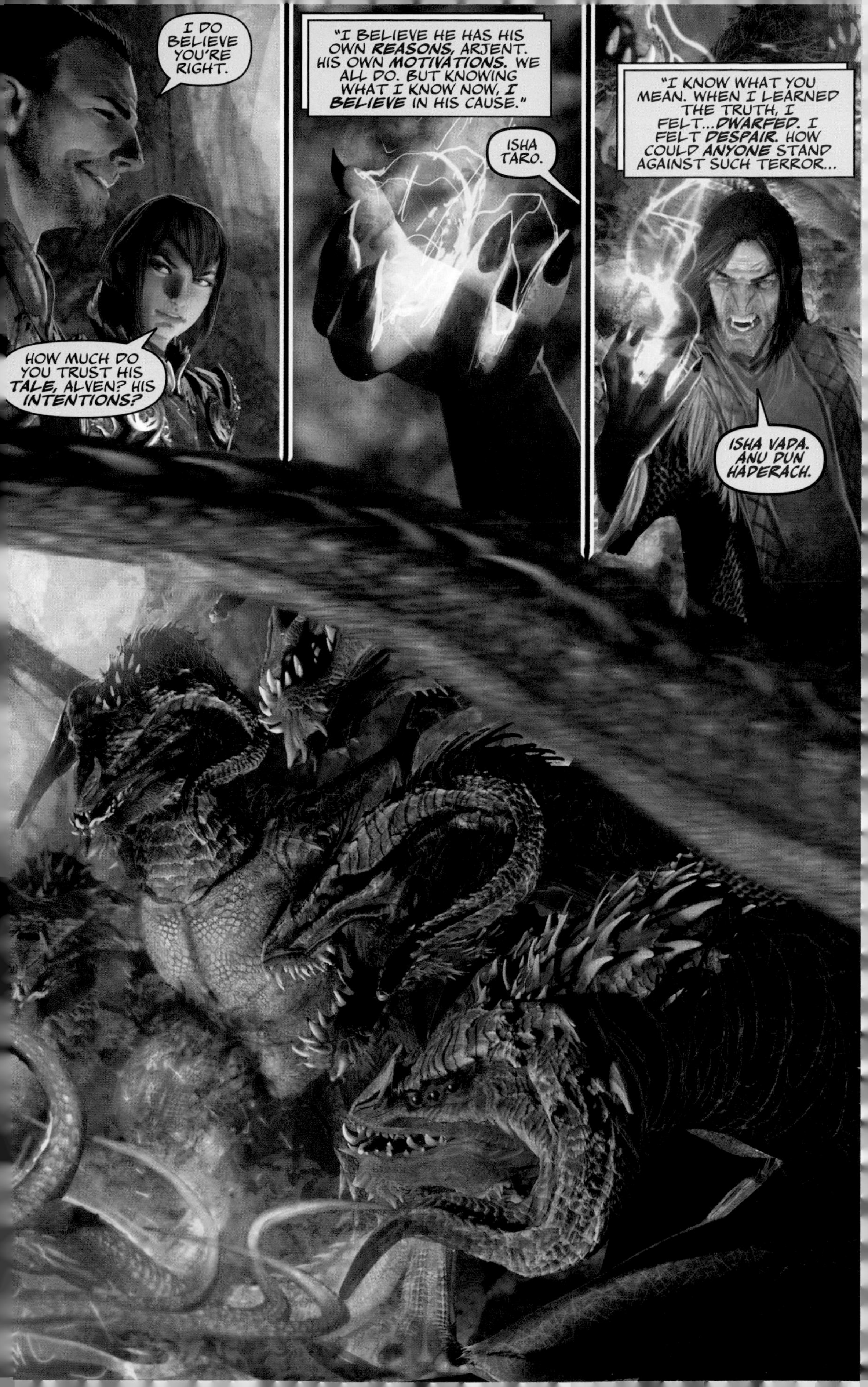
I DO BELIEVE YOU'RE RIGHT.
HOW MUCH DO YOU TRUST HIS TALE, ALVEN? HIS INTENTIONS?
"I BELIEVE HE HAS HIS OWN REASONS, ARJENT. HIS OWN MOTIVATIONS. WE ALL DO. BUT KNOWING WHAT I KNOW NOW, I BELIEVE IN HIS CAUSE."
ISHA TARO.
"I KNOW WHAT YOU MEAN. WHEN I LEARNED THE TRUTH, I FELT...DWARFED. I FELT DESPAIR. HOW COULD ANYONE STAND AGAINST SUCH TERROR...
ISHA VADA. ANU DUN HADERACH.

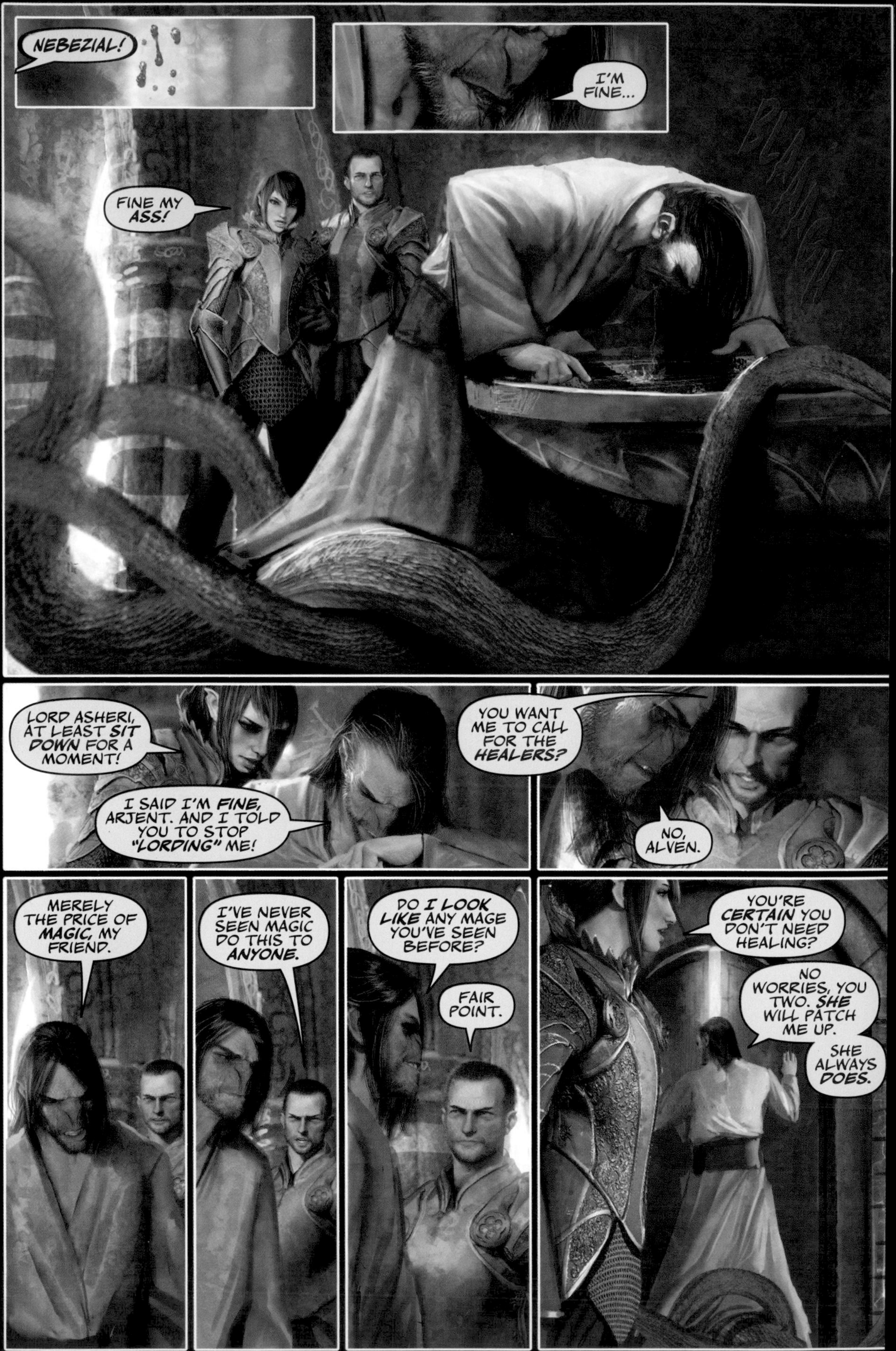
NEBEZIAL!
I'M FINE...
FINE MY ASS!
LORD ASHERI, AT LEAST SIT DOWN FOR A MOMENT!
I SAID I'M FINE, ARJENT. AND I TOLD YOU TO STOP "LORDING" ME!
YOU WANT ME TO CALL FOR THE HEALERS?
NO, ALVEN.
MERELY THE PRICE OF MAGIC, MY FRIEND.
I'VE NEVER SEEN MAGIC DO THIS TO ANYONE.
DO I LOOK LIKE ANY MAGE YOU'VE SEEN BEFORE?
FAIR POINT.
YOU'RE CERTAIN YOU DON'T NEED HEALING?
NO WORRIES, YOU TWO. SHE WILL PATCH ME UP.
SHE ALWAYS DOES.

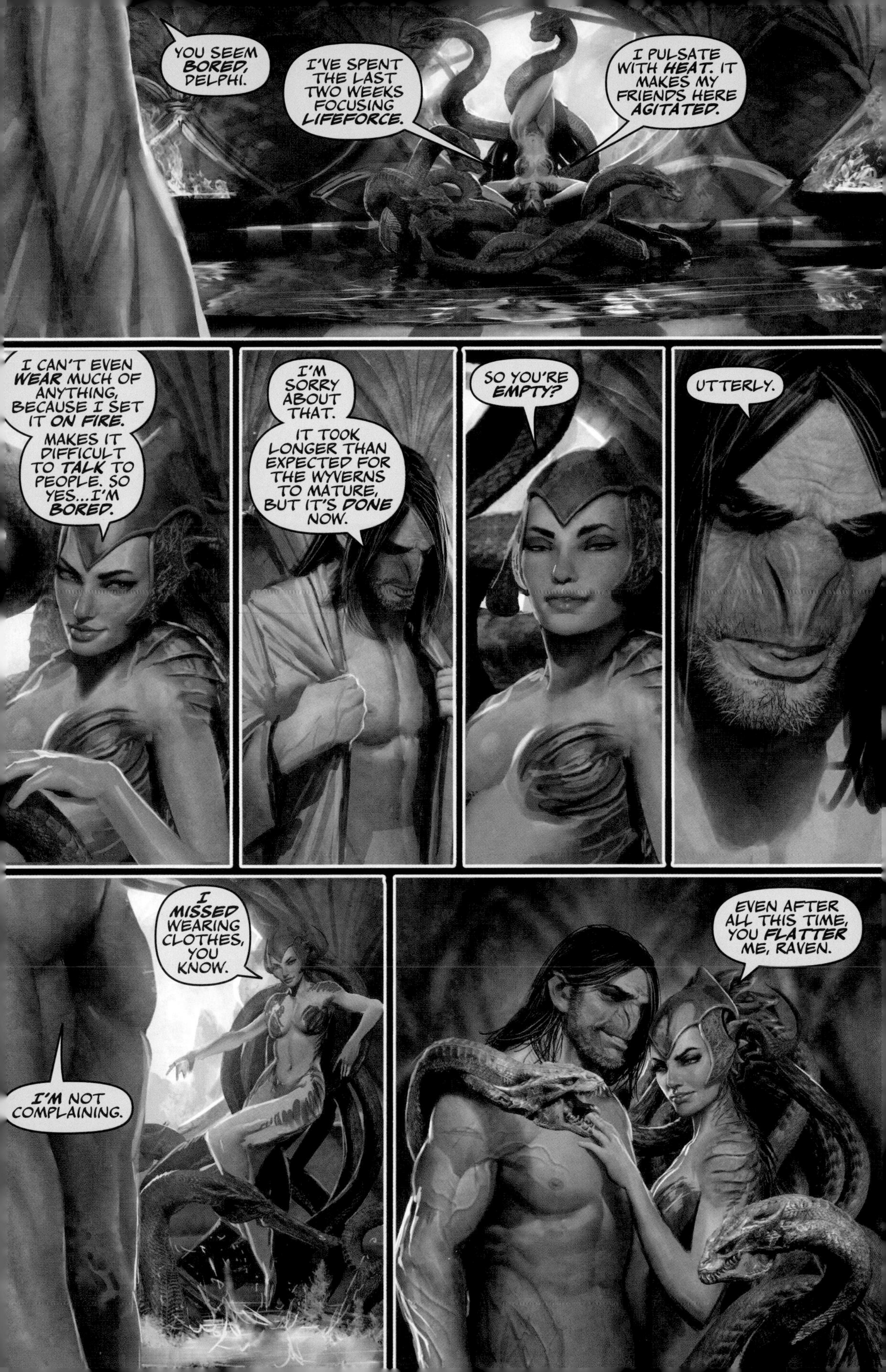
YOU SEEM BORED, DELPHI.
I'VE SPENT THE LAST TWO WEEKS FOCUSING LIFEFORCE.
I PULSATE WITH HEAT. IT MAKES MY FRIENDS HERE AGITATED.
I CAN'T EVEN WEAR MUCH OF ANYTHING, BECAUSE I SET IT ON FIRE.
MAKES IT DIFFICULT TO TALK TO PEOPLE. SO YES...I'M BORED.
I'M SORRY ABOUT THAT.
IT TOOK LONGER THAN EXPECTED FOR THE WYVERNS TO MATURE, BUT IT'S DONE NOW.
SO YOU'RE EMPTY?
UTTERLY.
I MISSED WEARING CLOTHES, YOU KNOW.
I'M NOT COMPLAINING.
EVEN AFTER ALL THIS TIME, YOU FLATTER ME, RAVEN.

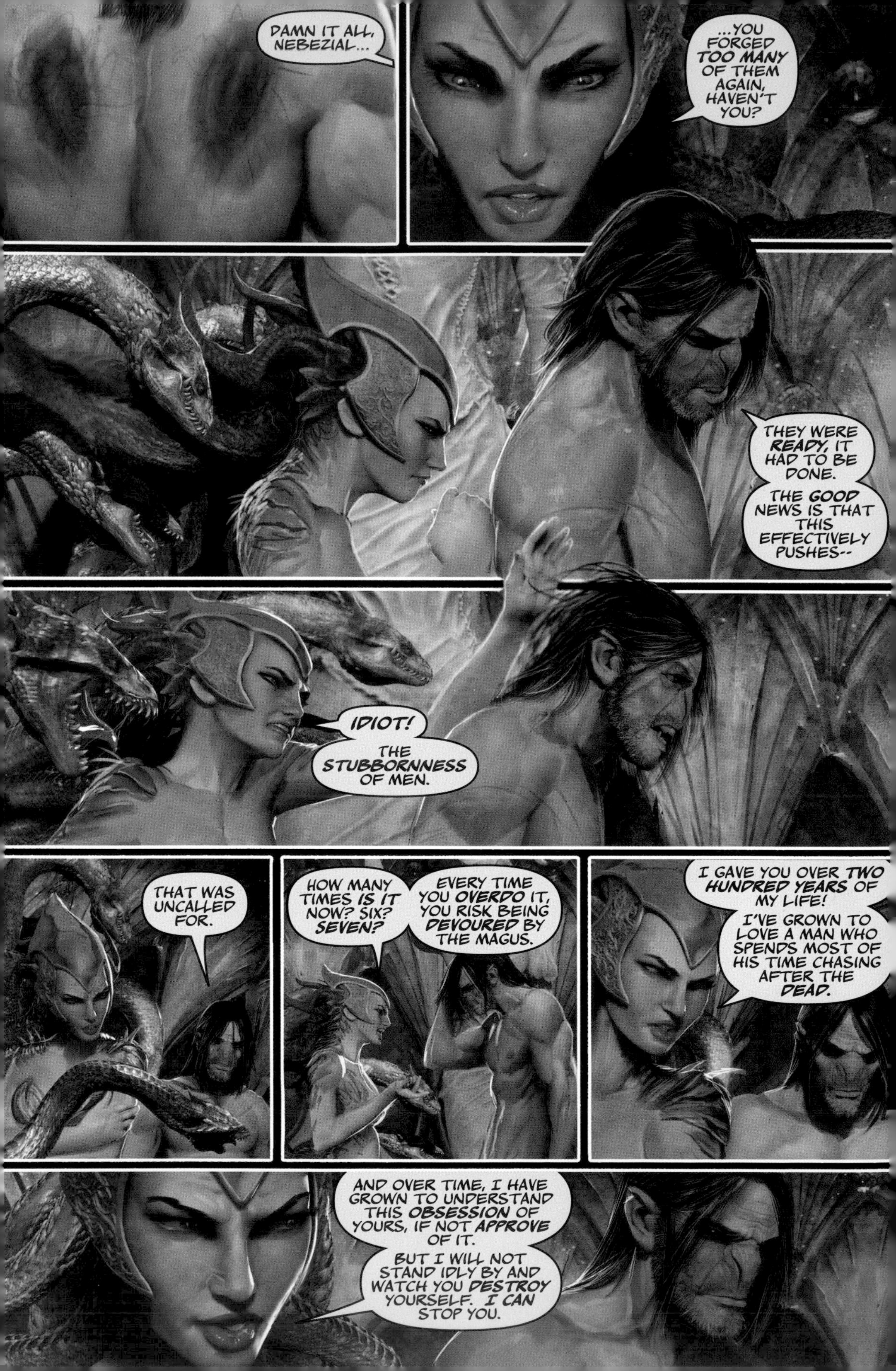
DAMN IT ALL, NEBEZIAL...
...YOU FORGED TOO MANY OF THEM AGAIN, HAVEN'T YOU?
THEY WERE READY, IT HAD TO BE DONE.
THE GOOD NEWS IS THAT THIS EFFECTIVELY PUSHES--
IDIOT!
THE STUBBORNNESS OF MEN.
THAT WAS UNCALLED FOR.
HOW MANY TIMES IS IT NOW? SIX? SEVEN?
EVERY TIME YOU OVERDO IT, YOU RISK BEING DEVOURED BY THE MAGUS.
I GAVE YOU OVER TWO HUNDRED YEARS OF MY LIFE!
I'VE GROWN TO LOVE A MAN WHO SPENDS MOST OF HIS TIME CHASING AFTER THE DEAD.
AND OVER TIME, I HAVE GROWN TO UNDERSTAND THIS OBSESSION OF YOURS, IF NOT APPROVE OF IT.
BUT I WILL NOT STAND IDLY BY AND WATCH YOU DESTROY YOURSELF. I CAN STOP YOU.

DELPHI, I MAY BE MANY THINGS, BUT I 'M NOT A *LIAR.* FROM DAY ONE, YOU KNEW *WHY* I STARTED ALL OF THIS.

FOR *FREYA.*

YES, BECAUSE THE WOMAN I LOVED WAS *TAKEN* FROM ME. THEN I FOUND OUT ABOUT YOU.

I PLANNED ON *USING* YOU, BUT I *LEARNED* THINGS. AND *TWO CENTURIES* IS A LONG TIME.

YOU COULD HAVE *SLAIN* ME THE DAY I TOLD YOU OF MY INTENTIONS. YET YOU DIDN'T. *WHY?*

I WAS *AMUSED* BY YOUR BLATANT HONESTY.

I'M NOT THE *SAME MAN* WHO SET YOU FREE THAT DAY. SO MUCH CHANGED. I CHANGED.

I LOVE YOU, DELPHI BELLARYA ASHERI.

IT KILLS YOU TO *SAY* IT, DOESN'T IT?

NO, IT KILLS ME THAT I *MEAN* IT.

THIS IS NOT ABOUT FREYA, NOT ANYMORE. THE TRUTH IS...

...I CAN'T REMEMBER HER *FACE* ANYMORE.

EVERY DEATH LEAVES A *MARK* ON THE KILLER. SHIVAS CAN EVEN *SEE* THESE MARKS. THEY CALL THEM THE *CROWS.*

A MURDER OF CROWS. SEEMS APPROPRIATE.

I ACCEPT THAT THE LIFE FRAGMENTS OF THOSE I'VE KILLED *ENCIRCLE* ME. MOST OF THEM FEEL JUSTIFIED.

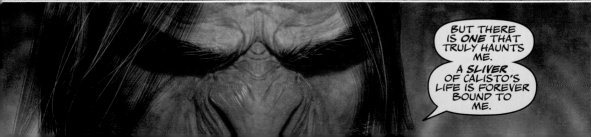

BUT THERE IS *ONE* THAT TRULY HAUNTS ME.

A *SLIVER* OF CALISTO'S LIFE IS FOREVER BOUND TO ME.

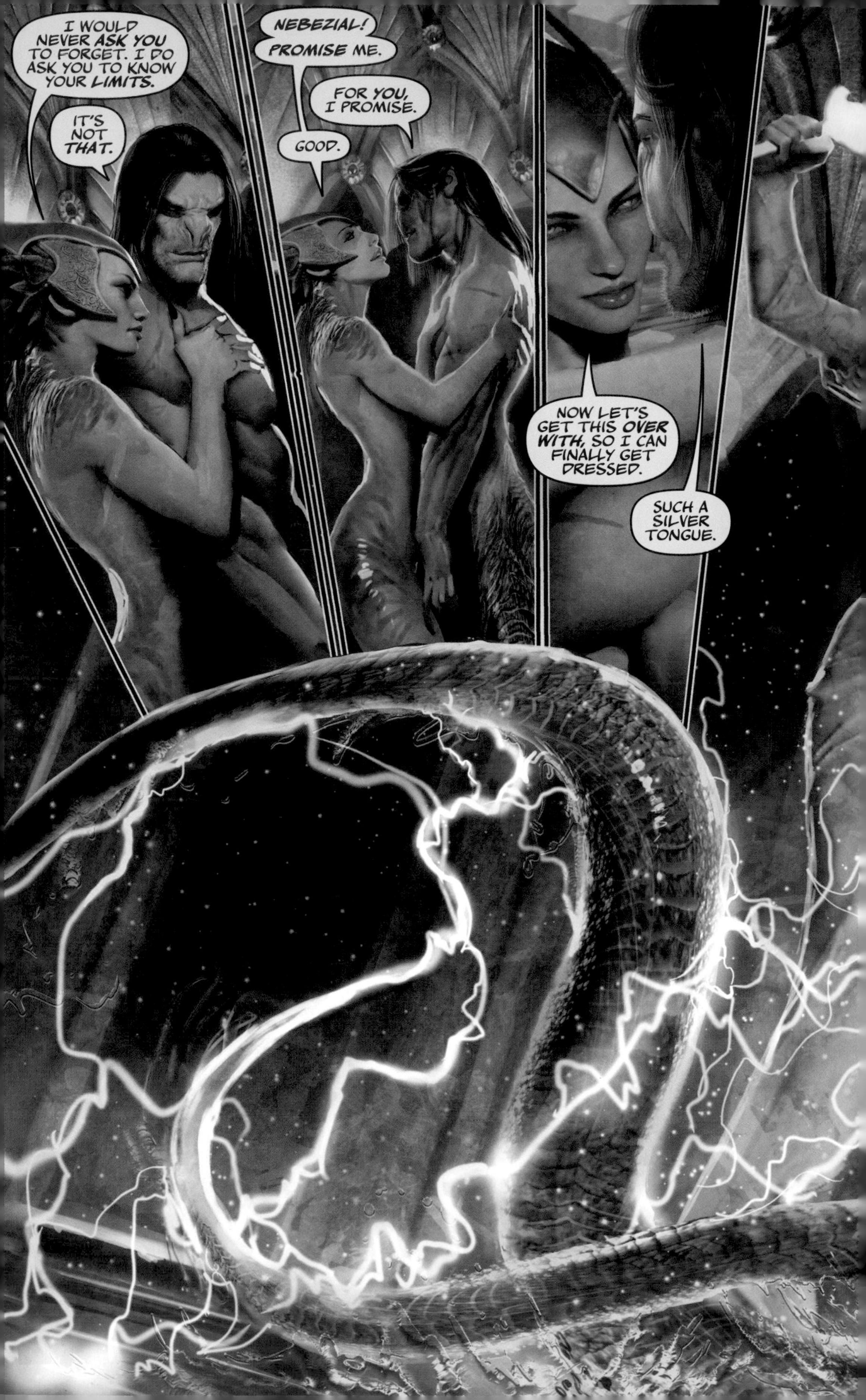
I WOULD NEVER ASK YOU TO FORGET. I DO ASK YOU TO KNOW YOUR LIMITS.
IT'S NOT THAT.
NEBEZIAL! PROMISE ME.
FOR YOU, I PROMISE.
GOOD.
NOW LET'S GET THIS OVER WITH, SO I CAN FINALLY GET DRESSED.
SUCH A SILVER TONGUE.

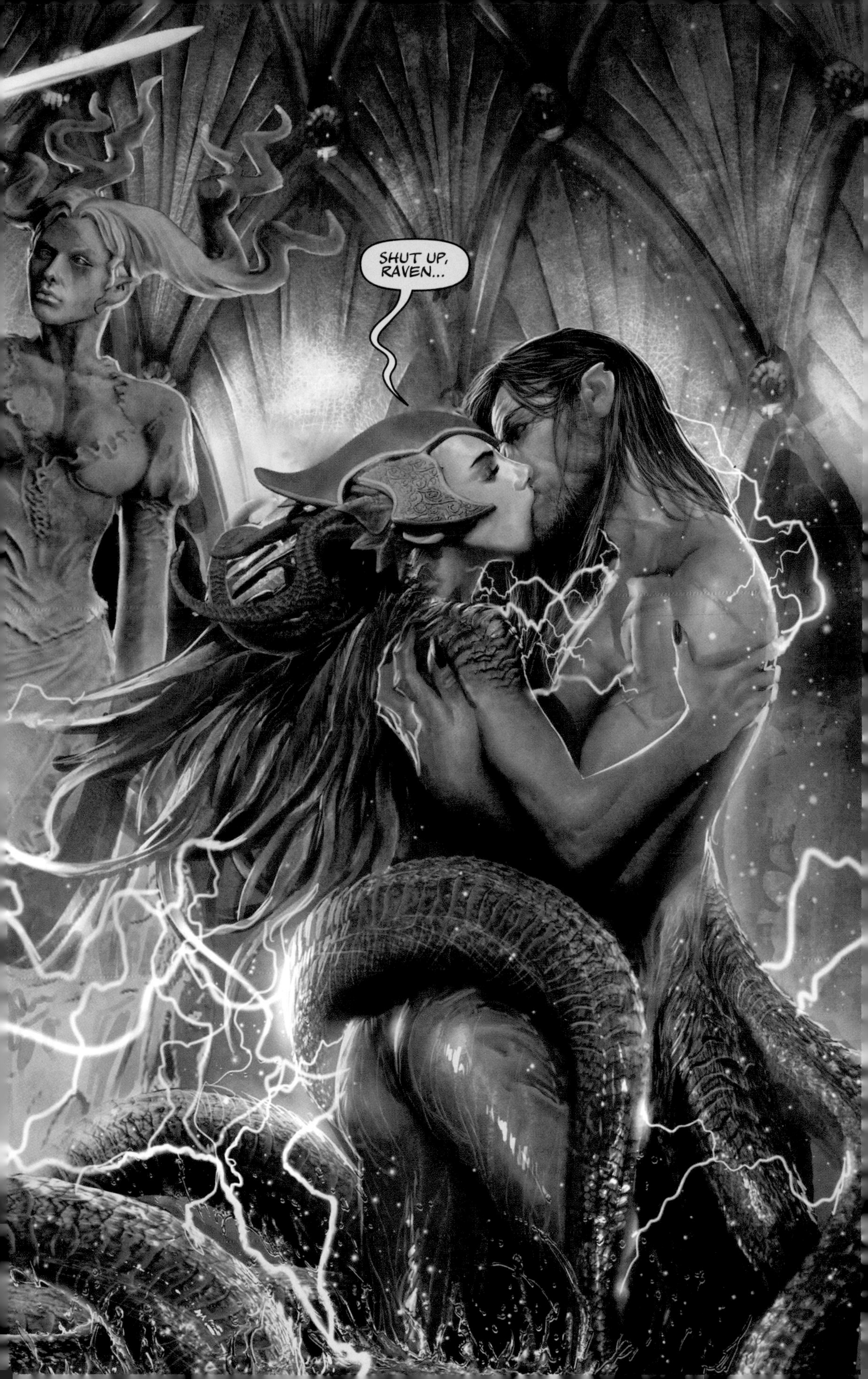
SHUT UP, RAVEN...

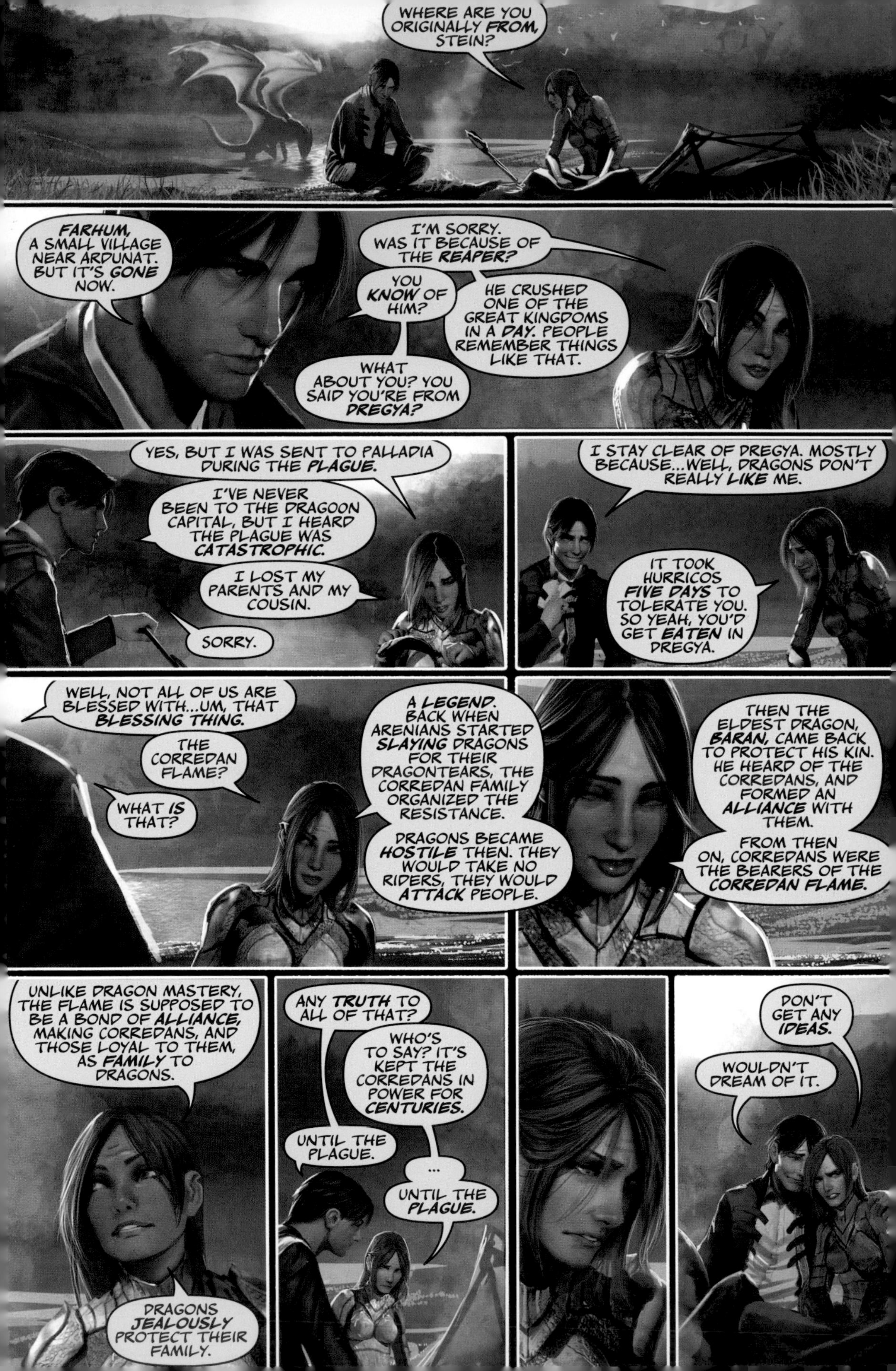
WHERE ARE YOU ORIGINALLY FROM, STEIN?
FARHUM, A SMALL VILLAGE NEAR ARDUNAT. BUT IT'S GONE NOW.
I'M SORRY. WAS IT BECAUSE OF THE REAPER?
YOU KNOW OF HIM?
HE CRUSHED ONE OF THE GREAT KINGDOMS IN A DAY. PEOPLE REMEMBER THINGS LIKE THAT.
WHAT ABOUT YOU? YOU SAID YOU'RE FROM DREGYA?
YES, BUT I WAS SENT TO PALLADIA DURING THE PLAGUE.
I'VE NEVER BEEN TO THE DRAGOON CAPITAL, BUT I HEARD THE PLAGUE WAS CATASTROPHIC.
I LOST MY PARENTS AND MY COUSIN.
SORRY.
I STAY CLEAR OF DREGYA. MOSTLY BECAUSE...WELL, DRAGONS DON'T REALLY LIKE ME.
IT TOOK HURRICOS FIVE DAYS TO TOLERATE YOU. SO YEAH, YOU'D GET EATEN IN DREGYA.
WELL, NOT ALL OF US ARE BLESSED WITH...UM, THAT BLESSING THING.
THE CORREDAN FLAME?
WHAT IS THAT?
A LEGEND. BACK WHEN ARENIANS STARTED SLAYING DRAGONS FOR THEIR DRAGONTEARS, THE CORREDAN FAMILY ORGANIZED THE RESISTANCE.
DRAGONS BECAME HOSTILE THEN. THEY WOULD TAKE NO RIDERS, THEY WOULD ATTACK PEOPLE.
THEN THE ELDEST DRAGON, BARAN, CAME BACK TO PROTECT HIS KIN. HE HEARD OF THE CORREDANS, AND FORMED AN ALLIANCE WITH THEM.
FROM THEN ON, CORREDANS WERE THE BEARERS OF THE CORREDAN FLAME.
UNLIKE DRAGON MASTERY, THE FLAME IS SUPPOSED TO BE A BOND OF ALLIANCE, MAKING CORREDANS, AND THOSE LOYAL TO THEM, AS FAMILY TO DRAGONS.
DRAGONS JEALOUSLY PROTECT THEIR FAMILY.
ANY TRUTH TO ALL OF THAT?
WHO'S TO SAY? IT'S KEPT THE CORREDANS IN POWER FOR CENTURIES.
UNTIL THE PLAGUE.
...
UNTIL THE PLAGUE.
DON'T GET ANY IDEAS.
WOULDN'T DREAM OF IT.

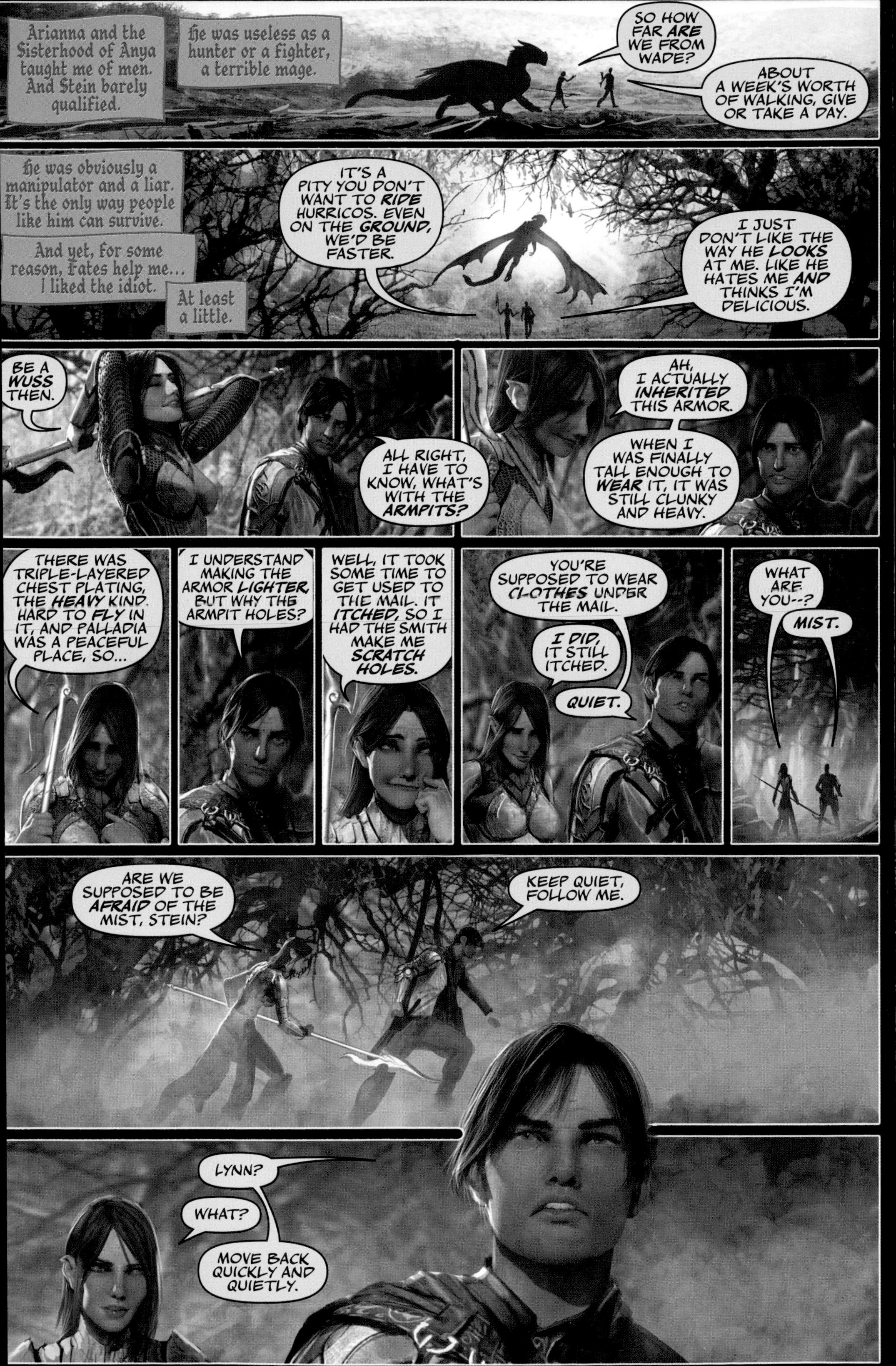
Arianna and the Sisterhood of Anya taught me of men. And Stein barely qualified.
He was useless as a hunter or a fighter, a terrible mage.
SO HOW FAR ARE WE FROM WADE?
ABOUT A WEEK'S WORTH OF WALKING, GIVE OR TAKE A DAY.
He was obviously a manipulator and a liar. It's the only way people like him can survive.
And yet, for some reason, Fates help me... I liked the idiot.
At least a little.
IT'S A PITY YOU DON'T WANT TO RIDE HURRICOS. EVEN ON THE GROUND, WE'D BE FASTER.
I JUST DON'T LIKE THE WAY HE LOOKS AT ME. LIKE HE HATES ME AND THINKS I'M DELICIOUS.
BE A WUSS THEN.
ALL RIGHT, I HAVE TO KNOW, WHAT'S WITH THE ARMPITS?
AH, I ACTUALLY INHERITED THIS ARMOR.
WHEN I WAS FINALLY TALL ENOUGH TO WEAR IT, IT WAS STILL CLUNKY AND HEAVY.
THERE WAS TRIPLE-LAYERED CHEST PLATING, THE HEAVY KIND. HARD TO FLY IN IT, AND PALLADIA WAS A PEACEFUL PLACE, SO...
I UNDERSTAND MAKING THE ARMOR LIGHTER, BUT WHY THE ARMPIT HOLES?
WELL, IT TOOK SOME TIME TO GET USED TO THE MAIL. IT ITCHED, SO I HAD THE SMITH MAKE ME SCRATCH HOLES.
YOU'RE SUPPOSED TO WEAR CLOTHES UNDER THE MAIL.
I DID, IT STILL ITCHED.
QUIET.
WHAT ARE YOU--?
MIST.
ARE WE SUPPOSED TO BE AFRAID OF THE MIST, STEIN?
KEEP QUIET, FOLLOW ME.
LYNN?
WHAT?
MOVE BACK QUICKLY AND QUIETLY.

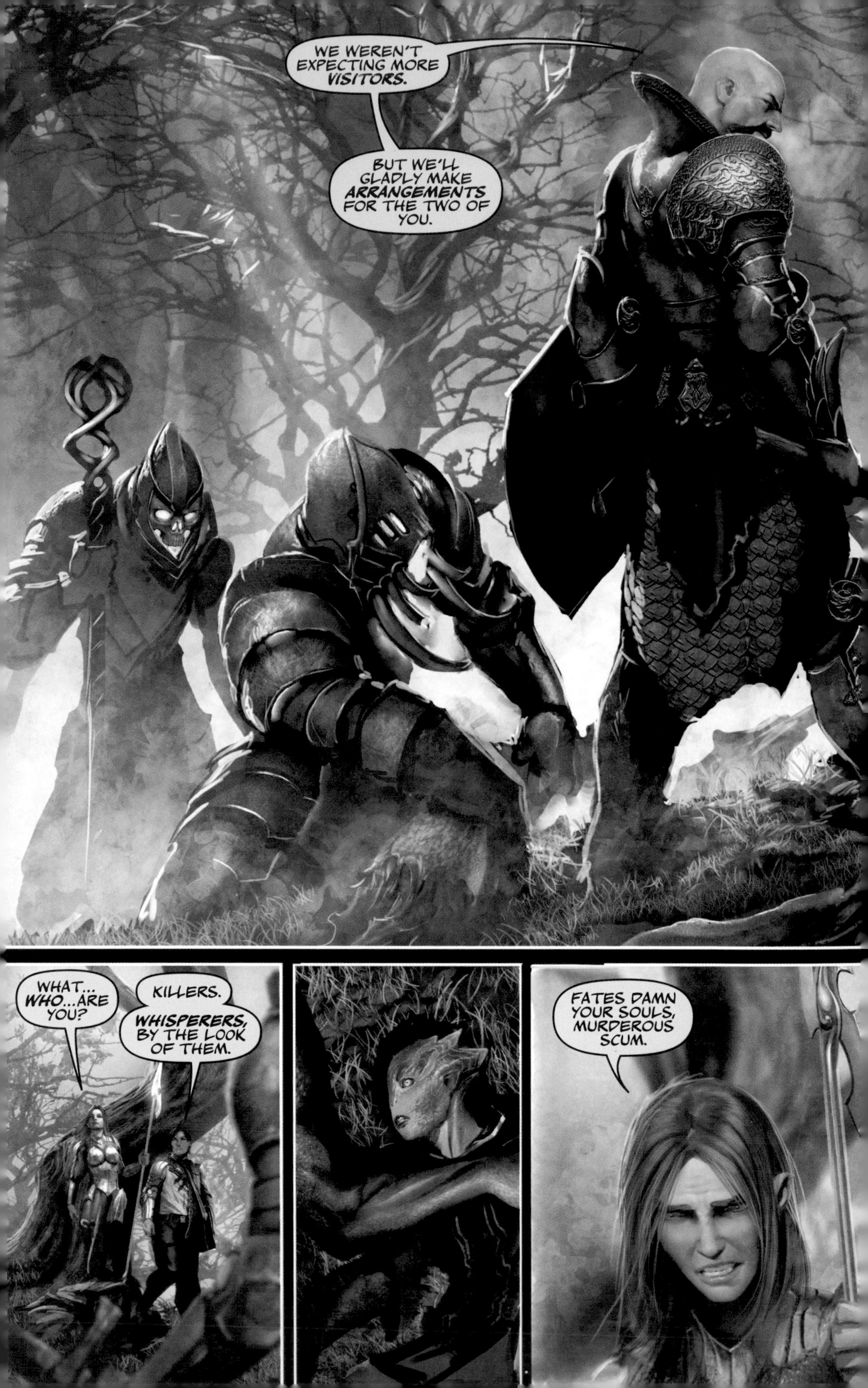
WE WEREN'T EXPECTING MORE VISITORS.
BUT WE'LL GLADLY MAKE ARRANGEMENTS FOR THE TWO OF YOU.
WHAT... WHO...ARE YOU?
KILLERS.
WHISPERERS, BY THE LOOK OF THEM.
FATES DAMN YOUR SOULS, MURDEROUS SCUM.

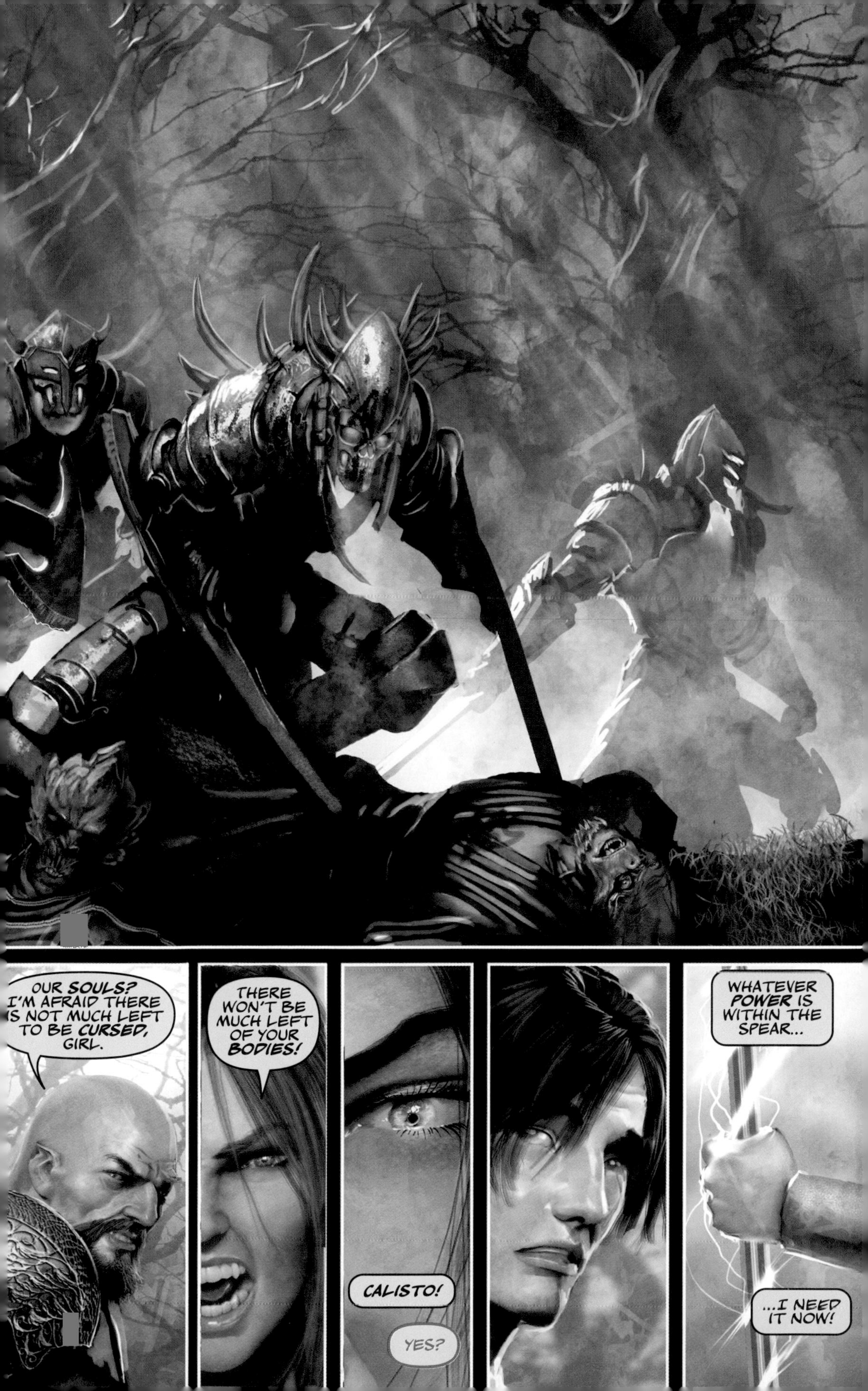
OUR SOULS? I'M AFRAID THERE IS NOT MUCH LEFT TO BE CURSED, GIRL.
THERE WON'T BE MUCH LEFT OF YOUR BODIES!
CALISTO!
YES?
WHATEVER POWER IS WITHIN THE SPEAR...
...I NEED IT NOW!

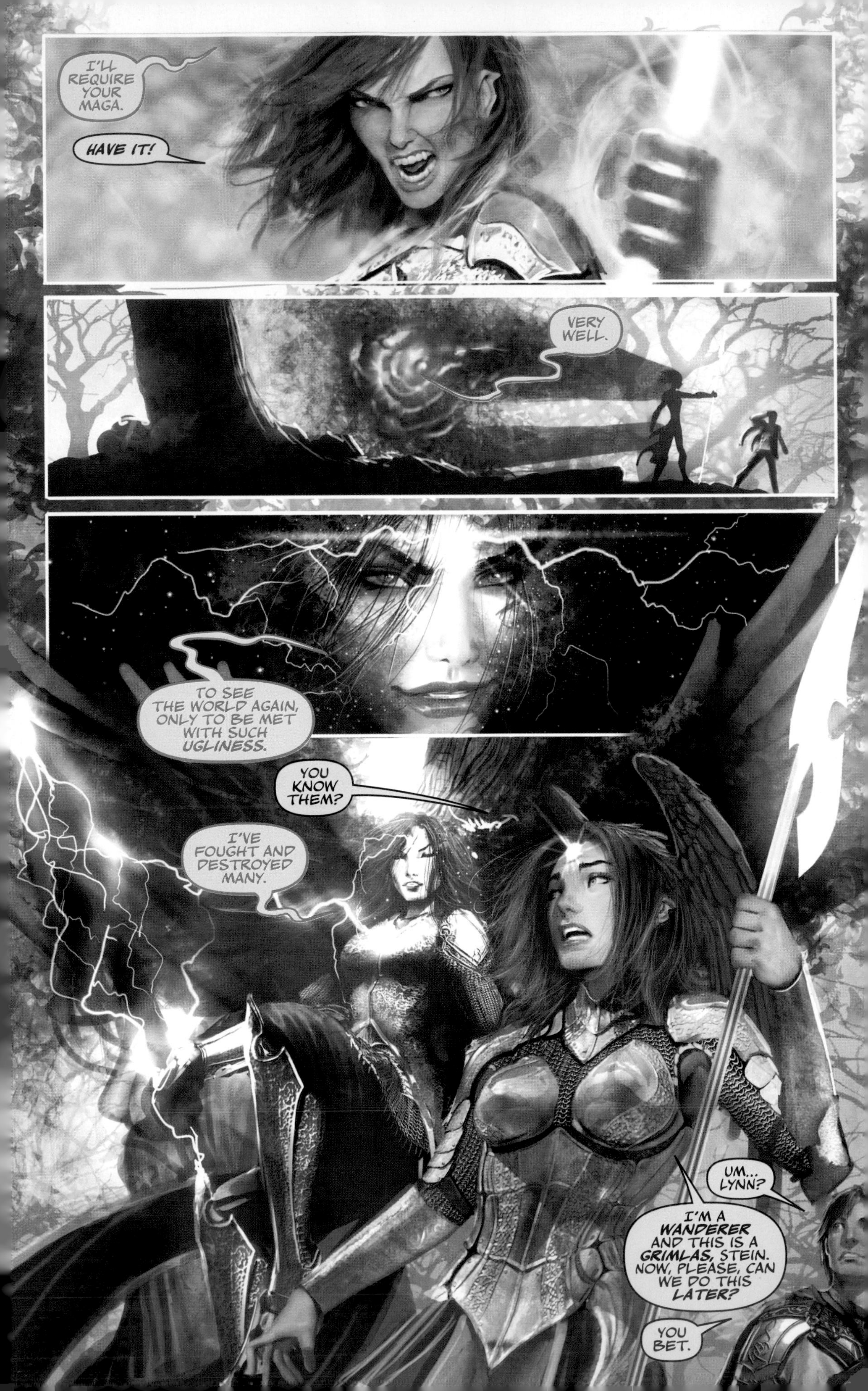
I'LL REQUIRE YOUR MAGA.
HAVE IT!
VERY WELL.
TO SEE THE WORLD AGAIN, ONLY TO BE MET WITH SUCH UGLINESS.
YOU KNOW THEM?
I'VE FOUGHT AND DESTROYED MANY.
UM... LYNN?
I'M A WANDERER AND THIS IS A GRIMLAS, STEIN. NOW, PLEASE, CAN WE DO THIS LATER?
YOU BET.

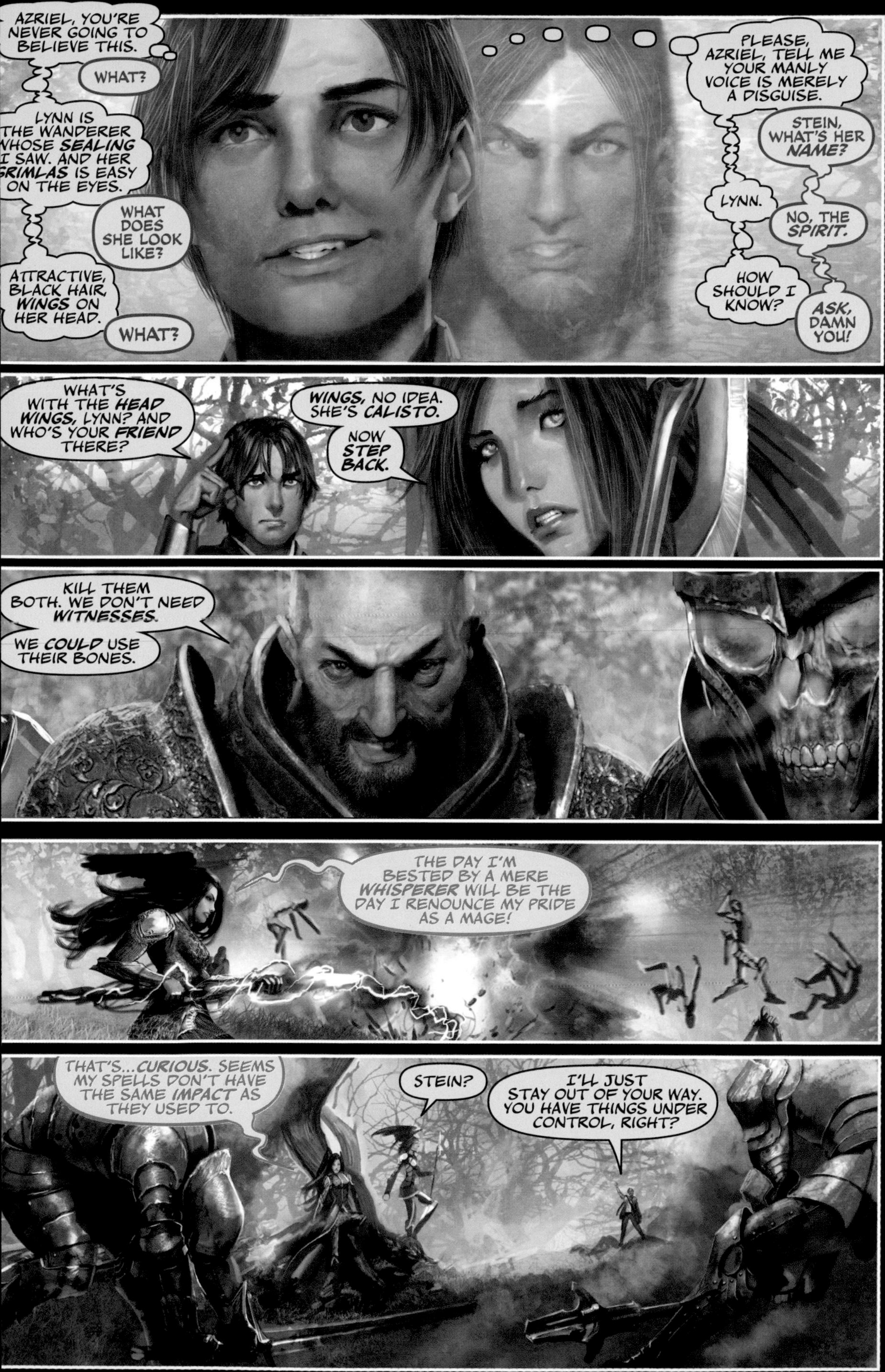
AZRIEL, YOU'RE NEVER GOING TO BELIEVE THIS.
WHAT?
LYNN IS THE WANDERER WHOSE SEALING I SAW. AND HER GRIMLAS IS EASY ON THE EYES.
WHAT DOES SHE LOOK LIKE?
ATTRACTIVE, BLACK HAIR, WINGS ON HER HEAD.
WHAT?
PLEASE, AZRIEL, TELL ME YOUR MANLY VOICE IS MERELY A DISGUISE.
STEIN, WHAT'S HER NAME?
LYNN.
NO, THE SPIRIT.
HOW SHOULD I KNOW?
ASK, DAMN YOU!
WHAT'S WITH THE HEAD WINGS, LYNN? AND WHO'S YOUR FRIEND THERE?
WINGS, NO IDEA. SHE'S CALISTO.
NOW STEP BACK.
KILL THEM BOTH. WE DON'T NEED WITNESSES.
WE COULD USE THEIR BONES.
THE DAY I'M BESTED BY A MERE WHISPERER WILL BE THE DAY I RENOUNCE MY PRIDE AS A MAGE!
THAT'S...CURIOUS. SEEMS MY SPELLS DON'T HAVE THE SAME IMPACT AS THEY USED TO.
STEIN?
I'LL JUST STAY OUT OF YOUR WAY. YOU HAVE THINGS UNDER CONTROL, RIGHT?

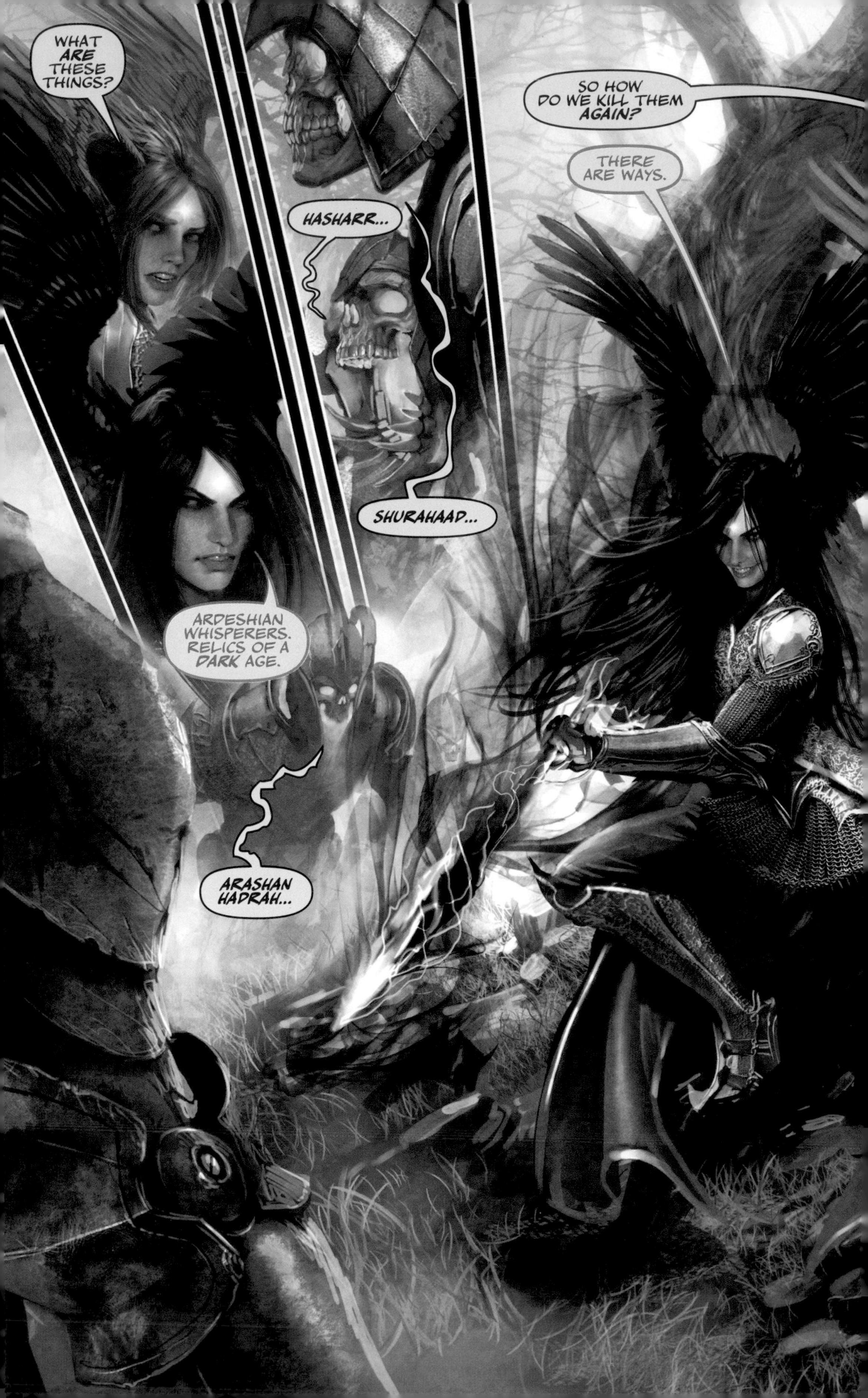
WHAT ARE THESE THINGS?
HASHARR...
SHURAHAAD...
ARDESHIAN WHISPERERS. RELICS OF A DARK AGE.
ARASHAN HADRAH...
SO HOW DO WE KILL THEM AGAIN?
THERE ARE WAYS.

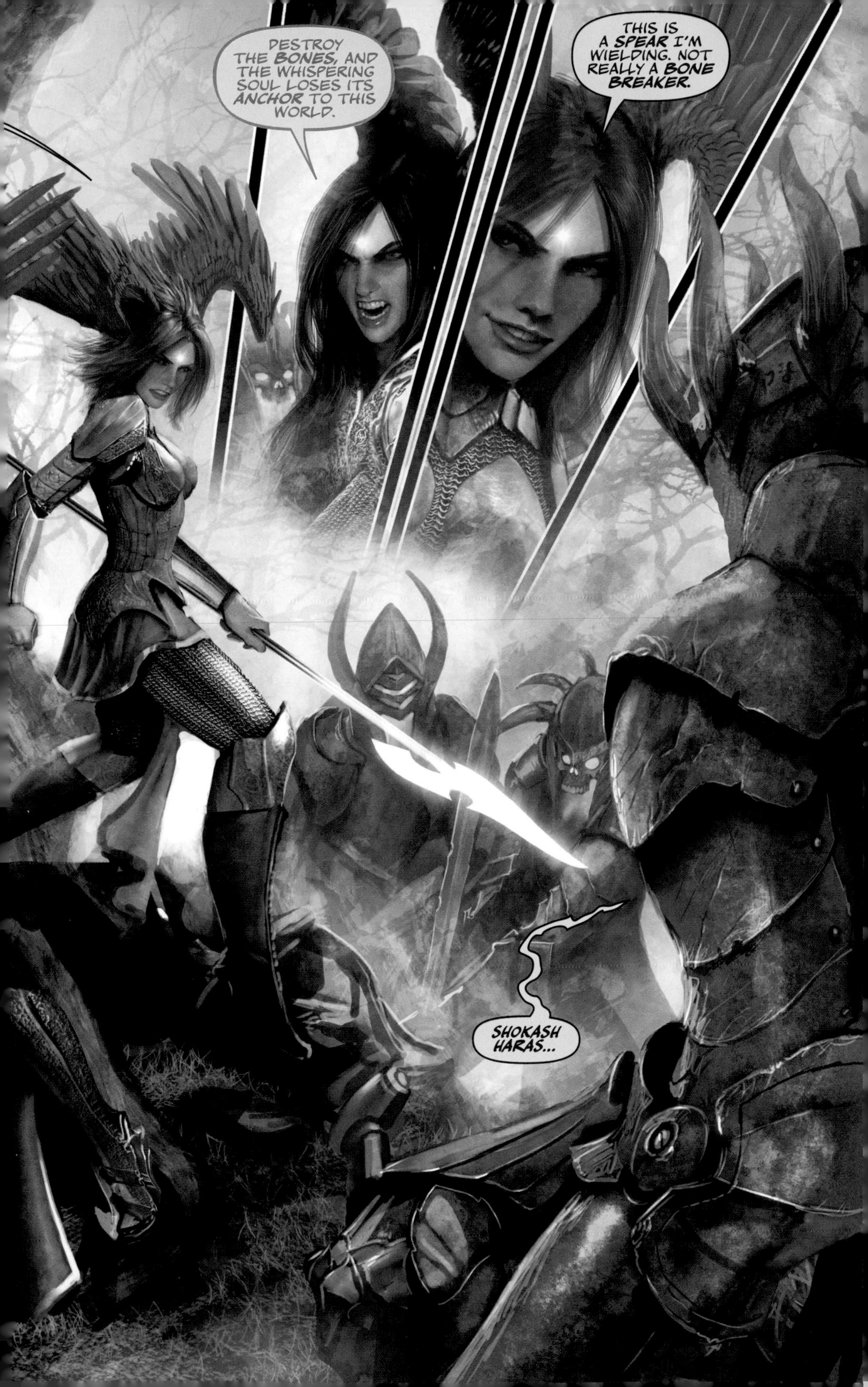
DESTROY THE BONES, AND THE WHISPERING SOUL LOSES ITS ANCHOR TO THIS WORLD.
THIS IS A SPEAR I'M WIELDING. NOT REALLY A BONE BREAKER.
SHOKASH HARAS...

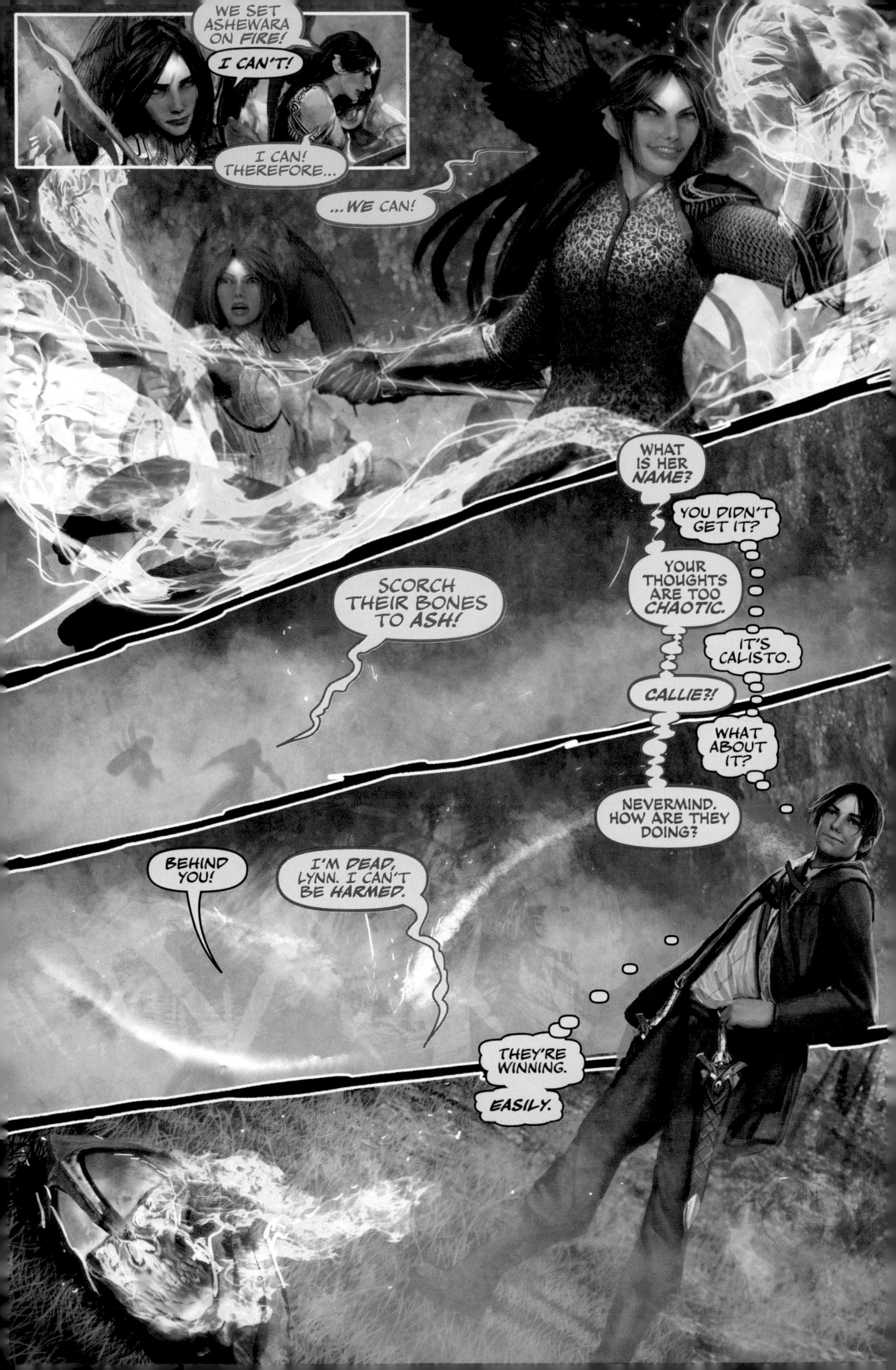
WE SET ASHEWARA ON FIRE!
I CAN'T!
I CAN! THEREFORE...
...WE CAN!
WHAT IS HER NAME?
YOU DIDN'T GET IT?
YOUR THOUGHTS ARE TOO CHAOTIC.
SCORCH THEIR BONES TO ASH!
IT'S CALISTO.
CALLIE?!
WHAT ABOUT IT?
NEVERMIND. HOW ARE THEY DOING?
BEHIND YOU!
I'M DEAD, LYNN. I CAN'T BE HARMED.
THEY'RE WINNING.
EASILY.

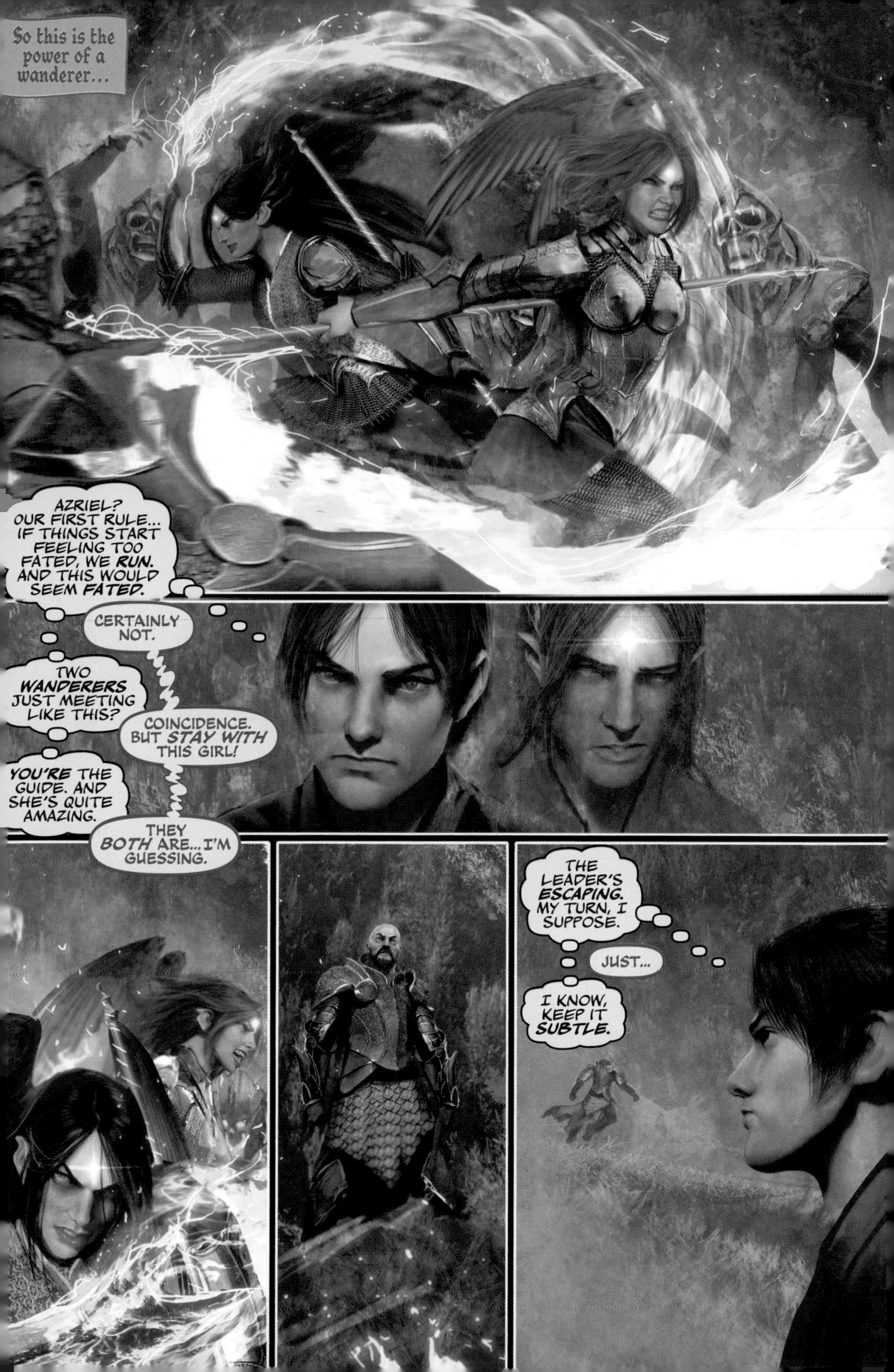
So this is the power of a wanderer...
AZRIEL? OUR FIRST RULE... IF THINGS START FEELING TOO FATED, WE RUN. AND THIS WOULD SEEM FATED.
CERTAINLY NOT.
TWO WANDERERS JUST MEETING LIKE THIS?
COINCIDENCE. BUT STAY WITH THIS GIRL!
YOU'RE THE GUIDE. AND SHE'S QUITE AMAZING.
THEY BOTH ARE... I'M GUESSING.
THE LEADER'S ESCAPING. MY TURN, I SUPPOSE.
JUST...
I KNOW, KEEP IT SUBTLE.

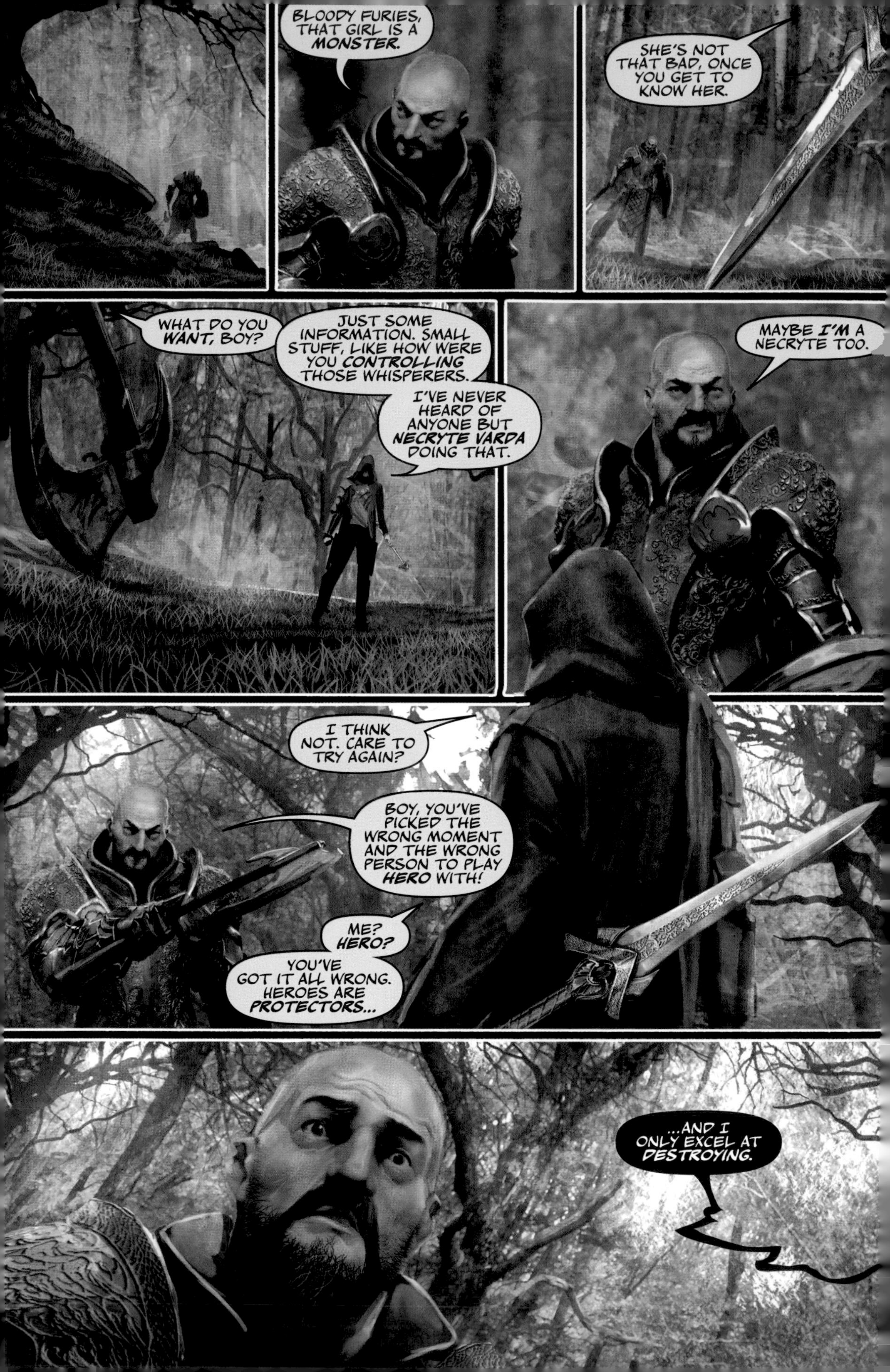
BLOODY FURIES, THAT GIRL IS A MONSTER.
SHE'S NOT THAT BAD, ONCE YOU GET TO KNOW HER.
WHAT DO YOU WANT, BOY?
JUST SOME INFORMATION. SMALL STUFF, LIKE HOW WERE YOU CONTROLLING THOSE WHISPERERS.
I'VE NEVER HEARD OF ANYONE BUT NECRYTE VARDA DOING THAT.
MAYBE I'M A NECRYTE TOO.
I THINK NOT. CARE TO TRY AGAIN?
BOY, YOU'VE PICKED THE WRONG MOMENT AND THE WRONG PERSON TO PLAY HERO WITH!
ME? HERO?
YOU'VE GOT IT ALL WRONG. HEROES ARE PROTECTORS...
...AND I ONLY EXCEL AT DESTROYING.

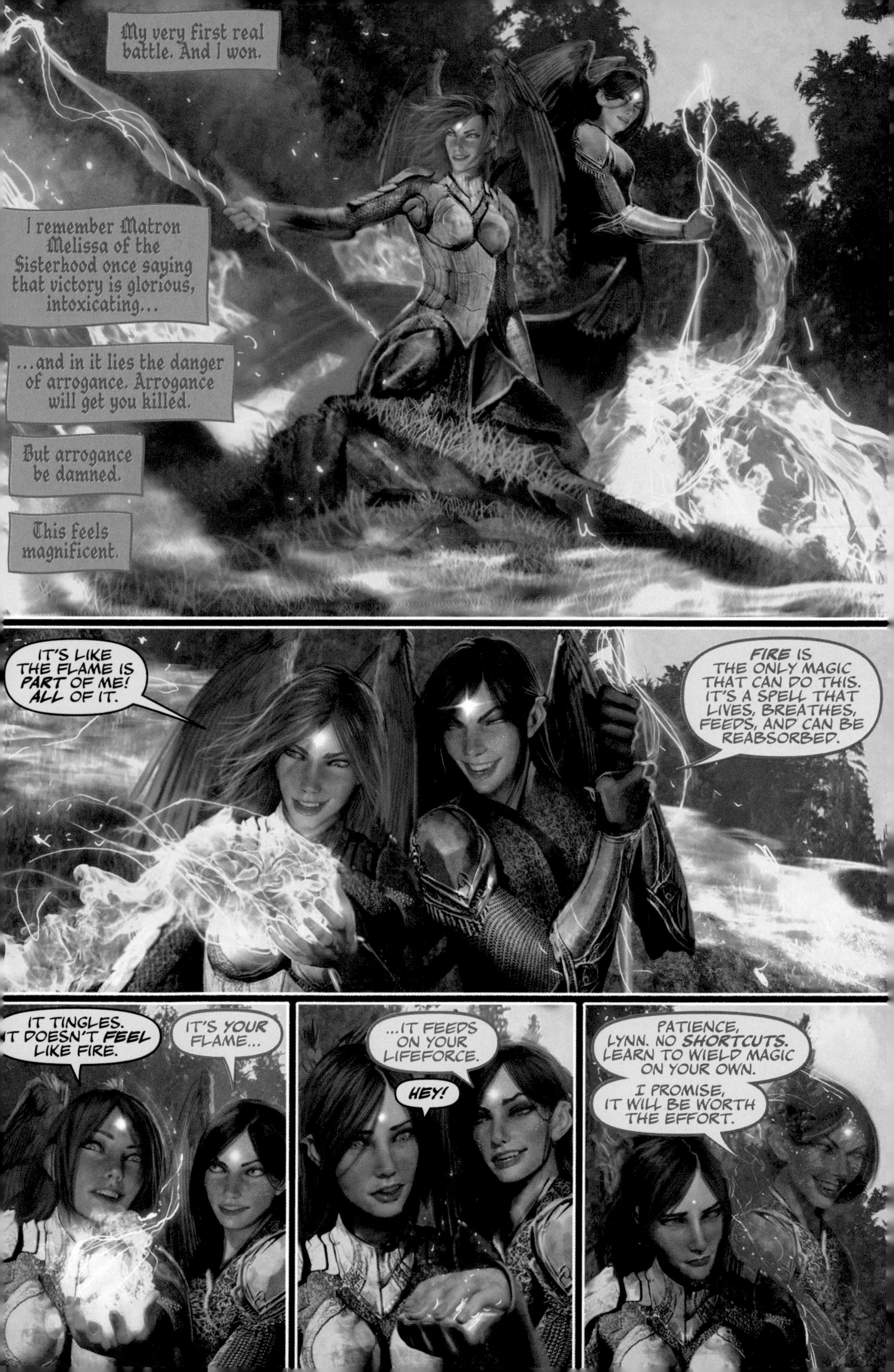

My very first real battle. And I won.
I remember Matron Melissa of the Sisterhood once saying that victory is glorious, intoxicating...
...and in it lies the danger of arrogance. Arrogance will get you killed.
But arrogance be damned.
This feels magnificent.
IT'S LIKE THE FLAME IS PART OF ME! ALL OF IT.
FIRE IS THE ONLY MAGIC THAT CAN DO THIS. IT'S A SPELL THAT LIVES, BREATHES, FEEDS, AND CAN BE REABSORBED.
IT TINGLES. IT DOESN'T FEEL LIKE FIRE.
IT'S YOUR FLAME...
...IT FEEDS ON YOUR LIFEFORCE.
HEY!
PATIENCE, LYNN. NO SHORTCUTS. LEARN TO WIELD MAGIC ON YOUR OWN.
I PROMISE, IT WILL BE WORTH THE EFFORT.

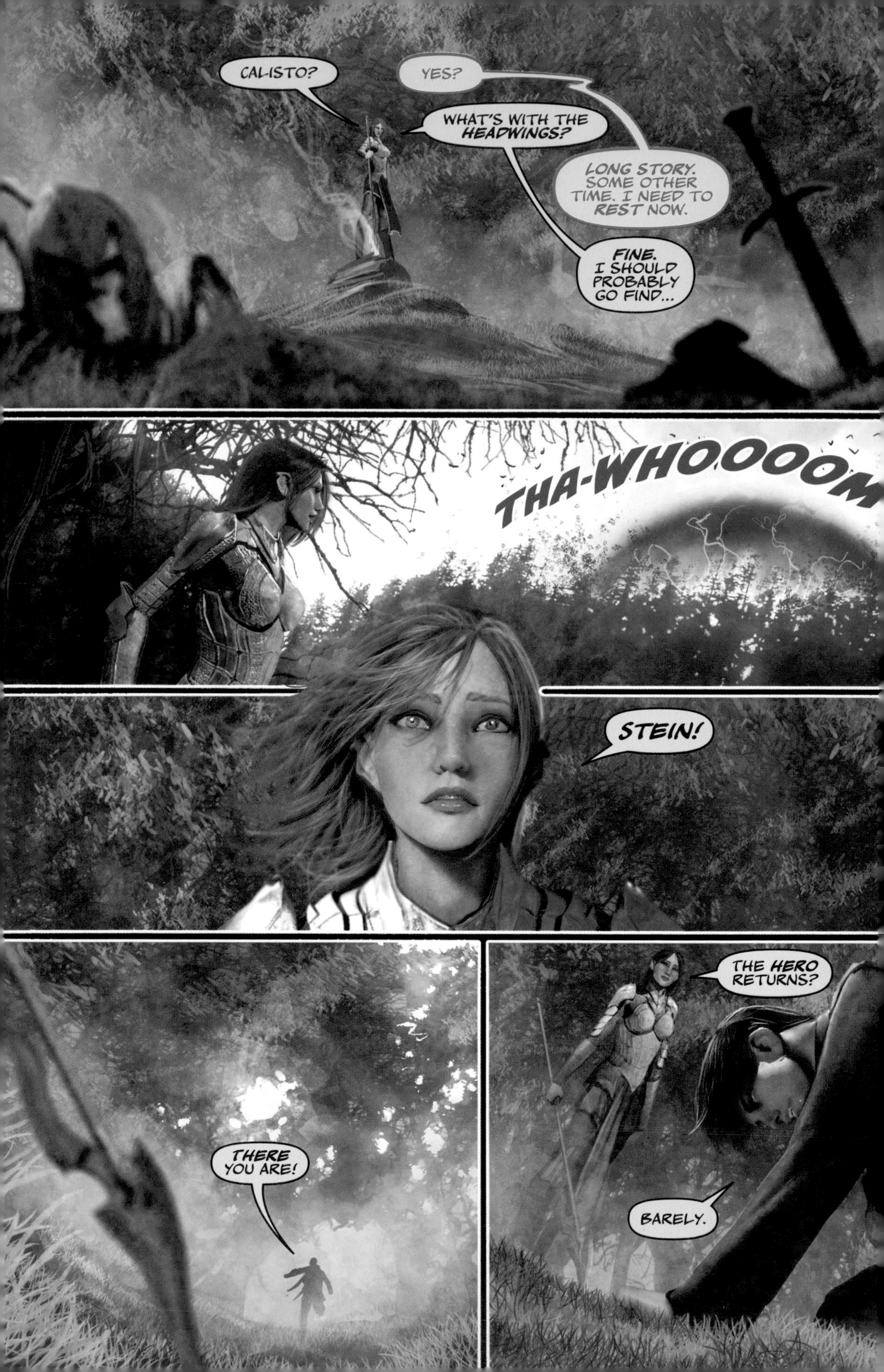
CALISTO?
YES?
WHAT'S WITH THE HEADWINGS?
LONG STORY. SOME OTHER TIME. I NEED TO REST NOW.
FINE. I SHOULD PROBABLY GO FIND...
THA-WHOOOOM
STEIN!
THERE YOU ARE!
THE HERO RETURNS?
BARELY.

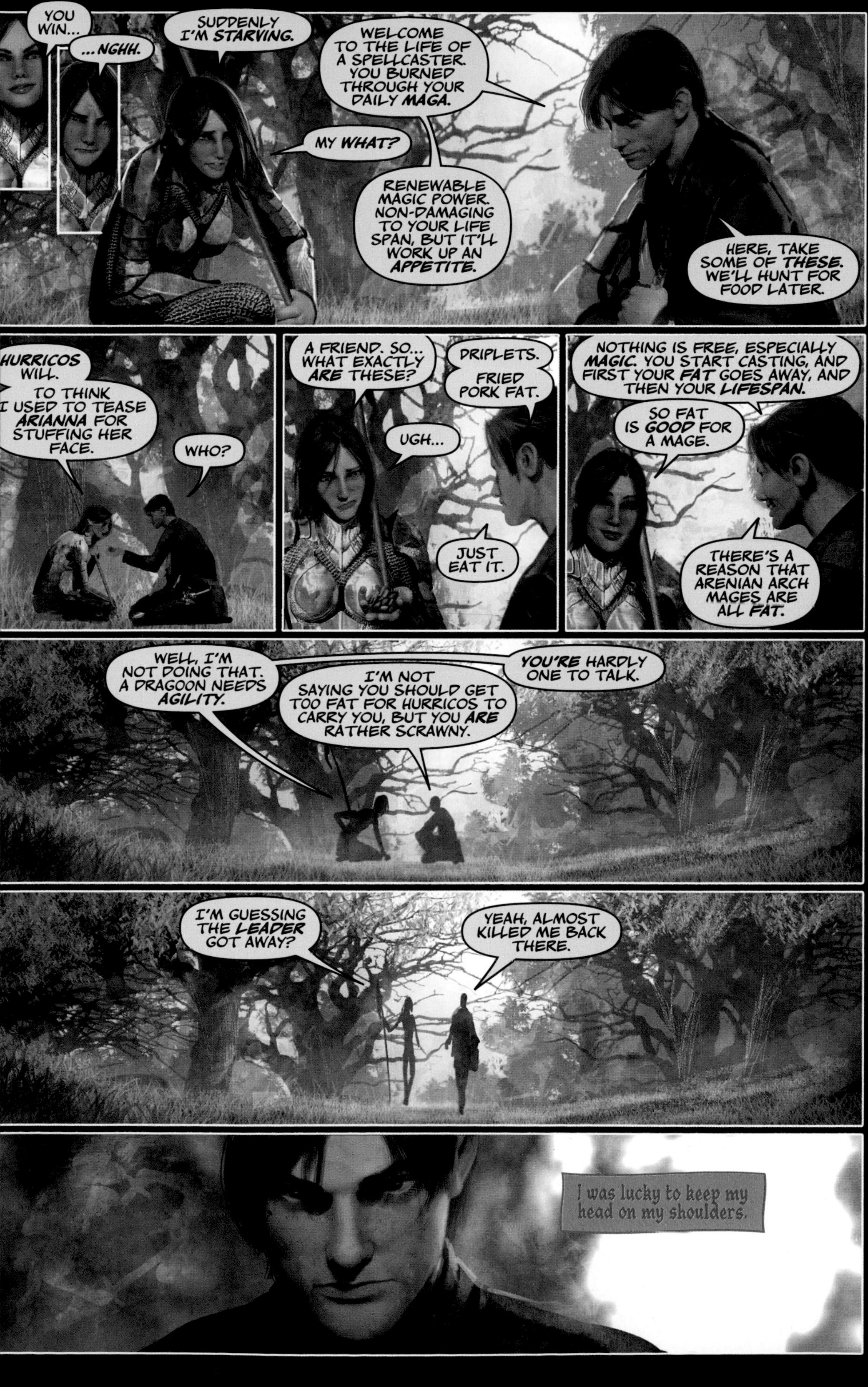
YOU WIN...
...NGHH.
SUDDENLY I'M STARVING.
WELCOME TO THE LIFE OF A SPELLCASTER. YOU BURNED THROUGH YOUR DAILY MAGA.
MY WHAT?
RENEWABLE MAGIC POWER. NON-DAMAGING TO YOUR LIFE SPAN, BUT IT'LL WORK UP AN APPETITE.
HERE, TAKE SOME OF THESE. WE'LL HUNT FOR FOOD LATER.
HURRICOS WILL.
TO THINK I USED TO TEASE ARIANNA FOR STUFFING HER FACE.
WHO?
A FRIEND. SO... WHAT EXACTLY ARE THESE?
DRIPLETS.
FRIED PORK FAT.
UGH...
JUST EAT IT.
NOTHING IS FREE, ESPECIALLY MAGIC. YOU START CASTING, AND FIRST YOUR FAT GOES AWAY, AND THEN YOUR LIFESPAN.
SO FAT IS GOOD FOR A MAGE.
THERE'S A REASON THAT ARENIAN ARCH MAGES ARE ALL FAT.
WELL, I'M NOT DOING THAT. A DRAGOON NEEDS AGILITY.
YOU'RE HARDLY ONE TO TALK.
I'M NOT SAYING YOU SHOULD GET TOO FAT FOR HURRICOS TO CARRY YOU, BUT YOU ARE RATHER SCRAWNY.
I'M GUESSING THE LEADER GOT AWAY?
YEAH, ALMOST KILLED ME BACK THERE.
I was lucky to keep my head on my shoulders.

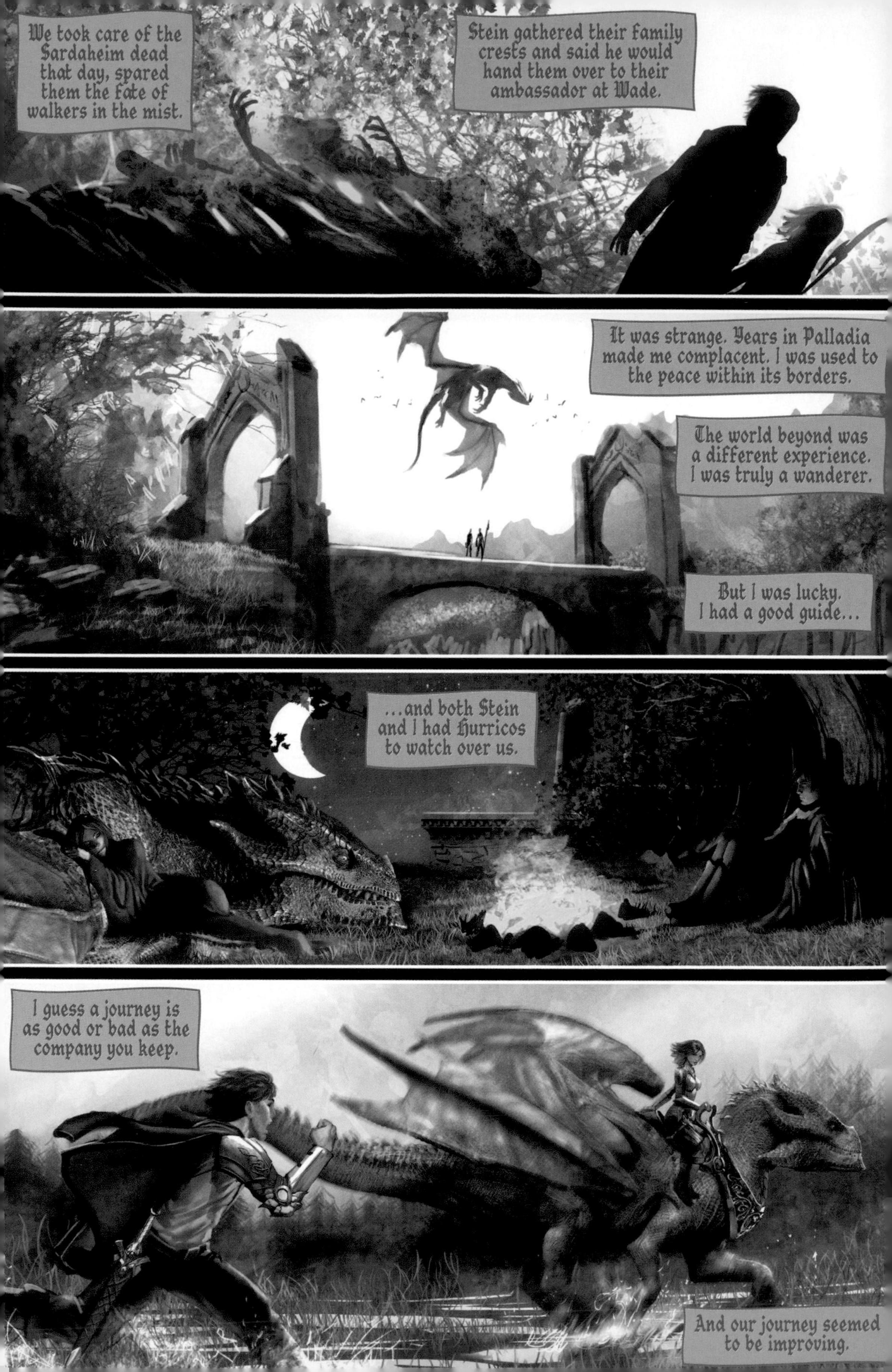
We took care of the Sardaheim dead that day, spared them the fate of walkers in the mist.
Stein gathered their family crests and said he would hand them over to their ambassador at Wade.
It was strange. Years in Palladia made me complacent. I was used to the peace within its borders.
The world beyond was a different experience. I was truly a wanderer.
But I was lucky. I had a good guide...
...and both Stein and I had Hurricos to watch over us.
I guess a journey is as good or bad as the company you keep.
And our journey seemed to be improving.

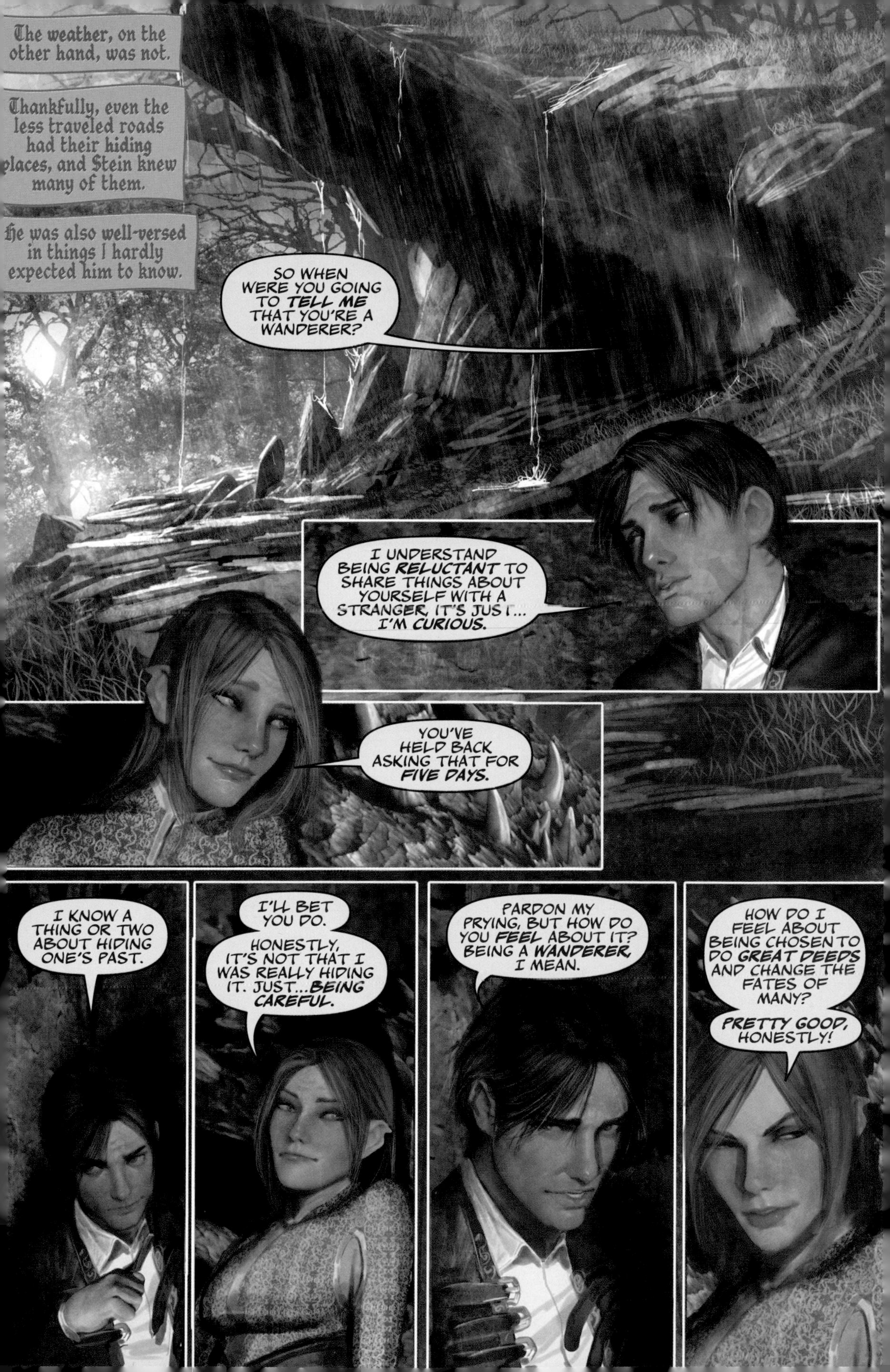

The weather, on the other hand, was not.
Thankfully, even the less traveled roads had their hiding places, and Stein knew many of them.
He was also well-versed in things I hardly expected him to know.
SO WHEN WERE YOU GOING TO TELL ME THAT YOU'RE A WANDERER?
I UNDERSTAND BEING RELUCTANT TO SHARE THINGS ABOUT YOURSELF WITH A STRANGER, IT'S JUST I... I'M CURIOUS.
YOU'VE HELD BACK ASKING THAT FOR FIVE DAYS.
I KNOW A THING OR TWO ABOUT HIDING ONE'S PAST.
I'LL BET YOU DO.
HONESTLY, IT'S NOT THAT I WAS REALLY HIDING IT. JUST...BEING CAREFUL.
PARDON MY PRYING, BUT HOW DO YOU FEEL ABOUT IT? BEING A WANDERER, I MEAN.
HOW DO I FEEL ABOUT BEING CHOSEN TO DO GREAT DEEDS AND CHANGE THE FATES OF MANY?
PRETTY GOOD, HONESTLY!

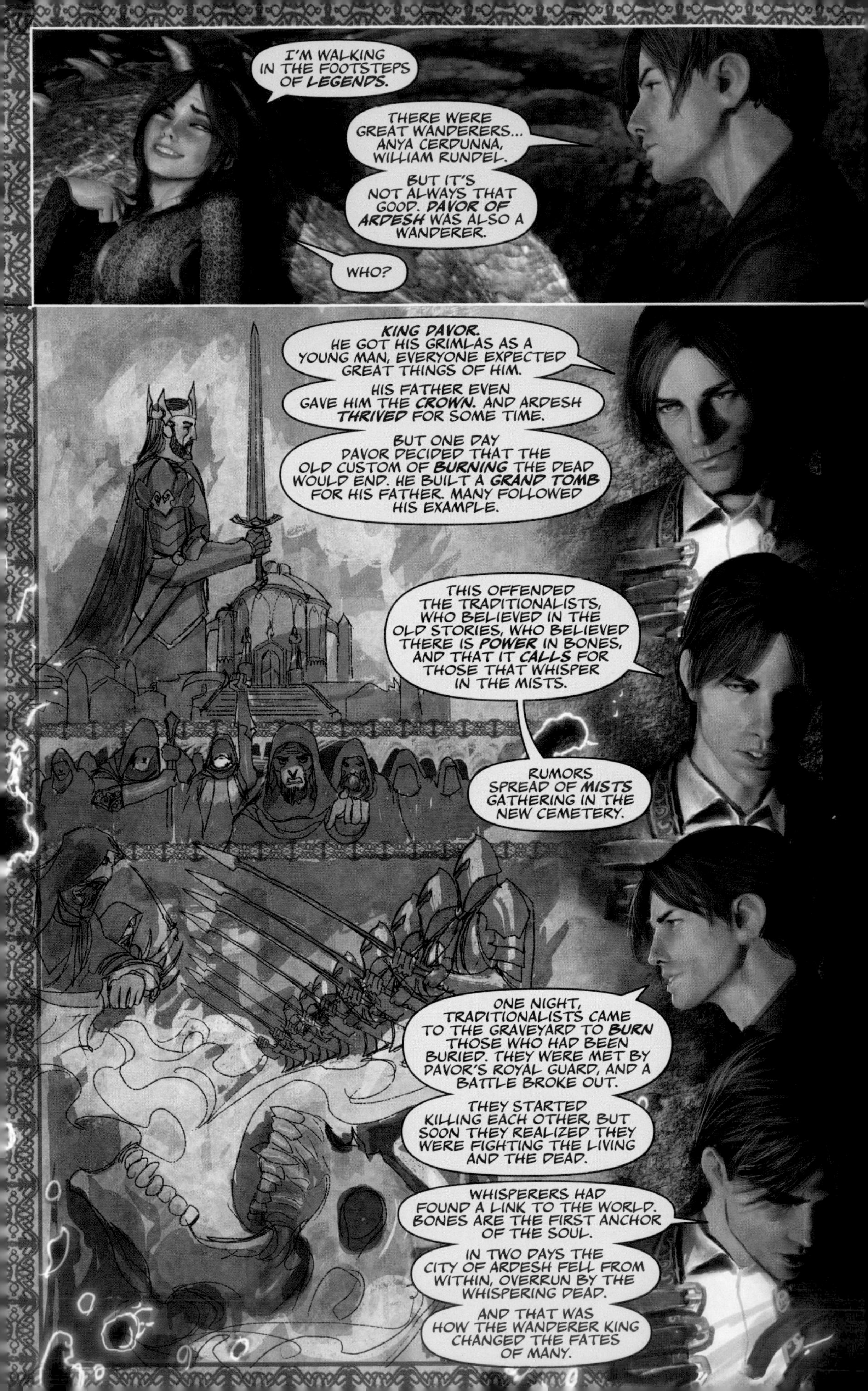
I'M WALKING IN THE FOOTSTEPS OF LEGENDS.
THERE WERE GREAT WANDERERS... ANYA CERDUNNA, WILLIAM RUNDEL.
BUT IT'S NOT ALWAYS THAT GOOD. DAVOR OF ARDESH WAS ALSO A WANDERER.
WHO?
KING DAVOR. HE GOT HIS GRIMLAS AS A YOUNG MAN, EVERYONE EXPECTED GREAT THINGS OF HIM.
HIS FATHER EVEN GAVE HIM THE CROWN. AND ARDESH THRIVED FOR SOME TIME.
BUT ONE DAY DAVOR DECIDED THAT THE OLD CUSTOM OF BURNING THE DEAD WOULD END. HE BUILT A GRAND TOMB FOR HIS FATHER. MANY FOLLOWED HIS EXAMPLE.
THIS OFFENDED THE TRADITIONALISTS, WHO BELIEVED IN THE OLD STORIES, WHO BELIEVED THERE IS POWER IN BONES, AND THAT IT CALLS FOR THOSE THAT WHISPER IN THE MISTS.
RUMORS SPREAD OF MISTS GATHERING IN THE NEW CEMETERY.
ONE NIGHT, TRADITIONALISTS CAME TO THE GRAVEYARD TO BURN THOSE WHO HAD BEEN BURIED. THEY WERE MET BY DAVOR'S ROYAL GUARD, AND A BATTLE BROKE OUT.
THEY STARTED KILLING EACH OTHER, BUT SOON THEY REALIZED THEY WERE FIGHTING THE LIVING AND THE DEAD.
WHISPERERS HAD FOUND A LINK TO THE WORLD. BONES ARE THE FIRST ANCHOR OF THE SOUL.
IN TWO DAYS THE CITY OF ARDESH FELL FROM WITHIN, OVERRUN BY THE WHISPERING DEAD.
AND THAT WAS HOW THE WANDERER KING CHANGED THE FATES OF MANY.

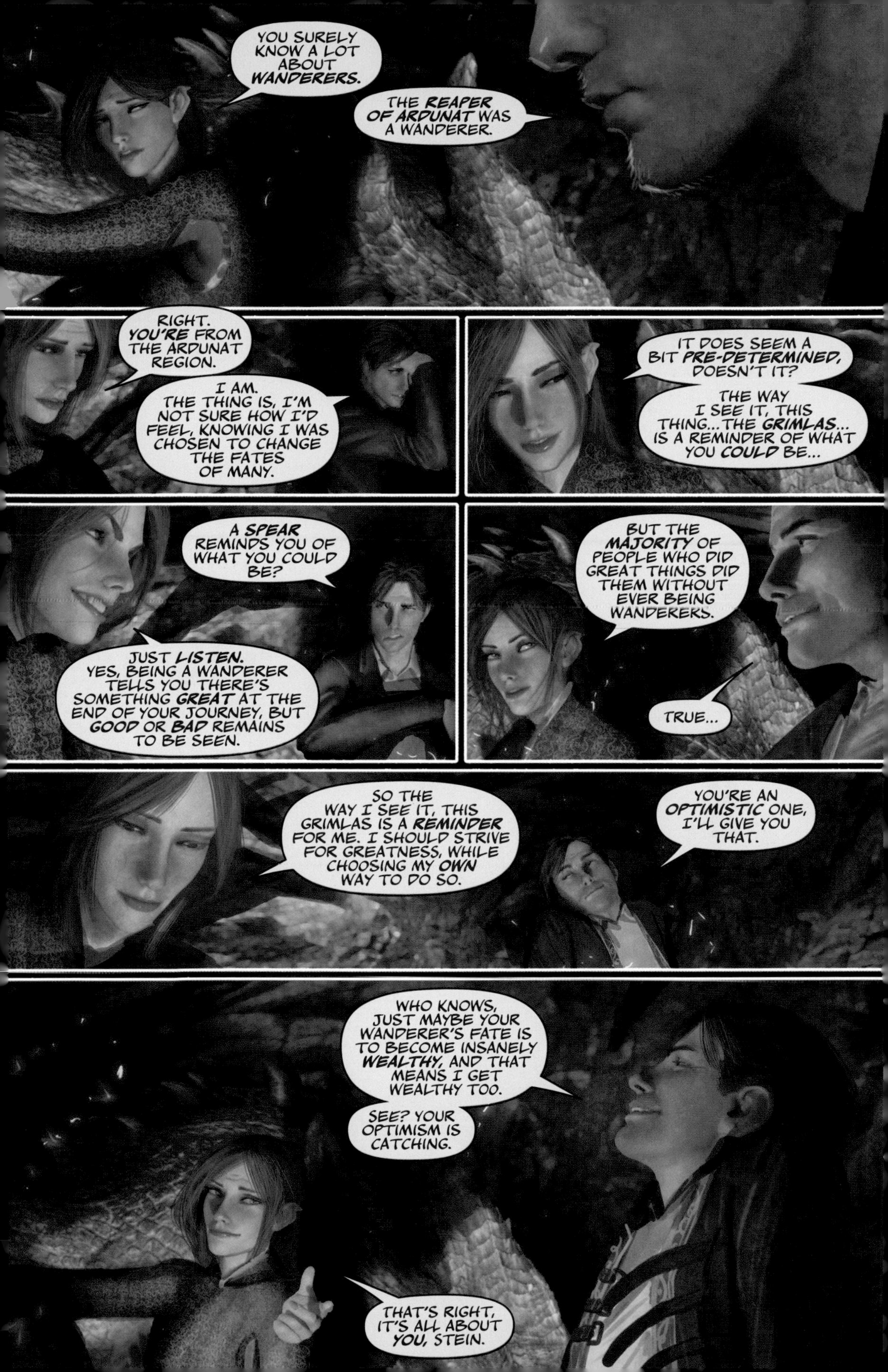
YOU SURELY KNOW A LOT ABOUT WANDERERS.
THE REAPER OF ARDUNAT WAS A WANDERER.
RIGHT. YOU'RE FROM THE ARDUNAT REGION.
I AM. THE THING IS, I'M NOT SURE HOW I'D FEEL, KNOWING I WAS CHOSEN TO CHANGE THE FATES OF MANY.
IT DOES SEEM A BIT PRE-DETERMINED, DOESN'T IT?
THE WAY I SEE IT, THIS THING... THE GRIMLAS... IS A REMINDER OF WHAT YOU COULD BE...
A SPEAR REMINDS YOU OF WHAT YOU COULD BE?
JUST LISTEN. YES, BEING A WANDERER TELLS YOU THERE'S SOMETHING GREAT AT THE END OF YOUR JOURNEY, BUT GOOD OR BAD REMAINS TO BE SEEN.
BUT THE MAJORITY OF PEOPLE WHO DID GREAT THINGS DID THEM WITHOUT EVER BEING WANDERERS.
TRUE...
SO THE WAY I SEE IT, THIS GRIMLAS IS A REMINDER FOR ME. I SHOULD STRIVE FOR GREATNESS, WHILE CHOOSING MY OWN WAY TO DO SO.
YOU'RE AN OPTIMISTIC ONE, I'LL GIVE YOU THAT.
WHO KNOWS, JUST MAYBE YOUR WANDERER'S FATE IS TO BECOME INSANELY WEALTHY, AND THAT MEANS I GET WEALTHY TOO.
SEE? YOUR OPTIMISM IS CATCHING.
THAT'S RIGHT, IT'S ALL ABOUT YOU, STEIN.

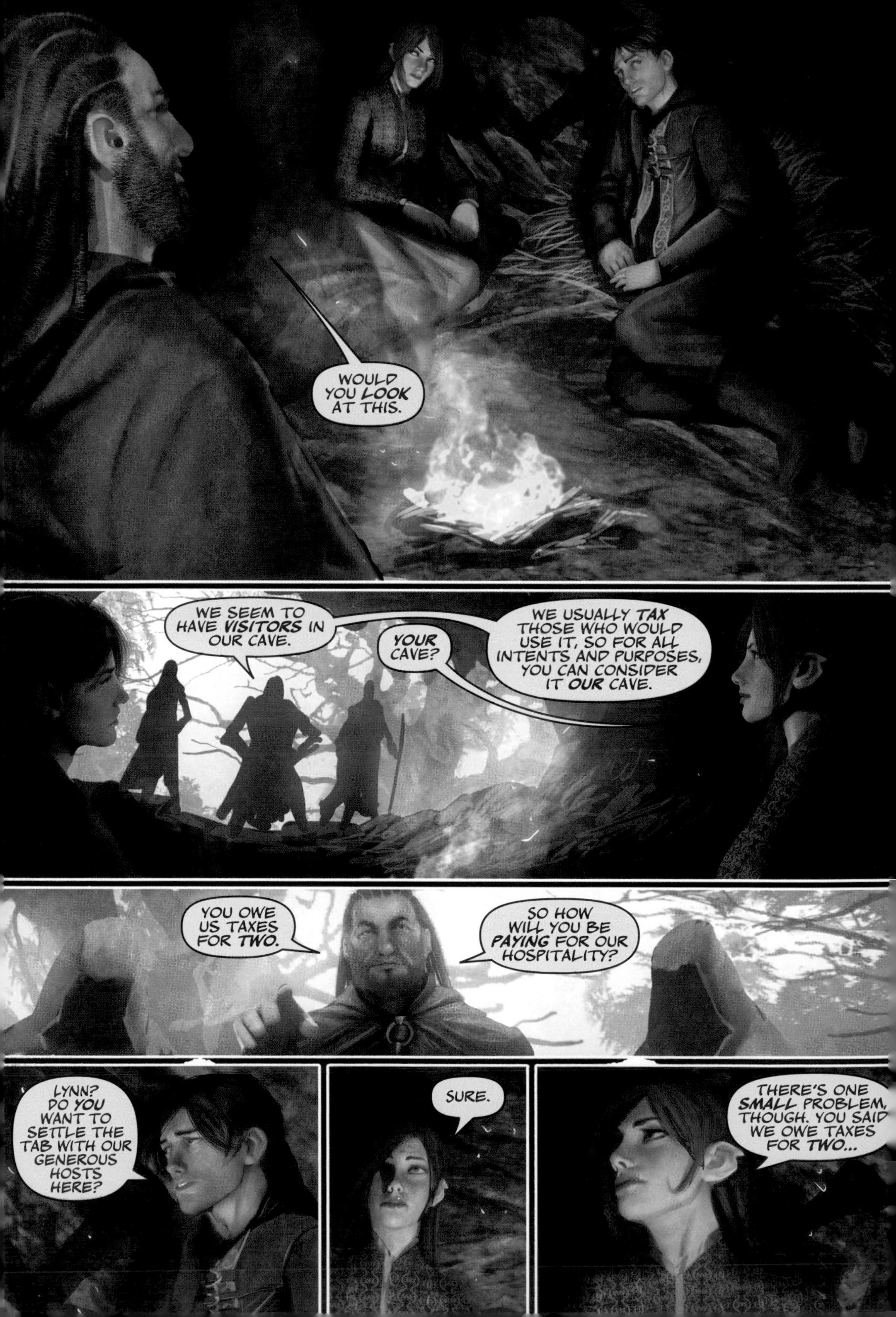
WOULD YOU LOOK AT THIS.
WE SEEM TO HAVE VISITORS IN OUR CAVE.
YOUR CAVE?
WE USUALLY TAX THOSE WHO WOULD USE IT, SO FOR ALL INTENTS AND PURPOSES, YOU CAN CONSIDER IT OUR CAVE.
YOU OWE US TAXES FOR TWO.
SO HOW WILL YOU BE PAYING FOR OUR HOSPITALITY?
LYNN? DO YOU WANT TO SETTLE THE TAB WITH OUR GENEROUS HOSTS HERE?
SURE.
THERE'S ONE SMALL PROBLEM, THOUGH. YOU SAID WE OWE TAXES FOR TWO...

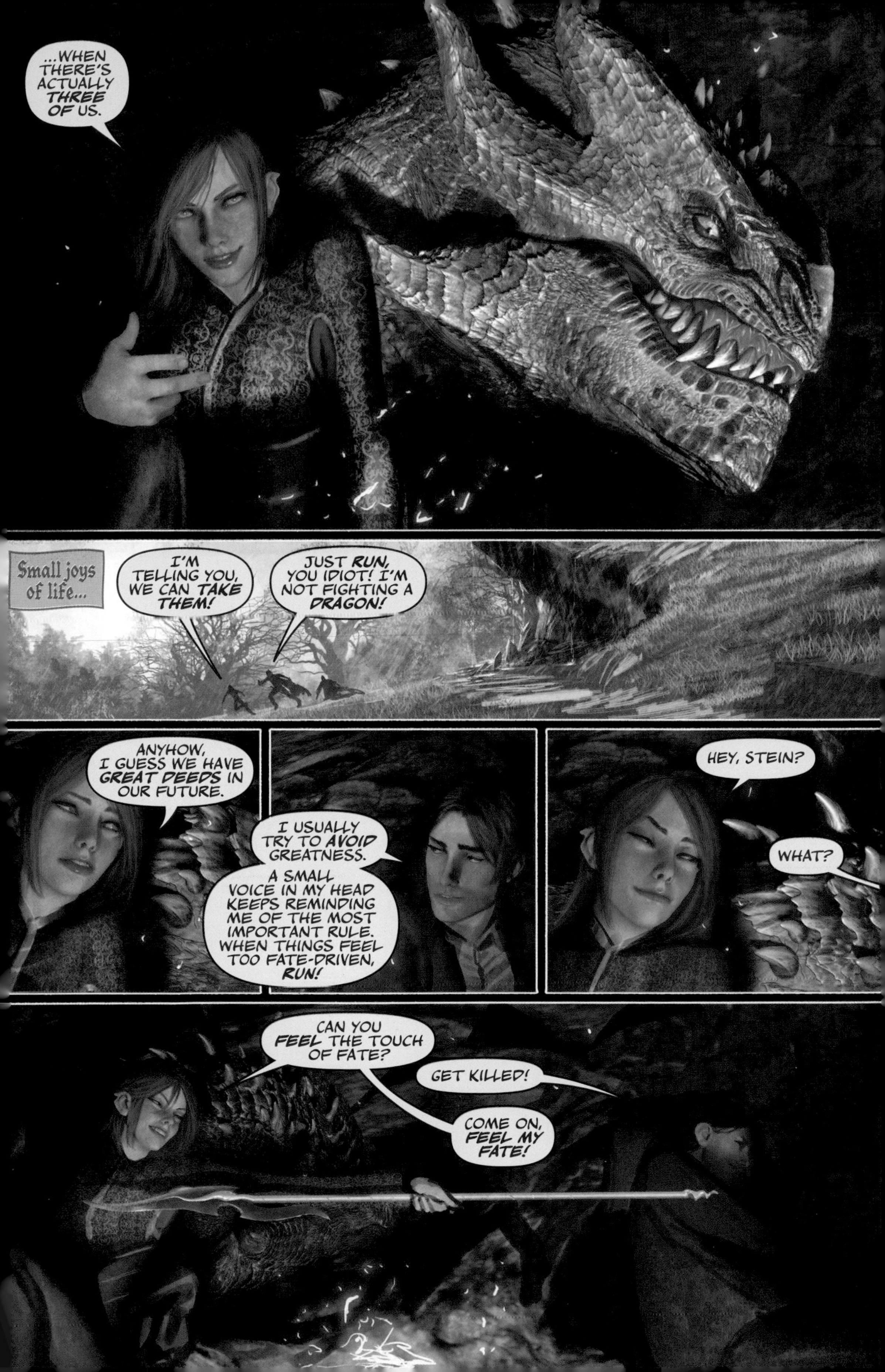
...WHEN THERE'S ACTUALLY THREE OF US.
Small joys of life...
I'M TELLING YOU, WE CAN TAKE THEM!
JUST RUN, YOU IDIOT! I'M NOT FIGHTING A DRAGON!
ANYHOW, I GUESS WE HAVE GREAT DEEDS IN OUR FUTURE.
I USUALLY TRY TO AVOID GREATNESS.
A SMALL VOICE IN MY HEAD KEEPS REMINDING ME OF THE MOST IMPORTANT RULE. WHEN THINGS FEEL TOO FATE-DRIVEN, RUN!
HEY, STEIN?
WHAT?
CAN YOU FEEL THE TOUCH OF FATE?
GET KILLED!
COME ON, FEEL MY FATE!

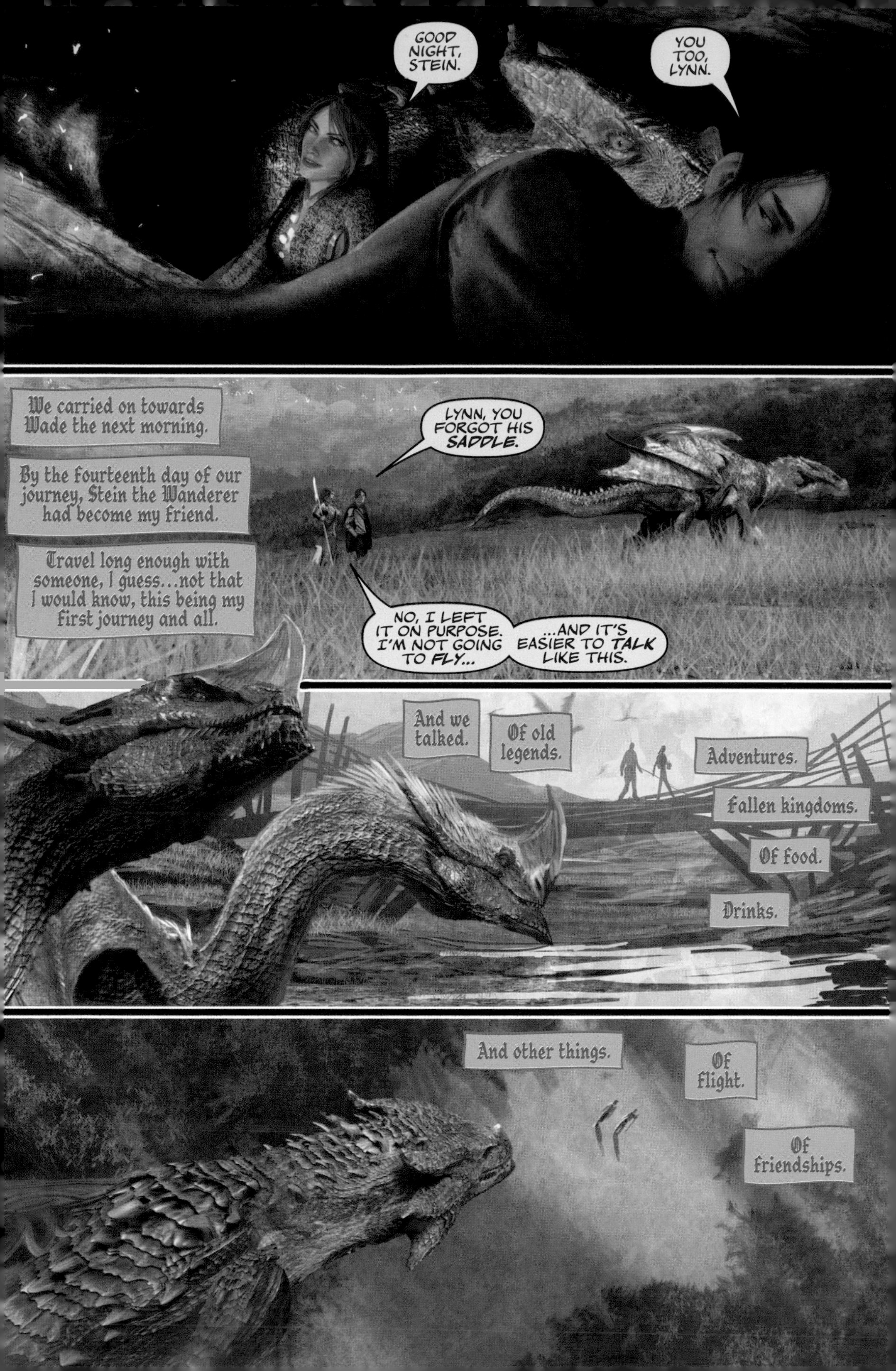
GOOD NIGHT, STEIN.
YOU TOO, LYNN.
We carried on towards Wade the next morning.
By the fourteenth day of our journey, Stein the Wanderer had become my friend.
Travel long enough with someone, I guess...not that I would know, this being my first journey and all.
LYNN, YOU FORGOT HIS SADDLE.
NO, I LEFT IT ON PURPOSE. I'M NOT GOING TO FLY...
...AND IT'S EASIER TO TALK LIKE THIS.
And we talked.
Of old legends.
Adventures.
Fallen kingdoms.
Of food.
Drinks.
And other things.
Of flight.
Of friendships.

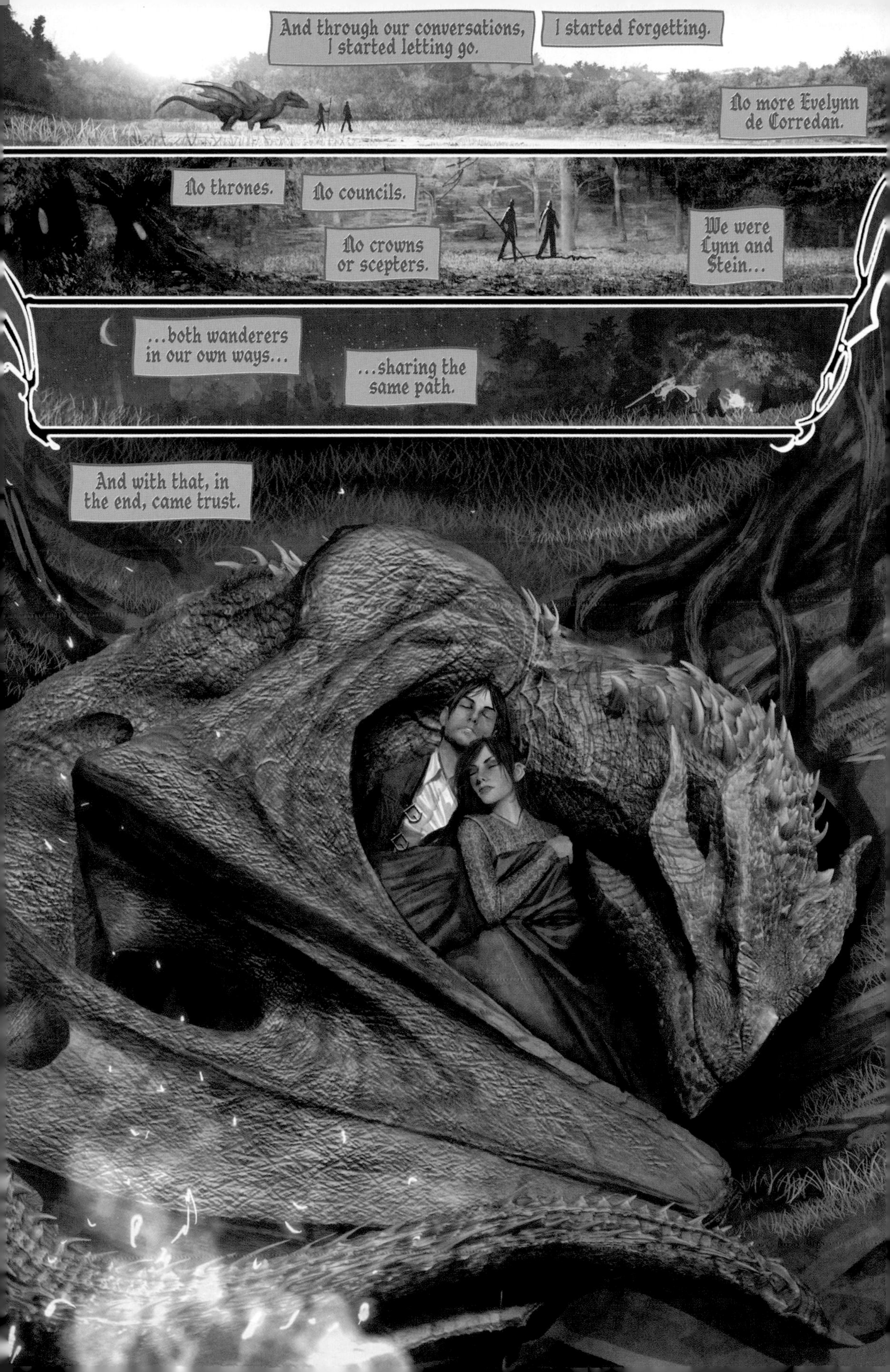
And through our conversations, I started letting go.
I started forgetting.
No more Evelynn de Corredan.
No thrones.
No councils.
No crowns or scepters.
We were Lynn and Stein...
...both wanderers in our own ways...
...sharing the same path.
And with that, in the end, came trust.

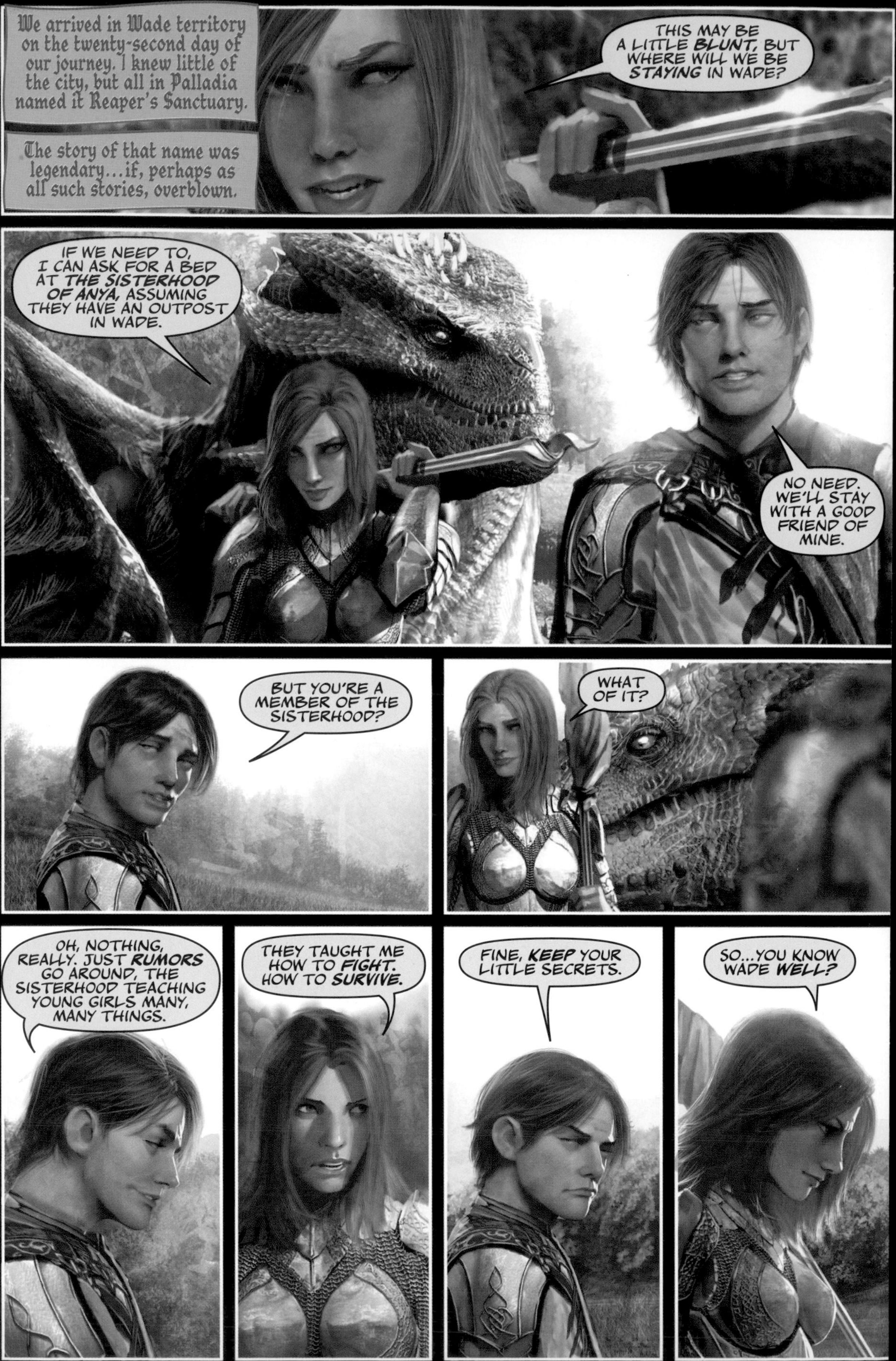
We arrived in Wade territory on the twenty-second day of our journey. I knew little of the city, but all in Palladia named it Reaper's Sanctuary.
The story of that name was legendary...if, perhaps as all such stories, overblown.
THIS MAY BE A LITTLE BLUNT, BUT WHERE WILL WE BE STAYING IN WADE?
IF WE NEED TO, I CAN ASK FOR A BED AT THE SISTERHOOD OF ANYA, ASSUMING THEY HAVE AN OUTPOST IN WADE.
NO NEED. WE'LL STAY WITH A GOOD FRIEND OF MINE.
BUT YOU'RE A MEMBER OF THE SISTERHOOD?
WHAT OF IT?
OH, NOTHING, REALLY. JUST RUMORS GO AROUND, THE SISTERHOOD TEACHING YOUNG GIRLS MANY, MANY THINGS.
THEY TAUGHT ME HOW TO FIGHT. HOW TO SURVIVE.
FINE, KEEP YOUR LITTLE SECRETS.
SO...YOU KNOW WADE WELL?

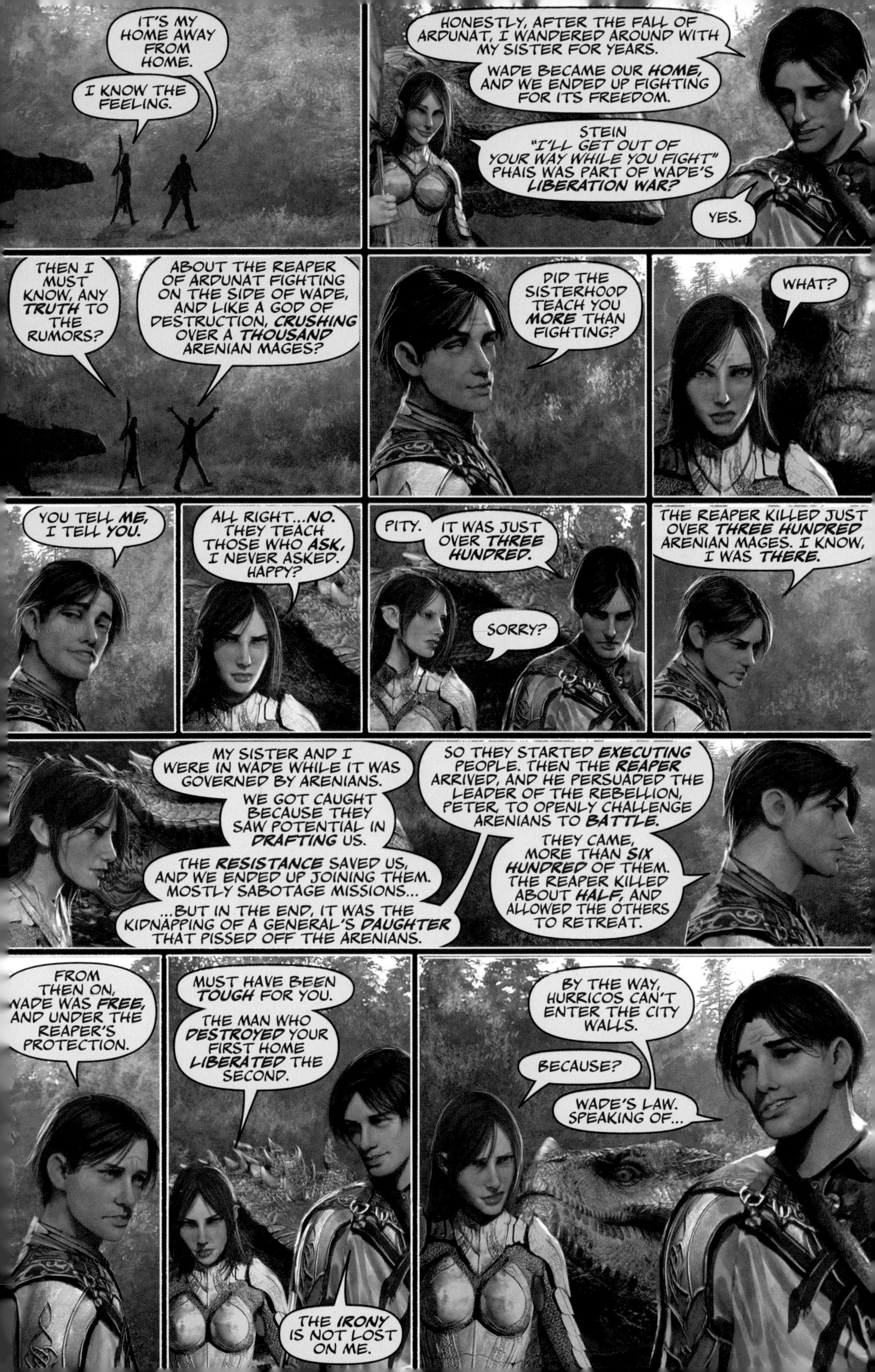
IT'S MY HOME AWAY FROM HOME.
I KNOW THE FEELING.
HONESTLY, AFTER THE FALL OF ARDUNAT, I WANDERED AROUND WITH MY SISTER FOR YEARS.
WADE BECAME OUR HOME, AND WE ENDED UP FIGHTING FOR ITS FREEDOM.
STEIN "I'LL GET OUT OF YOUR WAY WHILE YOU FIGHT" PHAIS WAS PART OF WADE'S LIBERATION WAR?
YES.
THEN I MUST KNOW, ANY TRUTH TO THE RUMORS?
ABOUT THE REAPER OF ARDUNAT FIGHTING ON THE SIDE OF WADE, AND LIKE A GOD OF DESTRUCTION, CRUSHING OVER A THOUSAND ARENIAN MAGES?
DID THE SISTERHOOD TEACH YOU MORE THAN FIGHTING?
WHAT?
YOU TELL ME, I TELL YOU.
ALL RIGHT...NO. THEY TEACH THOSE WHO ASK, I NEVER ASKED. HAPPY?
PITY.
IT WAS JUST OVER THREE HUNDRED.
SORRY?
THE REAPER KILLED JUST OVER THREE HUNDRED ARENIAN MAGES. I KNOW, I WAS THERE.
MY SISTER AND I WERE IN WADE WHILE IT WAS GOVERNED BY ARENIANS.
WE GOT CAUGHT BECAUSE THEY SAW POTENTIAL IN DRAFTING US.
THE RESISTANCE SAVED US, AND WE ENDED UP JOINING THEM. MOSTLY SABOTAGE MISSIONS...
...BUT IN THE END, IT WAS THE KIDNAPPING OF A GENERAL'S DAUGHTER THAT PISSED OFF THE ARENIANS.
SO THEY STARTED EXECUTING PEOPLE. THEN THE REAPER ARRIVED, AND HE PERSUADED THE LEADER OF THE REBELLION, PETER, TO OPENLY CHALLENGE ARENIANS TO BATTLE.
THEY CAME, MORE THAN SIX HUNDRED OF THEM. THE REAPER KILLED ABOUT HALF, AND ALLOWED THE OTHERS TO RETREAT.
FROM THEN ON, WADE WAS FREE, AND UNDER THE REAPER'S PROTECTION.
MUST HAVE BEEN TOUGH FOR YOU.
THE MAN WHO DESTROYED YOUR FIRST HOME LIBERATED THE SECOND.
THE IRONY IS NOT LOST ON ME.
BY THE WAY, HURRICOS CAN'T ENTER THE CITY WALLS.
BECAUSE?
WADE'S LAW. SPEAKING OF...

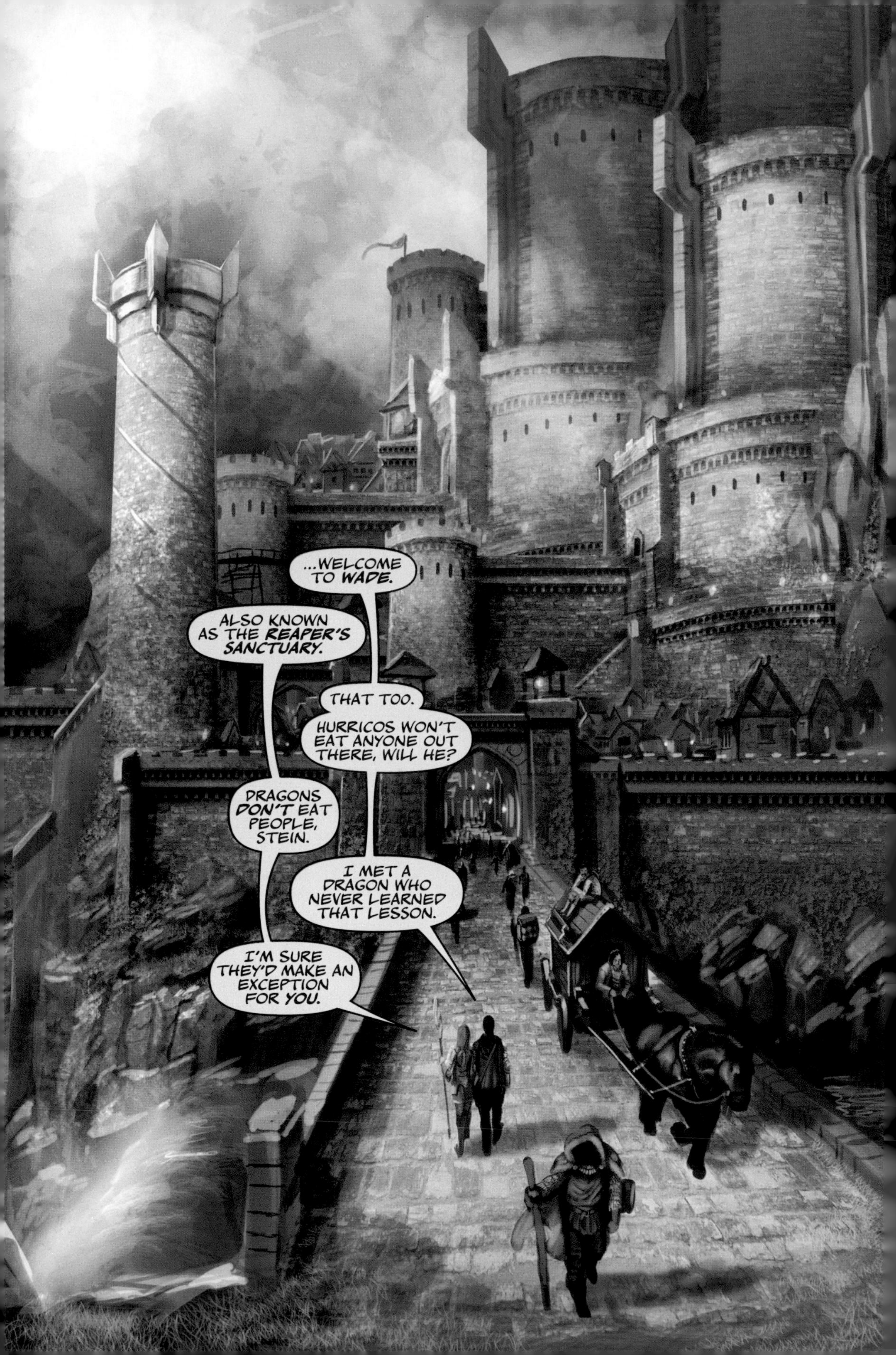
...WELCOME TO WADE.
ALSO KNOWN AS THE REAPER'S SANCTUARY.
THAT TOO.
HURRICOS WON'T EAT ANYONE OUT THERE, WILL HE?
DRAGONS DON'T EAT PEOPLE, STEIN.
I MET A DRAGON WHO NEVER LEARNED THAT LESSON.
I'M SURE THEY'D MAKE AN EXCEPTION FOR YOU.

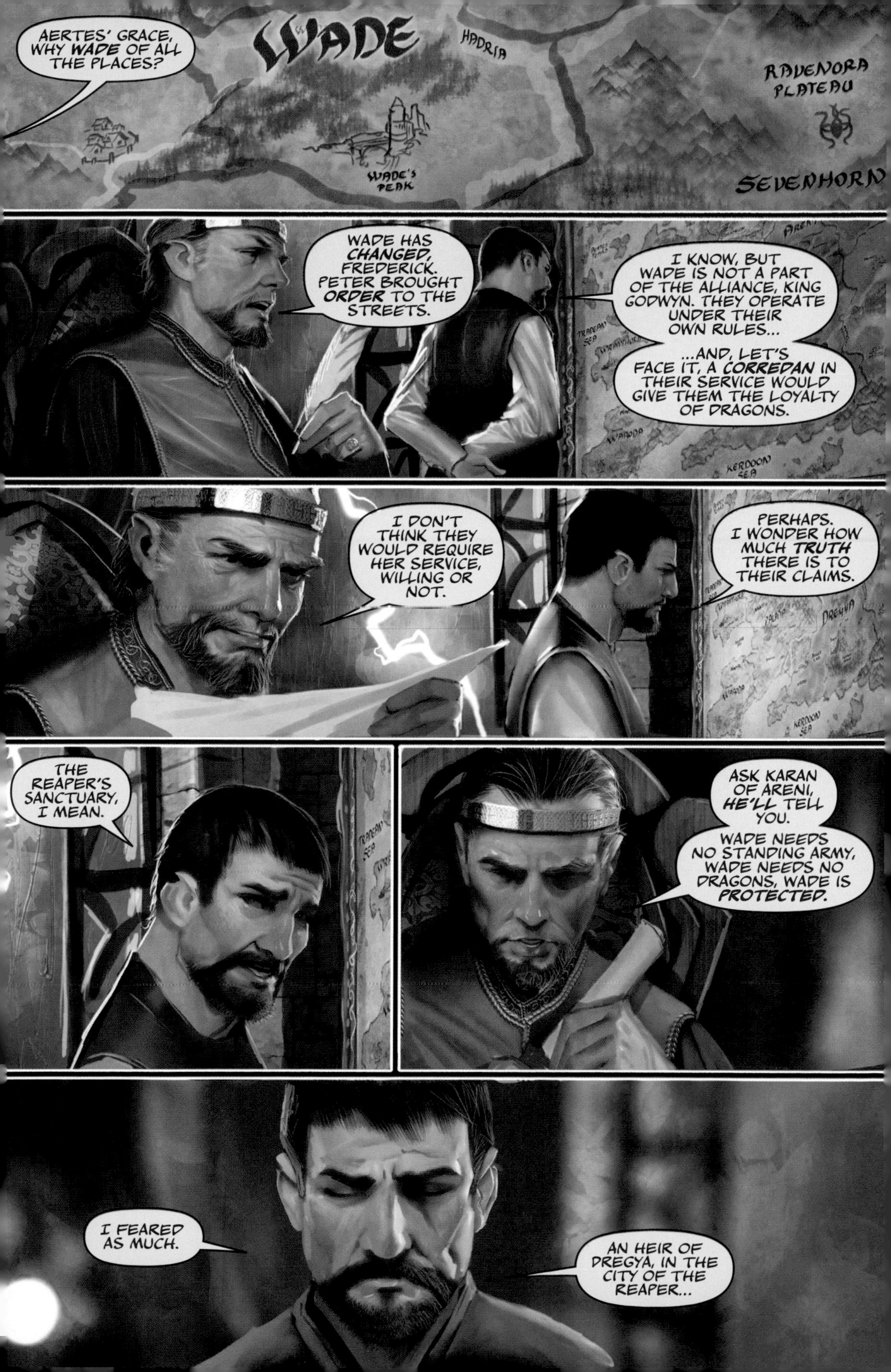

AERTES' GRACE, WHY WADE OF ALL THE PLACES?
WADE
HADRIA
RAVENORA PLATEAU
WADE'S PEAK
SEVENHORN
WADE HAS CHANGED, FREDERICK. PETER BROUGHT ORDER TO THE STREETS.
I KNOW, BUT WADE IS NOT A PART OF THE ALLIANCE, KING GODWYN. THEY OPERATE UNDER THEIR OWN RULES...
...AND, LET'S FACE IT, A CORREDAN IN THEIR SERVICE WOULD GIVE THEM THE LOYALTY OF DRAGONS.
I DON'T THINK THEY WOULD REQUIRE HER SERVICE, WILLING OR NOT.
PERHAPS. I WONDER HOW MUCH TRUTH THERE IS TO THEIR CLAIMS.
THE REAPER'S SANCTUARY, I MEAN.
ASK KARAN OF ARENI, HE'LL TELL YOU.
WADE NEEDS NO STANDING ARMY, WADE NEEDS NO DRAGONS, WADE IS PROTECTED.
I FEARED AS MUCH.
AN HEIR OF DREGYA, IN THE CITY OF THE REAPER...

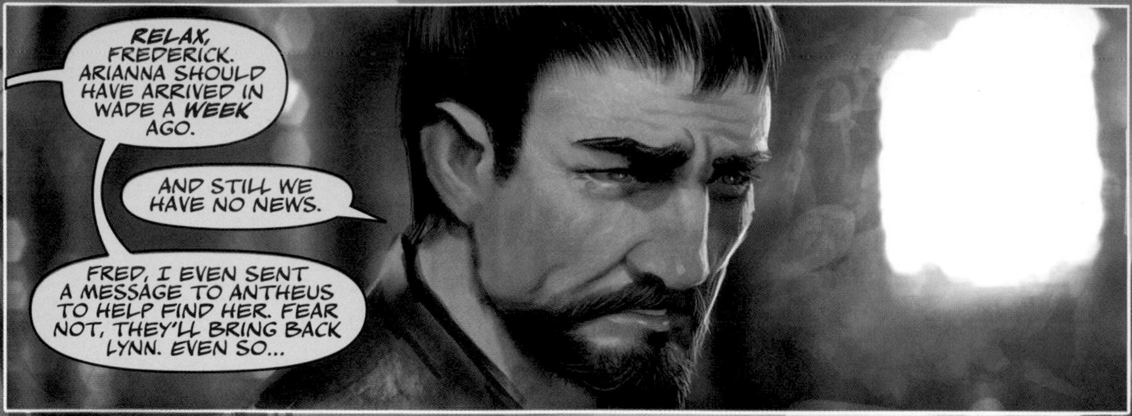
RELAX, FREDERICK. ARIANNA SHOULD HAVE ARRIVED IN WADE A WEEK AGO.
AND STILL WE HAVE NO NEWS.
FRED, I EVEN SENT A MESSAGE TO ANTHEUS TO HELP FIND HER. FEAR NOT, THEY'LL BRING BACK LYNN. EVEN SO...

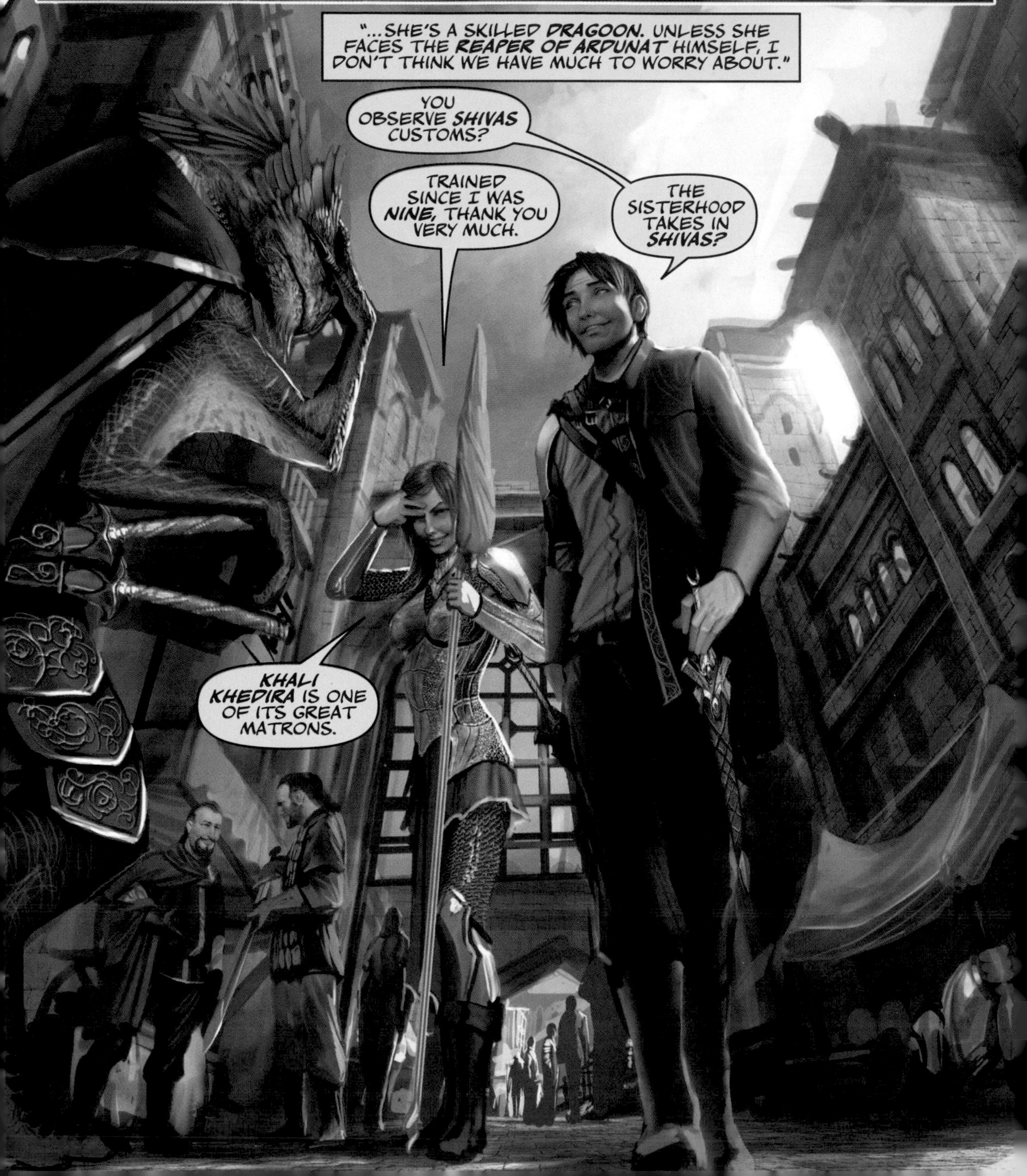
"...SHE'S A SKILLED DRAGOON. UNLESS SHE FACES THE REAPER OF ARDUNAT HIMSELF, I DON'T THINK WE HAVE MUCH TO WORRY ABOUT."
YOU OBSERVE SHIVAS CUSTOMS?
TRAINED SINCE I WAS NINE, THANK YOU VERY MUCH.
THE SISTERHOOD TAKES IN SHIVAS?
KHALI KHEDIRA IS ONE OF ITS GREAT MATRONS.

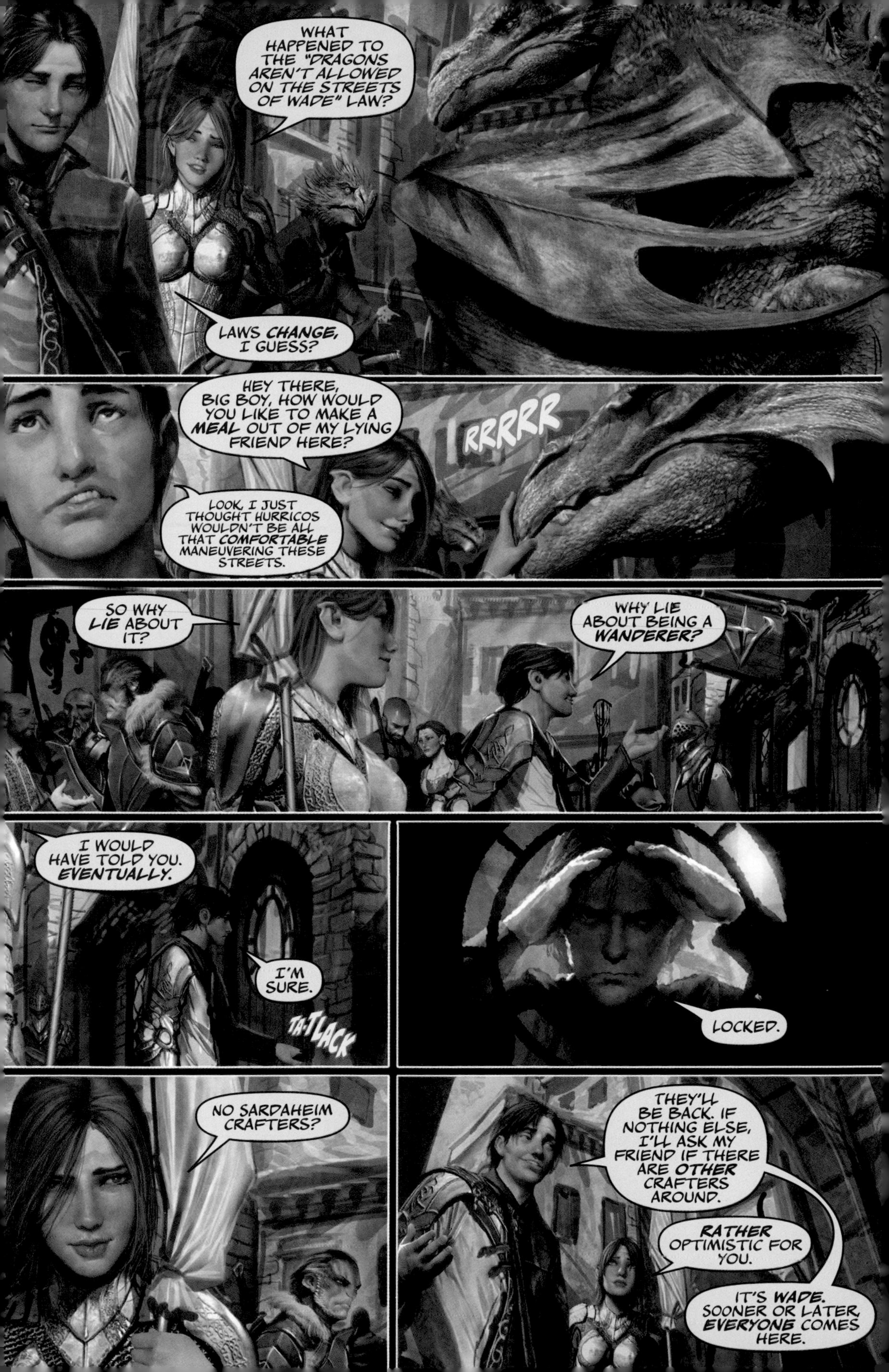
WHAT HAPPENED TO THE "DRAGONS AREN'T ALLOWED ON THE STREETS OF WADE" LAW?
LAWS CHANGE, I GUESS?
HEY THERE, BIG BOY, HOW WOULD YOU LIKE TO MAKE A MEAL OUT OF MY LYING FRIEND HERE?
RRRRR
LOOK, I JUST THOUGHT HURRICOS WOULDN'T BE ALL THAT COMFORTABLE MANEUVERING THESE STREETS.
SO WHY LIE ABOUT IT?
WHY LIE ABOUT BEING A WANDERER?
I WOULD HAVE TOLD YOU. EVENTUALLY.
I'M SURE.
TA-TLACK
LOCKED.
NO SARDAHEIM CRAFTERS?
THEY'LL BE BACK. IF NOTHING ELSE, I'LL ASK MY FRIEND IF THERE ARE OTHER CRAFTERS AROUND.
RATHER OPTIMISTIC FOR YOU.
IT'S WADE. SOONER OR LATER, EVERYONE COMES HERE.

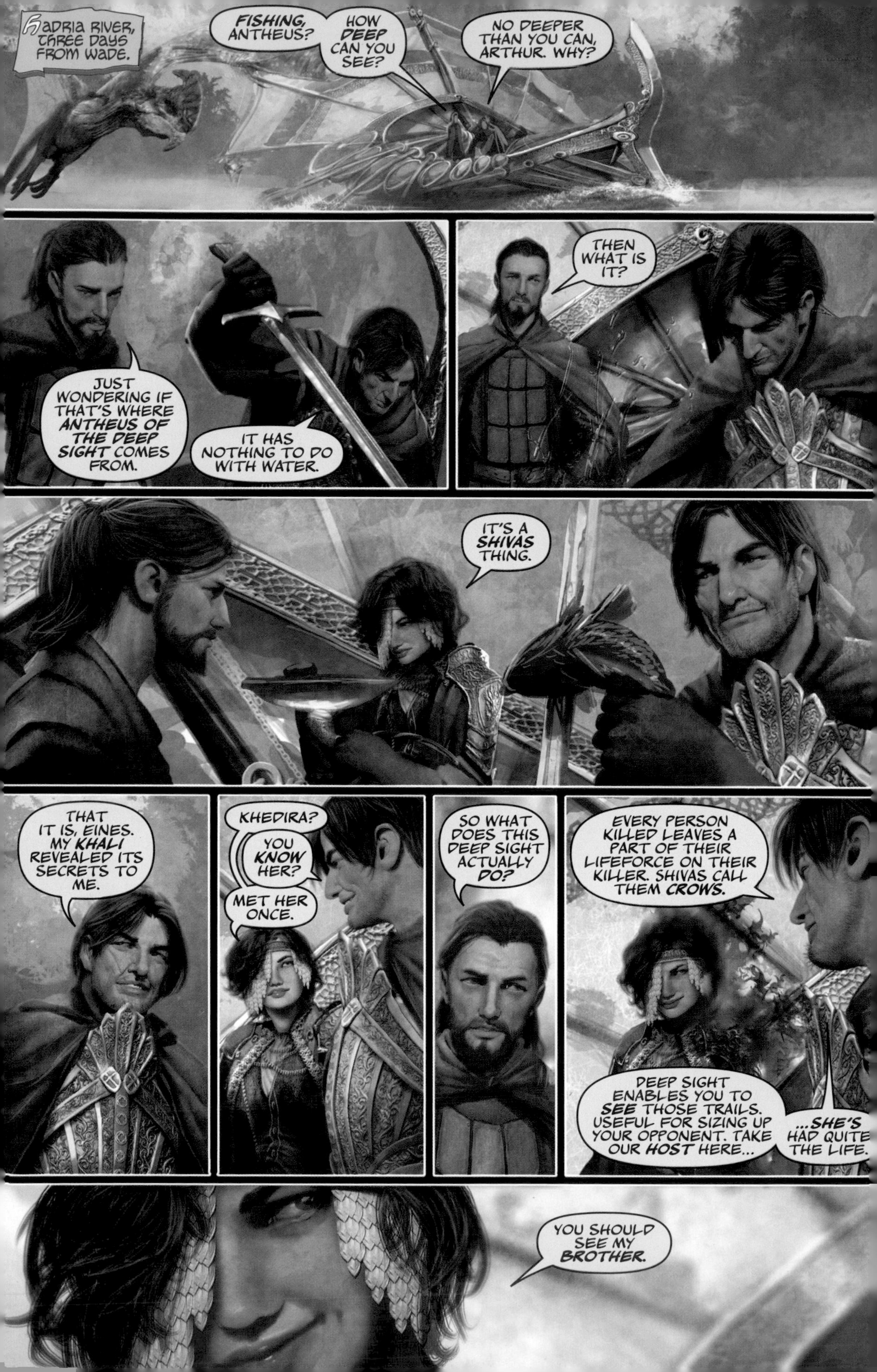
HADRIA RIVER, THREE DAYS FROM WADE.
FISHING, ANTHEUS?
HOW DEEP CAN YOU SEE?
NO DEEPER THAN YOU CAN, ARTHUR. WHY?
JUST WONDERING IF THAT'S WHERE ANTHEUS OF THE DEEP SIGHT COMES FROM.
IT HAS NOTHING TO DO WITH WATER.
THEN WHAT IS IT?
IT'S A SHIVAS THING.
THAT IT IS, EINES. MY KHALI REVEALED ITS SECRETS TO ME.
KHEDIRA?
YOU KNOW HER?
MET HER ONCE.
SO WHAT DOES THIS DEEP SIGHT ACTUALLY DO?
EVERY PERSON KILLED LEAVES A PART OF THEIR LIFEFORCE ON THEIR KILLER. SHIVAS CALL THEM CROWS.
DEEP SIGHT ENABLES YOU TO SEE THOSE TRAILS. USEFUL FOR SIZING UP YOUR OPPONENT. TAKE OUR HOST HERE...
...SHE'S HAD QUITE THE LIFE.
YOU SHOULD SEE MY BROTHER.

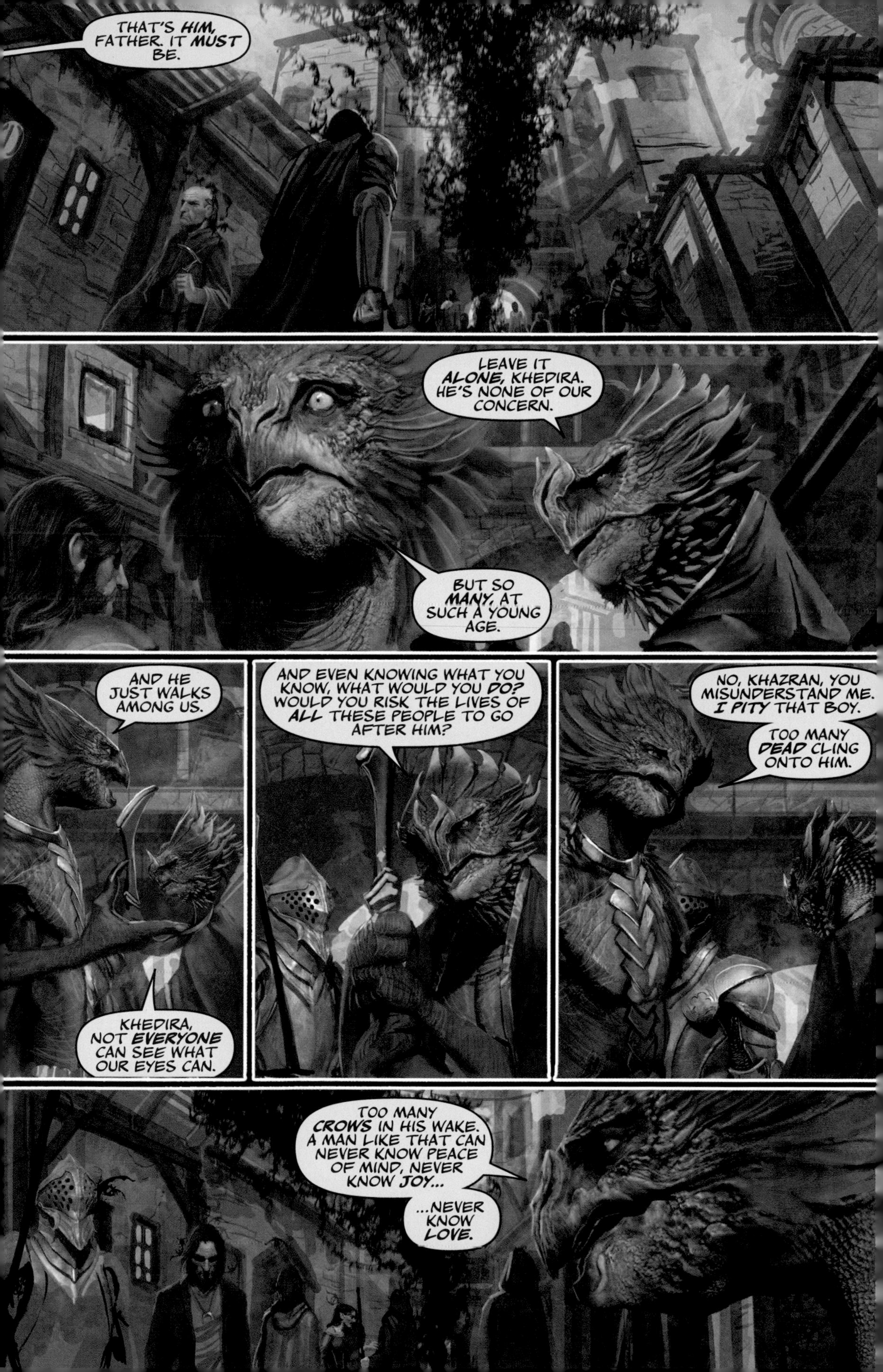
THAT'S HIM, FATHER. IT MUST BE.
LEAVE IT ALONE, KHEDIRA. HE'S NONE OF OUR CONCERN.
BUT SO MANY, AT SUCH A YOUNG AGE.
AND HE JUST WALKS AMONG US.
KHEDIRA, NOT EVERYONE CAN SEE WHAT OUR EYES CAN.
AND EVEN KNOWING WHAT YOU KNOW, WHAT WOULD YOU DO? WOULD YOU RISK THE LIVES OF ALL THESE PEOPLE TO GO AFTER HIM?
NO, KHAZRAN, YOU MISUNDERSTAND ME. I PITY THAT BOY.
TOO MANY DEAD CLING ONTO HIM.
TOO MANY CROWS IN HIS WAKE. A MAN LIKE THAT CAN NEVER KNOW PEACE OF MIND, NEVER KNOW JOY...
...NEVER KNOW LOVE.

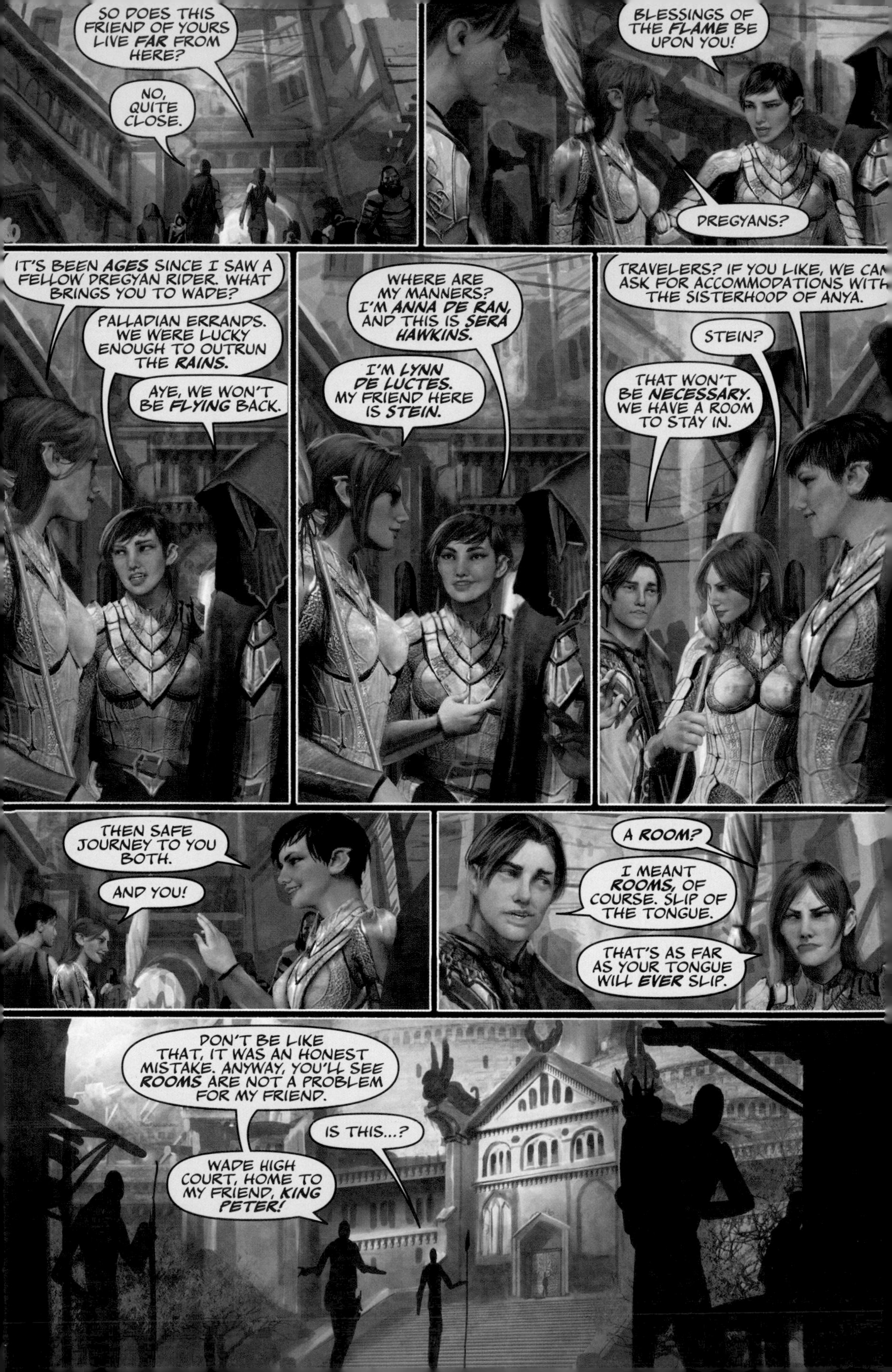

SO DOES THIS FRIEND OF YOURS LIVE FAR FROM HERE?
NO, QUITE CLOSE.
BLESSINGS OF THE FLAME BE UPON YOU!
DREGYANS?
IT'S BEEN AGES SINCE I SAW A FELLOW DREGYAN RIDER. WHAT BRINGS YOU TO WADE?
PALLADIAN ERRANDS. WE WERE LUCKY ENOUGH TO OUTRUN THE RAINS.
AYE, WE WON'T BE FLYING BACK.
WHERE ARE MY MANNERS? I'M ANNA DE RAN, AND THIS IS SERA HAWKINS.
I'M LYNN DE LUCTES. MY FRIEND HERE IS STEIN.
TRAVELERS? IF YOU LIKE, WE CAN ASK FOR ACCOMMODATIONS WITH THE SISTERHOOD OF ANYA.
STEIN?
THAT WON'T BE NECESSARY. WE HAVE A ROOM TO STAY IN.
THEN SAFE JOURNEY TO YOU BOTH.
AND YOU!
A ROOM?
I MEANT ROOMS, OF COURSE. SLIP OF THE TONGUE.
THAT'S AS FAR AS YOUR TONGUE WILL EVER SLIP.
DON'T BE LIKE THAT, IT WAS AN HONEST MISTAKE. ANYWAY, YOU'LL SEE ROOMS ARE NOT A PROBLEM FOR MY FRIEND.
IS THIS...?
WADE HIGH COURT, HOME TO MY FRIEND, KING PETER!

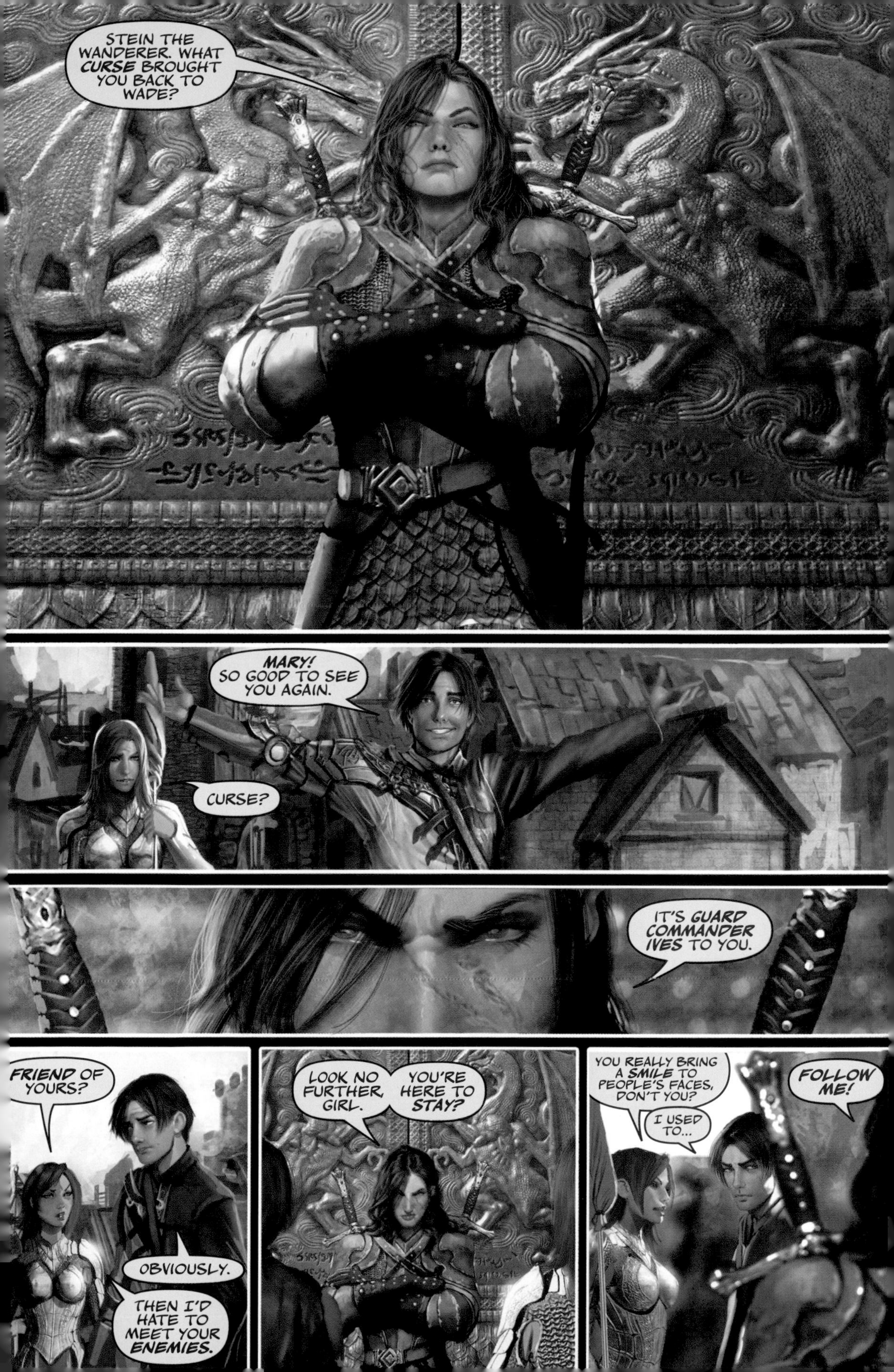
STEIN THE WANDERER. WHAT CURSE BROUGHT YOU BACK TO WADE?
MARY! SO GOOD TO SEE YOU AGAIN.
CURSE?
IT'S GUARD COMMANDER IVES TO YOU.
FRIEND OF YOURS?
OBVIOUSLY.
THEN I'D HATE TO MEET YOUR ENEMIES.
LOOK NO FURTHER, GIRL.
YOU'RE HERE TO STAY?
YOU REALLY BRING A SMILE TO PEOPLE'S FACES, DON'T YOU?
I USED TO...
FOLLOW ME!

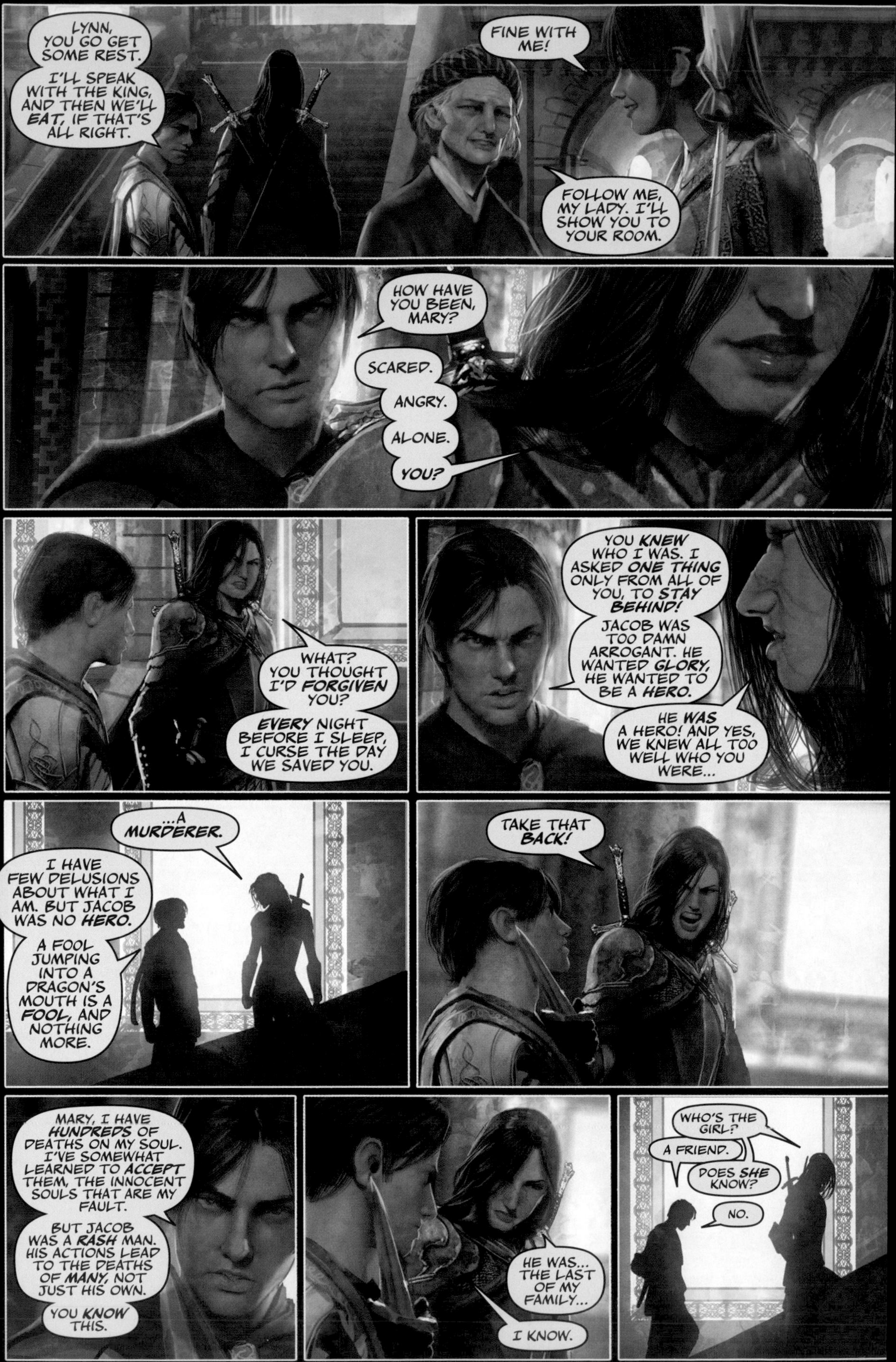
LYNN, YOU GO GET SOME REST.
I'LL SPEAK WITH THE KING, AND THEN WE'LL EAT, IF THAT'S ALL RIGHT.
FINE WITH ME!
FOLLOW ME, MY LADY. I'LL SHOW YOU TO YOUR ROOM.
HOW HAVE YOU BEEN, MARY?
SCARED.
ANGRY.
ALONE.
YOU?
WHAT? YOU THOUGHT I'D FORGIVEN YOU?
EVERY NIGHT BEFORE I SLEEP, I CURSE THE DAY WE SAVED YOU.
YOU KNEW WHO I WAS. I ASKED ONE THING ONLY FROM ALL OF YOU, TO STAY BEHIND!
JACOB WAS TOO DAMN ARROGANT. HE WANTED GLORY, HE WANTED TO BE A HERO.
HE WAS A HERO! AND YES, WE KNEW ALL TOO WELL WHO YOU WERE...
...A MURDERER.
I HAVE FEW DELUSIONS ABOUT WHAT I AM. BUT JACOB WAS NO HERO.
A FOOL JUMPING INTO A DRAGON'S MOUTH IS A FOOL, AND NOTHING MORE.
TAKE THAT BACK!
MARY, I HAVE HUNDREDS OF DEATHS ON MY SOUL. I'VE SOMEWHAT LEARNED TO ACCEPT THEM, THE INNOCENT SOULS THAT ARE MY FAULT.
BUT JACOB WAS A RASH MAN. HIS ACTIONS LEAD TO THE DEATHS OF MANY, NOT JUST HIS OWN.
YOU KNOW THIS.
HE WAS... THE LAST OF MY FAMILY...
I KNOW.
WHO'S THE GIRL?
A FRIEND.
DOES SHE KNOW?
NO.

PETER! YOU CERTAINLY ARE A SIGHT FOR...

WHAT MISFORTUNE BRINGS *YOU* BACK BEFORE MY EYES?

NOW *THIS* IS GETTING STUPID. WHAT'S WITH ALL THE *HOSTILITY* TODAY?

DOES MY PRESENCE TROUBLE *EVERYONE* ALL OF A SUDDEN?

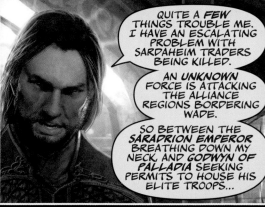

QUITE A *FEW* THINGS TROUBLE ME. I HAVE AN ESCALATING PROBLEM WITH SARDAHEIM TRADERS BEING KILLED.

AN *UNKNOWN* FORCE IS ATTACKING THE ALLIANCE REGIONS BORDERING WADE.

SO BETWEEN THE *SARADRION EMPEROR* BREATHING DOWN MY NECK, AND *GODWYN OF PALLADIA* SEEKING PERMITS TO HOUSE HIS ELITE TROOPS...

...I AM *INDEED* TROUBLED.

AND LEST I FORGET, THERE IS THIS...

...FRESH FROM PALLADIA, COPIED AND DISTRIBUTED AT THE REQUEST OF GODWYN HIMSELF.

I HAVE ENOUGH OF MY *OWN* PROBLEMS...

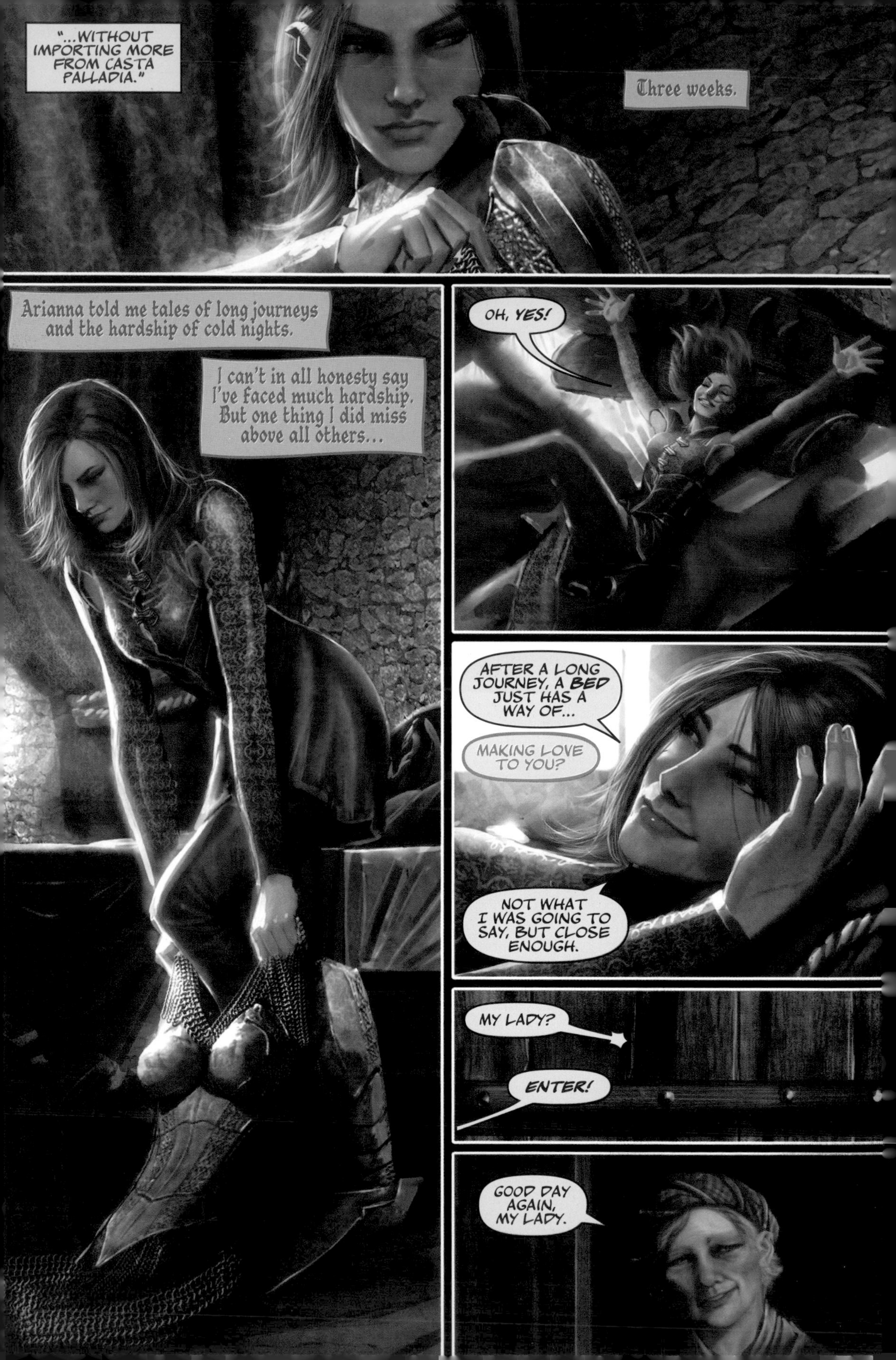
"...WITHOUT IMPORTING MORE FROM CASTA PALLADIA."
Three weeks.
Arianna told me tales of long journeys and the hardship of cold nights.
I can't in all honesty say I've faced much hardship. But one thing I did miss above all others...
OH, YES!
AFTER A LONG JOURNEY, A BED JUST HAS A WAY OF...
MAKING LOVE TO YOU?
NOT WHAT I WAS GOING TO SAY, BUT CLOSE ENOUGH.
MY LADY?
ENTER!
GOOD DAY AGAIN, MY LADY.

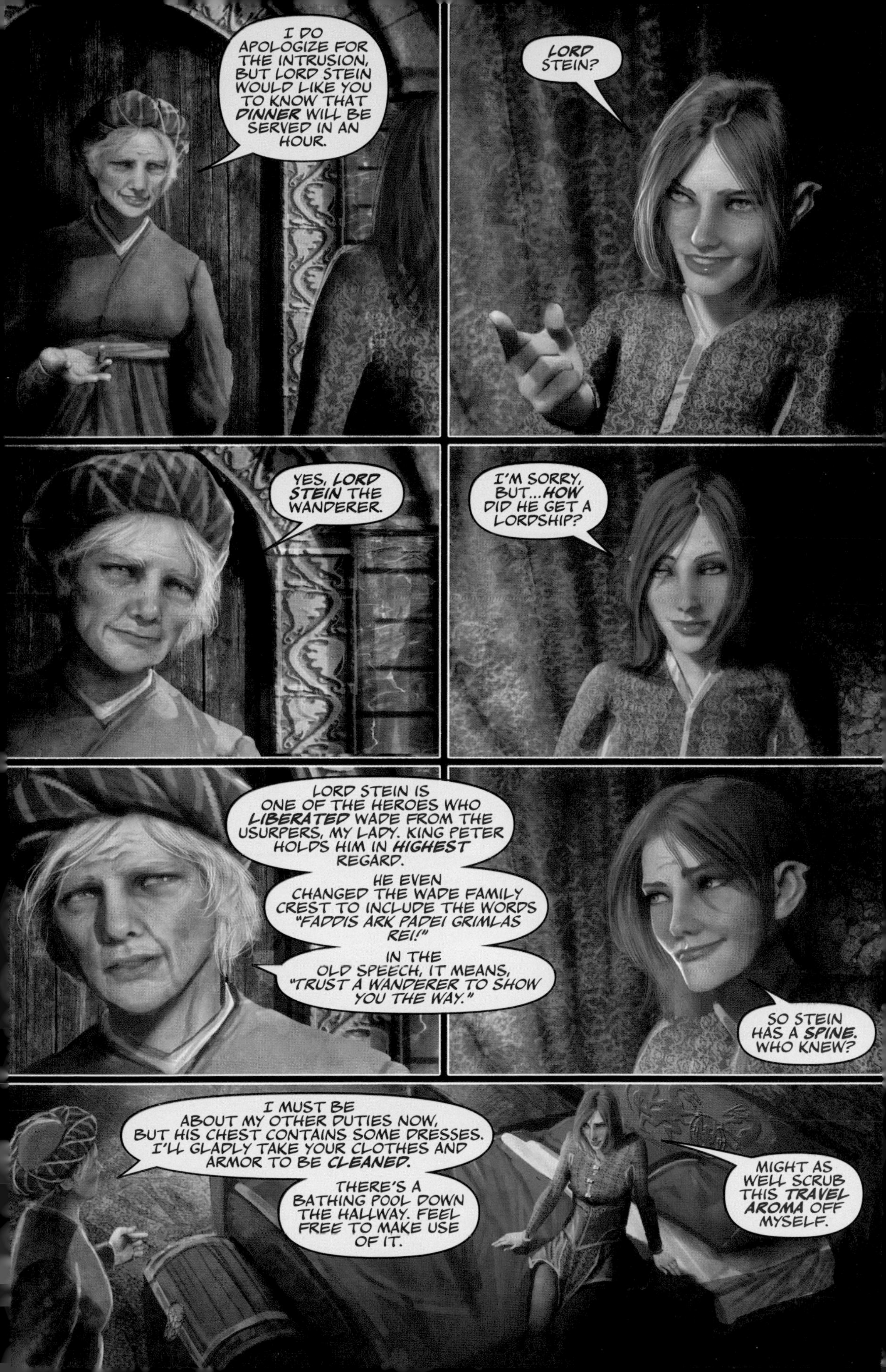
I DO APOLOGIZE FOR THE INTRUSION, BUT LORD STEIN WOULD LIKE YOU TO KNOW THAT DINNER WILL BE SERVED IN AN HOUR.
LORD STEIN?
YES, LORD STEIN THE WANDERER.
I'M SORRY, BUT...HOW DID HE GET A LORDSHIP?
LORD STEIN IS ONE OF THE HEROES WHO LIBERATED WADE FROM THE USURPERS, MY LADY. KING PETER HOLDS HIM IN HIGHEST REGARD.
HE EVEN CHANGED THE WADE FAMILY CREST TO INCLUDE THE WORDS "FADDIS ARK PADEI GRIMLAS REI!"
IN THE OLD SPEECH, IT MEANS, "TRUST A WANDERER TO SHOW YOU THE WAY."
SO STEIN HAS A SPINE. WHO KNEW?
I MUST BE ABOUT MY OTHER DUTIES NOW, BUT HIS CHEST CONTAINS SOME DRESSES. I'LL GLADLY TAKE YOUR CLOTHES AND ARMOR TO BE CLEANED.
THERE'S A BATHING POOL DOWN THE HALLWAY. FEEL FREE TO MAKE USE OF IT.
MIGHT AS WELL SCRUB THIS TRAVEL AROMA OFF MYSELF.

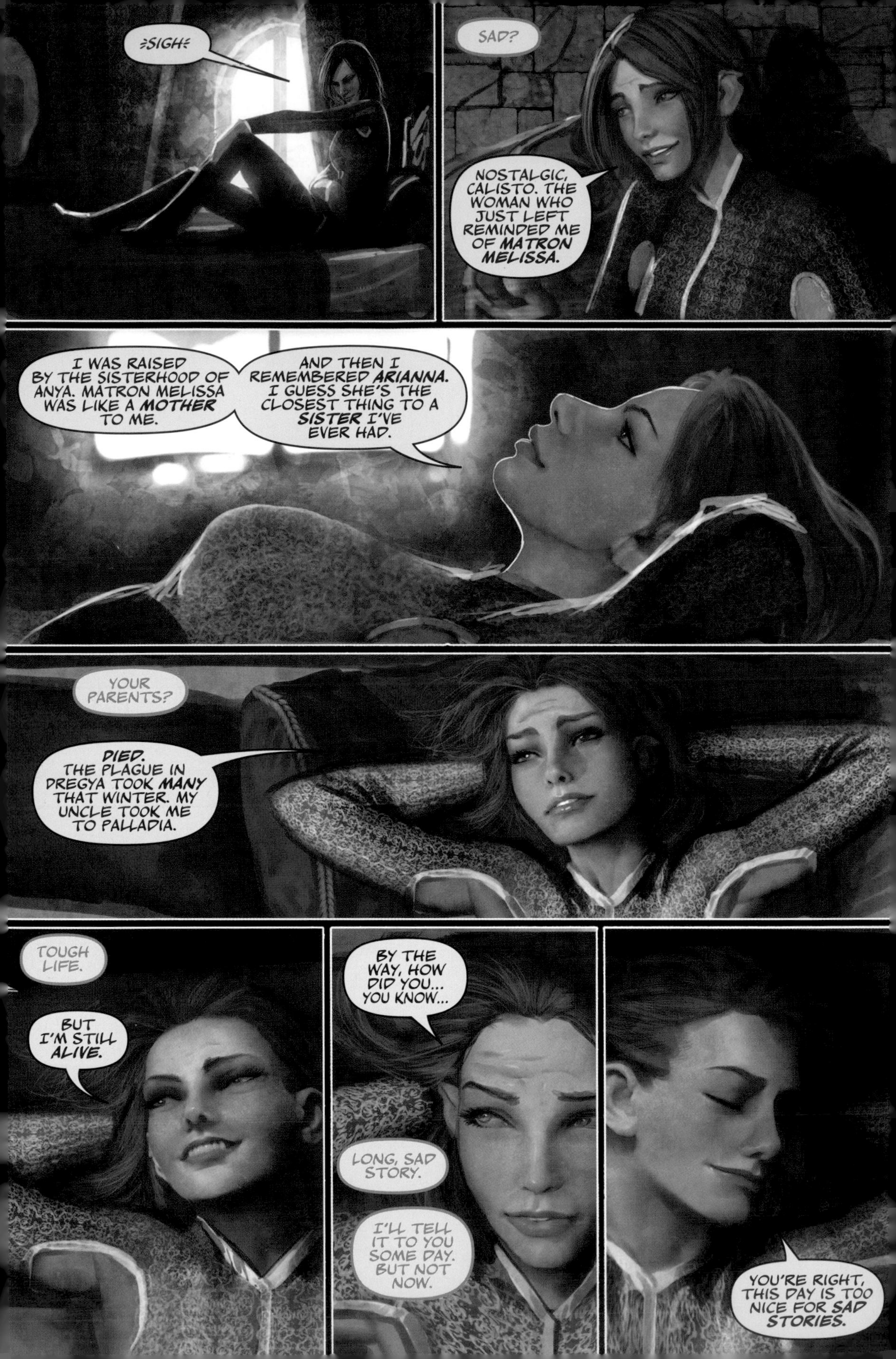

≈SIGH≈
SAD?
NOSTALGIC, CALISTO. THE WOMAN WHO JUST LEFT REMINDED ME OF MATRON MELISSA.
I WAS RAISED BY THE SISTERHOOD OF ANYA. MATRON MELISSA WAS LIKE A MOTHER TO ME.
AND THEN I REMEMBERED ARIANNA. I GUESS SHE'S THE CLOSEST THING TO A SISTER I'VE EVER HAD.
YOUR PARENTS?
DIED. THE PLAGUE IN DREGYA TOOK MANY THAT WINTER. MY UNCLE TOOK ME TO PALLADIA.
TOUGH LIFE.
BUT I'M STILL ALIVE.
BY THE WAY, HOW DID YOU... YOU KNOW...
LONG, SAD STORY.
I'LL TELL IT TO YOU SOME DAY. BUT NOT NOW.
YOU'RE RIGHT, THIS DAY IS TOO NICE FOR SAD STORIES.

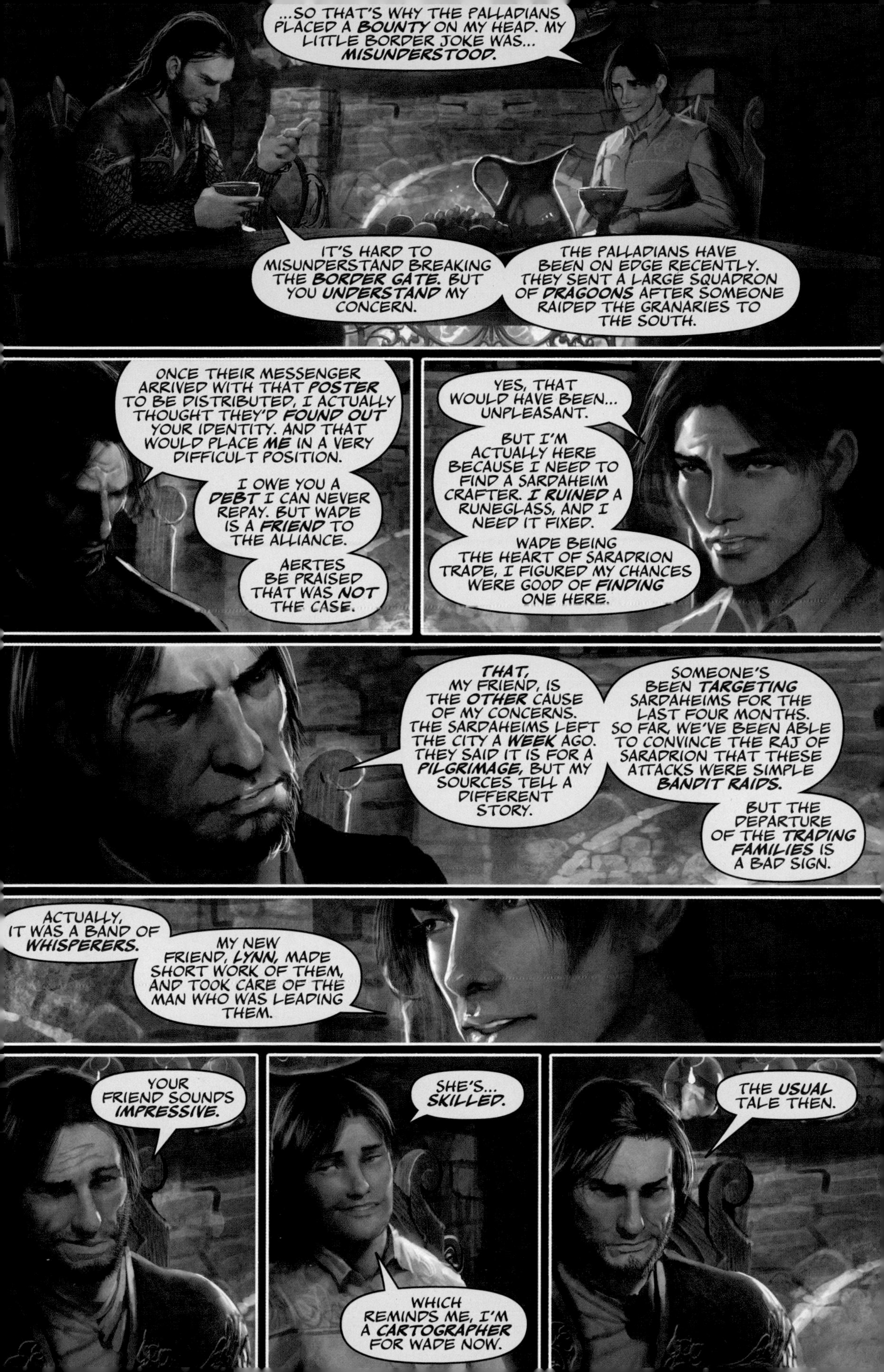
...SO THAT'S WHY THE PALLADIANS PLACED A BOUNTY ON MY HEAD. MY LITTLE BORDER JOKE WAS... MISUNDERSTOOD.
IT'S HARD TO MISUNDERSTAND BREAKING THE BORDER GATE. BUT YOU UNDERSTAND MY CONCERN.
THE PALLADIANS HAVE BEEN ON EDGE RECENTLY. THEY SENT A LARGE SQUADRON OF DRAGOONS AFTER SOMEONE RAIDED THE GRANARIES TO THE SOUTH.
ONCE THEIR MESSENGER ARRIVED WITH THAT POSTER TO BE DISTRIBUTED, I ACTUALLY THOUGHT THEY'D FOUND OUT YOUR IDENTITY. AND THAT WOULD PLACE ME IN A VERY DIFFICULT POSITION.
I OWE YOU A DEBT I CAN NEVER REPAY. BUT WADE IS A FRIEND TO THE ALLIANCE.
AERTES BE PRAISED THAT WAS NOT THE CASE.
YES, THAT WOULD HAVE BEEN... UNPLEASANT.
BUT I'M ACTUALLY HERE BECAUSE I NEED TO FIND A SARDAHEIM CRAFTER. I RUINED A RUNEGLASS, AND I NEED IT FIXED.
WADE BEING THE HEART OF SARADRION TRADE, I FIGURED MY CHANCES WERE GOOD OF FINDING ONE HERE.
THAT, MY FRIEND, IS THE OTHER CAUSE OF MY CONCERNS. THE SARDAHEIMS LEFT THE CITY A WEEK AGO. THEY SAID IT IS FOR A PILGRIMAGE, BUT MY SOURCES TELL A DIFFERENT STORY.
SOMEONE'S BEEN TARGETING SARDAHEIMS FOR THE LAST FOUR MONTHS. SO FAR, WE'VE BEEN ABLE TO CONVINCE THE RAJ OF SARADRION THAT THESE ATTACKS WERE SIMPLE BANDIT RAIDS.
BUT THE DEPARTURE OF THE TRADING FAMILIES IS A BAD SIGN.
ACTUALLY, IT WAS A BAND OF WHISPERERS.
MY NEW FRIEND, LYNN, MADE SHORT WORK OF THEM, AND TOOK CARE OF THE MAN WHO WAS LEADING THEM.
YOUR FRIEND SOUNDS IMPRESSIVE.
SHE'S... SKILLED.
WHICH REMINDS ME, I'M A CARTOGRAPHER FOR WADE NOW.
THE USUAL TALE THEN.

SO... DRAGONTOMBS?

AYE.

YOU *DO* KNOW...

THAT EVERYBODY WHO TRIED FINDING THEM GOT *KILLED?* I KNOW.

NO, THAT'S NOT WHAT I MEANT TO SAY. YOU *DO* KNOW YOU COULD JUST GIVE IT UP AND *SETTLE* IN WADE?

YOUR *LORDSHIP* IS THE *LEAST* WE COULD GRANT YOU. WADE WOULD GLADLY FINANCE AN EASY LIFE HERE.

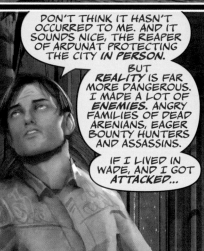

DON'T THINK IT HASN'T OCCURRED TO ME. AND IT SOUNDS NICE, THE REAPER OF ARDUNAT PROTECTING THE CITY *IN PERSON.*

BUT *REALITY* IS FAR MORE DANGEROUS. I MADE A LOT OF *ENEMIES.* ANGRY FAMILIES OF DEAD ARENIANS, EAGER BOUNTY HUNTERS AND ASSASSINS.

IF I LIVED IN WADE, AND I GOT *ATTACKED...*

YES, THE *CASUALTIES.* I SEE YOUR POINT.

ONE DEAD CITY IS MORE THAN ENOUGH FOR ME.

EVEN COMING TO WADE WAS A RISK DRIVEN BY *NEED.* ANY SHIVAS CAN EASILY SEE ME FOR WHO I AM.

THAT MAY BE A *BENEFIT.* RUMORS OF THE *REAPER* WALKING THE STREETS EVERY NOW AND THEN KEEP ENEMIES FROM OUR BORDERS.

BUT I UNDERSTAND.

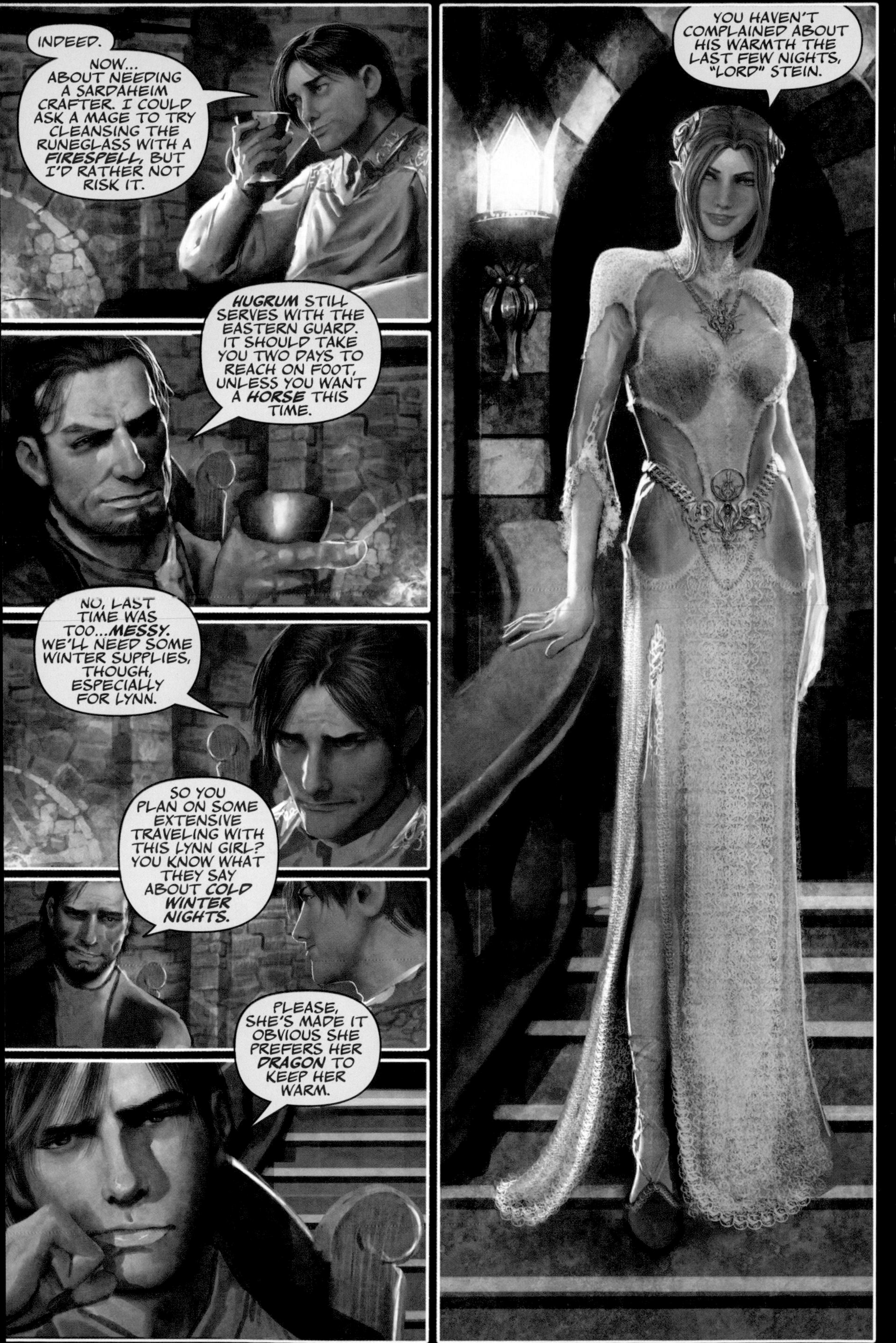
INDEED.
NOW... ABOUT NEEDING A SARDAHEIM CRAFTER. I COULD ASK A MAGE TO TRY CLEANSING THE RUNEGLASS WITH A FIRESPELL, BUT I'D RATHER NOT RISK IT.
HUGRUM STILL SERVES WITH THE EASTERN GUARD. IT SHOULD TAKE YOU TWO DAYS TO REACH ON FOOT, UNLESS YOU WANT A HORSE THIS TIME.
NO, LAST TIME WAS TOO...MESSY. WE'LL NEED SOME WINTER SUPPLIES, THOUGH, ESPECIALLY FOR LYNN.
SO YOU PLAN ON SOME EXTENSIVE TRAVELING WITH THIS LYNN GIRL? YOU KNOW WHAT THEY SAY ABOUT COLD WINTER NIGHTS.
PLEASE, SHE'S MADE IT OBVIOUS SHE PREFERS HER DRAGON TO KEEP HER WARM.
YOU HAVEN'T COMPLAINED ABOUT HIS WARMTH THE LAST FEW NIGHTS, "LORD" STEIN.

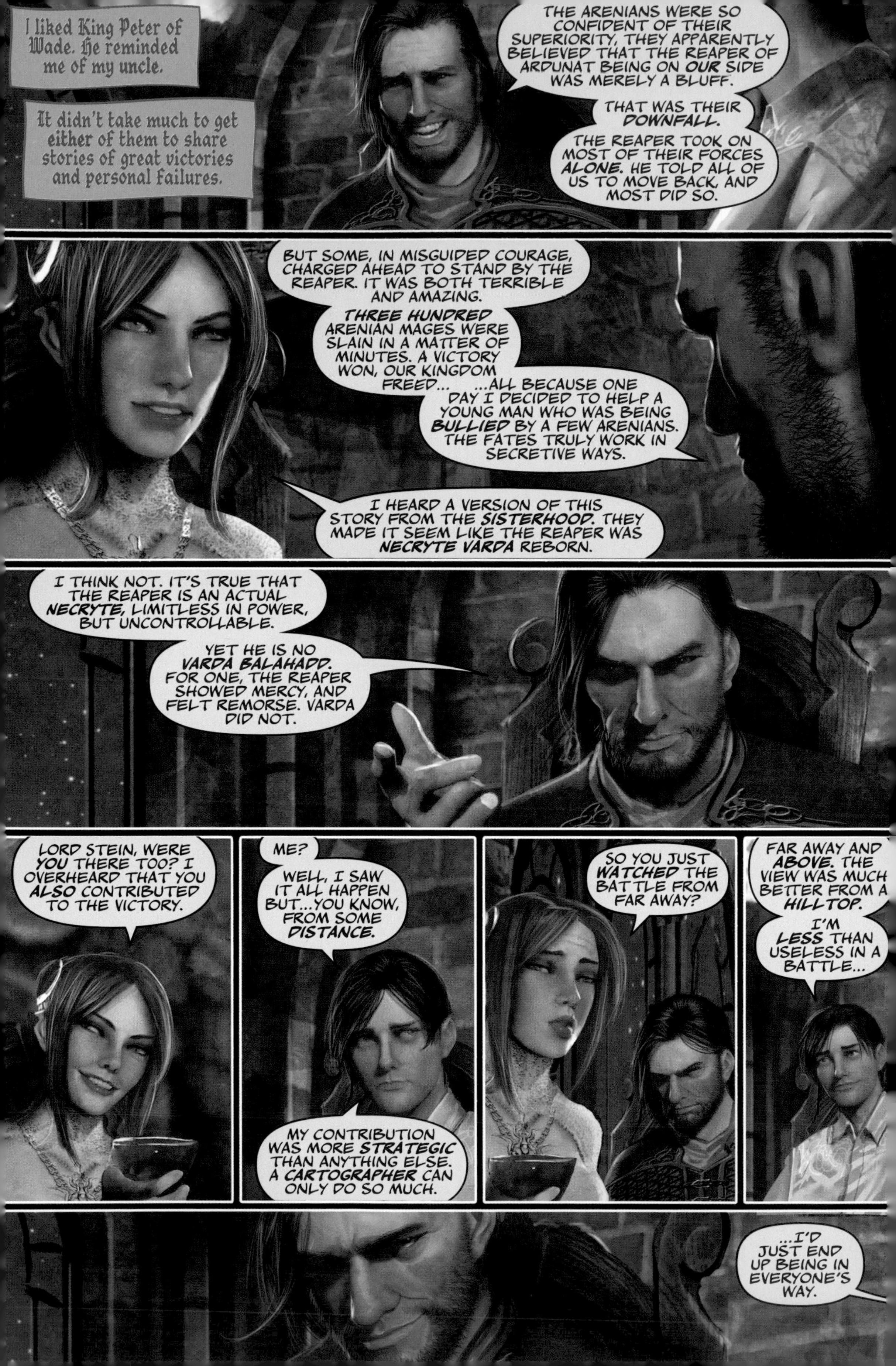
I liked King Peter of Wade. He reminded me of my uncle.
It didn't take much to get either of them to share stories of great victories and personal failures.
THE ARENIANS WERE SO CONFIDENT OF THEIR SUPERIORITY, THEY APPARENTLY BELIEVED THAT THE REAPER OF ARDUNAT BEING ON OUR SIDE WAS MERELY A BLUFF.
THAT WAS THEIR DOWNFALL.
THE REAPER TOOK ON MOST OF THEIR FORCES ALONE. HE TOLD ALL OF US TO MOVE BACK, AND MOST DID SO.
BUT SOME, IN MISGUIDED COURAGE, CHARGED AHEAD TO STAND BY THE REAPER. IT WAS BOTH TERRIBLE AND AMAZING.
THREE HUNDRED ARENIAN MAGES WERE SLAIN IN A MATTER OF MINUTES. A VICTORY WON, OUR KINGDOM FREED...
...ALL BECAUSE ONE DAY I DECIDED TO HELP A YOUNG MAN WHO WAS BEING BULLIED BY A FEW ARENIANS. THE FATES TRULY WORK IN SECRETIVE WAYS.
I HEARD A VERSION OF THIS STORY FROM THE SISTERHOOD. THEY MADE IT SEEM LIKE THE REAPER WAS NECRYTE VARDA REBORN.
I THINK NOT. IT'S TRUE THAT THE REAPER IS AN ACTUAL NECRYTE, LIMITLESS IN POWER, BUT UNCONTROLLABLE.
YET HE IS NO VARDA BALAHADD. FOR ONE, THE REAPER SHOWED MERCY, AND FELT REMORSE. VARDA DID NOT.
LORD STEIN, WERE YOU THERE TOO? I OVERHEARD THAT YOU ALSO CONTRIBUTED TO THE VICTORY.
ME?
WELL, I SAW IT ALL HAPPEN BUT...YOU KNOW, FROM SOME DISTANCE.
MY CONTRIBUTION WAS MORE STRATEGIC THAN ANYTHING ELSE. A CARTOGRAPHER CAN ONLY DO SO MUCH.
SO YOU JUST WATCHED THE BATTLE FROM FAR AWAY?
FAR AWAY AND ABOVE. THE VIEW WAS MUCH BETTER FROM A HILLTOP.
I'M LESS THAN USELESS IN A BATTLE...
...I'D JUST END UP BEING IN EVERYONE'S WAY.

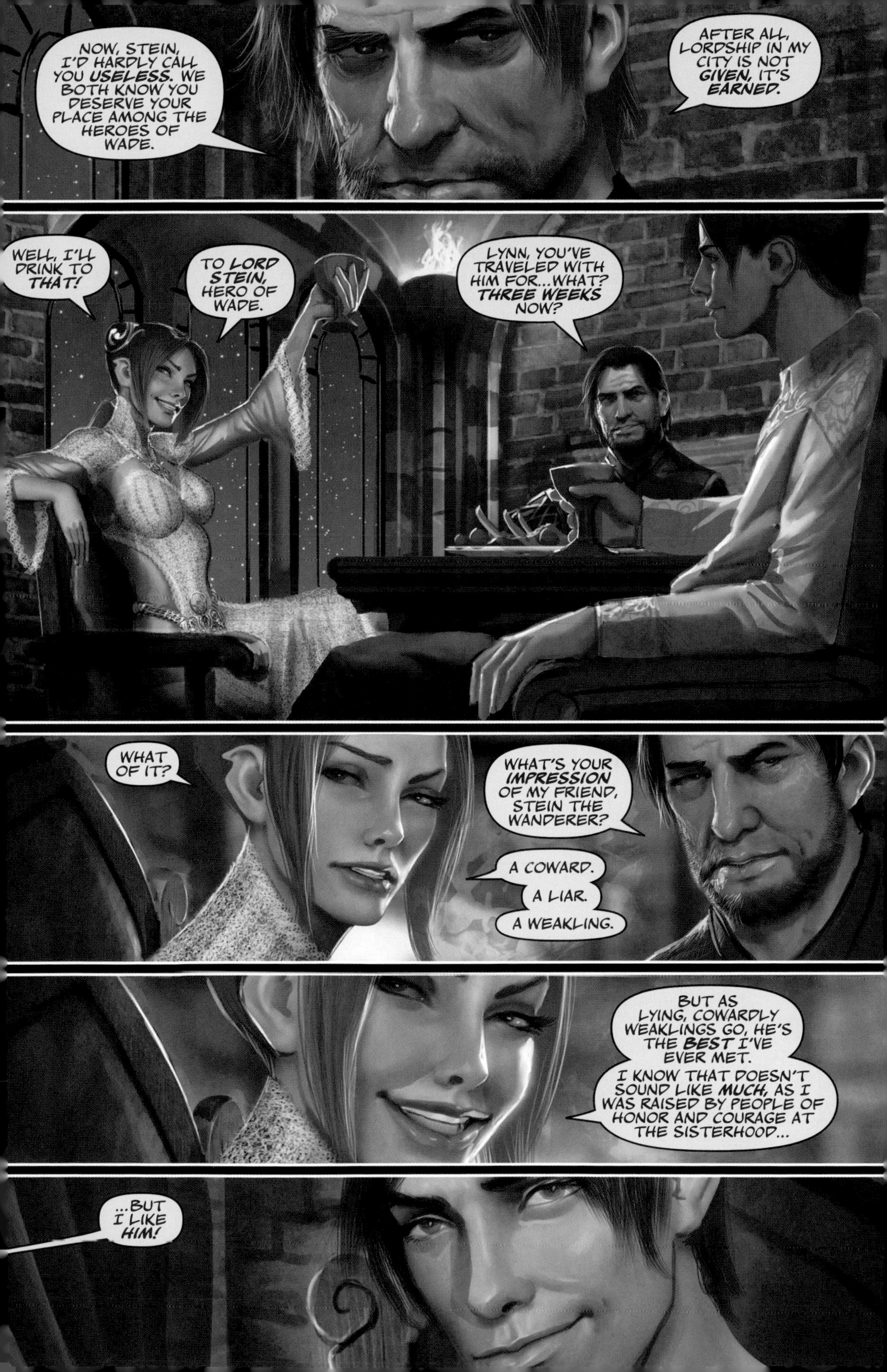
NOW, STEIN, I'D HARDLY CALL YOU USELESS. WE BOTH KNOW YOU DESERVE YOUR PLACE AMONG THE HEROES OF WADE.
AFTER ALL, LORDSHIP IN MY CITY IS NOT GIVEN, IT'S EARNED.
WELL, I'LL DRINK TO THAT!
TO LORD STEIN, HERO OF WADE.
LYNN, YOU'VE TRAVELED WITH HIM FOR...WHAT? THREE WEEKS NOW?
WHAT OF IT?
WHAT'S YOUR IMPRESSION OF MY FRIEND, STEIN THE WANDERER?
A COWARD.
A LIAR.
A WEAKLING.
BUT AS LYING, COWARDLY WEAKLINGS GO, HE'S THE BEST I'VE EVER MET.
I KNOW THAT DOESN'T SOUND LIKE MUCH, AS I WAS RAISED BY PEOPLE OF HONOR AND COURAGE AT THE SISTERHOOD...
...BUT I LIKE HIM!

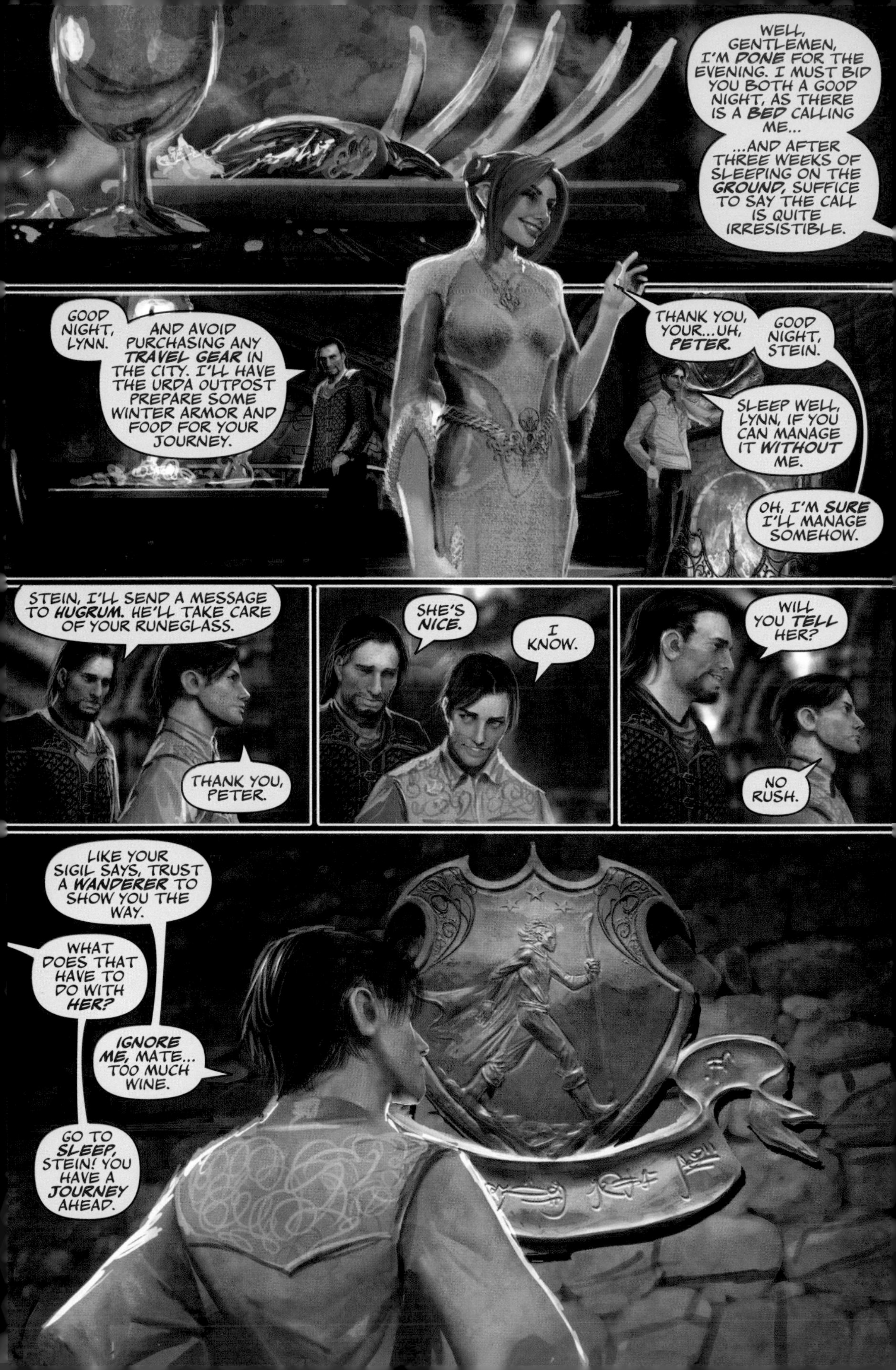
WELL, GENTLEMEN, I'M DONE FOR THE EVENING. I MUST BID YOU BOTH A GOOD NIGHT, AS THERE IS A BED CALLING ME...
...AND AFTER THREE WEEKS OF SLEEPING ON THE GROUND, SUFFICE TO SAY THE CALL IS QUITE IRRESISTIBLE.
GOOD NIGHT, LYNN.
AND AVOID PURCHASING ANY TRAVEL GEAR IN THE CITY. I'LL HAVE THE URDA OUTPOST PREPARE SOME WINTER ARMOR AND FOOD FOR YOUR JOURNEY.
THANK YOU, YOUR...UH, PETER.
GOOD NIGHT, STEIN.
SLEEP WELL, LYNN, IF YOU CAN MANAGE IT WITHOUT ME.
OH, I'M SURE I'LL MANAGE SOMEHOW.
STEIN, I'LL SEND A MESSAGE TO HUGRUM. HE'LL TAKE CARE OF YOUR RUNEGLASS.
THANK YOU, PETER.
SHE'S NICE.
I KNOW.
WILL YOU TELL HER?
NO RUSH.
LIKE YOUR SIGIL SAYS, TRUST A WANDERER TO SHOW YOU THE WAY.
WHAT DOES THAT HAVE TO DO WITH HER?
IGNORE ME, MATE... TOO MUCH WINE.
GO TO SLEEP, STEIN! YOU HAVE A JOURNEY AHEAD.

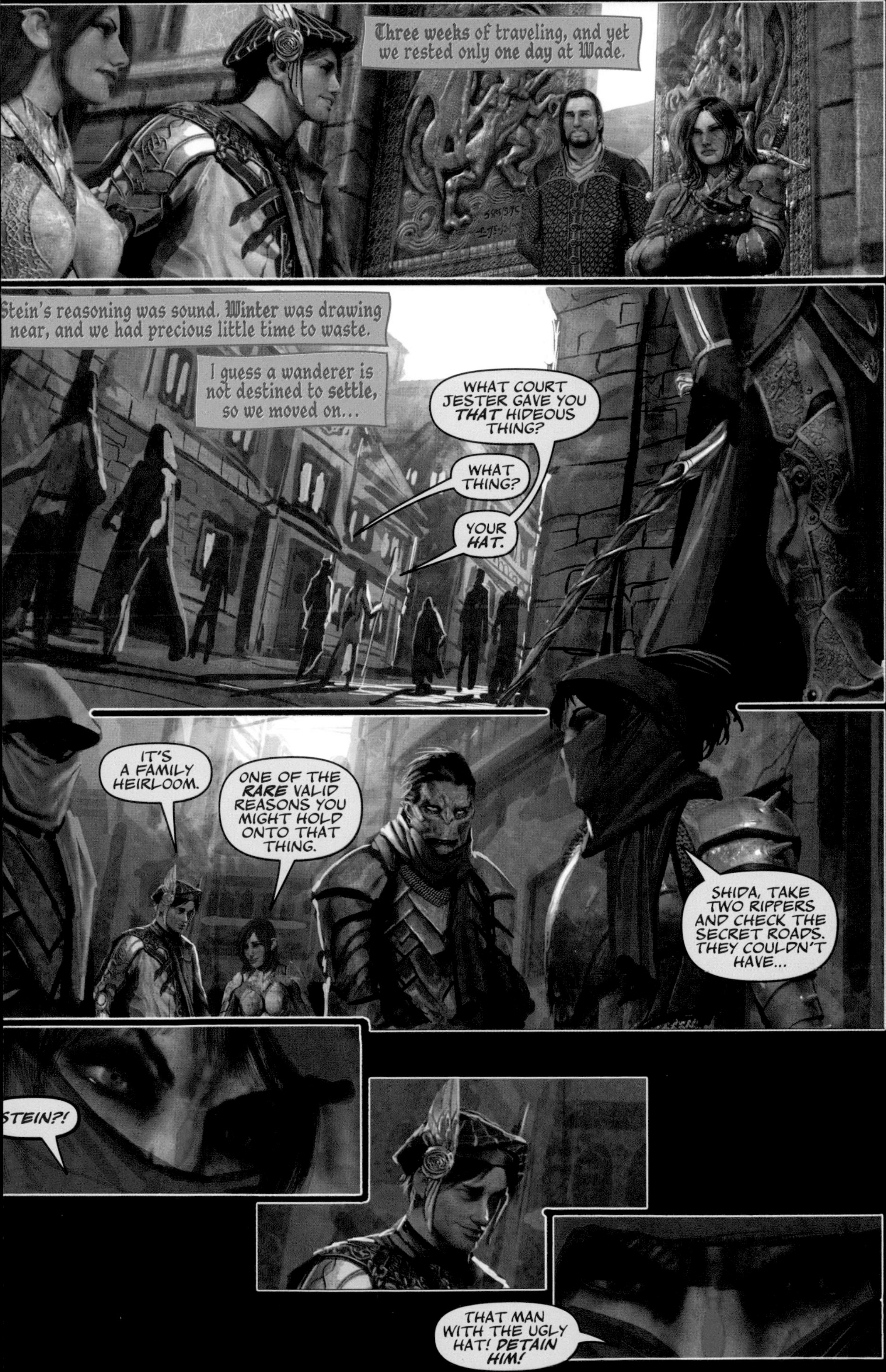
Three weeks of traveling, and yet we rested only one day at Wade.
Stein's reasoning was sound. Winter was drawing near, and we had precious little time to waste.
I guess a wanderer is not destined to settle, so we moved on...
WHAT COURT JESTER GAVE YOU THAT HIDEOUS THING?
WHAT THING?
YOUR HAT.
IT'S A FAMILY HEIRLOOM.
ONE OF THE RARE VALID REASONS YOU MIGHT HOLD ONTO THAT THING.
SHIDA, TAKE TWO RIPPERS AND CHECK THE SECRET ROADS. THEY COULDN'T HAVE...
STEIN?!
THAT MAN WITH THE UGLY HAT! DETAIN HIM!

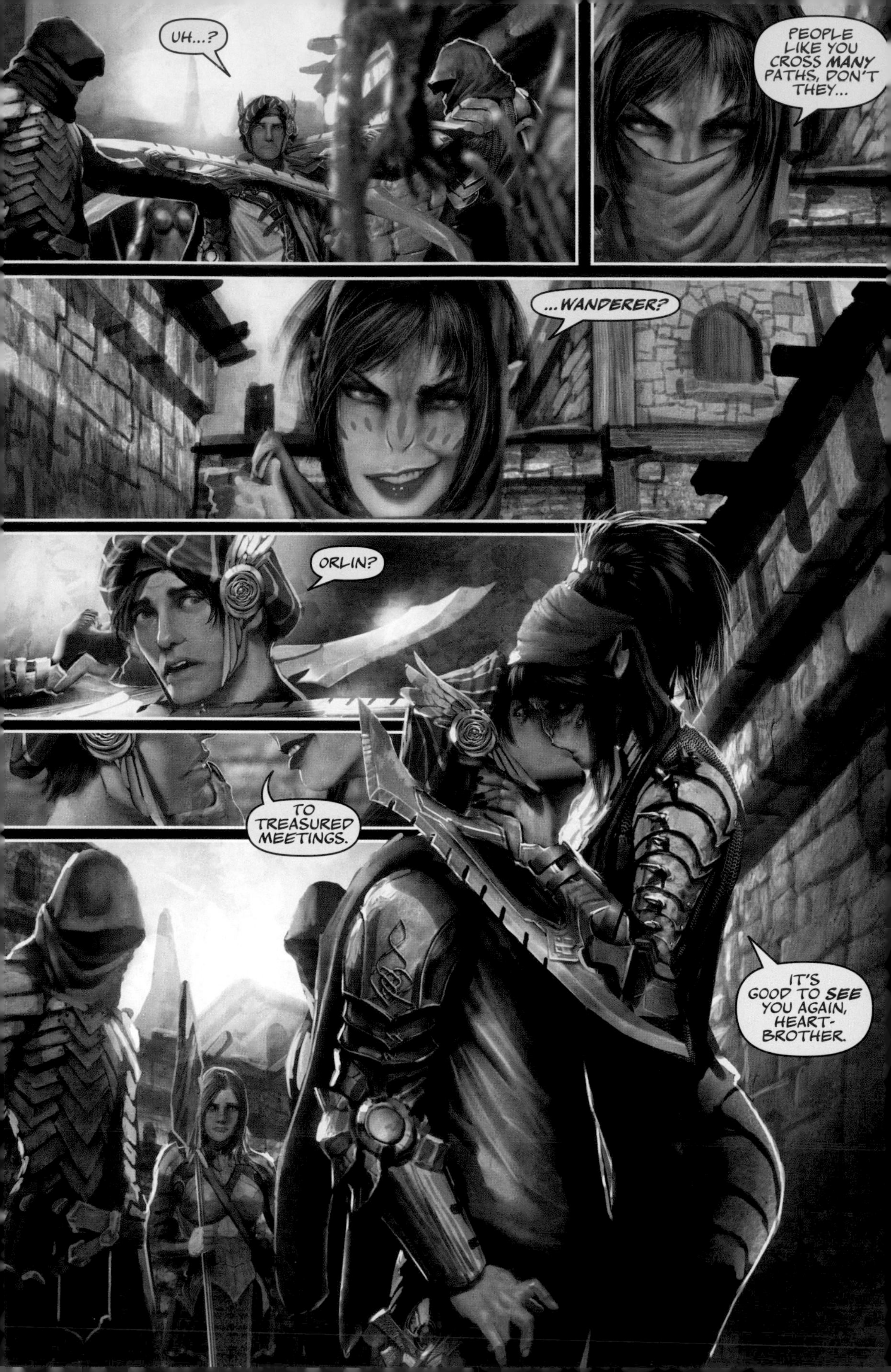
UH...?
PEOPLE LIKE YOU CROSS MANY PATHS, DON'T THEY...
...WANDERER?
ORLIN?
TO TREASURED MEETINGS.
IT'S GOOD TO SEE YOU AGAIN, HEART-BROTHER.

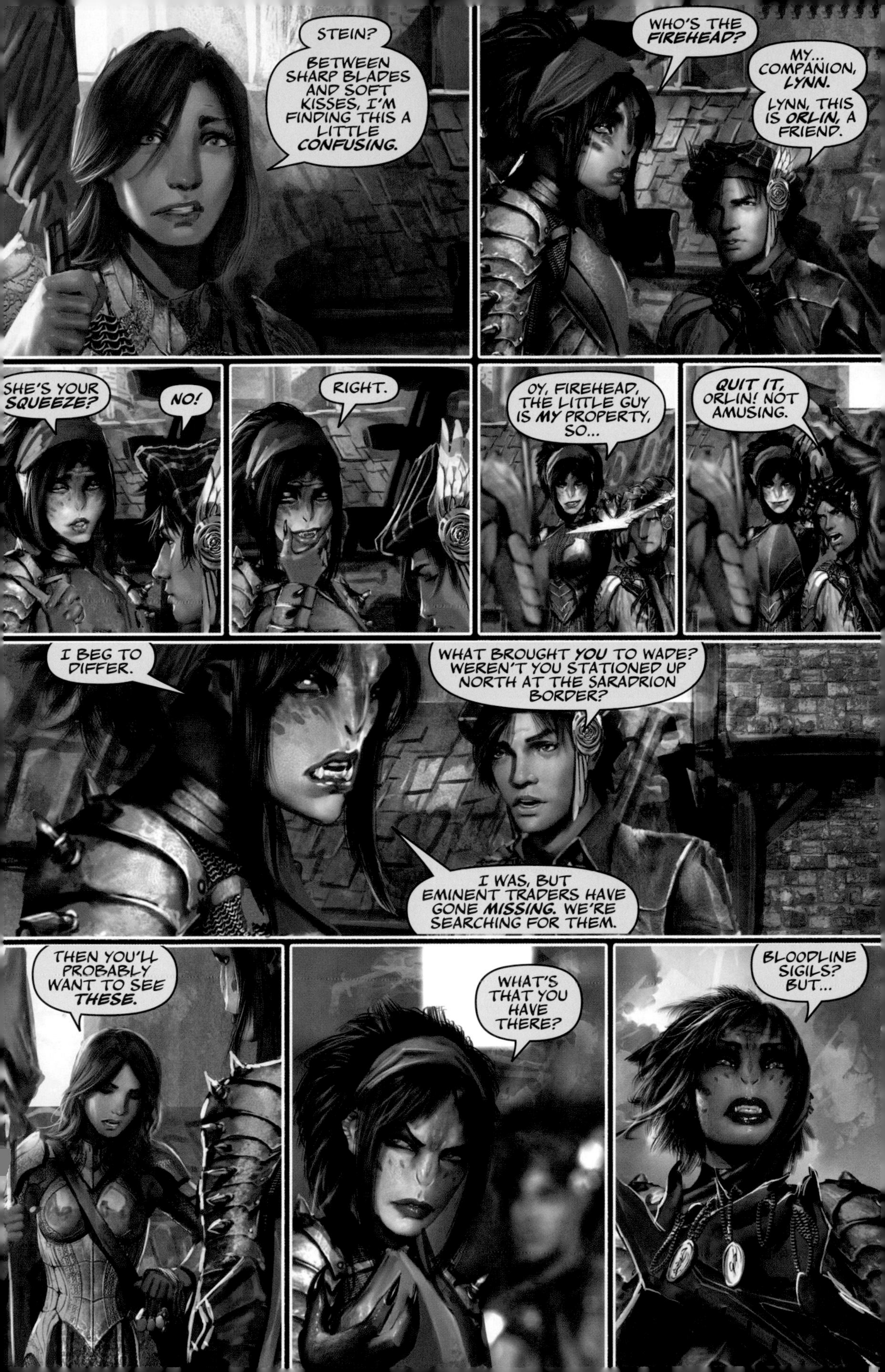
STEIN?
BETWEEN SHARP BLADES AND SOFT KISSES, I'M FINDING THIS A LITTLE CONFUSING.
WHO'S THE FIREHEAD?
MY... COMPANION, LYNN.
LYNN, THIS IS ORLIN, A FRIEND.
SHE'S YOUR SQUEEZE?
NO!
RIGHT.
OY, FIREHEAD, THE LITTLE GUY IS MY PROPERTY, SO...
QUIT IT, ORLIN! NOT AMUSING.
I BEG TO DIFFER.
WHAT BROUGHT YOU TO WADE? WEREN'T YOU STATIONED UP NORTH AT THE SARADRION BORDER?
I WAS, BUT EMINENT TRADERS HAVE GONE MISSING. WE'RE SEARCHING FOR THEM.
THEN YOU'LL PROBABLY WANT TO SEE THESE.
WHAT'S THAT YOU HAVE THERE?
BLOODLINE SIGILS? BUT...

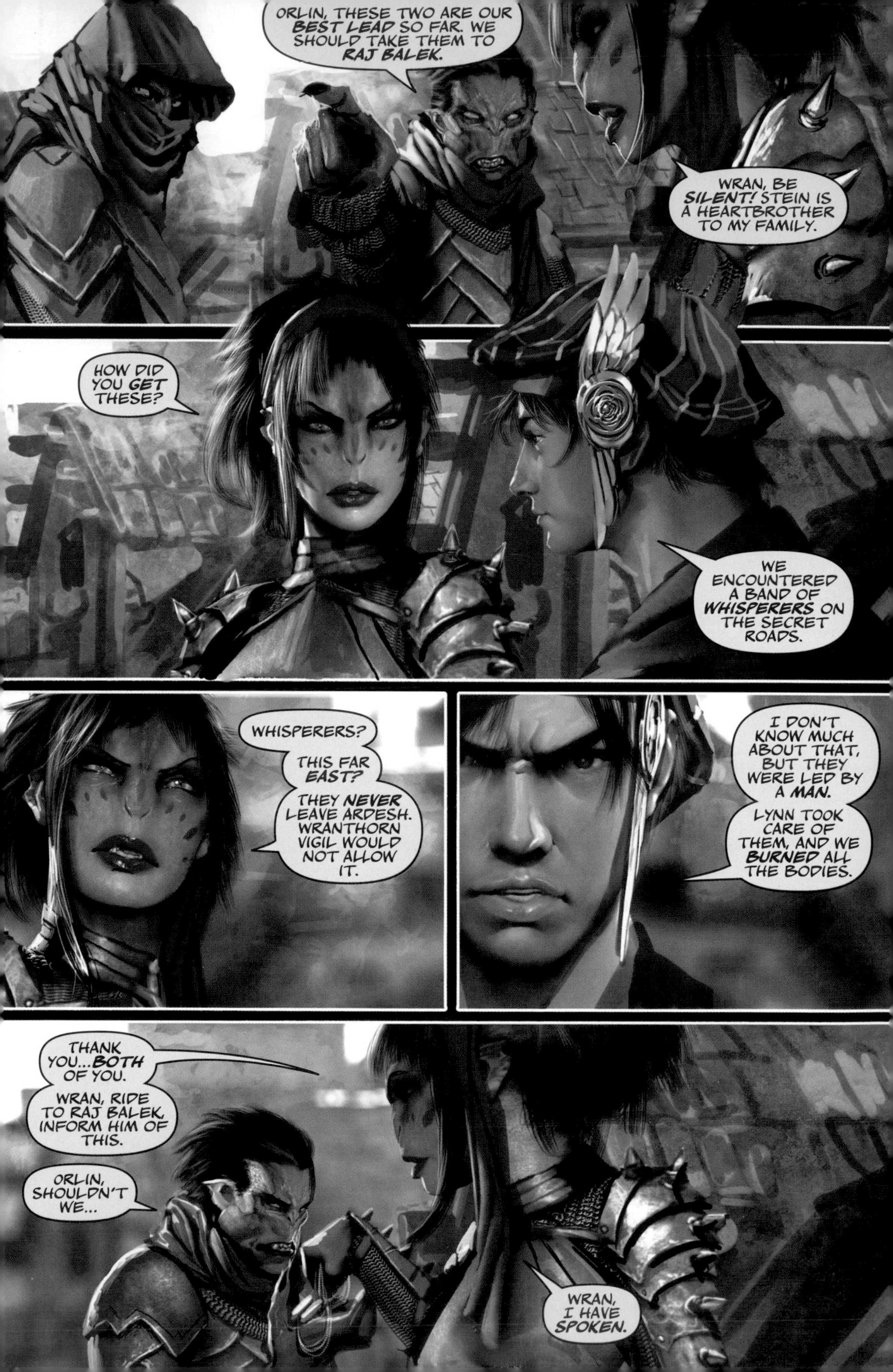
ORLIN, THESE TWO ARE OUR BEST LEAD SO FAR. WE SHOULD TAKE THEM TO RAJ BALEK.
WRAN, BE SILENT! STEIN IS A HEARTBROTHER TO MY FAMILY.
HOW DID YOU GET THESE?
WE ENCOUNTERED A BAND OF WHISPERERS ON THE SECRET ROADS.
WHISPERERS?
THIS FAR EAST?
THEY NEVER LEAVE ARDESH. WRANTHORN VIGIL WOULD NOT ALLOW IT.
I DON'T KNOW MUCH ABOUT THAT, BUT THEY WERE LED BY A MAN.
LYNN TOOK CARE OF THEM, AND WE BURNED ALL THE BODIES.
THANK YOU...BOTH OF YOU.
WRAN, RIDE TO RAJ BALEK, INFORM HIM OF THIS.
ORLIN, SHOULDN'T WE...
WRAN, I HAVE SPOKEN.

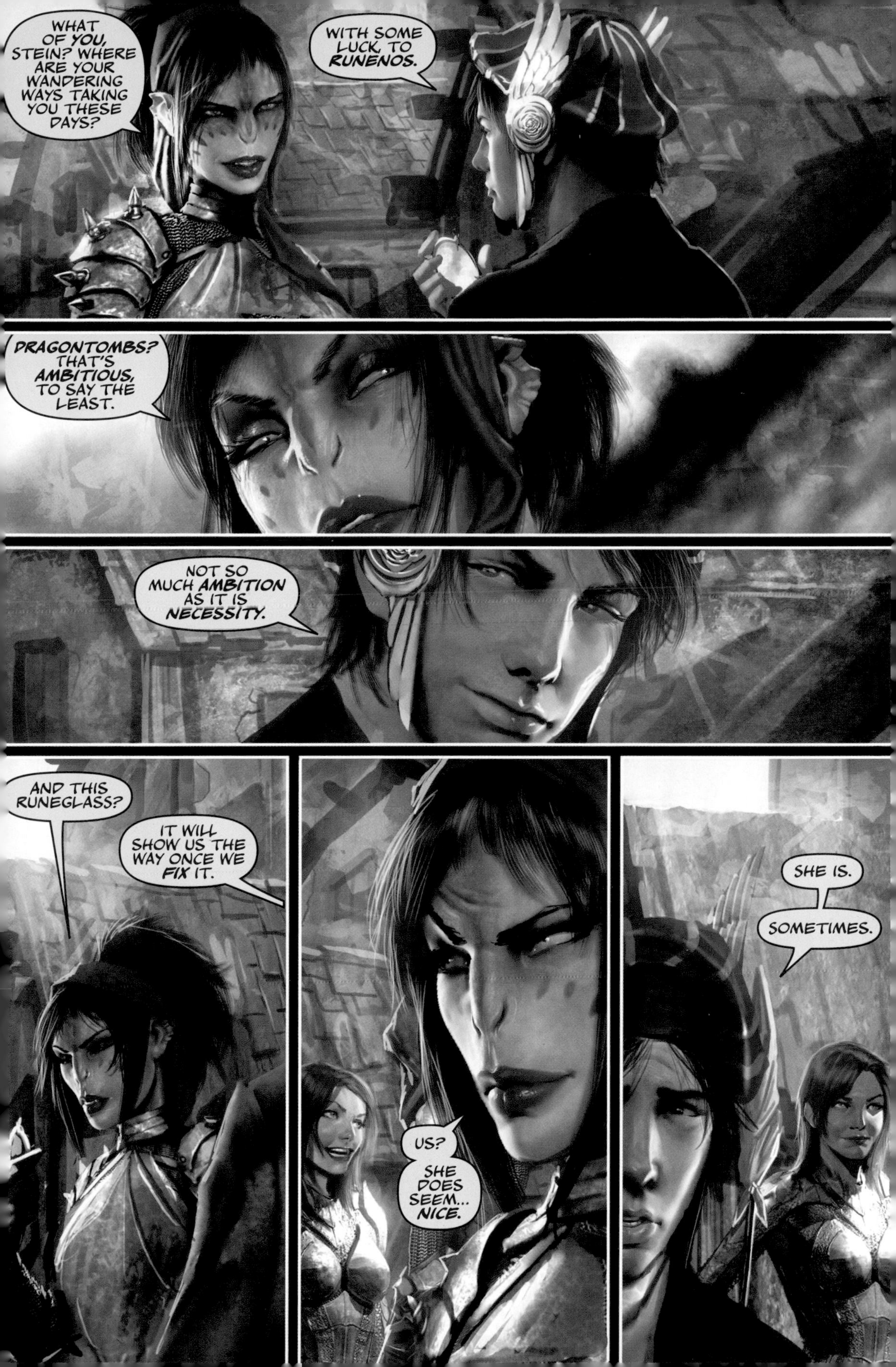
WHAT OF YOU, STEIN? WHERE ARE YOUR WANDERING WAYS TAKING YOU THESE DAYS?
WITH SOME LUCK, TO RUNENOS.
DRAGONTOMBS? THAT'S AMBITIOUS, TO SAY THE LEAST.
NOT SO MUCH AMBITION AS IT IS NECESSITY.
AND THIS RUNEGLASS?
IT WILL SHOW US THE WAY ONCE WE FIX IT.
US?
SHE DOES SEEM... NICE.
SHE IS.
SOMETIMES.

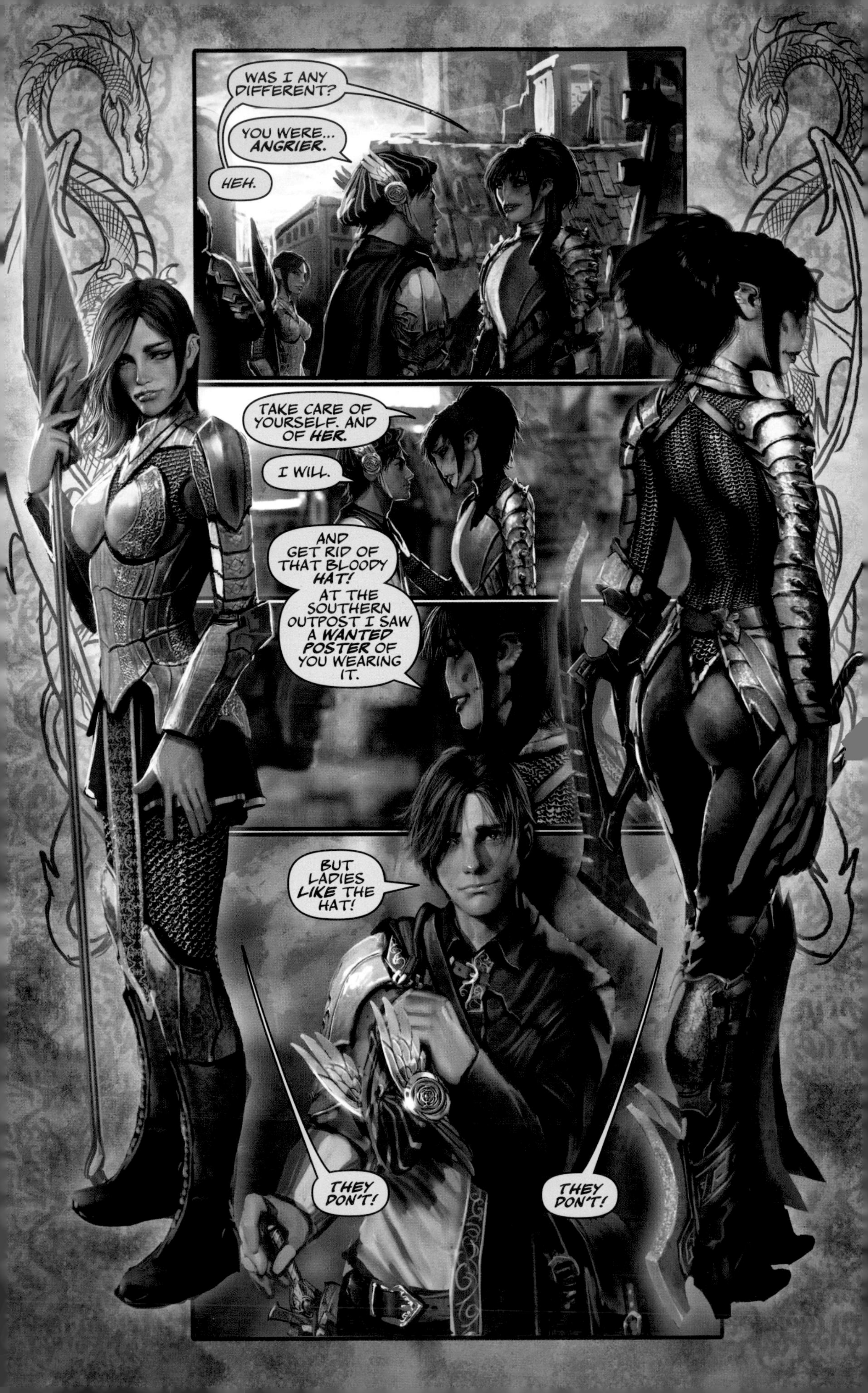
WAS I ANY DIFFERENT?
YOU WERE... ANGRIER.
HEH.
TAKE CARE OF YOURSELF. AND OF HER.
I WILL.
AND GET RID OF THAT BLOODY HAT!
AT THE SOUTHERN OUTPOST I SAW A WANTED POSTER OF YOU WEARING IT.
BUT LADIES LIKE THE HAT!
THEY DON'T!
THEY DON'T!

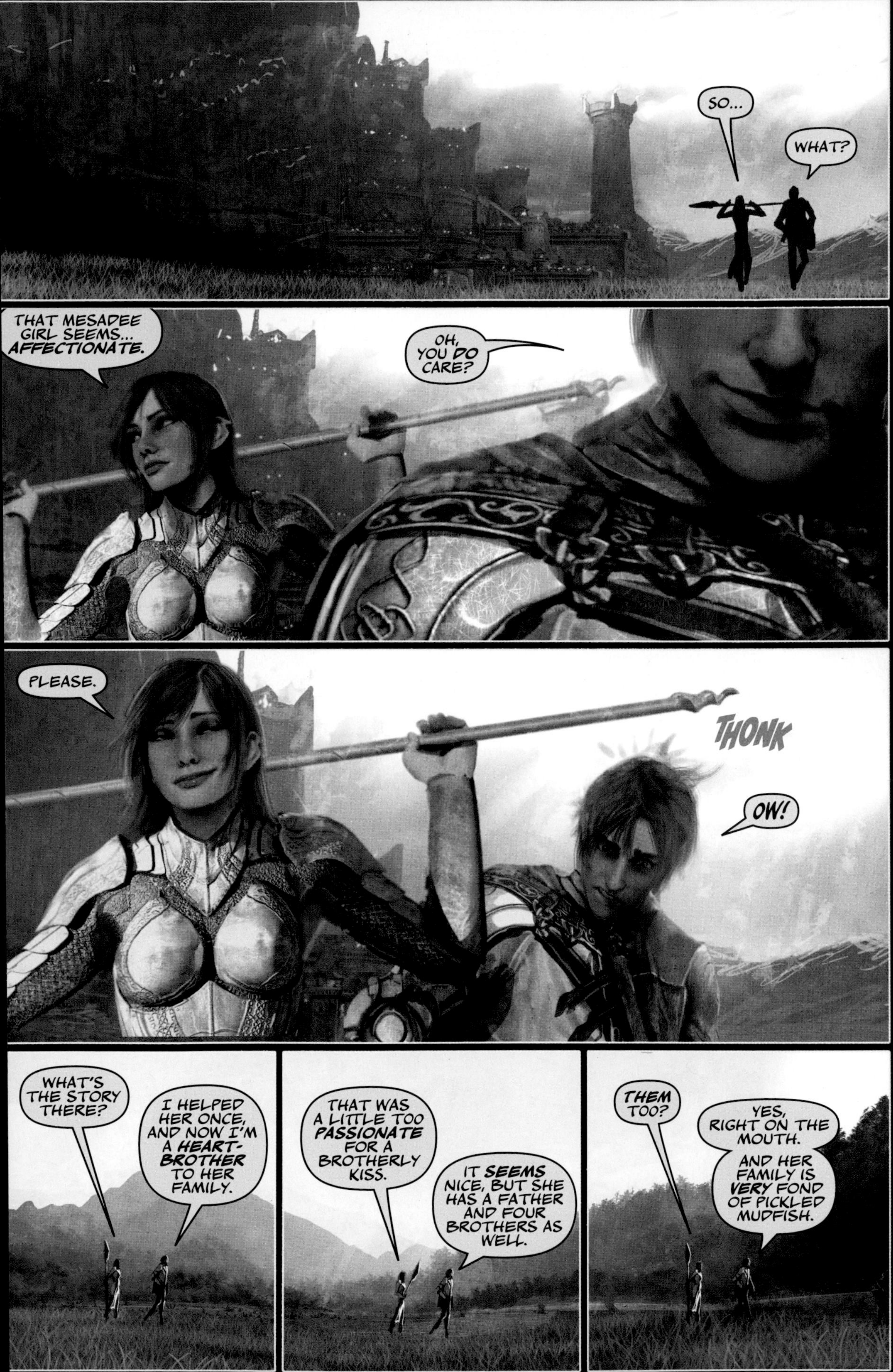
SO...
WHAT?
THAT MESADEE GIRL SEEMS... AFFECTIONATE.
OH, YOU DO CARE?
PLEASE.
THONK
OW!
WHAT'S THE STORY THERE?
I HELPED HER ONCE, AND NOW I'M A HEART-BROTHER TO HER FAMILY.
THAT WAS A LITTLE TOO PASSIONATE FOR A BROTHERLY KISS.
IT SEEMS NICE, BUT SHE HAS A FATHER AND FOUR BROTHERS AS WELL.
THEM TOO?
YES, RIGHT ON THE MOUTH.
AND HER FAMILY IS VERY FOND OF PICKLED MUDFISH.

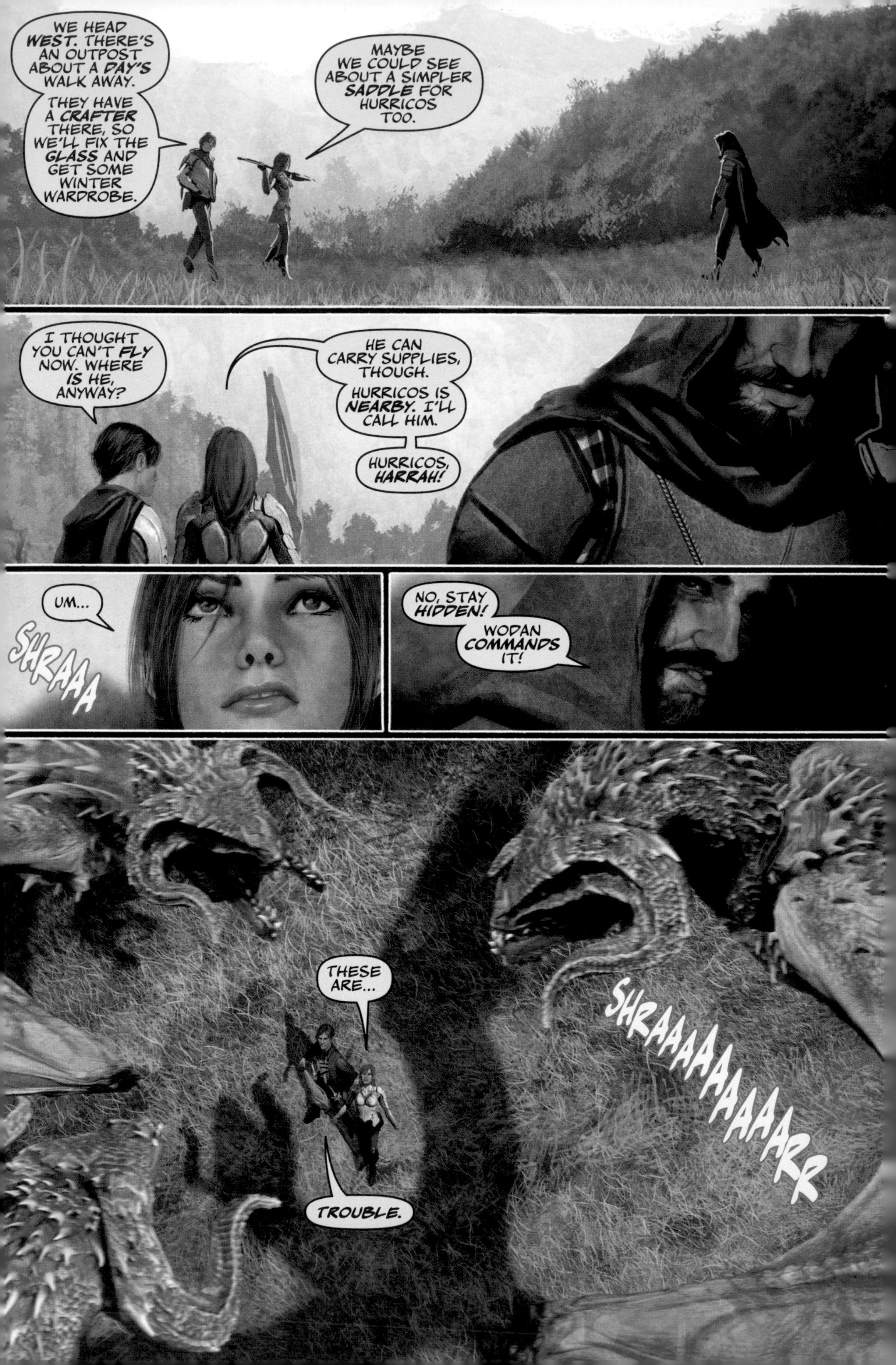
WE HEAD WEST. THERE'S AN OUTPOST ABOUT A DAY'S WALK AWAY.
THEY HAVE A CRAFTER THERE, SO WE'LL FIX THE GLASS AND GET SOME WINTER WARDROBE.
MAYBE WE COULD SEE ABOUT A SIMPLER SADDLE FOR HURRICOS TOO.
I THOUGHT YOU CAN'T FLY NOW. WHERE IS HE, ANYWAY?
HE CAN CARRY SUPPLIES, THOUGH.
HURRICOS IS NEARBY. I'LL CALL HIM.
HURRICOS, HARRAH!
UM...
SHRAAA
NO, STAY HIDDEN!
WODAN COMMANDS IT!
THESE ARE...
SHRAAAAAAAAAARR
TROUBLE.

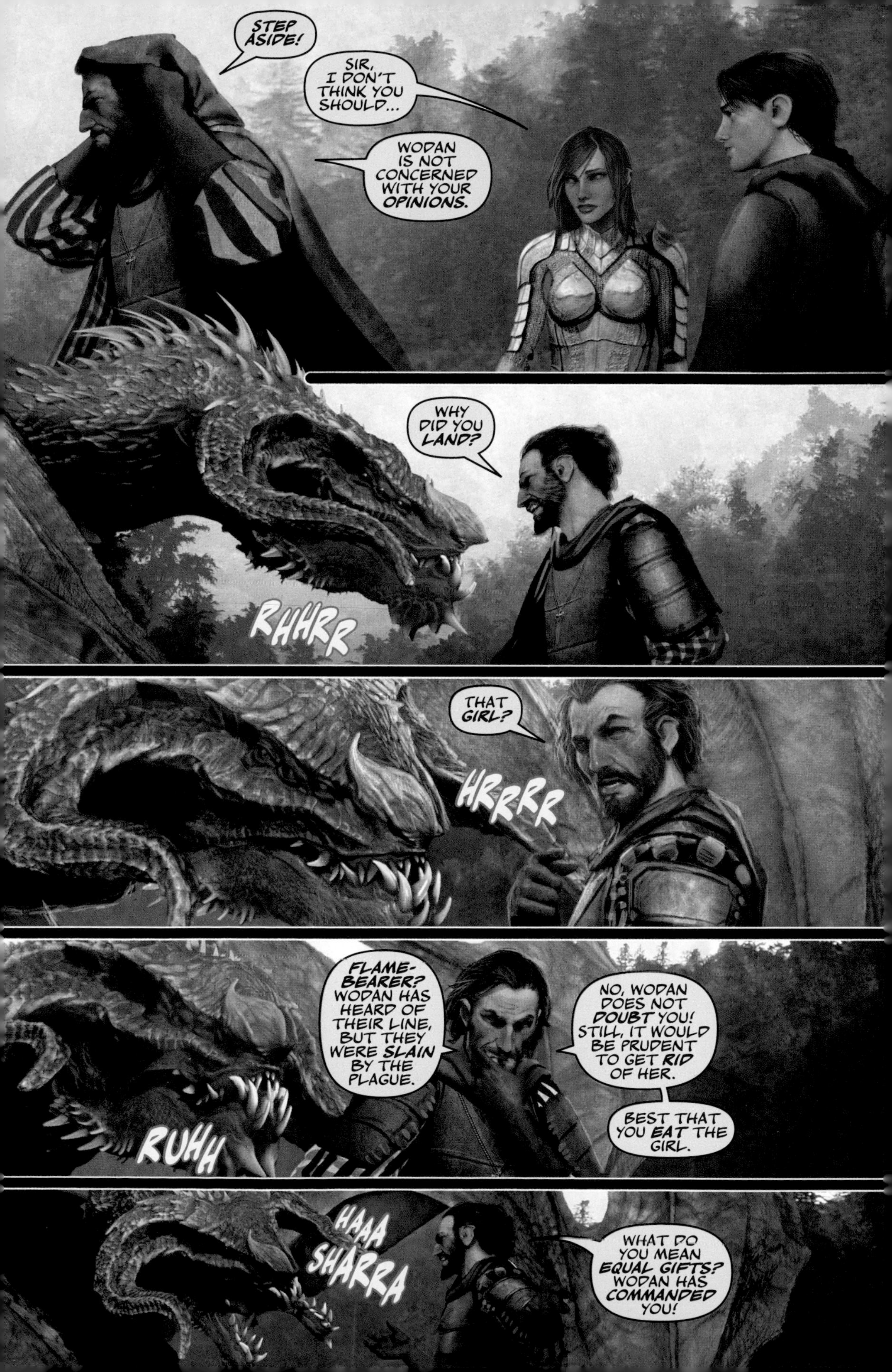
STEP ASIDE!
SIR, I DON'T THINK YOU SHOULD...
WODAN IS NOT CONCERNED WITH YOUR OPINIONS.
WHY DID YOU LAND?
RHHRR
THAT GIRL?
HRRRR
FLAME-BEARER? WODAN HAS HEARD OF THEIR LINE, BUT THEY WERE SLAIN BY THE PLAGUE.
RUHH
NO, WODAN DOES NOT DOUBT YOU! STILL, IT WOULD BE PRUDENT TO GET RID OF HER.
BEST THAT YOU EAT THE GIRL.
HAAA SHARRA
WHAT DO YOU MEAN EQUAL GIFTS? WODAN HAS COMMANDED YOU!

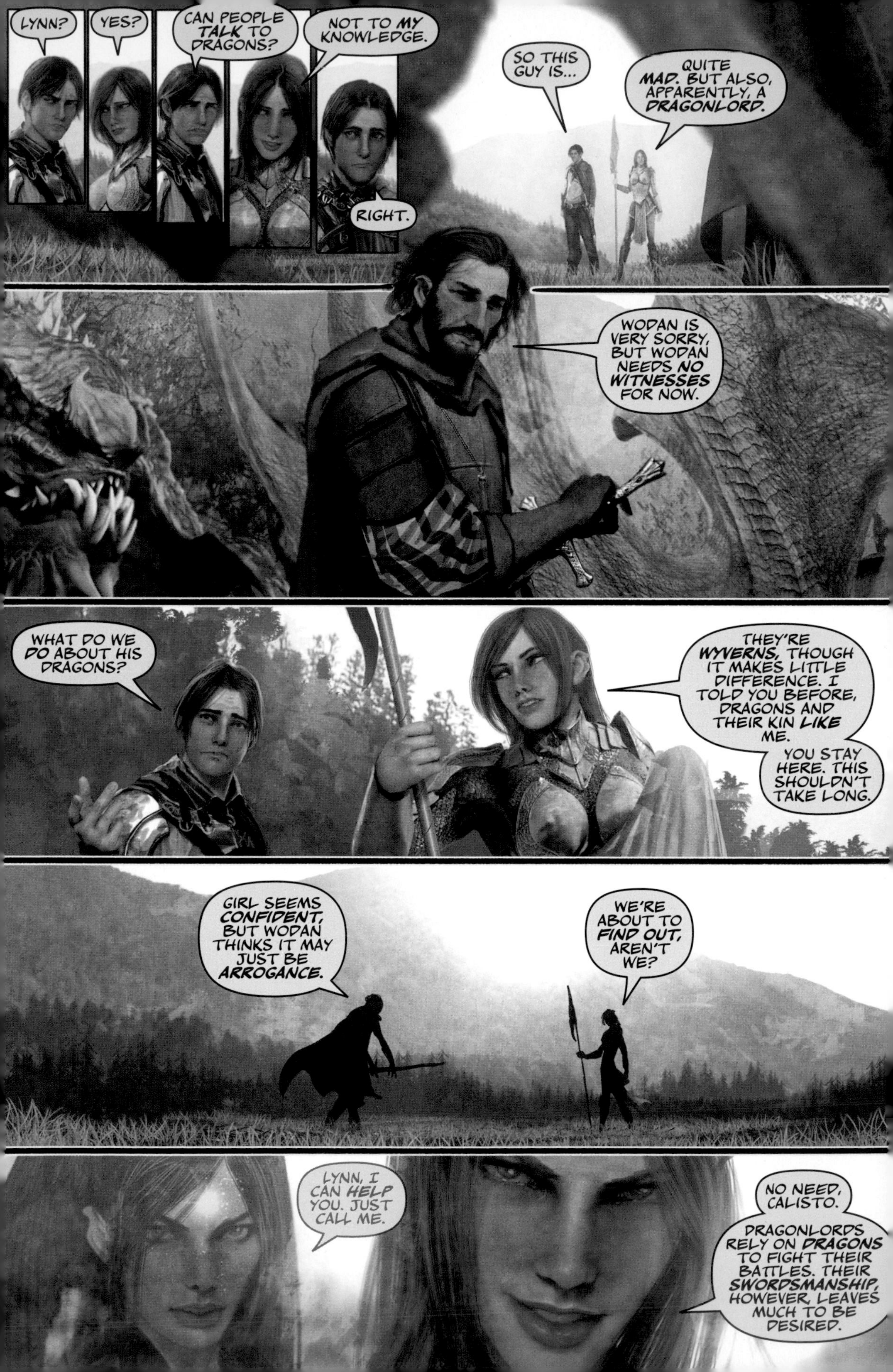
LYNN?
YES?
CAN PEOPLE TALK TO DRAGONS?
NOT TO MY KNOWLEDGE.
RIGHT.
SO THIS GUY IS...
QUITE MAD. BUT ALSO, APPARENTLY, A DRAGONLORD.
WODAN IS VERY SORRY, BUT WODAN NEEDS NO WITNESSES FOR NOW.
WHAT DO WE DO ABOUT HIS DRAGONS?
THEY'RE WYVERNS, THOUGH IT MAKES LITTLE DIFFERENCE. I TOLD YOU BEFORE, DRAGONS AND THEIR KIN LIKE ME.
YOU STAY HERE. THIS SHOULDN'T TAKE LONG.
GIRL SEEMS CONFIDENT, BUT WODAN THINKS IT MAY JUST BE ARROGANCE.
WE'RE ABOUT TO FIND OUT, AREN'T WE?
LYNN, I CAN HELP YOU. JUST CALL ME.
NO NEED, CALISTO.
DRAGONLORDS RELY ON DRAGONS TO FIGHT THEIR BATTLES. THEIR SWORDSMANSHIP, HOWEVER, LEAVES MUCH TO BE DESIRED.

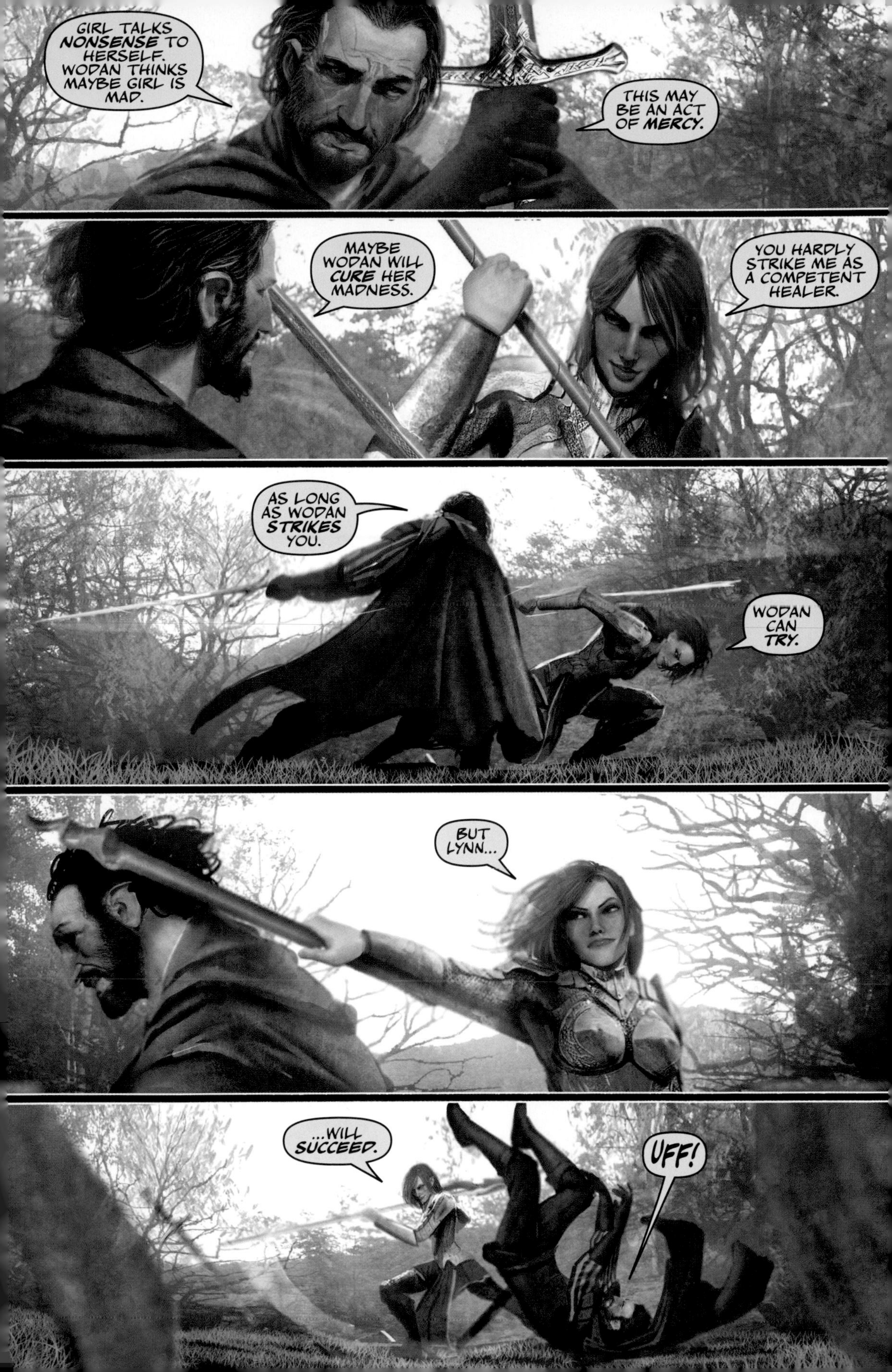
GIRL TALKS NONSENSE TO HERSELF. WODAN THINKS MAYBE GIRL IS MAD.
THIS MAY BE AN ACT OF MERCY.
MAYBE WODAN WILL CURE HER MADNESS.
YOU HARDLY STRIKE ME AS A COMPETENT HEALER.
AS LONG AS WODAN STRIKES YOU.
WODAN CAN TRY.
BUT LYNN...
...WILL SUCCEED.
UFF!

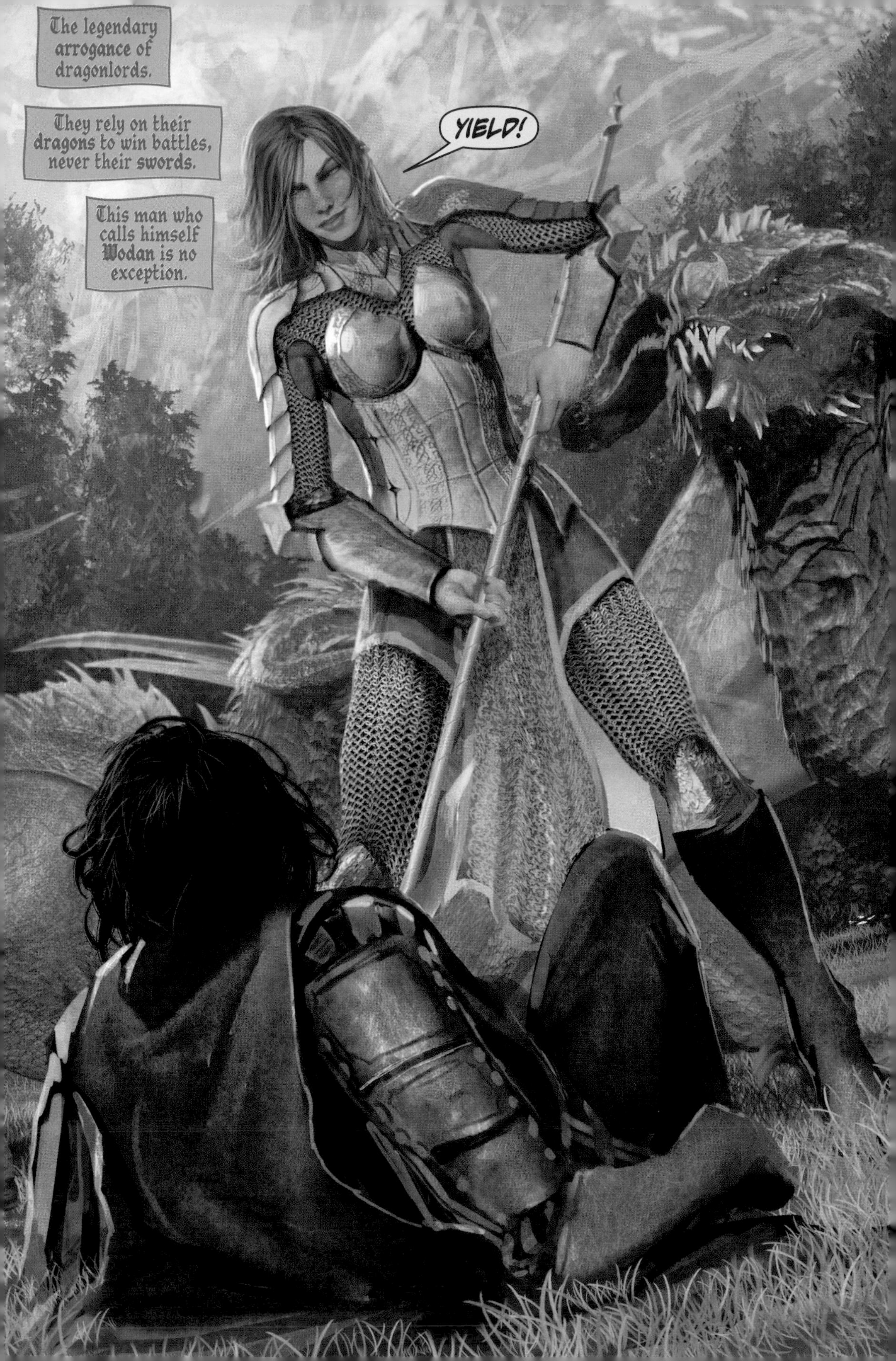
The legendary arrogance of dragonlords.
They rely on their dragons to win battles, never their swords.
YIELD!
This man who calls himself Wodan is no exception.

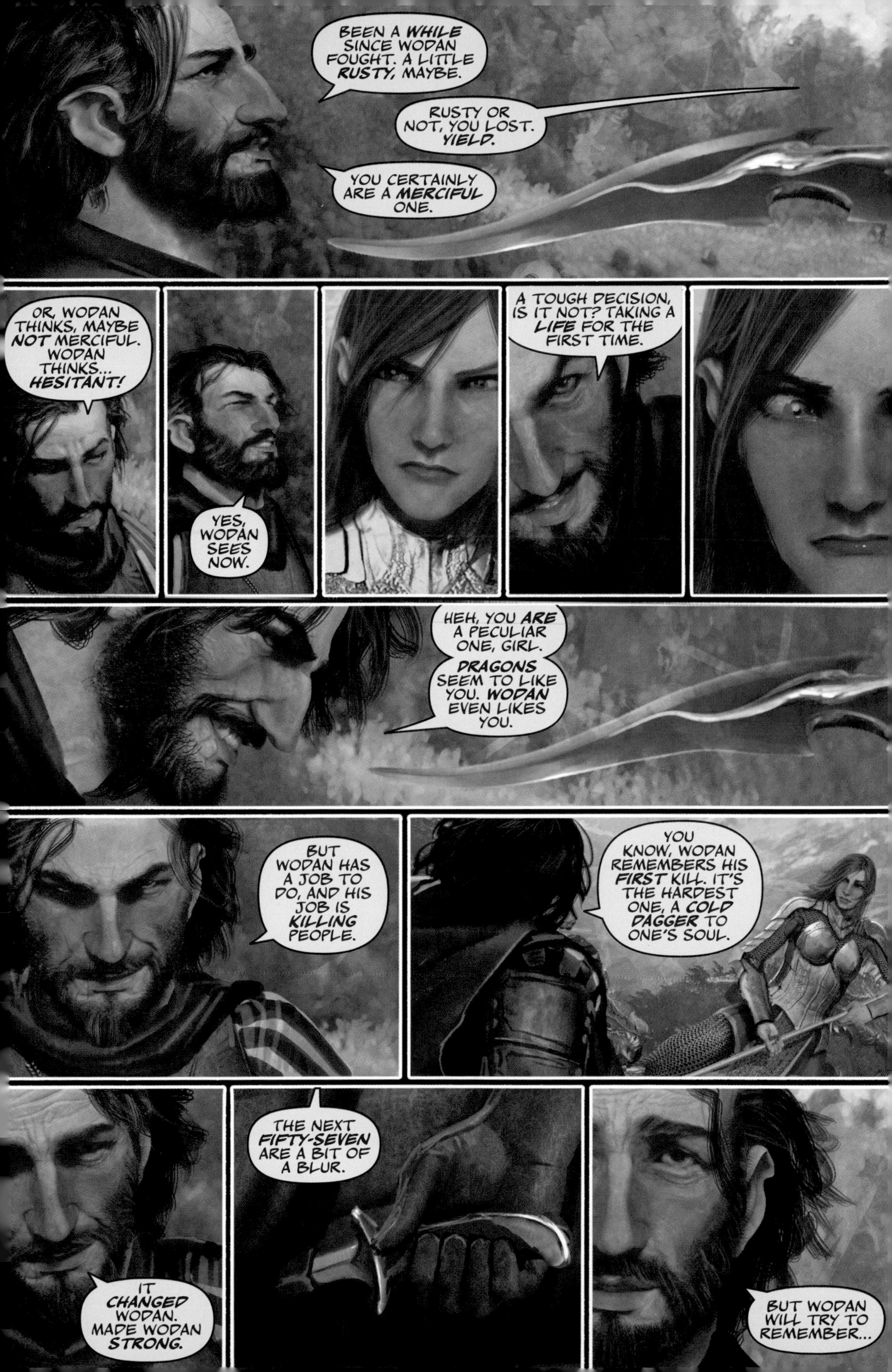

BEEN A WHILE SINCE WODAN FOUGHT. A LITTLE RUSTY, MAYBE.
RUSTY OR NOT, YOU LOST. YIELD.
YOU CERTAINLY ARE A MERCIFUL ONE.
OR, WODAN THINKS, MAYBE NOT MERCIFUL. WODAN THINKS... HESITANT!
YES, WODAN SEES NOW.
A TOUGH DECISION, IS IT NOT? TAKING A LIFE FOR THE FIRST TIME.
HEH, YOU ARE A PECULIAR ONE, GIRL. DRAGONS SEEM TO LIKE YOU. WODAN EVEN LIKES YOU.
BUT WODAN HAS A JOB TO DO, AND HIS JOB IS KILLING PEOPLE.
YOU KNOW, WODAN REMEMBERS HIS FIRST KILL. IT'S THE HARDEST ONE, A COLD DAGGER TO ONE'S SOUL.
IT CHANGED WODAN. MADE WODAN STRONG.
THE NEXT FIFTY-SEVEN ARE A BIT OF A BLUR.
BUT WODAN WILL TRY TO REMEMBER...

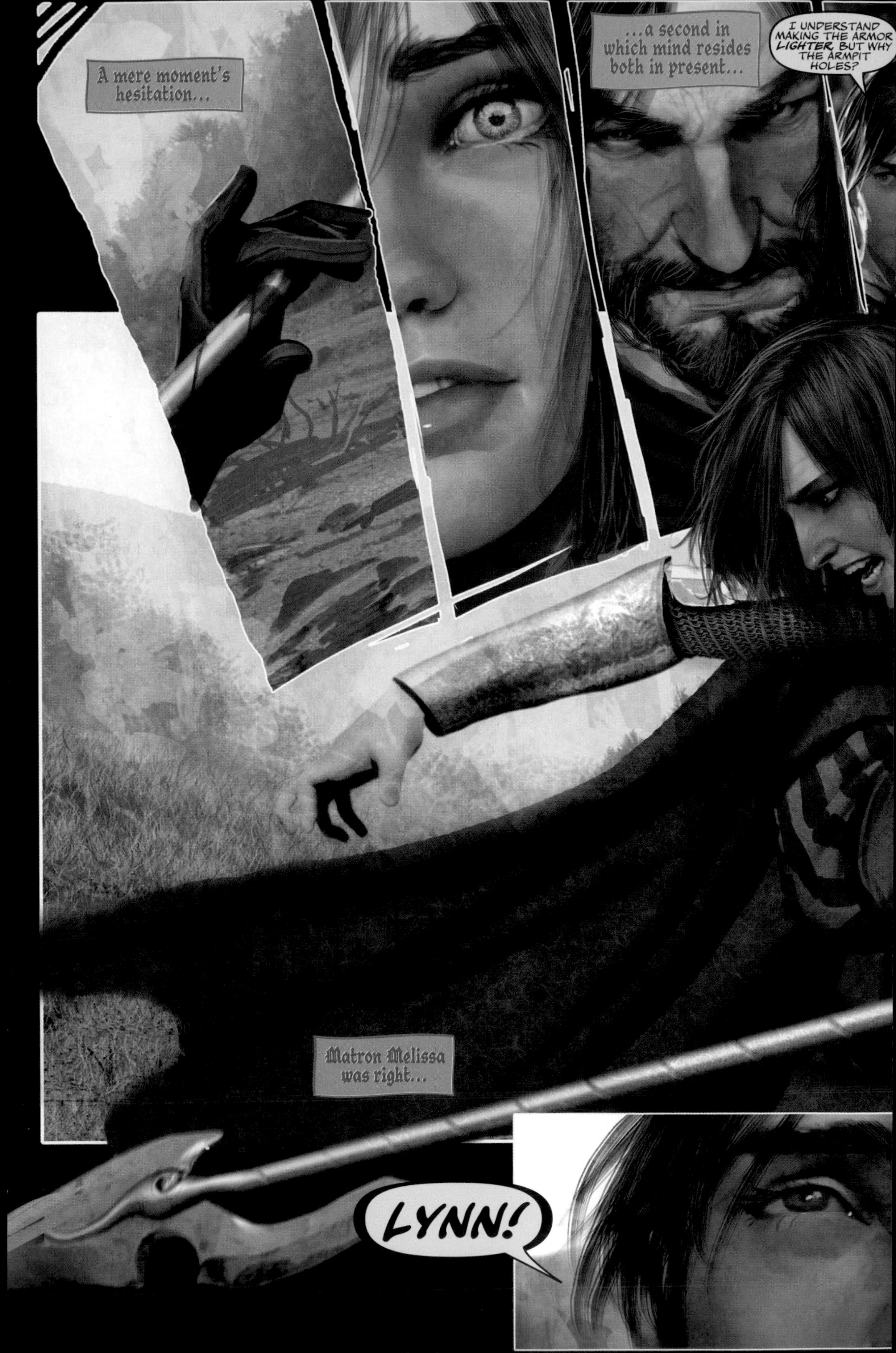
A mere moment's hesitation...
...a second in which mind resides both in present...
I UNDERSTAND MAKING THE ARMOR LIGHTER, BUT WHY THE ARMPIT HOLES?
Matron Melissa was right...
LYNN!

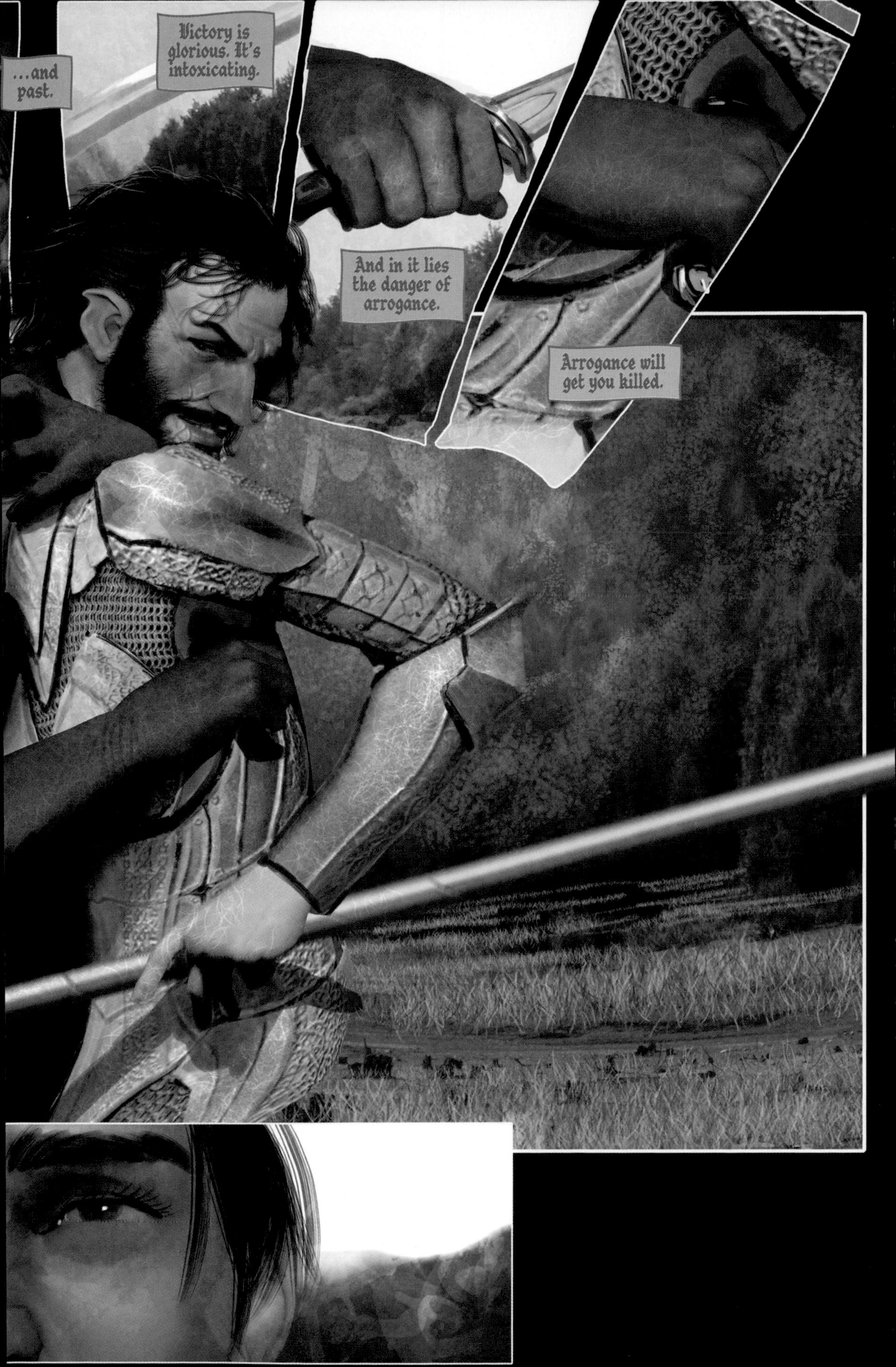
...and past.
Victory is glorious. It's intoxicating.
And in it lies the danger of arrogance.
Arrogance will get you killed.

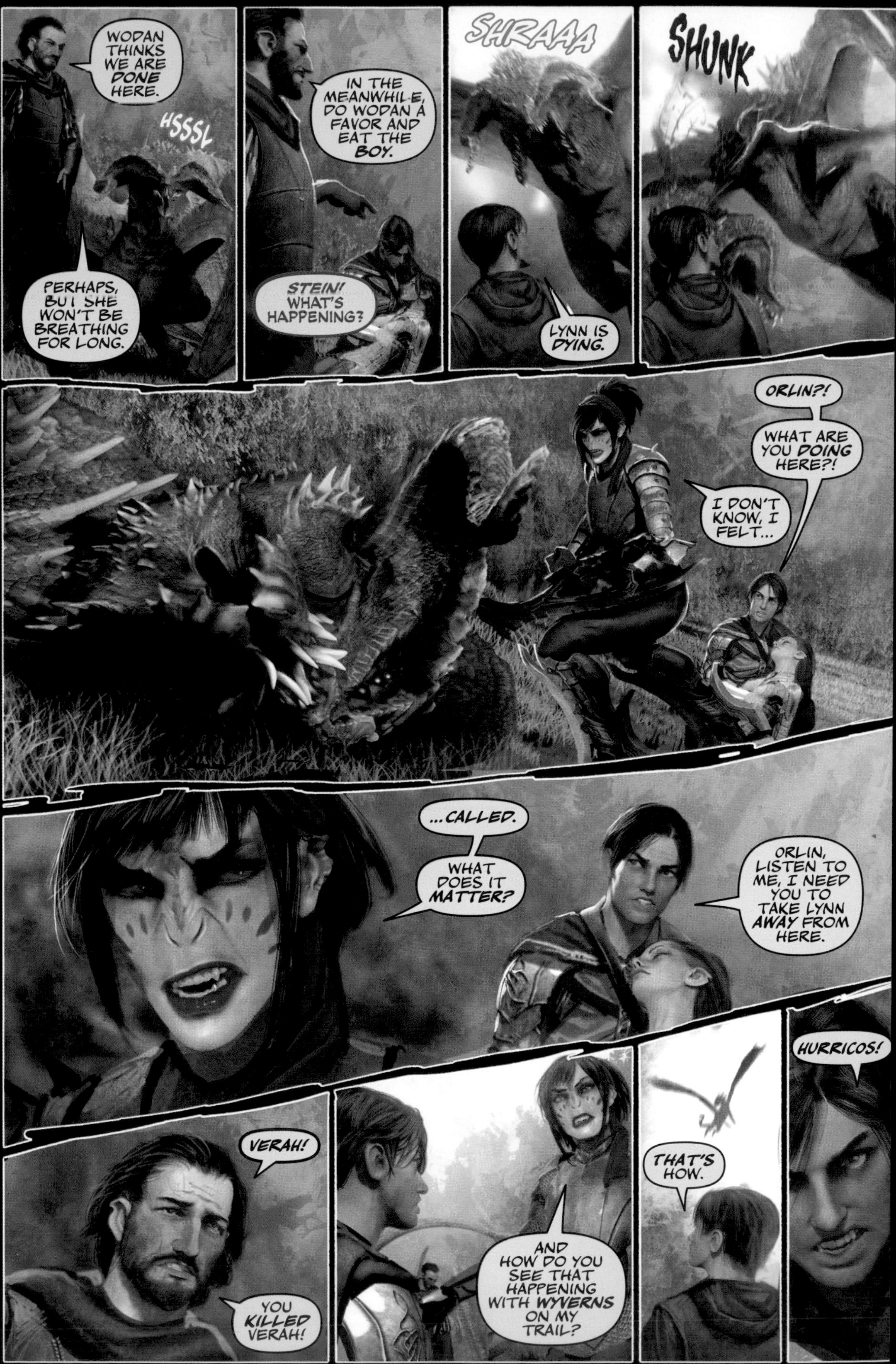

WODAN THINKS WE ARE DONE HERE.
HSSSL
PERHAPS, BUT SHE WON'T BE BREATHING FOR LONG.
IN THE MEANWHILE, DO WODAN A FAVOR AND EAT THE BOY.
STEIN! WHAT'S HAPPENING?
SHRAAA
LYNN IS DYING.
SHUNK
ORLIN?!
WHAT ARE YOU DOING HERE?!
I DON'T KNOW, I FELT...
...CALLED.
WHAT DOES IT MATTER?
ORLIN, LISTEN TO ME, I NEED YOU TO TAKE LYNN AWAY FROM HERE.
VERAH!
YOU KILLED VERAH!
AND HOW DO YOU SEE THAT HAPPENING WITH WYVERNS ON MY TRAIL?
THAT'S HOW.
HURRICOS!

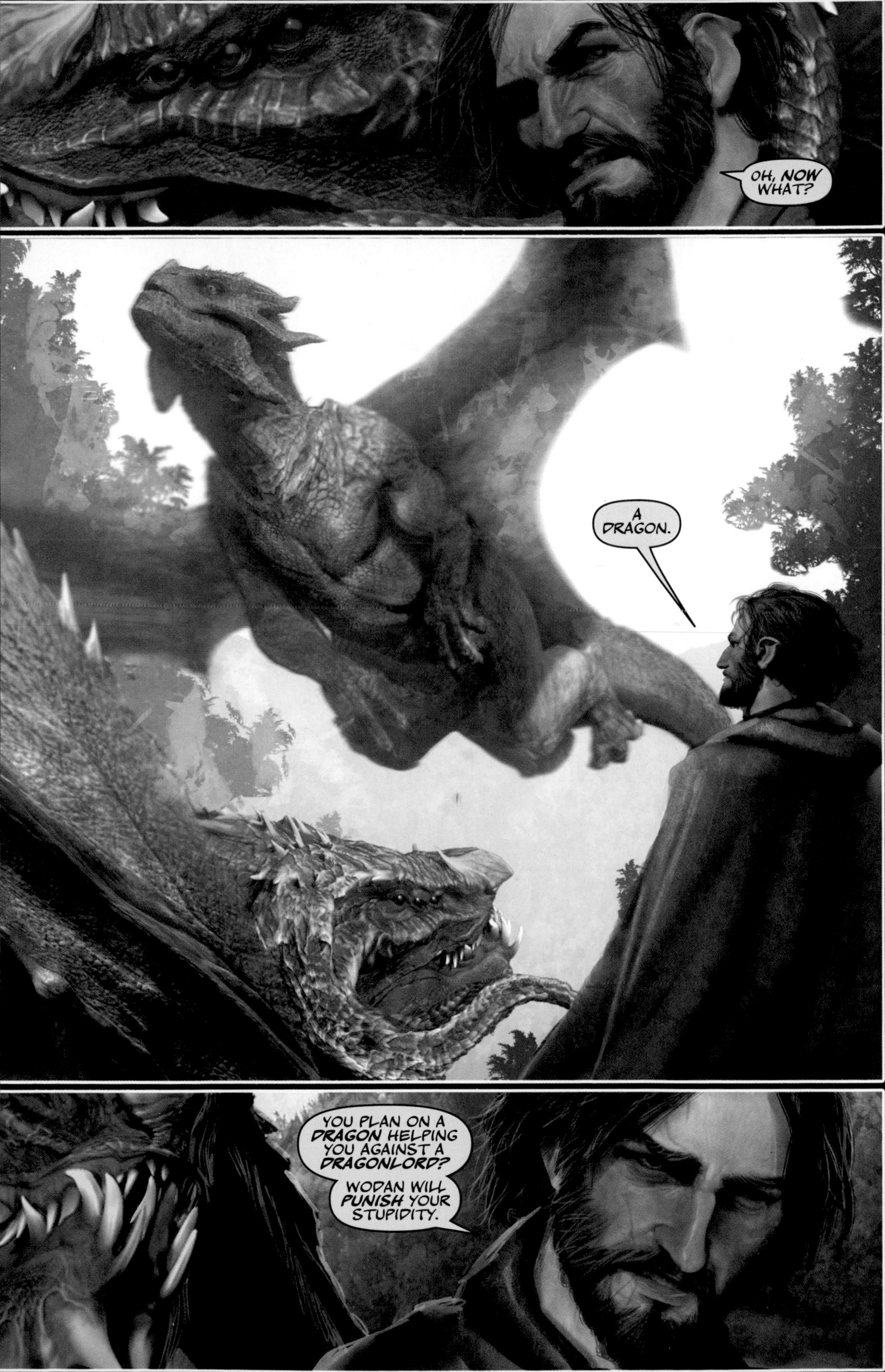
OH, NOW WHAT?
A DRAGON.
YOU PLAN ON A DRAGON HELPING YOU AGAINST A DRAGONLORD?
WODAN WILL PUNISH YOUR STUPIDITY.

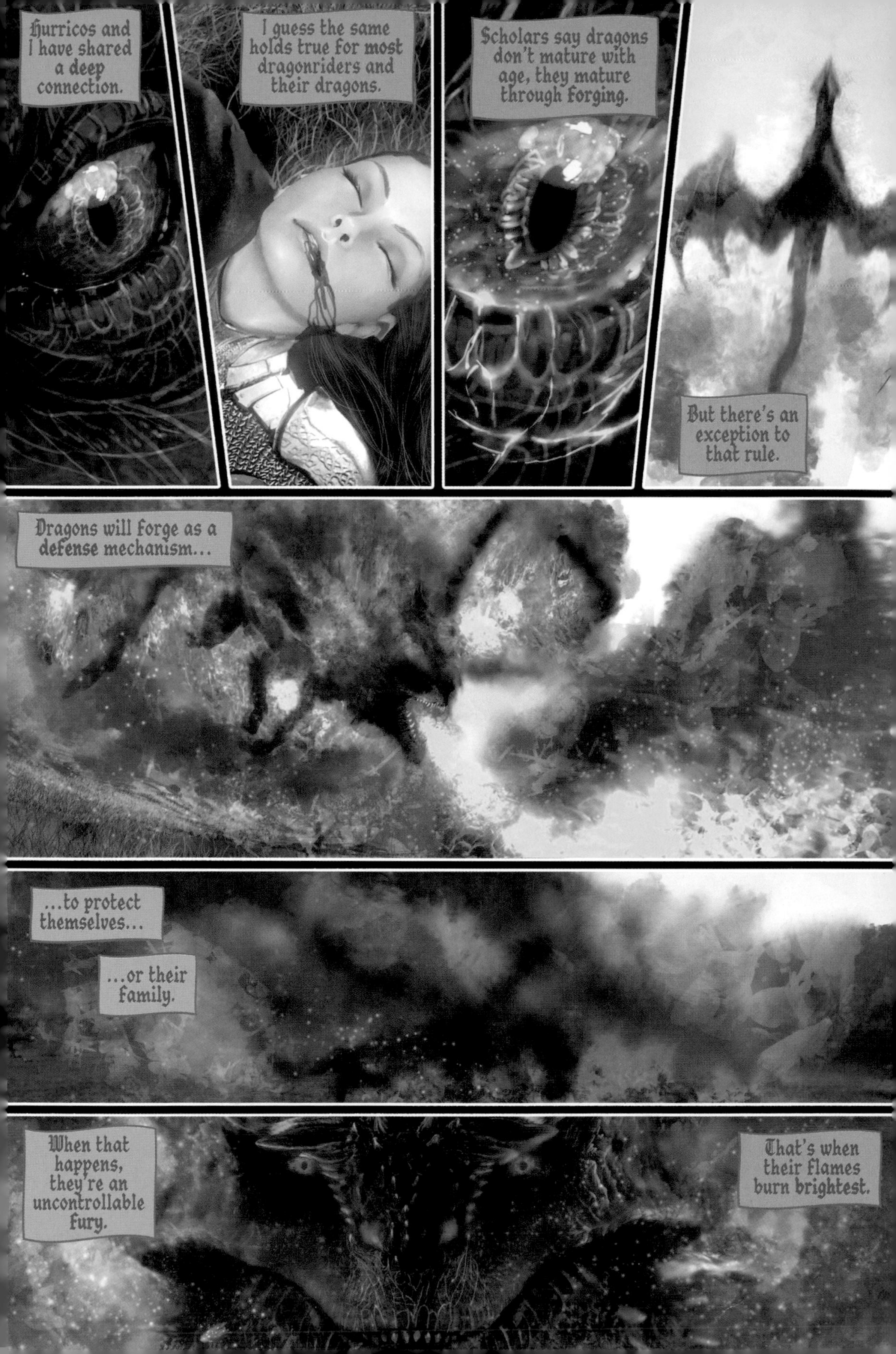
Hurricos and I have shared a deep connection.
I guess the same holds true for most dragonriders and their dragons.
Scholars say dragons don't mature with age, they mature through forging.
But there's an exception to that rule.
Dragons will forge as a defense mechanism...
...to protect themselves...
...or their family.
When that happens, they're an uncontrollable fury.
That's when their flames burn brightest.

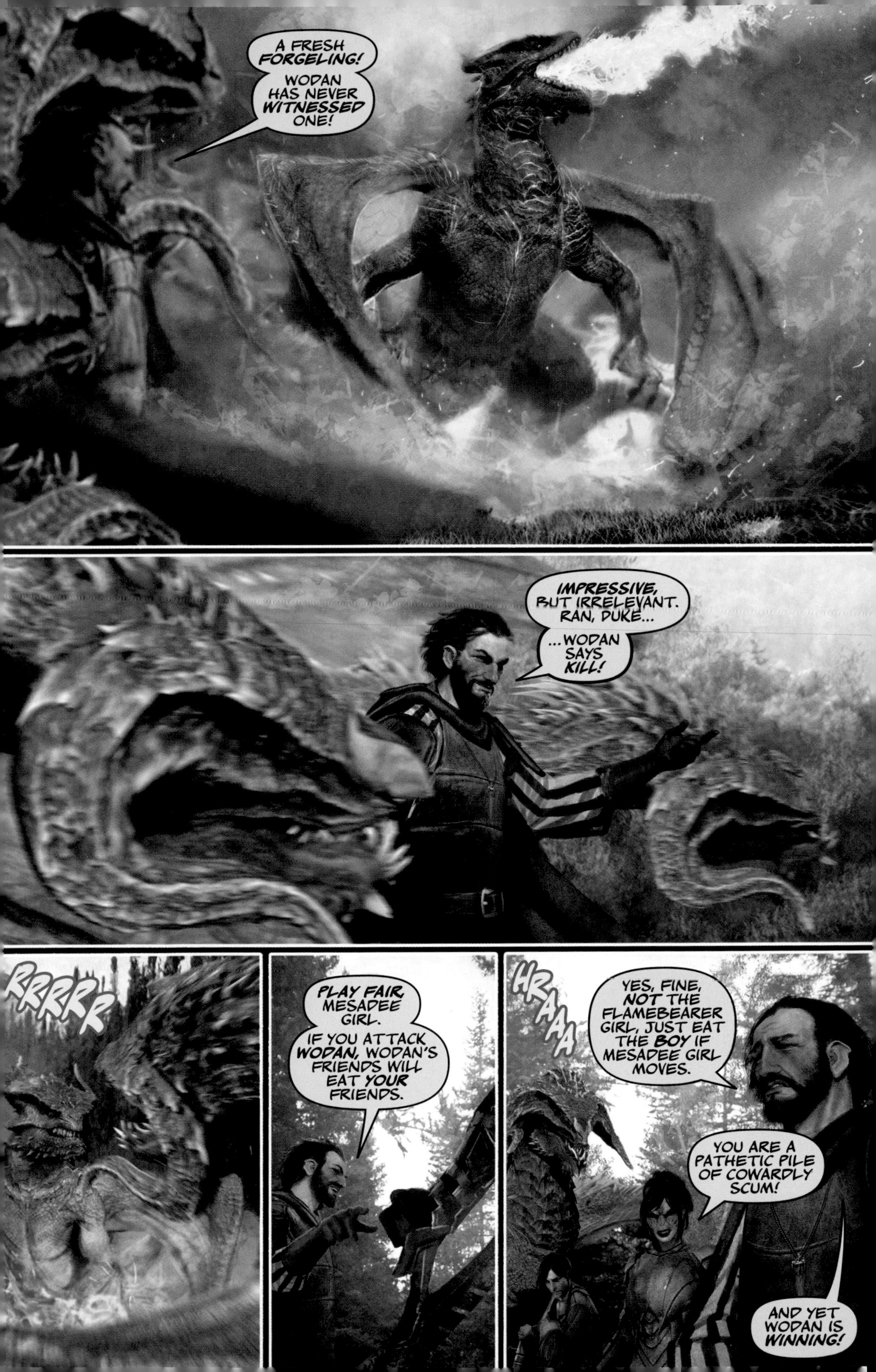
A FRESH FORGELING!
WODAN HAS NEVER WITNESSED ONE!
IMPRESSIVE, BUT IRRELEVANT. RAN, DUKE...
...WODAN SAYS KILL!
RRRRR
PLAY FAIR, MESADEE GIRL.
IF YOU ATTACK WODAN, WODAN'S FRIENDS WILL EAT YOUR FRIENDS.
HRAAA
YES, FINE, NOT THE FLAMEBEARER GIRL, JUST EAT THE BOY IF MESADEE GIRL MOVES.
YOU ARE A PATHETIC PILE OF COWARDLY SCUM!
AND YET WODAN IS WINNING!

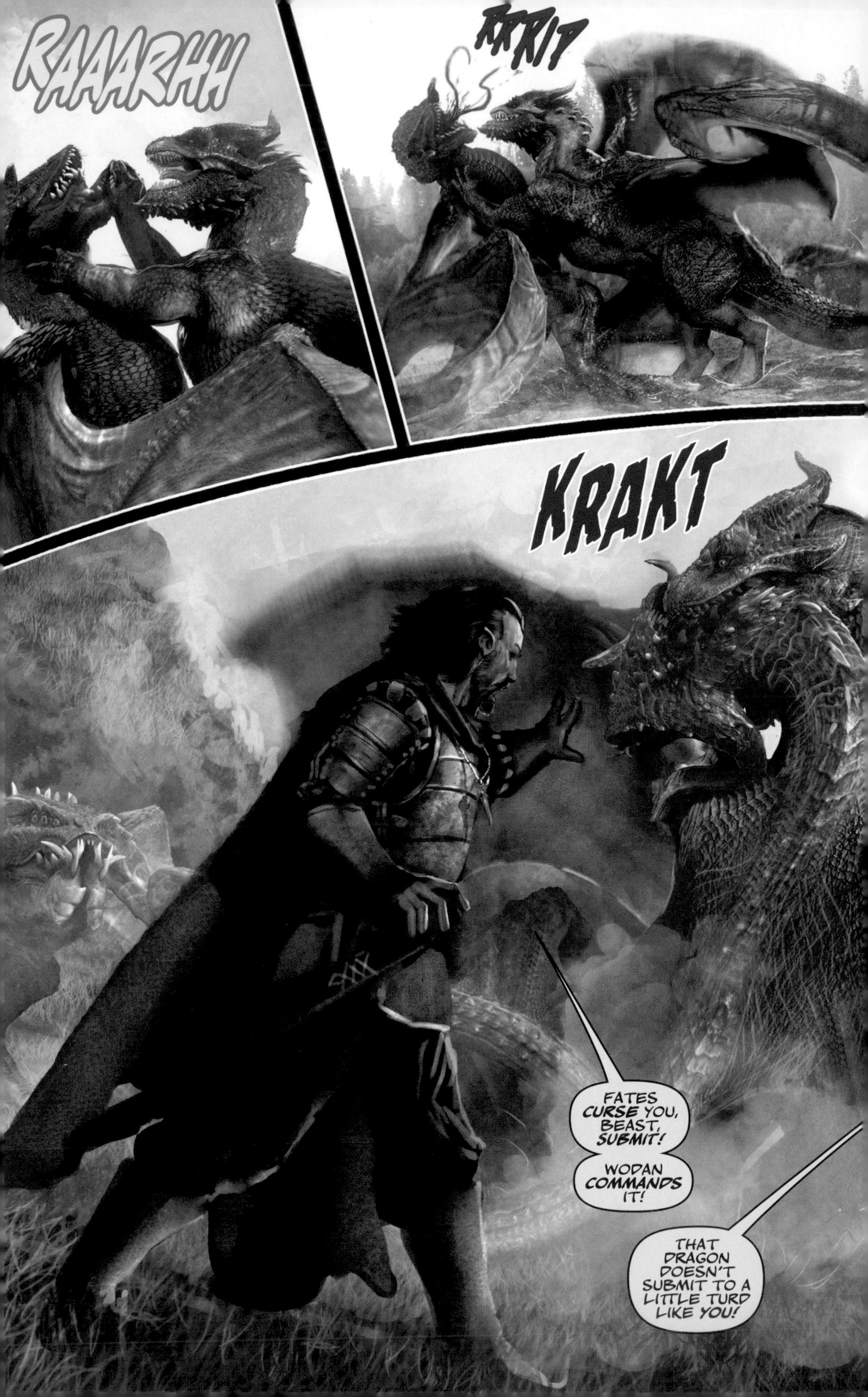
RAAARHH
RRRRIP
KRAKT
FATES CURSE YOU, BEAST, SUBMIT!
WODAN COMMANDS IT!
THAT DRAGON DOESN'T SUBMIT TO A LITTLE TURD LIKE YOU!

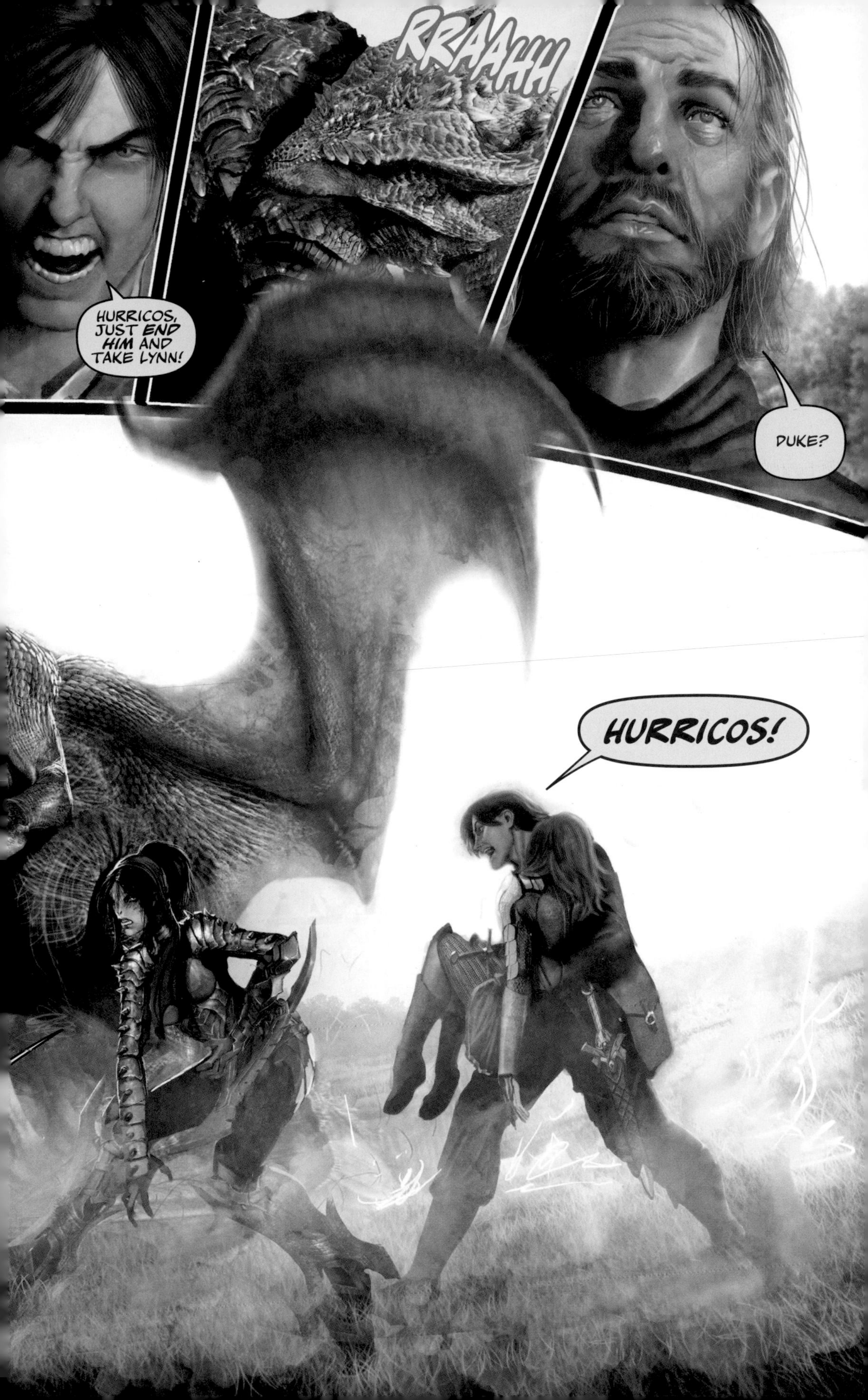
RRAAHH
HURRICOS, JUST END HIM AND TAKE LYNN!
DUKE?
HURRICOS!

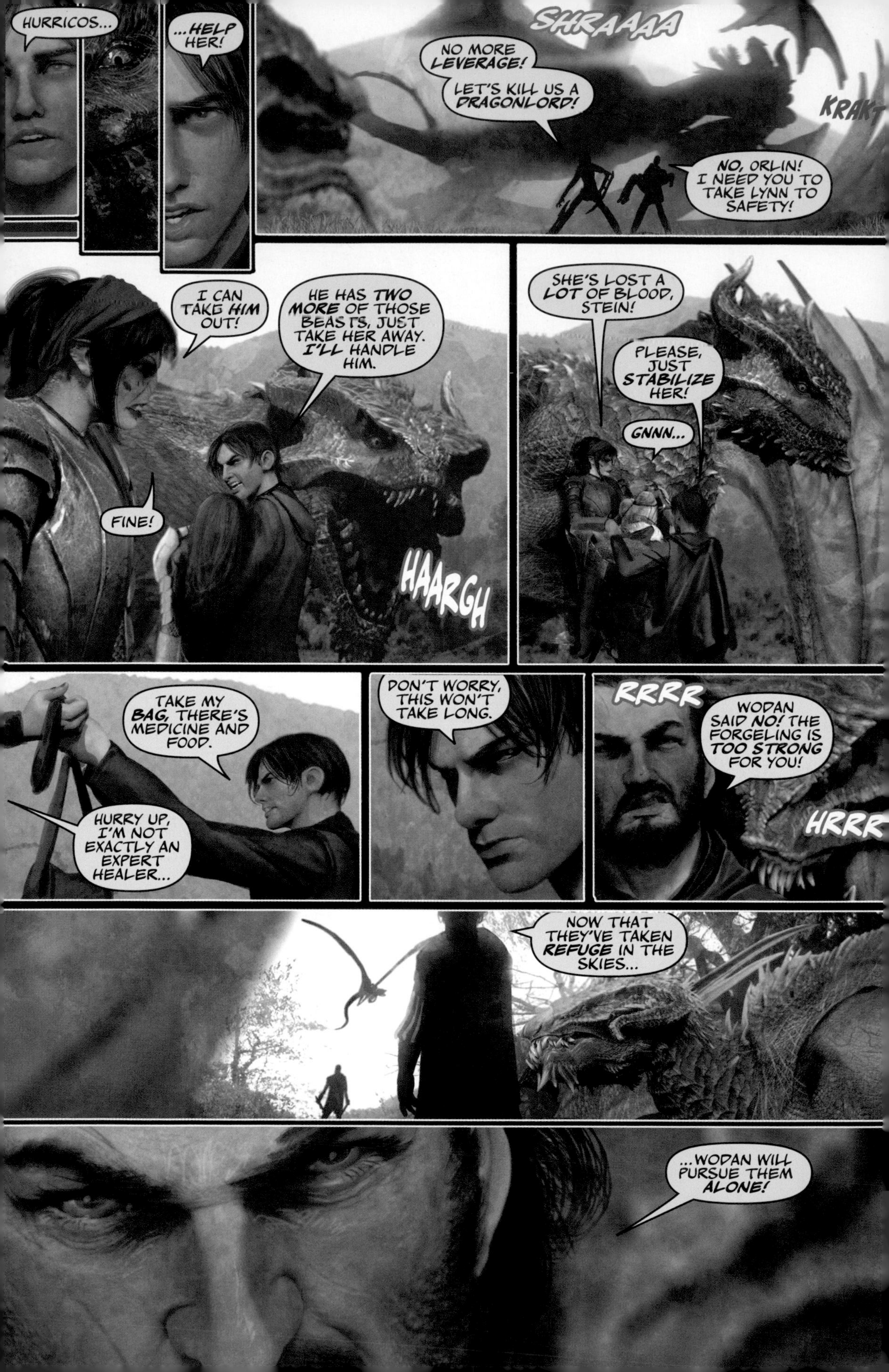
HURRICOS...
...HELP HER!
SHRAAAA
NO MORE LEVERAGE!
LET'S KILL US A DRAGONLORD!
KRAKT
NO, ORLIN! I NEED YOU TO TAKE LYNN TO SAFETY!
I CAN TAKE HIM OUT!
HE HAS TWO MORE OF THOSE BEASTS, JUST TAKE HER AWAY. I'LL HANDLE HIM.
FINE!
HAARGH
SHE'S LOST A LOT OF BLOOD, STEIN!
PLEASE, JUST STABILIZE HER!
GNNN...
TAKE MY BAG, THERE'S MEDICINE AND FOOD.
HURRY UP, I'M NOT EXACTLY AN EXPERT HEALER...
DON'T WORRY, THIS WON'T TAKE LONG.
RRRR
WODAN SAID NO! THE FORGELING IS TOO STRONG FOR YOU!
HRRR
NOW THAT THEY'VE TAKEN REFUGE IN THE SKIES...
...WODAN WILL PURSUE THEM ALONE!

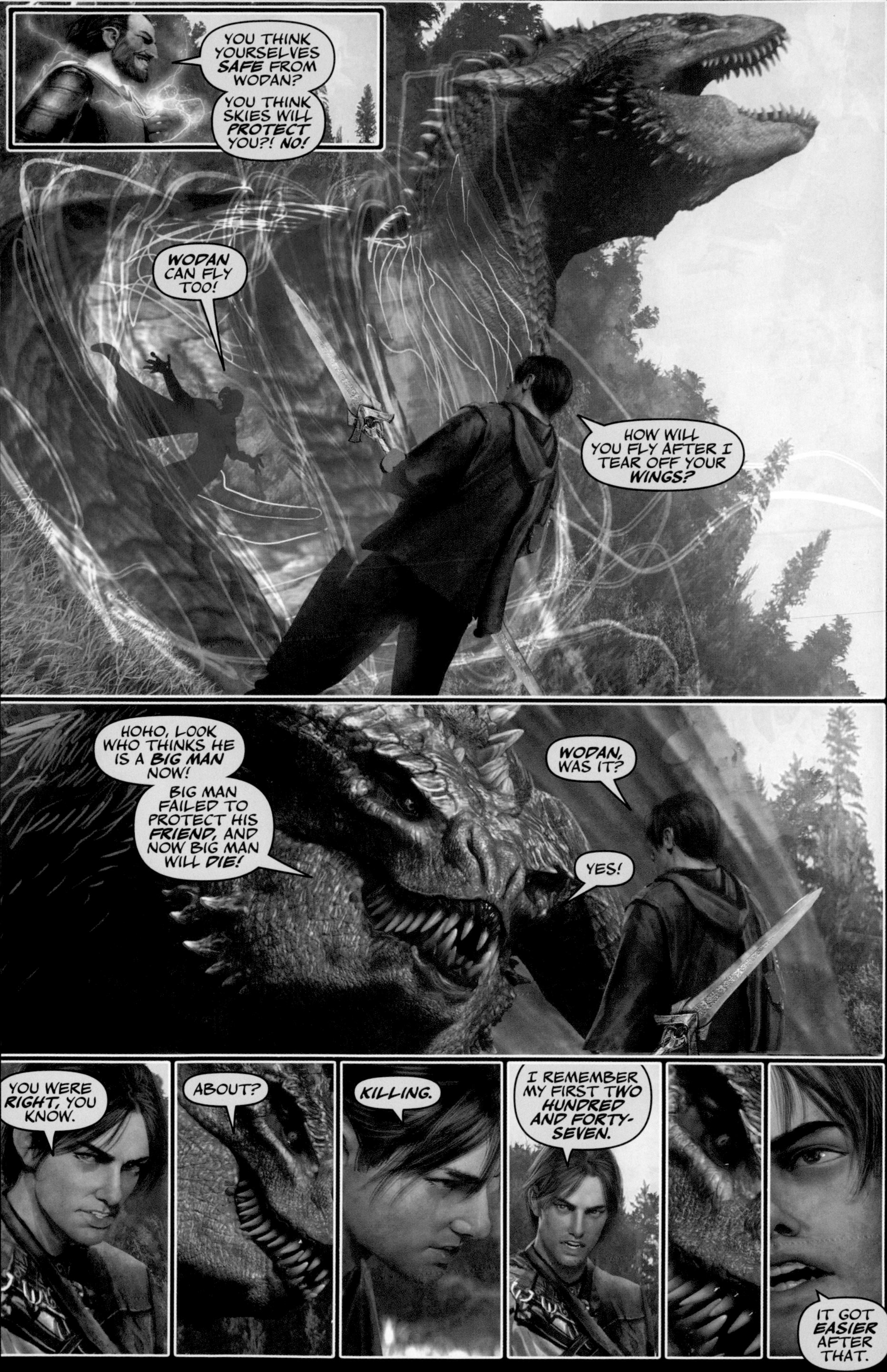
YOU THINK YOURSELVES SAFE FROM WODAN?
YOU THINK SKIES WILL PROTECT YOU?! NO!
WODAN CAN FLY TOO!
HOW WILL YOU FLY AFTER I TEAR OFF YOUR WINGS?
HOHO, LOOK WHO THINKS HE IS A BIG MAN NOW!
BIG MAN FAILED TO PROTECT HIS FRIEND, AND NOW BIG MAN WILL DIE!
WODAN, WAS IT?
YES!
YOU WERE RIGHT, YOU KNOW.
ABOUT?
KILLING.
I REMEMBER MY FIRST TWO HUNDRED AND FORTY-SEVEN.
IT GOT EASIER AFTER THAT.

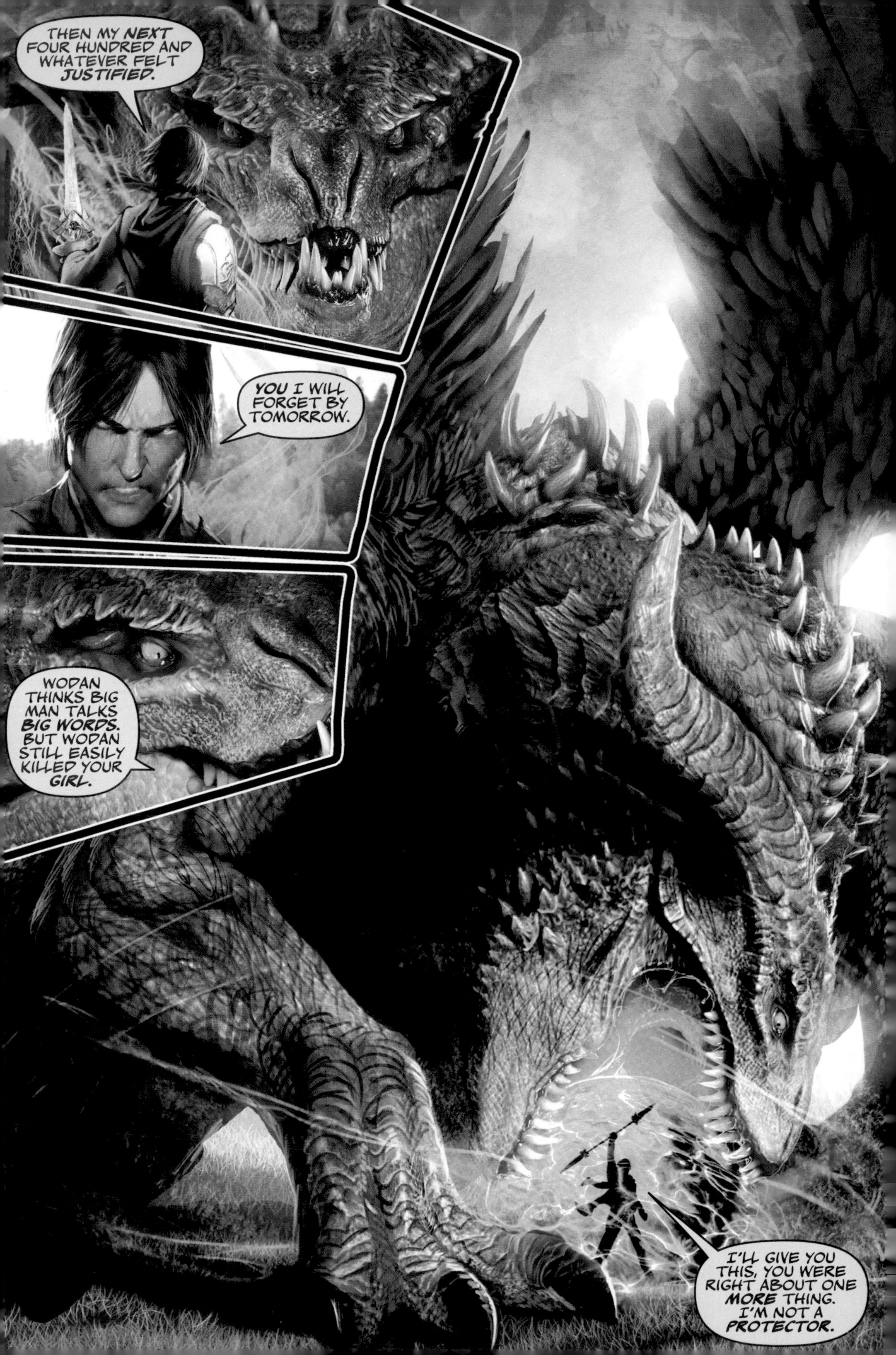
THEN MY NEXT FOUR HUNDRED AND WHATEVER FELT JUSTIFIED.
YOU I WILL FORGET BY TOMORROW.
WODAN THINKS BIG MAN TALKS BIG WORDS. BUT WODAN STILL EASILY KILLED YOUR GIRL.
I'LL GIVE YOU THIS, YOU WERE RIGHT ABOUT ONE MORE THING. I'M NOT A PROTECTOR.

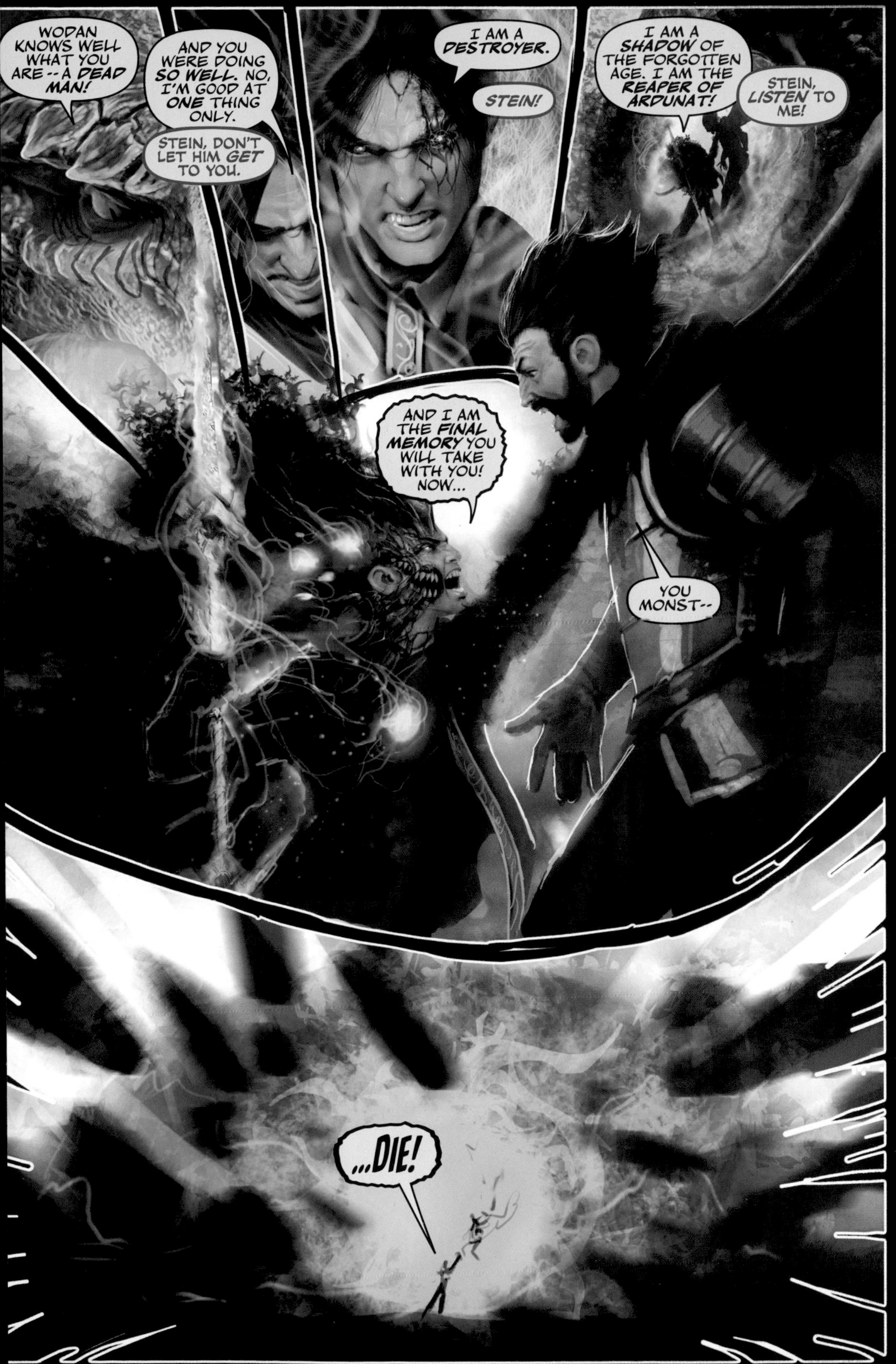
WODAN KNOWS WELL WHAT YOU ARE--A DEAD MAN!
AND YOU WERE DOING SO WELL. NO, I'M GOOD AT ONE THING ONLY.
STEIN, DON'T LET HIM GET TO YOU.
I AM A DESTROYER.
STEIN!
I AM A SHADOW OF THE FORGOTTEN AGE. I AM THE REAPER OF ARDUNAT!
STEIN, LISTEN TO ME!
AND I AM THE FINAL MEMORY YOU WILL TAKE WITH YOU! NOW...
YOU MONST--
...DIE!

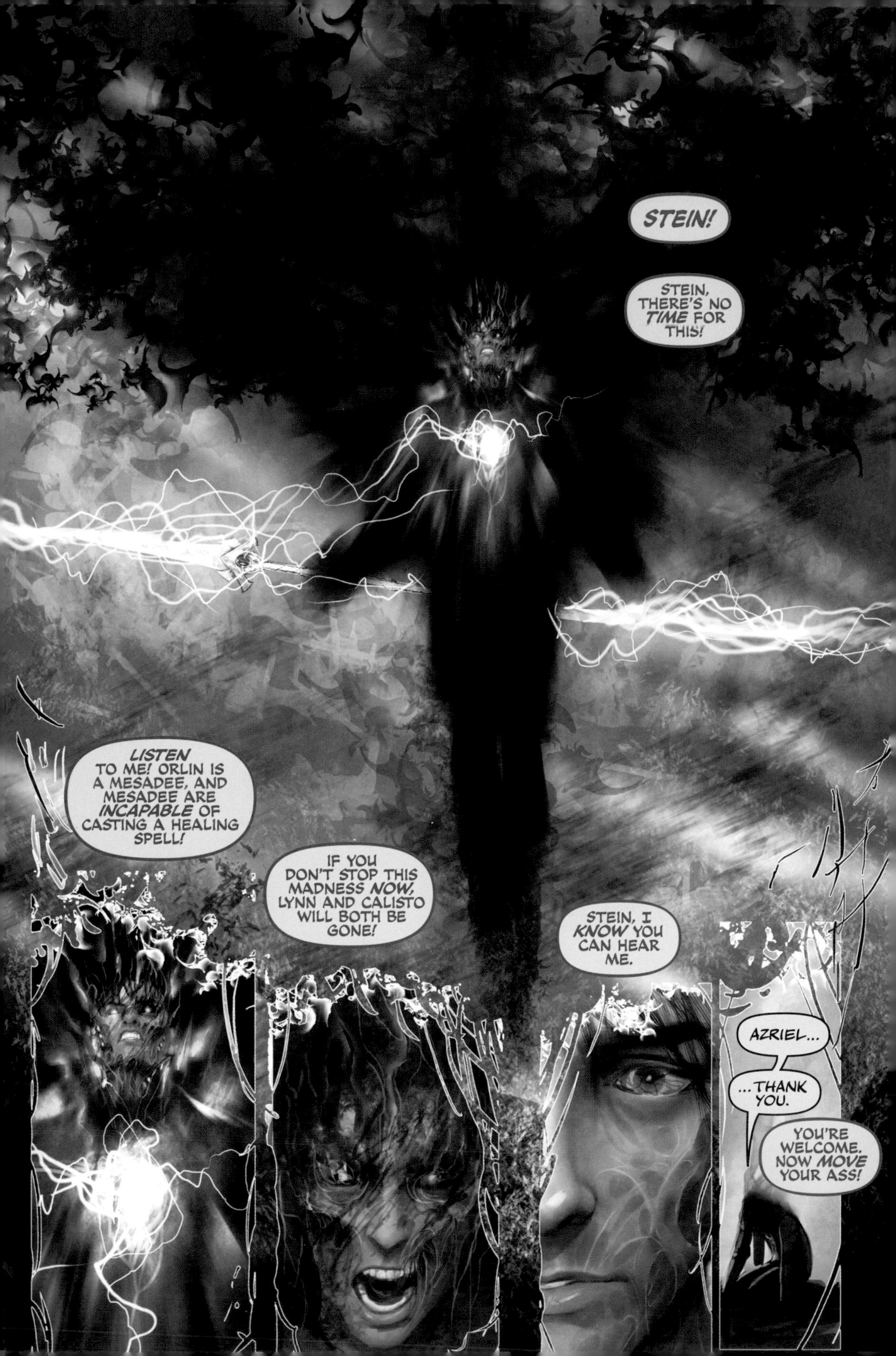
STEIN!
STEIN, THERE'S NO TIME FOR THIS!
LISTEN TO ME! ORLIN IS A MESADEE, AND MESADEE ARE INCAPABLE OF CASTING A HEALING SPELL!
IF YOU DON'T STOP THIS MADNESS NOW, LYNN AND CALISTO WILL BOTH BE GONE!
STEIN, I KNOW YOU CAN HEAR ME.
AZRIEL...
...THANK YOU.
YOU'RE WELCOME. NOW MOVE YOUR ASS!

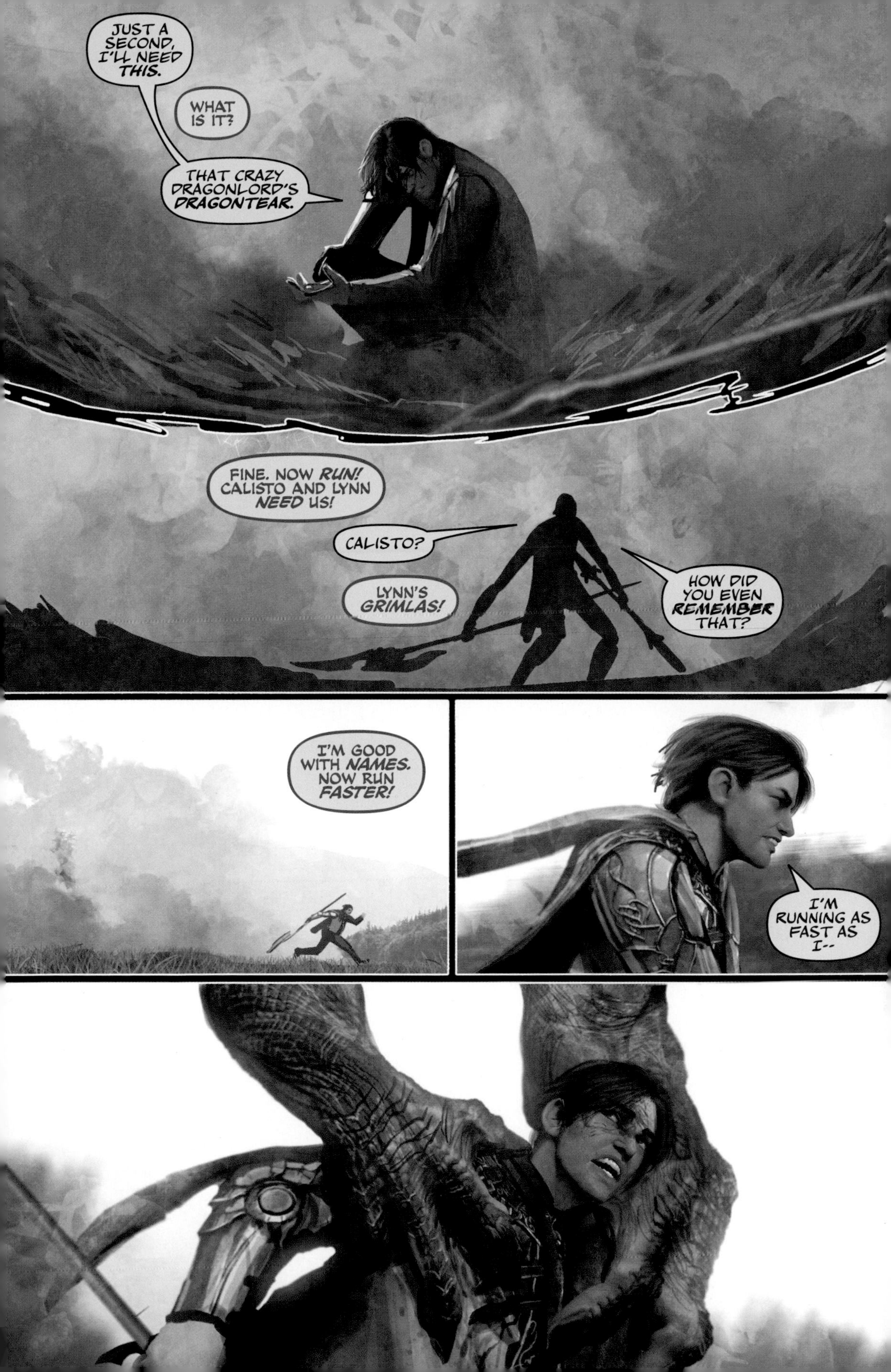
JUST A SECOND, I'LL NEED THIS.
WHAT IS IT?
THAT CRAZY DRAGONLORD'S DRAGONTEAR.
FINE. NOW RUN! CALISTO AND LYNN NEED US!
CALISTO?
LYNN'S GRIMLAS!
HOW DID YOU EVEN REMEMBER THAT?
I'M GOOD WITH NAMES. NOW RUN FASTER!
I'M RUNNING AS FAST AS I--

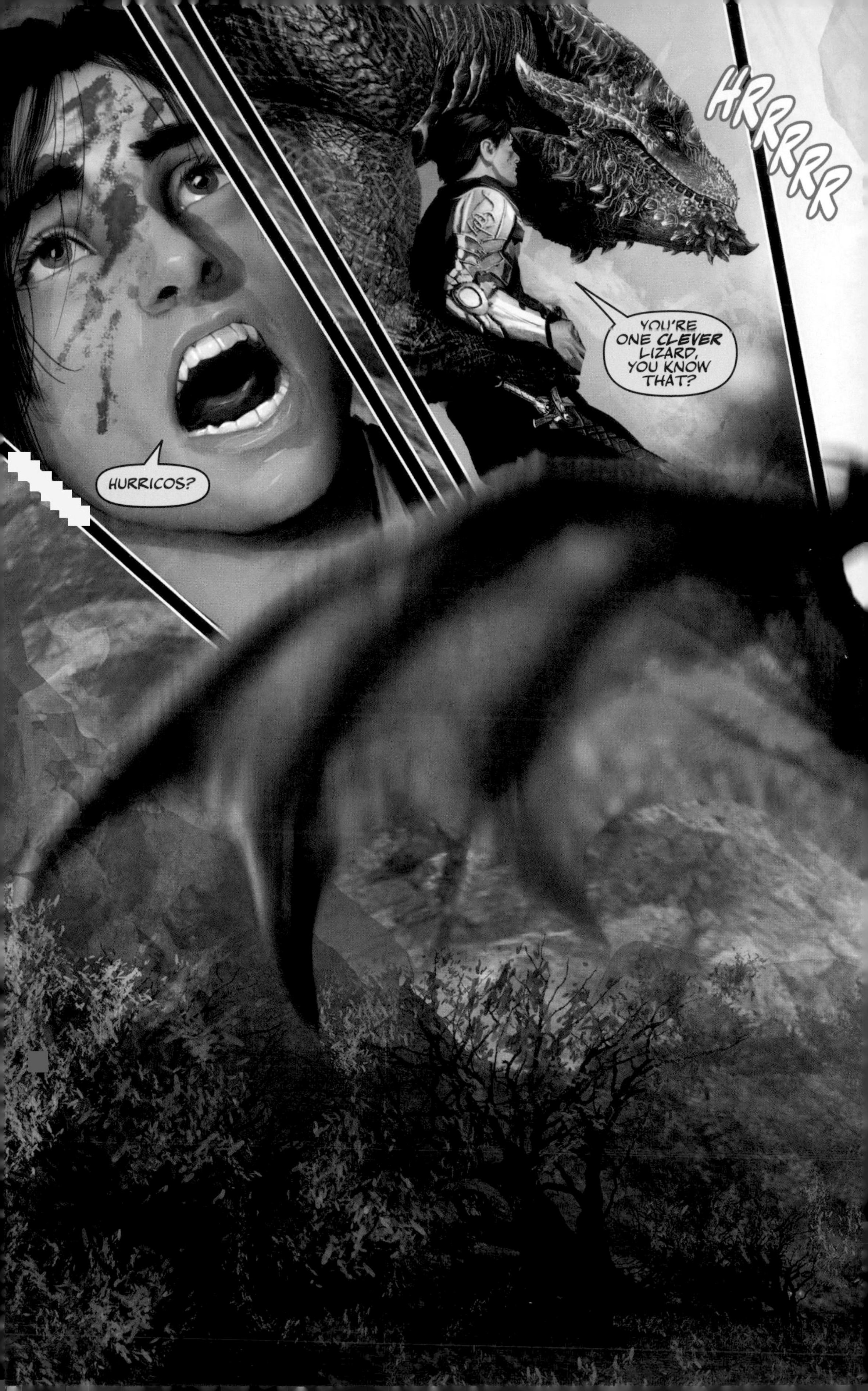
HRRRRRR
YOU'RE ONE CLEVER LIZARD, YOU KNOW THAT?
HURRICOS?

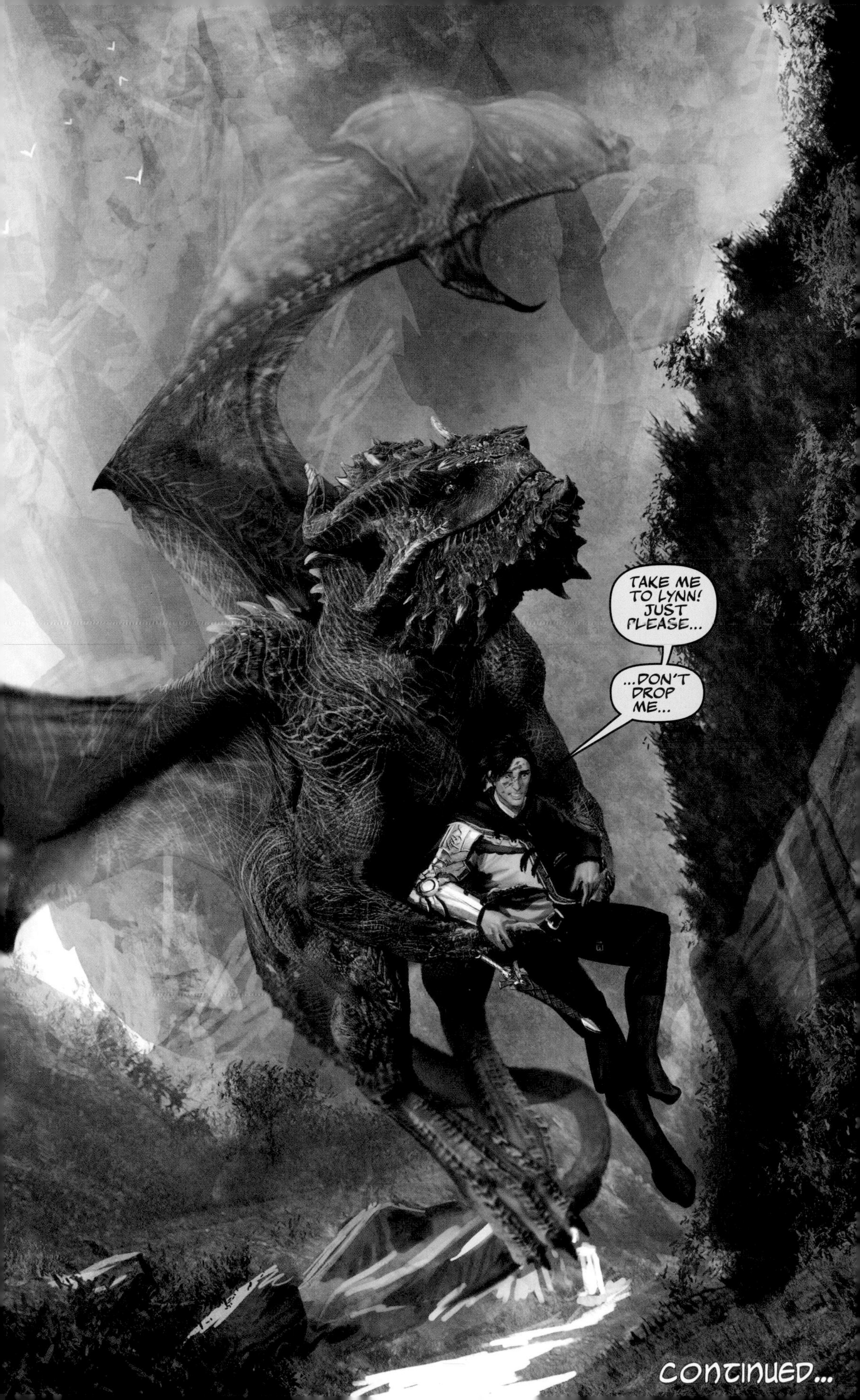
TAKE ME TO LYNN! JUST PLEASE...
...DON'T DROP ME...
CONTINUED...

APPENDIX

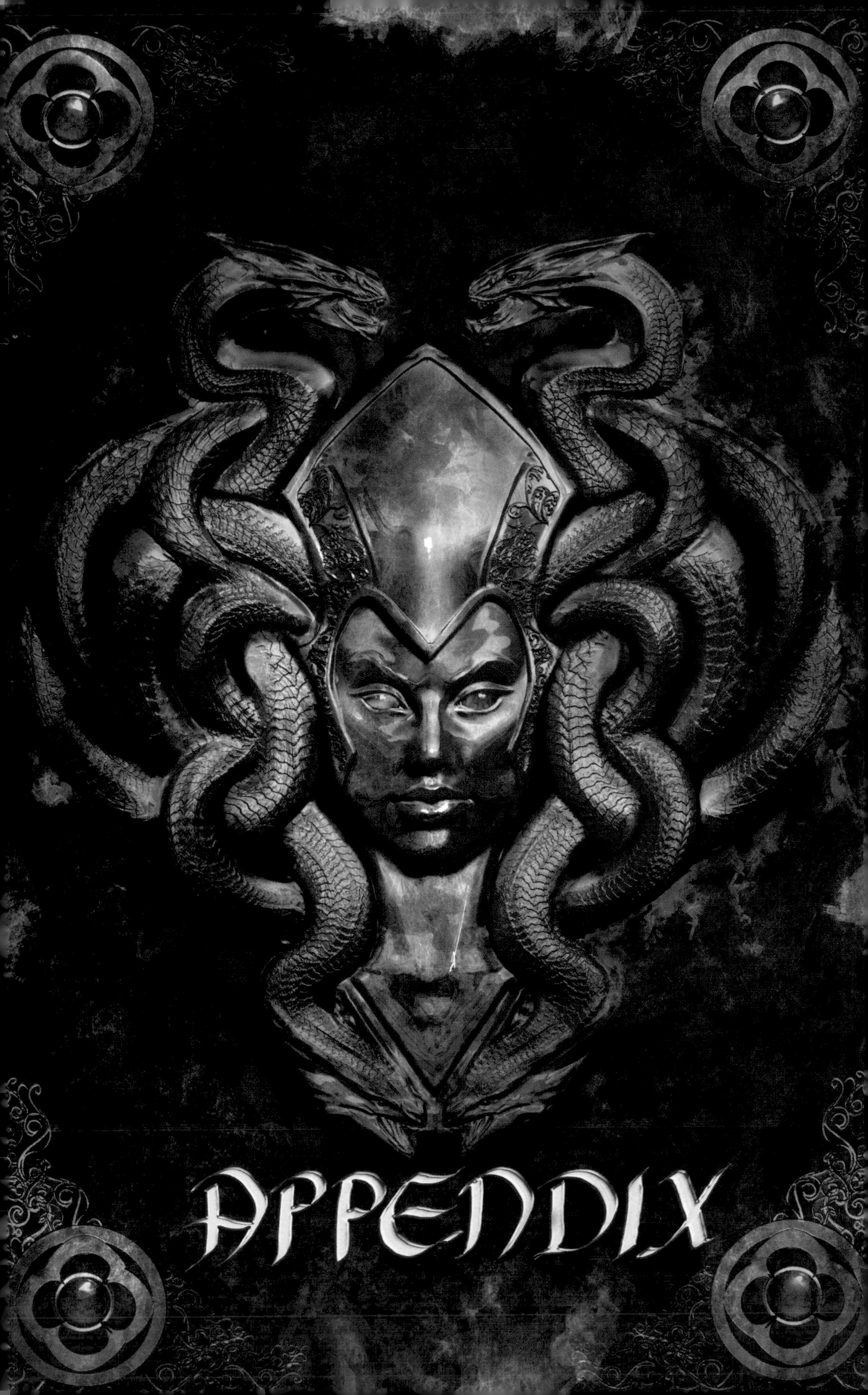

Glossary

Aertes: Called Aertes of the Fates, goddess and servant of destiny. She is referred to by Damanulites as the deaf goddess, as she is unlikely to answer prayers.

Ardunat: One of the two fallen kingdoms of Ravine, destroyed by the second Necryte, known only as the Reaper of Ardunat.

Arenian Wraith: A magic- and wind-controlled warboat of the Arenian empire. Arenians successfully controlled all the great rivers of their empire.

Badrunim Priest: High-ranking warrior priest in the service of Azhi Damanul.

Casta Palladia: Kingdom and fortress bearing the same name since the time of the Muraman barbarian kings. Considered unconquerable because of the presence of the god under the mountain. Muraman translation: unbroken star.

Crows: Fragments of souls of the dead that attach themselves to the killer. They are harmless by nature, and invisible to the naked eye.

Damanul: Living god of the mountain, sealed under Mount Palladron. He protects Palladia, and is considered the hidden power of the Alliance.

Deep Sight: A complex, hard-to-master technique inherently linked to the Shivas. Users can agitate necra within their eyes, and see the crows that follow anyone who has ever killed a person.

Dragonlord: Of the bloodline of Worgal, gifted with the ability of dragonmind, enabling them to give simple orders to dragons, and organize their actions in battle.

Dragoon's Boon: A Dregyan medicine based on old Sardaheim recipes. It is used to preempt sky illness, although it has a violent impact on the digestive system of anyone who takes it.

Dragontear: A crystalline formation within a dragon's throat, used to generate the firebreath. It grows stronger with a dragon's forging. In time, other traits have been discovered.

Dragoon: Dragon rider. The kingdom of Dregya is known for producing the best dragoons.

Driplets: Chunks of deep-fried pig fat. Often referred to as mage's salvation, because daily maga is regenerated through food and rest. An efficient snack like driplets is highly valued by all spellcasters.

Eani: Also called starfolk, people of the old world who followed the great exodus of dragons. Immortal, though weaker in spellcasting than people of Ravine.

Faetree: Massive tree in Palladia that judges those who would seal the weapons embedded in it. It's said the roots reach to the heart of all worlds.

Forging: Natural process of dragon maturation. The first forge gives dragons their breath, and layers their scales with tellas. It also gives them stronger bones, enabling them to wingwalk.

Grimlas: Weapon of another world, those who seal it become wanderers. Muraman translation: fated.

Grimlas Avendati: Spirit chosen by fates to serve as a wanderer's guide. Muraman translation: fated spirit.

Hannum: Official title of the ruler of Waroda, most technologically-developed kingdom of the Alliance.

Maga: Muraman translation: life force.

Magic: Manipulation of necra through use of one's life force.

Necra: That of which all is made. Muraman translation: matter.

Necryte: An abberation of magic, a mage who neither pays for spells with life force, nor can aim spells. The lonely nature of their existence makes them prone to madness.

Palladian Alliance: Formed to oppose the threat of the Necryte, Varda Ballahad, it originally included the kingdoms of Palladia, Wranthorn, Waroda , Dregya, Areni, Kaddan and Ardunat.

Praetorian Guard: Elite guard to King Godwyn of Palladia, led by High Praetorean Antheus Prayne.

Raj: A Sardaheim high emissary, functioning as an ambassador.

Ravine: Name by which most call the continent of Harrak. Thus renamed because of the ravine in the Saradrion Empire, through which the old world's denizens first entered.

Rimad Gregorius: Leader of the church of Damanul. Muraman translation: mountain blessed.

Ripper: A Mesadee elite guard and assassin in the service of Saradrion empire.

Runeglass: Originally a Sardaheim creation, but copied by many. A tracker that is used in combination with maga branding, also called a tracking rune.

Runenos: Long rumored to be the location of dragon tombs, but never found. Dragons jealously guard their dead.

Sealing: The act of marking a weapon with one's own life force. It synchronizes the user and the weapon for balanced spellwork.

Sky Illness: Dragonflight has a way of reducing the rider's body temperature drastically, even in summertime. For this reason, dragonflight generally is avoided at all costs once the rains arrive. Coldness bites at a rider's very breath, stealing it away, along with the rider's life.

Tellas: Metallic substance derived from dragon scales, strengthened each time a dragon forges. Tellas of fifth rank (forging) is more valuable than any other metal. Harvested from molting dragons, it's said that the Runenos tomb holds the greatest concentration of tellas.

Trueform: The ability of a dragonlord to use the dragontear of a dead dragon to claim the beast's form.

Wade: A trading metropolis that has been a center of trade routes for the entire continent of Harrak. It had been held for centuries by Arenian invaders, only to be freed from them seven years ago through the combined efforts of rebels and the Reaper of Ardunat.

Wanderer: Paragon of fate, changer of destinies, who bears the grimlas weapon.

Wyvern: Lesser dragonkin. They are savage, faster than dragons, but unable to forge. They are born with a static dragontear, which means their firebreath does not gain power with age.

Cast of Characters

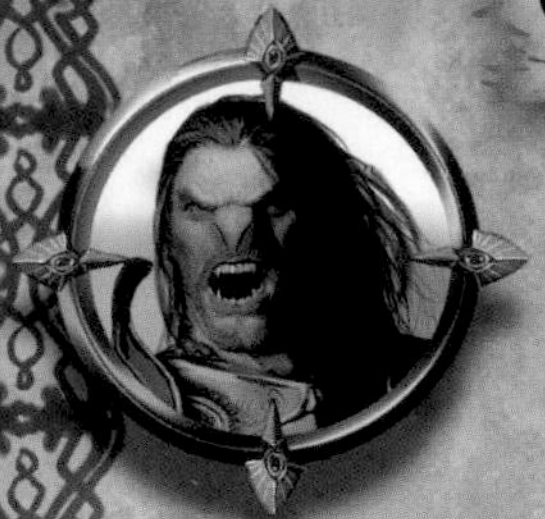

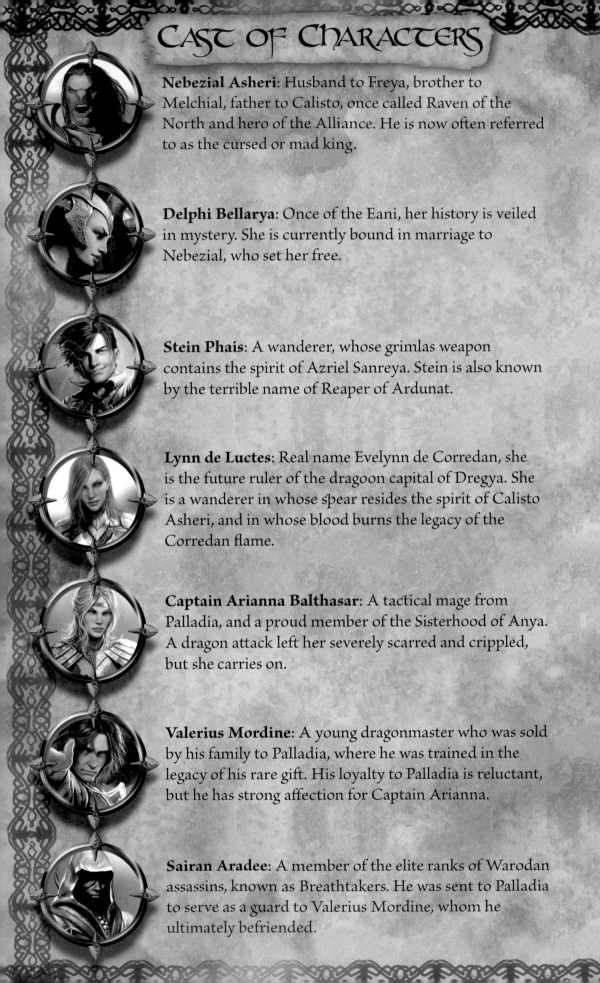

Nebezial Asheri: Husband to Freya, brother to Melchial, father to Calisto, once called Raven of the North and hero of the Alliance. He is now often referred to as the cursed or mad king.

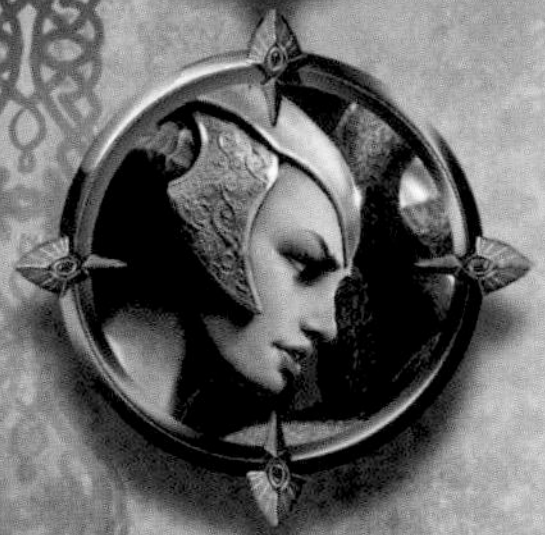

Delphi Bellarya: Once of the Eani, her history is veiled in mystery. She is currently bound in marriage to Nebezial, who set her free.

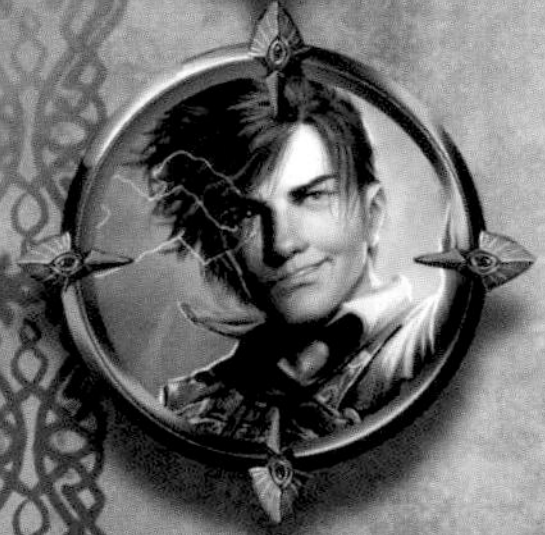

Stein Phais: A wanderer, whose grimlas weapon contains the spirit of Azriel Sanreya. Stein is also known by the terrible name of Reaper of Ardunat.

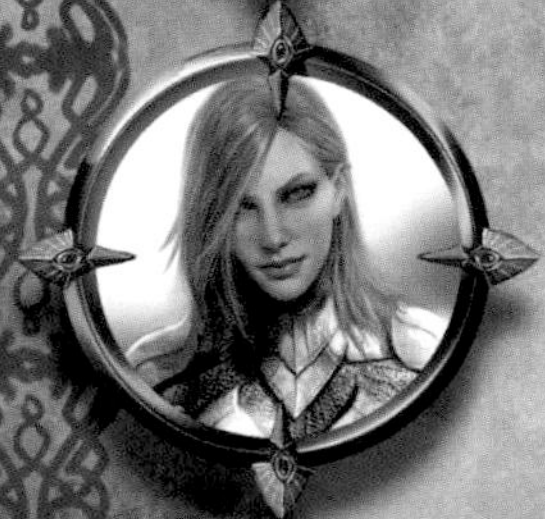

Lynn de Luctes: Real name Evelynn de Corredan, she is the future ruler of the dragoon capital of Dregya. She is a wanderer in whose spear resides the spirit of Calisto Asheri, and in whose blood burns the legacy of the Corredan flame.

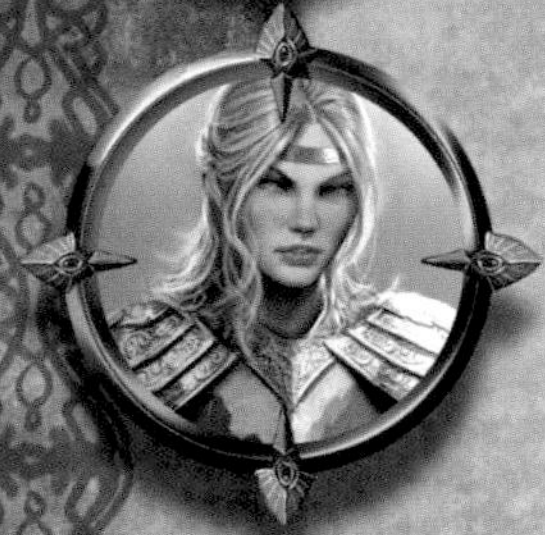

Captain Arianna Balthasar: A tactical mage from Palladia, and a proud member of the Sisterhood of Anya. A dragon attack left her severely scarred and crippled, but she carries on.

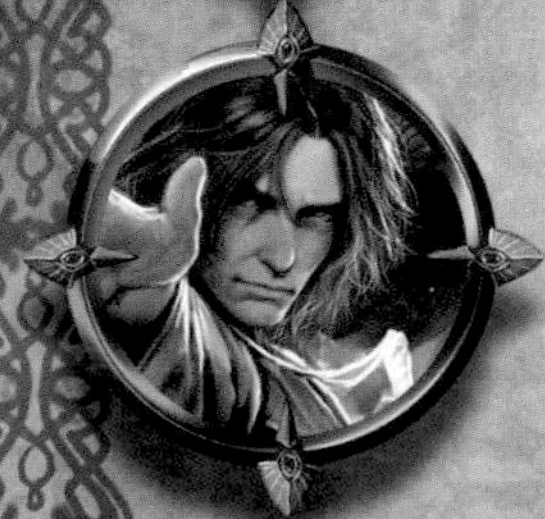

Valerius Mordine: A young dragonmaster who was sold by his family to Palladia, where he was trained in the legacy of his rare gift. His loyalty to Palladia is reluctant, but he has strong affection for Captain Arianna.

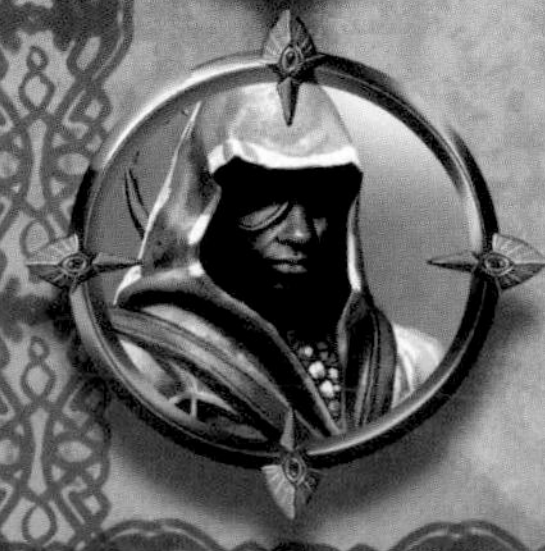

Sairan Aradee: A member of the elite ranks of Warodan assassins, known as Breathtakers. He was sent to Palladia to serve as a guard to Valerius Mordine, whom he ultimately befriended.

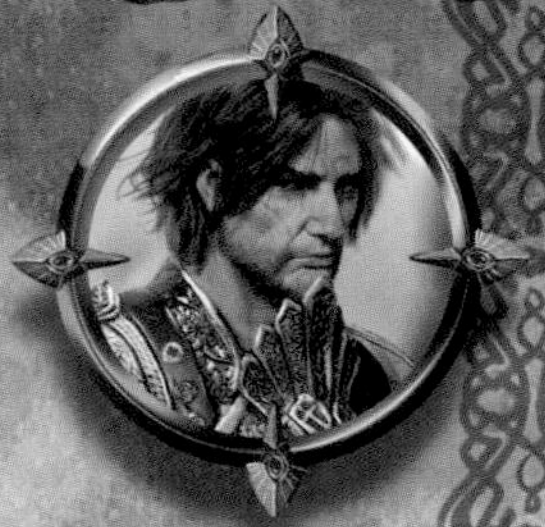

Antheus Prayne: Praetorean Guard to King Godwyn, also known as Antheus of the Deep Sight, due to his mastery of Shivas swordsmanship.

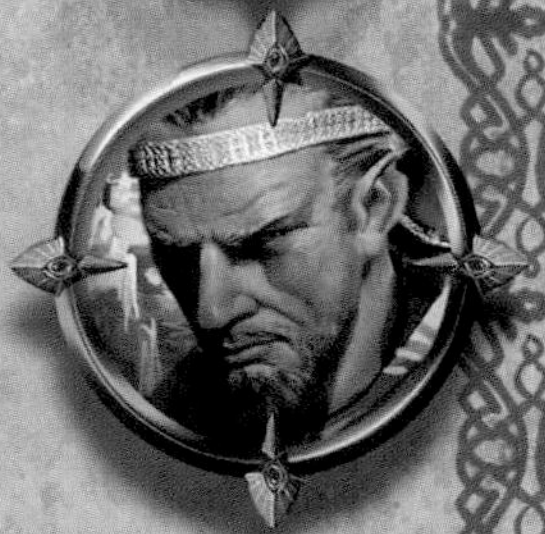

King Godwyn Bardensturm: Ruler of Palladia, former general to King Ardan. He was chosen by the Council of Lords to take the throne of Palladia.

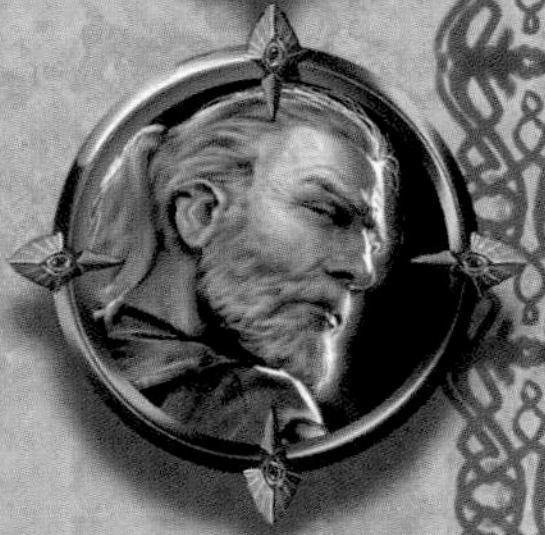

Melchial Asheri: Brother to Nebezial, slayer of the Necryte Varda Balahad, and current leader or Rimad Gregorius of the Church of Damanul.

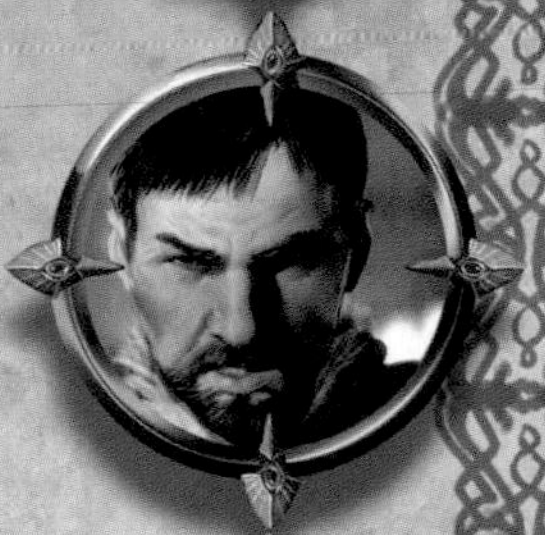

Frederick de Ruddan of Dregya: Uncle to Lynn de Luctes, and lord and throne keeper of Dregya.

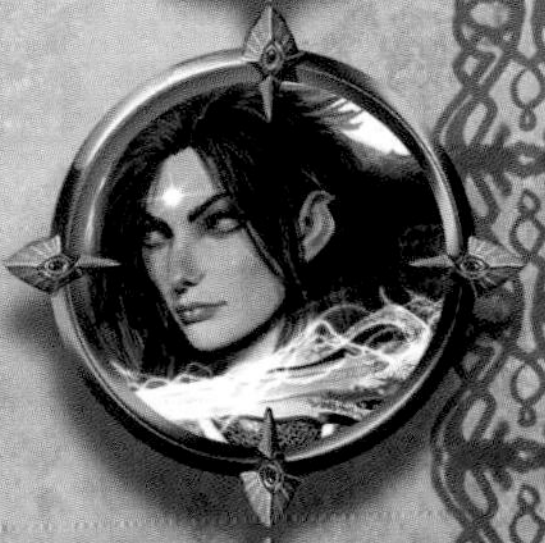

Calisto Asheri: Daughter of Nebezial and Freya, princess of Aphelion, half-Eani on her mother's side, fiancee to Azriel. After death, she was chosen as grimlas avendati, guiding spirit to Lynn de Luctes.

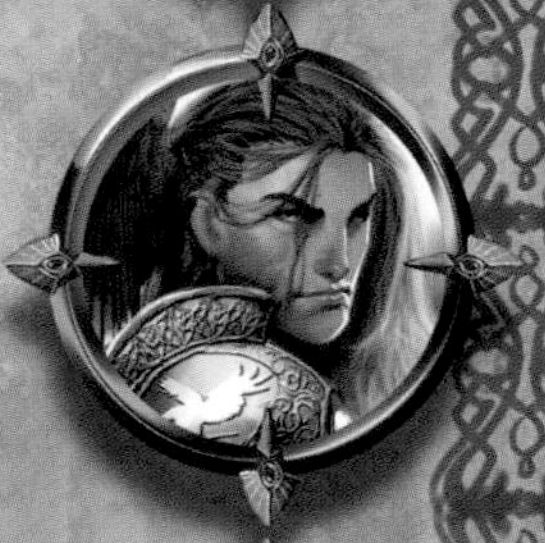

Azriel Sanreya: General for the armies of Aphelion, fiance to Calisto Asheri, a pureblood Eani of the old world. After death, he was granted a chance for redemption by becoming grimlas avendati to Stein Phais.

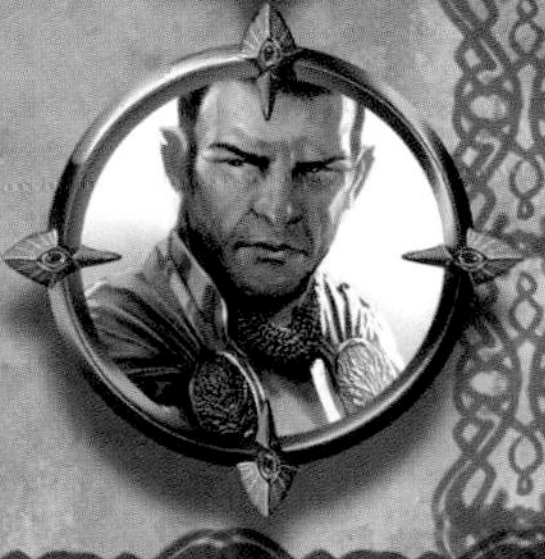

Alven Silverlake: Following the fall of the lordship of Lochenburg, Alven has faithfully served the Shinreyus family of Wranthorn. For this loyalty, Alven is included in their most secret councils.

Arthur Feldenstrom: Initially a guard at Buran Mine outpost, he is now a traveling companion of Antheus Prayne on his mission to track down the source of wyvern attacks.

Eines of Hadria: A mysterious ship captain on the River Hadria, in possession of an Arenian wraith battleship. Rumored to be quite dangerous.

Peter Bowen of House Wade: Current ruler of recently-liberated city kingdom of Wade. Good friend to Stein the Wanderer.

Orlin Bar Harr: A Mesadee ripper woman, heartsister to Stein the Wanderer.

Lara Walden de Corredan: Last known bearer of the Corredan bloodline, cousin to Lynn. Her health was ravaged by the plague.

Lord Ormu Walden of Dregya: One of the high lords of Dregya. His daughter Lara is next in line to rule Dregya.

Mikhail Wodan: Mad Dragonlord of Wranthorn. Though his mastery of dragons is among the greatest, his sanity is often questioned due to his habit of talking to his dragons, which is considered to be a very one-sided conversation.

THE SILENT DUCHESS

During the Second Arenian Expansion, Lady Ophelia, ruler of the Corredan dukedom, was on her own after the death of her husband. Many worried how the usually silent duchess, who rarely spoke in any political meetings, would hold the reins of one of the greatest lordships on the continent.

Some thought the silent duchess might be manipulated, used in the schemes of others. During the first year of her reign, she met the expectations of the nobles, maintaining order as well as she could in a time of war.

Rumors spread. The Corredan dukedom bordered the Arenian expanse, and with many messengers from Areni spotted, the lords presumed that Lady Ophelia would ally the Corredan lands with Areni.

Little did they suspect that silent Lady Ophelia listened. While many shouted and argued, she pondered, she worried. She was a smart woman, versed in history and lore. And a great worry burdened her. It was more than a year since the Arenians started slaying dragons, and harvesting their tears for the purpose of gaining greater military advantage.

Most said that the sole danger was the Arenians. Ophelia had her own opinions. She knew of old alliances dragons had made with the people of Ravine, of old promises sealed in blood and fire. She saw the recent mistrust in dragons, even aggression. She heard them roaring toward the west, calling.

It would be an understatement to say that the lords and kings of the lands that opposed the Arenians were shocked to receive a summons from Lady Ophelia. Yet most of them answered it. So on an autumn night, Ophelia Corredan shared her fears with them.

The Arenians broke the pact with dragons, an old code that said man would not slay a dragon, nor would a dragon slay a man. Now dragons called for justice, they called for blood. Ophelia thought there was one who might answer: Baran, the eldest living dragon, giver of magic, son of Mergarand the Dragonfather and Barahea the Dragonmother. Of the eldest, he alone still lived, somewhere in the west.

Ophelia proposed that they must stand alongside dragons, show their allegiance, and stop the bloodshed. Some of the lords agreed, possibly more for personal interests. A united alliance is far more efficient at scaring off an opponent. Others said they would consider it. And so the Corredans organized raids in which dragons were released and saved again and again.

Still, the Arenians were relentless. The dragons kept calling.

It was late winter that Baran finally answered their call, obliterating the Arenian borders. He then called his kin, and from them learned that not all had broken the code. Many defended it with their very lives. Baran learned of Lady Ophelia, and with her the final pact, that of Corredan Flame; not a pact of mastery, but of protection. Just as the Corredans had protected his kind, so would his kind treat the Corredans, and all blessed by them, as family.

And dragons take good care of their family.

Ophelia's wisdom saved many lives that year. Later, she was inducted as an honorary matriarch of the Sisterhood of Anya. What was once the Dukedom of Corredan had become a great city. Its name was Dregya, and it was protected.

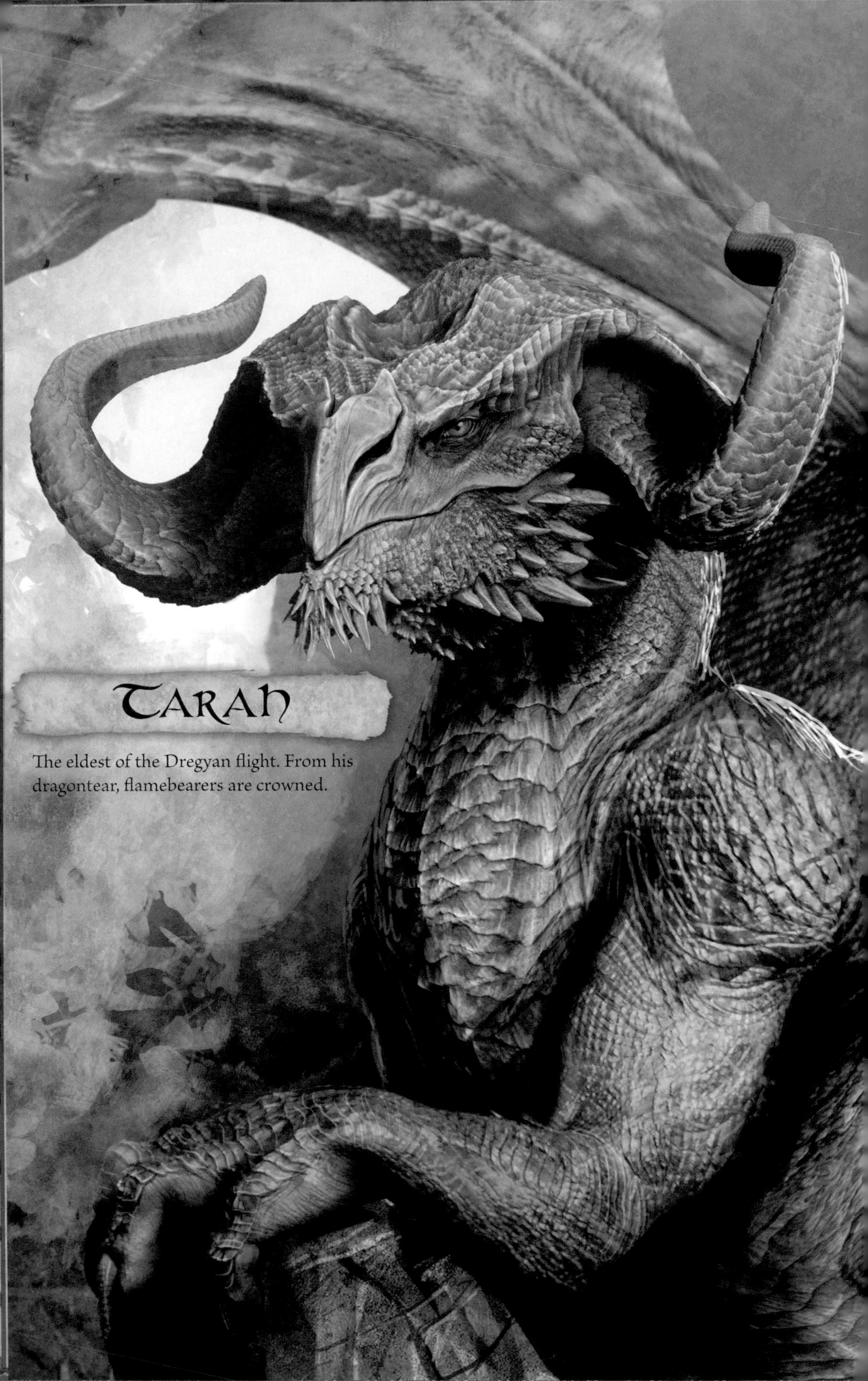

Tarah

The eldest of the Dregyan flight. From his dragontear, flamebearers are crowned.

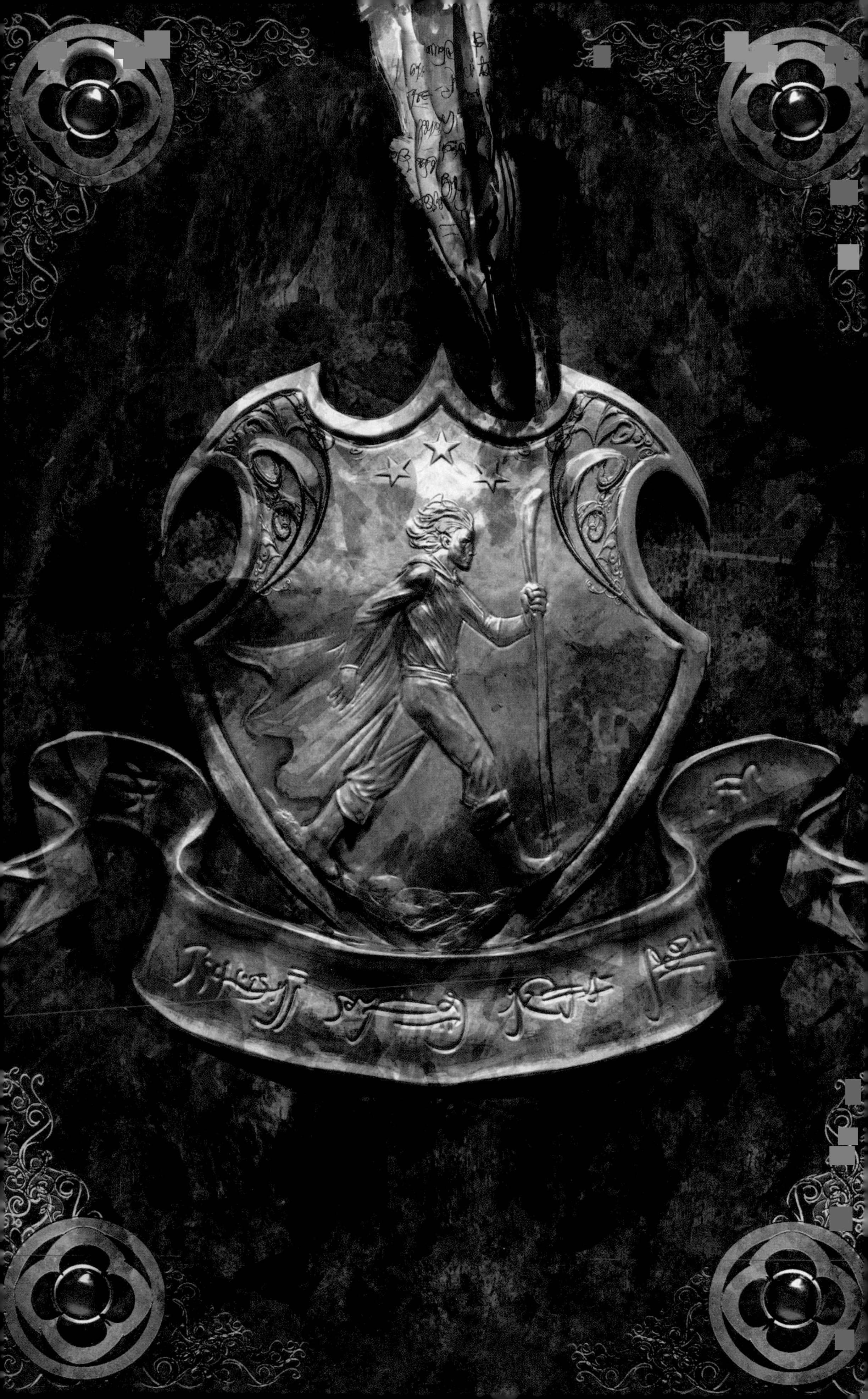

LIBERATION WAR

The boy was about nineteen. A young man, really, but his face made him look younger. The girl was younger, maybe fifteen or sixteen. Peter Bowen kept his distance, considering the situation, studying the people involved.

The city of Wade had been under Arenian occupation for more than three centuries now. Arenian trackers seeking out mages to be drafted to their military force was hardly an unusual event. Most people who were learned in spellcasting kept their skills hidden, and their weapons were creatively concealed.

Still, given enough time, any trickery will stand revealed. Trackers were quite skilled in noticing anything engraved with the spellcasting spiral. A ring, a stick, the smallest of things. They knew what they were looking for.

This was what baffled Peter as he studied the unfolding situation. The boy was blatantly wearing two short swords with the casting spiral boldly and prominently visible on their handles. He was either a fool, or a foreigner who had decided to seek his fortune in the city known to be the heart of the merchant routes of Ravine.

Control the trading routes and you control the gold. For that very reason, Arenians made sure Wade was well controlled.

A mage hunter pushed the boy, and Peter noticed that there was no fight in him. Panic, yes. Fear, definitely. But no fight.

Sigh.

"If those bastards are desperate enough for reinforcements to take such obvious wimps, the day of our victory is at hand," Peter said, a sad grin on his face, a grin full of painful memories of friends and lost allies that never reached his eyes.

Mary silently observed him, then glanced back at the four guards pushing around the young man and the girl.

So?

Peter turned to face her. She was young and beautiful, with black hair and pale, cold eyes that had seen too much evil. He remembered there were nights when she gave him comfort, but there was never love between them. There was comradery and there was absolute trust. And Aertes' grace, there was fight in her ... too much fight, he sometimes thought.

"There are four of them and two of us," Peter said, with a slightly amused look on his face.

"If you want, I can call a few more to make it interesting for you," she replied, eyebrow impishly raised.

"Which escape route do we take afterwards, and what do we do with … them?" he asked, glancing to the two foreigners.

"We go home. If they wish, they can follow," she said, in a disinterested way. "The girl seems strong. The guy, who knows?"

"Very well," Peter sighed, with a distinct tone of resignation in his voice. So distinct, in fact, that it was obviously exaggerated. He had every intention of helping the foreigners. Wade was, after all, his town. Arenians were merely borrowing it.

The street was relatively narrow. In a way, that made everything easier. They were fast and they were silent. It was the carelessness of the guards that did it. Over time, the guards grew complacent, so sure of their dominion over the streets that they could enjoy the mage hunter interrogating the foreigners, even laughing at the trembling young man, who begged for them to be left alone. Sadistic behavior comes easy in the right kind of environment, and Wade had, over time, become the best kind of environment for it.

That was the reason for their swift downfall; the guard who was supposed to watch the street behind them was far too amused with the goings-on. He fell first, a well-placed dagger in the temple. Mary mused about the arrogance of the guard not wearing his helmet, and a part of her felt the rage of the underestimated. The Arenians were so sure of their supremacy that the rebellion building in the dark corners went unnoticed.

Peter slit the throats of the other two guards in one swift motion. He was a large man, but training made him quick. And so accurate. The mage hunter turned around, a casting dagger in hand. In one smooth motion, the foreign girl produced what appeared to be a pipe with a spellcasting Baran spiral, and blasted a lightning bolt at the hunter. He fell to the ground, instantly dead.

The young man watched his companion in shock, then hugged her. Mary noticed he was crying.

A wimp, Mary thought.

"I'm so sorry, Eines," the boy said. "I ... I should have done it."

"You should not have taken a life. Not you too."

"Are you all right?" Peter asked, louder, to get their attention.

"Yes," came the answer.

"Listen well, you two," said Peter. "You can either run away, flee this city. You may make it, you may not. Or you can come with us."

They stared blankly at Peter, surrounded by the bloodbath that had occurred.

"We don't have all day," said Peter. "We're leaving now!"

"If you wish, follow!" Peter added, then took out a short casting dagger and set the dead bodies ablaze. He knew it was a certain sign to anyone that death had occurred there, but he'd be damned if the city he was striving to liberate ended up falling to Whisperers.

Immediately after, they ran.

The girl was the first to move, the young man followed.

After meandering through a labyrinth of streets and passages, they ended up in the tunnels, and eventually they came to a house. Peter took the foreigners to an empty room, where Mary joined them after a while.

"I am Peter Bowen, and the lady here is Mary Ives," Peter said. "And you two are?"

"Eines," the girl said.

"Eines...?" Peter asked.

"Just Eines," the girl replied.

"Very well," Peter said. "And you?"

"Stein. Stein Phais," the boy responded.

"Stein the Wanderer?"

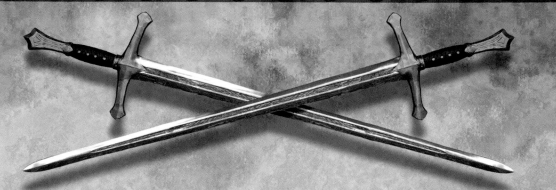

Stein twitched for a moment.

"Phais means wanderer in Muraman," Peter said in an amused tone. "So, Stein the Wanderer and ... Eines, what ill wind brought you two to Wade?"

The boy seemed to regain his composure, as he began a story Peter had heard on quite a few occasions.

They were refugees from Ardunat. He'd heard rumors, how much actual truth there was to them, he never knew. But even the Arenian Council of Mages had fled the fallen city.

Apparently a Necryte had been reborn there, and had leveled the city. Some said dozens died, while others said the fallen numbered in the hundreds. Such is the way of rumors.

If Stein's story was to be trusted, there was an event in Ardunat. It happened during the sealing of a Grimlas when the man (now dubbed the Reaper of Ardunat) lost control and revealed himself as a Necryte. Two hundred forty-seven people died. The boy must have lost someone dear that day, Peter thought. People like that remember the exact body count.

After the fall of Ardunat, Stein and his sister, Eines, wandered the kingdoms, doing work where work was to be found. Apparently, the girl was a competent mage, and Stein was a schooled cartographer. Still, in the end, the road took them to Wade. All roads lead to Wade, at one point or another. There they thought of finding work and even settling down. Until they were ambushed.

Peter glanced down at Stein's swords.

"You go around showing those blades, and you'll be marked by the mage trackers," said Peter. "Arenians always need mages for their armies, as a mage's life is a short endeavor, relatively speaking."

Stein seemed to study his own swords for a moment. "It never occurred to me that things were that bad in Wade," he said.

"Oh, yes," replied Mary. "My brothers were drafted, all but one. They weren't as ... lucky ... as you were today."

"You have my gratitude," Stein said. Then, after a pause spent carefully looking at both Peter and Mary, he continued, "Would I be wrong to presume that you two are opposing the Arenian rule?"

Peter and Mary shared a look.

"What gives you that idea?" Mary asked, noticing that Stein's demeanor had changed completely. Where once his eyes had seemed fearful, they were now cunning. A grin shined on lips that a mere hour ago had begged for mercy. He was an attractive young man, as opposed to the sniveling coward he had seemed so recently.

Stein grinned. "You mean besides the lack of hesitation in the way you killed those guards?" he said. "Your outfits, the way you hide your armor and weaponry, the way you dull its shine, so it doesn't attract attention. And of course the fact that Peter here has a crest of the House of Wade. They were the previous rulers and founders of the city, and only those who defy the present rule would hold to the crests of the old."

Eines rolled her eyes.

"What my brother is trying to say is that this house still has the crest of the former ruler engraved on the wall here. As a cartographer, he's quite familiar with it, as it used to signify Wade on trading maps," she said.

Stein shot a hurt look towards Eines, adding, "It sounded more clever the way I said it."

Peter laughed heartily. "I don't know about cartographers, but if you want, we're always looking for capable people to aid our battle."

Stein stiffened upon hearing the word battle. It was hard not to notice it. Peter put an arm around his shoulder and said, "There are different ways to fight this battle, Stein. Even a cartographer might find a purpose."

Stein remained silent.

"If you help us with food and a roof over our heads, we'll help in any way we can," said Eines.

Stein looked pleadingly at his sister, who shot him a cold look. He shrugged after a moment and said, "Very well, we'll help in any way we can."

"Excellent!" Peter said. "Then let us break bread and drink. More will come this night, and we'll see about finding some work for the two of you!"

After Peter and Mary left the room, and Stein turned to Eines.

"Why?"

"Because they helped us!" she responded. "They didn't ask who we were, they saw people in trouble and they helped. I plan on returning the favor."

Stein studied his sister, but there was no longer any true fight in him that day. He knew better by now.

"I'll be pretty much useless, you know that?" Stein questioned.

"You said it yourself," Eines replied. "You seek to redeem yourself, and who knows, maybe this is exactly the way you start."

"And what of the first rule?" asked Stein. "If things start feeling too fate-driven, we run?"

Eines smiled, and hugged her brother.

"How can you find redemption when you're running away from it?" she asked. "This doesn't feel fate-driven, Stein. This, to me, feels driven by people. But, hey, you can always ask Azriel."

Deep in the back of Stein's mind, a voice only he could hear said, "Usually I would advise you to run, but you already made your decision, Stein. The moment those people saved your sister when you couldn't protect her, you made a decision. You would repay them."

"Very well," Stein said. "We help them liberate Wade. Somehow."

2

About a dozen more people arrived by nightfall, and Stein found the company of a few of them to be quite pleasant.

Durdan was a short, half-blooded cartographer, maybe four feet tall, and not of Sardaheim or Shivas bloodlines. He lacked the height and grace of the one, and the ferocity of the other. No, Durdan was definitely of the old tribes, whose origins and legends are veiled in mystery. He was, however, easy to talk to, and so Stein and Durdan went on and on about the noble art of cartography. Durdan was the resistance's main spy at the general's table in Wade. And Stein definitely saw why.

Stein and Durdan's conversation was so energetic that soon, most of the room was observing them drinking, laughing and debating cartographical measurements. Suffice to say that the room's attention was based, not so much on interest in the topic, but instead on sheer bafflement.

Farad, a man of many talents (as he referred to himself), was the first to interrupt them: "This is the first time in years I've seen Durdan talk this much. If you're capable of doing that, Stein, then I do believe I'll be joining your side of the table." Farad sat beside Stein, who, confused by the interruption, paused before regaining his composure.

"Well, um, we were actually discussing just what ways a cartographer can derail plans of generals," said Stein, adding, "tweaking the scaling on the maps being the most obvious one, of course. But at the same time, the most traceable one. Trade route maps, though, now that's a whole different business altogether.."

Stein took one of Durdan's maps, while the people in the room observed him with amusement and quite a bit of interest. Stein pointed at the roads marked to and from Wade.

"These roads here, all of them, are taxed," Stein said. "And not too cheaply, I might add. Traders have been, for years, making their own paths, the secret roads. It is, by them, that they tend to transport their goods to avoid taxation."

Stein continued, "Now, any army of the city has its own supplies. You hit those first, you create the need for more, then you block the trade roads and keep the supplies from coming."

Peter observed Stein with interest. Useless in battle as this man might be, there was a cunning streak in him.

Eines joined in the discussion. "Lady Mary tells me that you've been having problems truly acting within the city, because you want to avoid innocent people getting hurt in the process."

"Yes," Peter said with a grumpy tone.

"Durdan, was it?" Eines asked, redirecting her attention to the cartographer.

"It is," Durdan said, smiling.

"Do you have a detailed map of Wade?" Eines asked with a half-amused look.

"Several," he replied.

Durdan took the map out of his bag and unfolded it. It was a beautiful, intricately detailed map, and Stein admired the craftsmanship until he felt a hearty slap on the back of his head.

"You're in the way," Eines said, as she looked over the map. She studied it for a while, then took a few coins and placed them on the map.

"Here is where you get them," she said.

The room studied the locations, and little by little, realization dawned. The coins were placed upon bridges, secluded tunnels, and foundation walls of the old Wade.

Peter said, "We've thought of that as well, but we have nothing that they want. Arenians wouldn't send their forces after just anyone."

Eines grinned as she took out her pipe wand and illuminated the room with a controlled, hovering fireball. "You do now," she said.

Stein stood up, looked at his sister with a stern expression, and said, "No. Any other way."

Eines glanced at him for a moment, and said, "Oh yes, and you and your fancy blades are coming with me."

Farad looked at them and laughed. "Peter, you really brought us some interesting reinforcements this time."

Peter laughed as well, then said, "Blame Mary, she made me do it."

Mary hugged Stein and joined in laughing. "I had to!" she said. "He was blubbering, begging for mercy, the poor boy was so scared!"

Stein turned to Mary with a half-angry, half-hurt expression on his face, only to see one of the warmest smiles he'd seen in ages. He wondered how a woman with such cold eyes could have such a warm smile. He smiled back, and then to his surprise, Mary kissed him quite passionately. The room erupted in laughter after seeing his confused face.

Mary then patted him on the cheek, loudly proclaiming, "He may be a coward, but he has a sly tongue and the skin of a woman! Farad, you might like him!"

Farad laughed, and said, "Pay no attention to Mary. My friend here, she likes to make fun of people, but she does have a kind heart hidden somewhere deep behind her forked tongue." Then Farad turned to Eines, studying her pipe wand. "Were you trained by the sisterhood?"

"No, my parents and grandfather," she replied, while producing small dancing flames.

Farad contemplated for a moment, then continued, "This idea of yours, of luring them, if you were of the sisterhood, it wouldn't have worked. But as it is ... it seems doable."

Eines looked at him inquisitively. "They don't touch the sisters?"

"Oh no, not even Arenians are crazy enough to mess with the sisterhood," Farad said. "I hear that Khali Khedira of the Shivas is now one of the grand matrons, and no mage is foolish enough to dance with Shivas. And let's face it, with the training and disciplined skill of the Sisters of Anya, Arenians would invite fury upon themselves as they haven't seen since the days of Ophelia Corredan and the dragons uprising."

Farad continued, "No, Arenians certainly don't want trouble in the last colony they hold. We're living in the last battlefield. Once Wade is liberated, it's the official demise of the Arenian expansion. Five centuries of conquerors, and it all ends."

"I hear Karan of Areni is a good man," said Stein.

Peter replied with a grim tone. "That he may be, but he's a good man who rules over a nation of people used to having things done their way. He may have proclaimed the equality of Wade's citizens, but Karan does not rule this city, his four generals do. And they come from a long line of oppressors."

"Children are what their parents and their society teaches them to be, and these four are well versed in the arts of oppression and tyranny," Peter continued. "Unfortunately, our numbers are too few to simply overthrow them, or challenge them openly on the fields of Wade in a glorious battle to end it all."

Stein and Eines shared a look, a meaningful look of two people who knew each other's pasts and secrets.

Eines then said, "So we erode them from within."

Stein looked at her with a crooked grin. "You're certainly eager to join a battle you knew nothing of until today."

With a sour look, Eines replied, "Those bastards wanted to take my brother. I can't allow that."

Mary laughed loudly at that. Stein looked at her with feigned sulkiness, and then burst into laughter himself. They drank deep into the night, they ate, they plotted and planned. And that night, Stein and Eines slept with a feeling of belonging somewhere again. Stein was happy, and even Azriel, the small voice only he could hear, told him, "This one time, maybe it's good that you stayed."

3

Four generals were not happy. That was the first thing James Bordin heard when he entered the General Court. He had been the caretaker of Wade for thirty years, and took great pride in the efficiency of how he ran the city. Besides small incidents, the people were kept in order. Taxes were collected, trading performed, all under his supervision. Never in his life had he heard that sentence before.

"Four generals were not happy," his assistant said matter-of-factly.

The tone of her voice irked him as he walked to the council room. He wondered why, of all things, he was annoyed at the woman, who had served as his assistant for a dozen years now. Then it hit him. She said it as if it was something that was a recurring event, not at all an exception to the monotony of his perfect record. It was the tone of voice one would use to heap scorn upon a sloppy lieutenant.

He entered the council room, leaving the assistant behind. That was good. Her company at this moment merely agitated him. Bah, they were not happy. Never has a conquered kingdom been run so orderly, so impeccably, and James Bordin was the reason for that. His unique balance of discipline and diplomacy ran this city like a well-oiled machine.

He opened the doors of the inner chamber as he was called to enter. The four generals sat behind their desks and offered him a seat.

"I was called," Bordin said.

"That you were!" said Mara Wilkes. She was a corpulent woman, a well-known arch mage who made sure she had more than enough energy to burn in battle. It's said that mages are short-lived, like candles that burn too bright. But this woman made sure that her candle wax was plentiful. The same could be said, to a lesser extent, for any of the four generals.

"So, Sir Bordin," Mara continued, while looking at the ledger in her hands. "For the last six weeks we have lost more than eighty guardsmen, seventeen mage hunters, and our weaponry cache in the northern part of the city. And let's not forget the military rations that were stolen."

James Bordin clenched his fist so tightly that the nails broke the skin of his palm. "There was no way..."

"I wasn't finished, Sir Bordin," Mara said. "You will be given a chance to explain yourself."

Mara then proceeded to read a lengthy list of the military supplies and weaponry shipments that had been intercepted and lost on the secret roads.

Bordin felt the cold sweat under his armor. When faced with the compilation of his failures in the last few weeks, he felt panic taking over. Was it really that bad, he thought?

Yes, there were attacks before. People claimed to be with the rebellion, but they were so insignificant that their activities were undetected. Now, though, it was different. He knew of most of these incidents. It was difficult not to. But not all. He knew nothing of the trading routes. And even his informers knew little to nothing. Word was that the rebellion was now led by a devil woman, but he knew nothing more of her. Was he going to tell that to the generals? Not if he valued his life. No, he would lie, and hopefully they would believe the lie for a while, at least until he--

"Sir Bordin!" said General Mara, tearing him away from his thoughts.

"Yes, General Mara?" he responded.

"How do you justify all of this?"

"I ... there is an insurrection building."

Nervous whispering among the generals.

"But have no fear," Bordin explained. "Our spies have infiltrated their ranks." One lie at a time, he thought. "And soon after we mark their leaders, we will destroy them from within."

"I see," said General Mara, leaning forward. "And these spies of yours were the ones who hid some of the stolen cargo in the basement of your home?"

"What... cargo?" Bordin stood frozen.

"Some of the more valuable items," continued the general. "Tributes to General Milo's daughter, her wedding gift. We received information that you were involved. Your house was searched, and we found ... a lot."

"General Mara, I'm obviously being framed! This is the work of the insurrectionists," Bordin said. "I can find them,

bring them to you!"

"That won't be necessary," the general responded.

Mara stood up from her chair. Quite an accomplishment, considering her size. She took her walking stick and pointed it to Bordin. He knew what was about to happen, and he was ready for it. A bolt of lightning shot across the room, only to be met with a shielding spell.

Mara laughed, as she pressed on with her attack. "Bordin, you should know better than to battle an arch mage. I can keep pressing you, and pressing, and pressing, and waste nothing more than fat. But you, you're a soldier, a fit man, a strong man, and all you have to burn is your lifespan."

Bordin gritted his teeth. He knew she was right, he knew well the nature of magic. Magic is a force one pays with one's lifespan. And while some can be done without tapping into one's lifespan, past a certain limit, you burn out all the energy you've gotten from food and sleep. From then on, you burn.

But Mara had the energy to burn, plenty of it. All Arenian arch mages did. They were smart, they cared little for their public appearance. They were fat slobs, but they were powerful. What did they care of their own appearance? They could burn all that fat in a day. But in that day, they would have the power to outstrip any regular mage.

Bordin knew all that, but he also knew something else. He knew that a mage can't both attack and defend.

"Your power must be waning, General Mara," Bordin said with a grin on his face.

"Let us test it then," said the general. Mara ceased the lightning bolts and started charging another spell. Bordin knew the spell. It was a pulverizing crush; she planned to literally crush both him and his shield. But this spell required a moment, and a moment was all he needed.

Bordin invested all of his remaining lifespan in a last attack. He knew that his family would be hunted down if he failed to slay all four generals here and now. They wouldn't have spread their suspicions, and have doubts cast on their own leadership skills. So Bordin would tear apart the whole room. He dropped the shield, and with a smile, he pointed his casting dagger.

But it was too late. General Milo was ready, and struck down Bordin with a lightning bolt. His charred corpse collapsed to the floor.

Mara glanced at Milo, who merely said, "So who do we appoint to be the new city overseer?"

4

Stein was awakened that morning by Peter, who rushed into the room. Both Stein and Mary were naked. She visited him often. After the first night, when she took his virginity and taught him about lovemaking, he presumed her relentless teasing would stop. It did not. He was forever a coward, but he was fine with that.

"Get dressed," Peter said. "The others are already here."

Stein dressed quickly. Mary was still fast asleep. He pondered whether to wake her, but remembered she was leading the night raids. They'd been in Wade six weeks now, and the city was in chaos.

The Arenians were powerless to stop it. He grinned. Who knew? He was actually helpful. His cartographical prowess enabled him to read the secret signs that pointed towards secret roads, and the damage they inflicted upon the Arenian military was tremendous. Eines was brilliant. Arenians had only twelve trained mage hunters left, and more and more mages joined the rebels. Things were good.

"Things are bad," said Peter, with a grim look.

Stein sipped on a cup of hot Arenian coffee. He liked the brew, one of the few good things Arenians brought to the kingdoms. "What happened?" he asked.

Mary's brother, Jacob, stood before the room and shared the fresh information. "The four generals have decided to purge the city, and they've brought military reinforcements, including more than a hundred berserker mages from the homeland," he said. "There are also twenty elite trackers, capable of finding a mage by using his or her residual spell force."

After a pause, Jacob continued, "Last night, twelve of our secret outposts were destroyed, and our brethren slain. More than a hundred fell in one night."

Stein reeled, shocked. "Eines?"

"She escaped. Farad and Durdan too," answered Jacob. "They should be on their way to the outer walls by now, and will meet up with our forces outside the city. We should leave too."

Stein stood silent, and then whispered, "So sudden…"

Jacob looked to the ground and said, "Actually, it's a reprisal. We kidnapped General Milo's daughter."

"You what?" Peter shouted.

"We ... thought she would make good bargaining leverage," said Jacob. "We miscalculated."

The room was silent for a moment, and then Peter said, "We're moving to the outer camps."

Stein went back to his room. Azriel saw his thoughts as a vortex of fear, panic and anger. "Stein, what happened?" she asked.

"I sense a lot of angry thoughts," said Azriel. "You aren't planning…"

"More than one hundred died," Stein growled through gritted teeth. "All for the sake of the greed and arrogance of those who seek dominion over the conquered."

Stein stopped in front of the doors to his room. "What could I do?" he said. "If I was to face them alone, on the battlefield maybe. But to do that, I would have to tell them, tell all of them. I ... can't do that."

Sigh.

Stein woke Mary, and told her what had happened. Soon they all snuck through the hidden tunnels that lead to the secret roads. In a matter of hours, they reached the outside camp. Beyond the city walls, the raiders of the trade routes sat around campfires, grim and cheerless. Peter followed Jacob to where the general's daughter was being kept.

Stein had no patience for such things. He was more concerned with finding his sister. He found her by a campfire, eating. She's been doing that a lot, he mused. It did wonders for her combat abilities. The Arenians referred to her as the devil woman, an arch mage in her own right. What she lacked in the corpulence of an Arenian arch mage, she more than made up for with skill and resourcefulness. And she was only sixteen.

A twinge of guilt stabbed the back of Stein's mind. He was only sixteen when he killed for the first time. Two hundred forty-seven people. Now Eines was a killer too. He sat next to his sister and shook off grim thoughts. He knew they would only take him to bad places. In the light of the fire, he noticed the redness in her eyes. She was crying.

"What?" she said, looking at him almost spitefully. He hugged her. She relaxed, and they sat like that until Peter arrived. His face revealed that this night was made of bad news

"Scouts just reported that the roads from Wade are blocked, and the army will come at dawn to purge these woods," he informed them. "Thankfully, they have no dragon riders, as no dragon would take an Arenian, but unfortunately, neither do we."

Peter continued, "We're a little over a hundred here, and there are currently about six hundred of them preparing to crush us in the morning. And every single one of them a mage."

Stein seemed thoughtful for a moment. "Many of them are of Wade, forcibly drafted, aren't they?" he asked.

"Aye," Peter said. "That they are, but any mage in the Arenian military is family-bound to the kingdom. If one was to desert or rebel, their family would be slain for their transgressions. They will fight us."

"So what are our options?" Stein asked.

Peter looked to the stars, silent for a moment. "We can run away, break one of the road blocks and leave Wade. Or we can fight a hopeless battle."

"Those are not options," said Eines. "That's just one option."

"What?" said Peter, pulled out of his thoughts.

"You would never leave Wade," continued Eines. "None of these men and women would, so that real leaves one option, and a fanciful fantasy for the other."

Peter laughed. "You've gotten to know us well, which is what I wanted to talk to you about."

"Here it comes," said Eines, an expression of deep anger slowly flooded her face.

"The two of you are not of Wade," Peter said. "You could leave, two people on the road wouldn't--"

He was slammed into a tree by the forceful blast of Eines's spell.

"That's what I do to people who annoy me, Peter," Eines said. "Would you like to find out what I do to those who truly enrage me?"

Peter got up off the ground, caught his breath, and started laughing. "You two really are something."

Mary and Durdan joined them, Farad followed.

"So I guess their answer was no," Mary said, smiling. Peter nodded.

"Well, I was sure Eines would refuse, but Stein is the wimpier one," Mary continued, laughing, as she sat next to Stein. She hugged him and said, "So we die together then."

Mary added, "I can't say that I love you, we were never that close. At best, you were what I needed."

"Thrilled to hear that," Stein replied.

Mary grabbed Stein's face and made him face her. "However, I'm glad to have met you, I'm glad to have called you my friend, and yes, I'm very glad to have shared my bed with you. Tomorrow, if the fates see fit, I'll be glad to die beside you, Stein the Wanderer."

"All that from me too," Peter said, "except for sharing the bed."

They all laughed.

Stein looked at Eines. His look told her everything. She had seen it before. A look of deep regret, of old pain. But this time, also a resolute look.

She nodded.

Stein said, "What if we could win this?" Everyone turned toward him, baffled expressions on their faces.

Peter spoke with the tone of someone bringing a dazed person back to reality. "A hundred and twelve of us, five

mages among us, no breath-takers dragonlords or dragoons. Traps and trickery won't work if they just set the woods afire."

Stein stood silent for a few seconds as everyone regarded him with curiosity.

5

The dawn broke, and it was beautiful. Stein stood alone on the field, facing the city of Wade. The woods were behind him, and in the woods, many eyes were upon him. Eyes that used to look at him with amusement were now alert, even fearful. They had every reason to be.

Autumn was just around the corner, and fields were poised for that final glory, rich in colors and smells. Birds chirped, a soft breeze blew, a day fit for a pleasant nap.

Somehow it felt wrong. It should be grim, Stein thought. Many would die today. Nature should have some decency and make the day feel appropriate. He watched as the great southern gate of Wade opened, and the army made its way out. There were so many soldiers. So many of them had families.

Azriel told him, "So do the people you're trying to protect right now." It helped. Not just for the obvious reason of soothing the killer's remorse. It was the word "protect." Stein was never a protector. How could he be?

Come to think of it, he was never much of anything. His father tried teaching him magic when he was younger. He came from a long line of skilled and smart spellcasters. The saying holds that a mage's life is that of a candle burning too bright. But his family knew how to keep the flame in check.

Stein still remembered his training.

"The world and the universe around us are made of necra," his father had said, grabbing a handful of sand. "Necra is as the tiniest grain of sand, bound together to form matter. Scholars say there's a trinity of forces in action when one becomes a mage. A soul, or anu, uses life-force, or maga, to manipulate matter, or necra."

Stein was twelve then, and had broken about fifty practice wands that day alone.

"You use a caster weapon to weave a spell," his father continued. "Look at this spiral on it."

Stein glanced at the wand with only a half-interested look. He knew all this already, of course, but his father hoped it was the theory that made him fail over and over.

"You use this to channel your maga and mix it with necra," his father said. "This results in the formation of the spell. Now, why did the wands break?"

Stein looked at the pile of shattered wands on the ground. "Because they're crap?" he responded.

His father laughed, but got serious quickly. "No!" he said. "The danger in untrained magic is that with a strong caster weapon, a novice mage would use up his permanent life force too fast. The goal of using magic wisely is to merely use the daily maga, that which can be regenerated by food and sleep. That's why practice wands have a thin and breakable spiral engraved, to stop you from releasing too much maga and hurting your lifespan."

Stein kept trying … and failing. Even then, it was clear that he could not control his spell work at all. His sister could, she was a prodigy. Stein wasn't.

It soon became apparent that magic was not his domain. His father asked for a favor from the scholars at the University of Ardunat, and so Stein was schooled in cartography instead.

It was interesting, and he liked it. He found his place in the world, and all was good. But then he turned sixteen, the age everyone was allowed to pull a weapon from the faetree of Ardunat. He could not have cared less about

weaponry. His swordsmanship was laughable anyway, but customs were customs. So he too came to the tree.

Stein wasn't terribly interested in which weapon he would pull. They were all heavy-looking swords and spears and axes. He looked for the lightest ones he could see. Two light short swords were embedded right at the top of the tree. They seemed to be a matching set. Why not, Stein figured.

That day, two hundred forty-seven died. He realized why his spellcasting was so erratic and uncontrollable too.

That day, with the best spellcasting weapons in his hands, his power was unleashed. Afterwards, he ran. His sister found him, and told him no one knew who did it, but the people of Ardunat were fleeing. Their family was too, and she'd come to bring him back. Stein refused. He knew what he was now. A voice only he could hear told him all about it. He couldn't go back.

Instead, Eines came with him.

Back from his memories, Stein smiled.

Last night, when he shared this tale around the campfire, he had to repeat parts of it as more and more came to listen. By its end, there was dead silence. Many didn't believe him, so he had to show them.

Over the last three years, he'd learned to control it. Not aim, of course, he could never aim his spells and pulses. But at least he knew how to stop them. He knew how to unravel his form to become what the rare few who had seen it called the Reaper of Ardunat. That was what he had shown them last night. He saw fear in the faces of his friends as he pulsated in between, in and out of existence, a mirage of death and all the terrors of the night.

Then he promised them he would liberate Wade this day.

All they needed to do was stay in the woods. Stay far away.

They did just that. Stein was alone on that field, the army fast approaching. He cast one last glance around the field. Such a shame. It was so beautiful.

He saw a woman in elaborate armor step forward. Not one of the top officers, he thought. Arenian arch mages rely on gorging themselves to fuel their spells. This woman was slender.

"We demand the daughter of General Milo be returned," the female lieutenant said. "This and only this will give you any chance of survival."

Stein nodded, and signaled to the rebels in the woods. Soon a young woman came out of the woods. As she passed Stein, he said, "Don't linger. As soon as you pass the army, run as far as you can."

She shot him a dirty look and whispered, "I would have no interest in seeing your puny rebellion massacred. I've seen your numbers, and they're unimpressive."

She moved away, and Stein gave her a sad smile. Still, he noted that once she reached their ranks, she ran, and fast for a privileged brat.

He knew what came next. Such was the way of the world. You didn't bargain with an enemy you found both weaker and more dangerous at the same time. Without a warning, a fireball flew his way. He shielded himself, and with no small irony, he noticed that for once, that was enough. Other mages were in the forest.

The lieutenant laughed. "A fellow spellcaster, I see. Pity, we could use more in our ranks. Still, our numbers will quickly drain you of your life."

The mages started pummeling Stein, who merely stood there observing them.

After a while, confusion dawned on their faces. The combination of their attacks should have placed so much stress on his shield that they expected him to be dead by now, his lifespan fully drained. And yet here they were, dangerously close to tapping into their own lifespans. The boy just smiled.

The barrage stopped.

Then Stein spoke: "We want the Arenian forces to leave the free city of Wade." After waiting for the laughter to subside, he continued, "You will be granted safe passage. None of you need to die."

The lieutenant studied him for a moment, unsure what to make of him. He was scrawny for a man, entirely unimpressive. But he had blocked enough firepower to drop an arch mage, and there was not a single sign of fatigue in him. Something was amiss here.

"We know your numbers," she said. "And we know you are limited in sheer mage firepower. We, on the other hand, number six hundred fifty-two. You are severely outmatched."

"You're right about the numbers," said Stein. "You're wrong about the limitations of our mage firepower."

"Really?" she smirked. "Impress me."

"It's unlimited ... if a little hard to control," he said in response.

A confused look.

Stein surveyed the forces in front of him.

"We have six mages," he told her. "But to destroy you, we need only me."

"What makes you so impressive? she asked him.

"Hardly impressive. More like defective," said Stein. "You might say I was born a little damaged."

The lieutenant narrowed her eyes as a terrible thought occurred to her. "Who are you?"

At that moment, a corpulent woman broke through their ranks, shouting, "What's the delay, lieutenant?" She shot Stein a disgusted look, observed his shielding, and said, "What are you waiting for? Hammer him down and move on!"

"We tried that, General Mara," said the lieutenant.

Stein interrupted, "I heard stories about you, Mara. Nothing good."

"And you would be?" Mara said, readying her weapon.

"Me?" Stein said. "I'm Stein. Stein the Wanderer."

"Stein the Dead Man seems more appropriate," she said.

"I prefer my other name," Stein said.

He noticed the lieutenant pulling back, revelation dawning in her eyes. He saw her fear, and smiled.

"The Reaper of Ardunat," Stein proclaimed, and created a single pulse that sent Mara sprawling back into her troops. A dozen people cushioned her fall.

Mara frothed with rage, screaming, "Destroy him! Kill him now!"

All hell broke loose. Fire and lightning engulfed the field, and soon only dust clouds were visible. Mara got up, looking at the place where Stein had been, and then several things happened at once.

Jacob ran out of the forest, then a few other rebels, and then his sister, Mary. Somewhere behind them, Eines screamed for them to stop. Their intentions were good, but they had made a horrible mistake.

Stein felt the familiar tingling feeling of unraveling. His body was in unstable form, pulsating in and out of existence, a dark specter of death flickering in front of Mara. Terror dawned in her eyes. It was the last thing to ever dawn for her.

The pulse was swift, unleashing destruction in all directions. Stein slew more than three hundred Arenian soldiers in a single pulse that day, along with six rebels. Mary's brother, Jacob, was one of them. Mary escaped with injuries.

In the forest, Eines, Peter and the rest of the rebels handled a second smaller wave of elite forces led by General Milo. Eines herself defeated him, and made the general face the reality of defeat when she showed him the destruction Stein had caused.

Stein stopped, and once again asked for the Arenians to surrender. They were paralyzed with fear, hiding behind

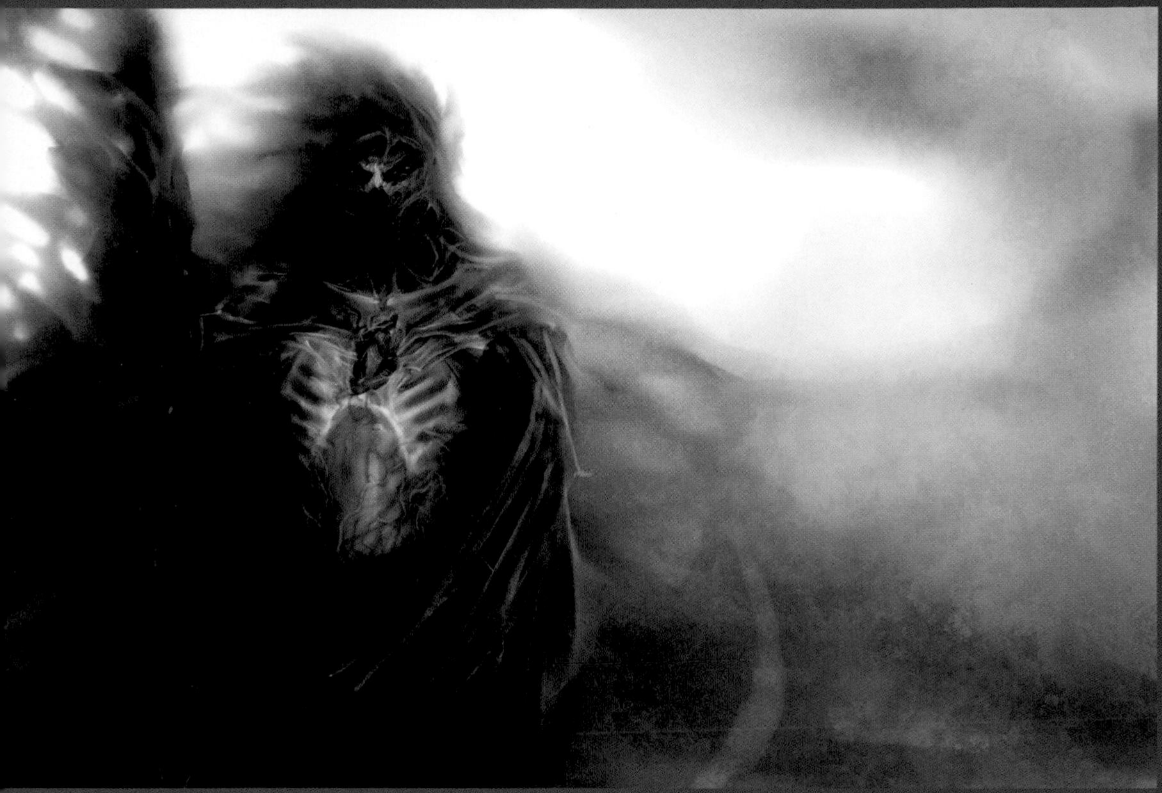

spell shields. From the woods, General Milo screamed, "We surrender!"

It ended. Wade was liberated. Only later did Stein learn of the allies who had perished because of him. When he faced Mary, the look in her remaining good eye was enough to tell him that it was highly unlikely she would ever forgive him.

He'd have to accept that, but he'd had to accept worse things in his life. And for once, he knew this was not his fault. He didn't need Azriel to tell him that.

The remaining three generals left Wade and took their forces with them, carrying a message to Karan of Areni: Wade is a free city, protected by the Reaper of Ardunat.

Peter took control of the city, and soon was made king. Stein and Eines left shortly after. They knew it was for the best. Staying meant facing the risk of paid assassins, hired by unhappy families of Arenians, or the people of Ardunat.

Still, friendships remained strong, and Wade was free. Free under the sigil of the Wanderer.

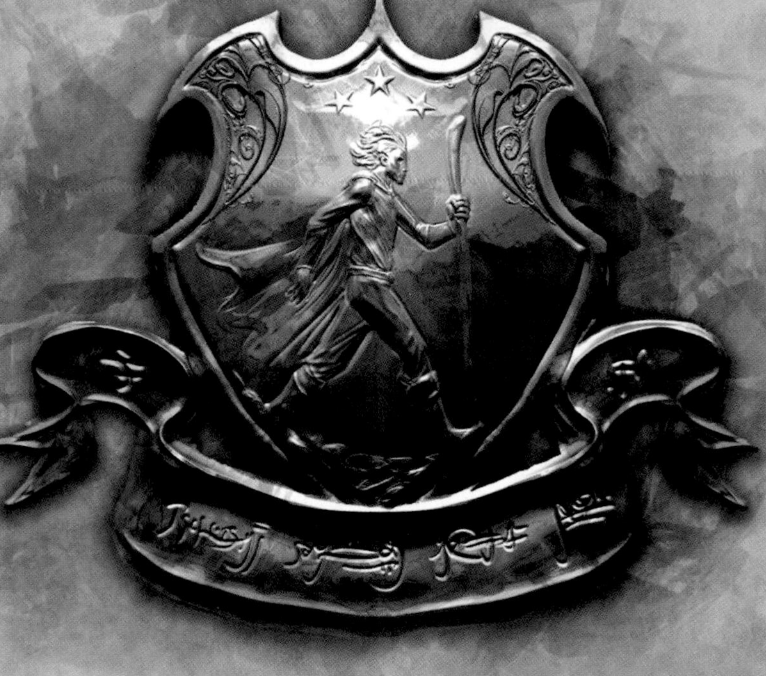

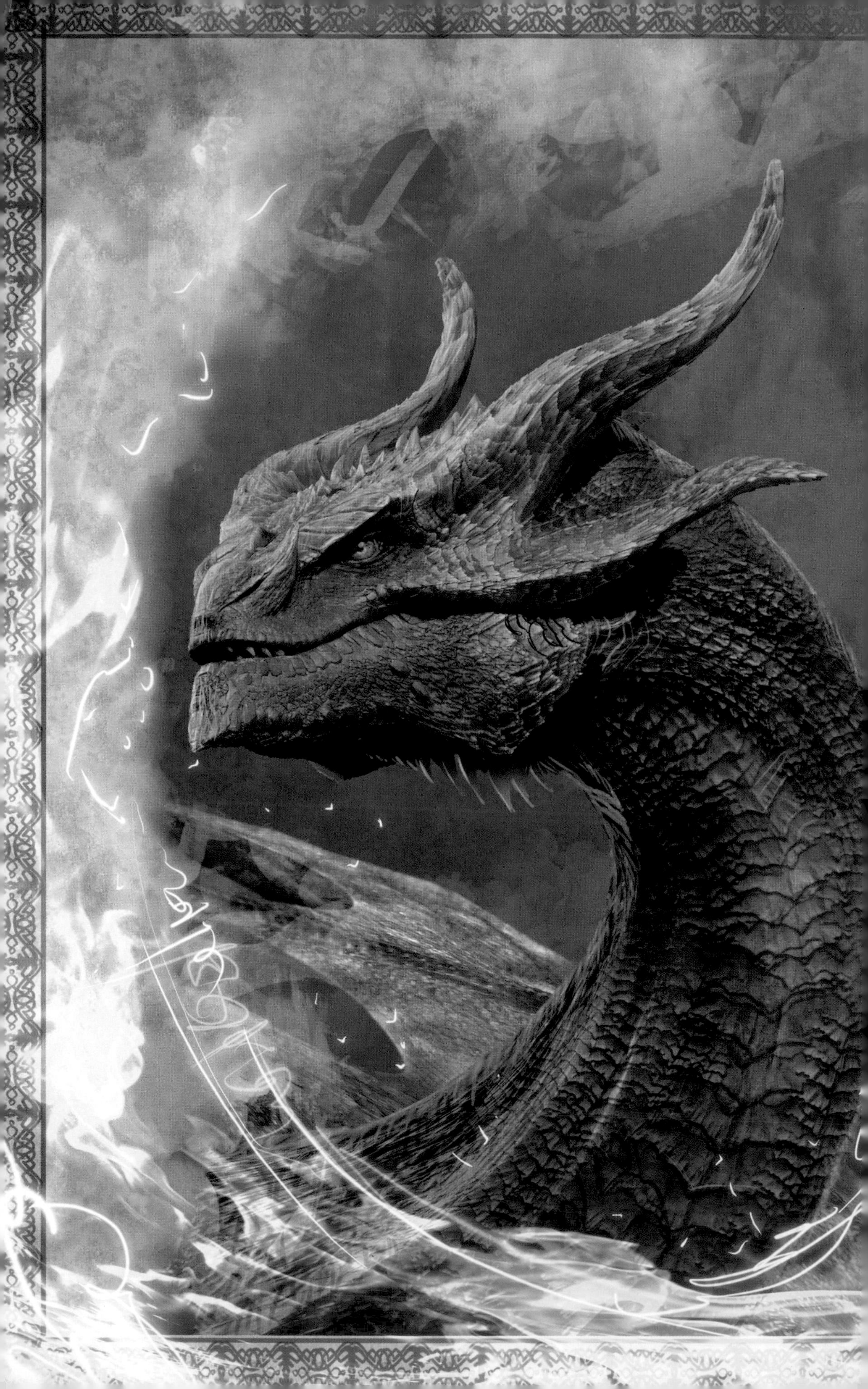

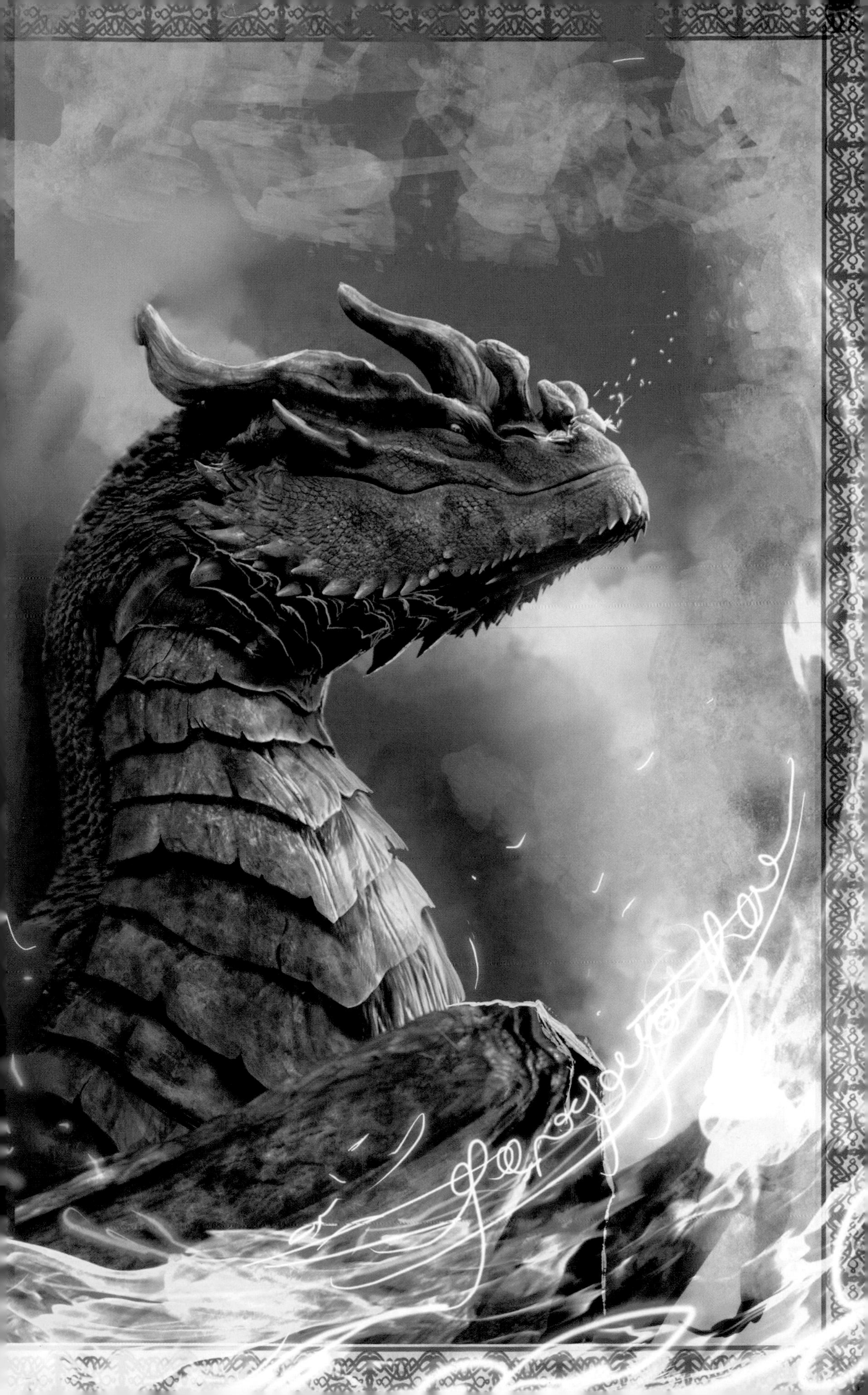

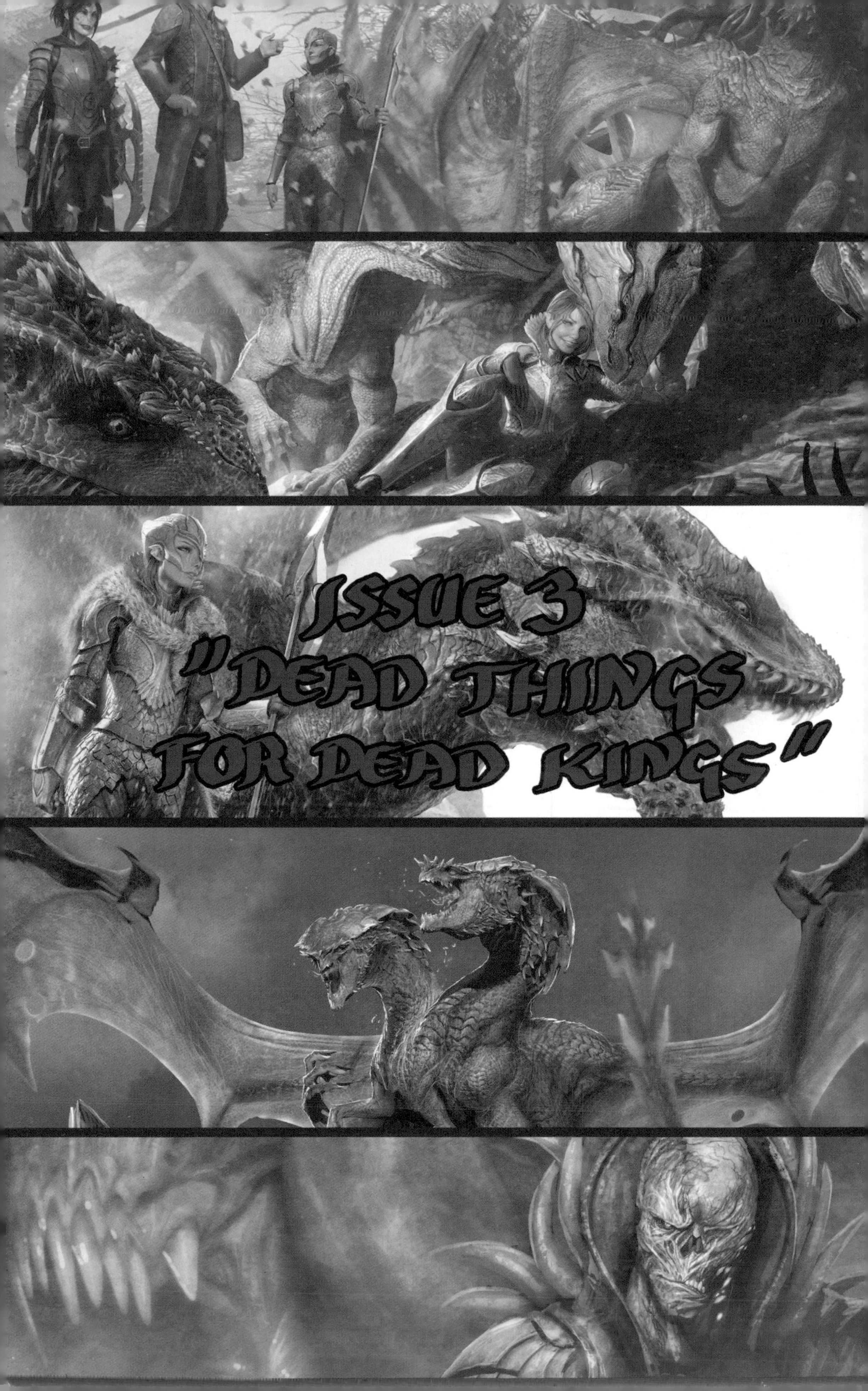
ISSUE 3
"DEAD THINGS
FOR DEAD KINGS"